GUINNESS WORLD RECORDS 2023

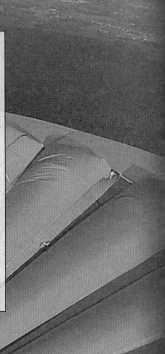

HIGHEST ALTITUDE STANDING ATOP A HOT-AIR BALLOON
Welcome to *Guinness World Records 2023*! Begin your out-of-this-world journey through record breaking by taking in the views from 4 km (2.5 mi) above Earth, courtesy of Rémi Ouvrard (FRA). On 10 Nov 2021, daredevil Rémi dressed as an astronaut to take a sky-high selfie 4,016 m (13,175 ft) above Châtellerault in Vienne, France. He was standing on top of a balloon piloted by his father, Jean-Daniel, for a stunt in aid of France's annual Téléthon fundraiser.

Missions

3... 2... 1... We have lift-off on another fully revised and updated *Guinness World Records* annual! The 2023 edition will take you on a journey that's out of this world, revealing the latest and greatest record-breaking achievements both here on Earth and across space via nine superlative-packed "Missions" (chapters). It's time to explore the final frontier...

Bizarre Beasts

Galleries packed with epic photography

Infographic panels visually convey the facts

Central & South America

YOUNG ACHIEVERS

Back by popular demand is the Young Achievers section, which this year honours nine record-breaking newcomers. Look out for exclusive Q&As from these inspirational under-16s, who share their experience on topics as diverse as becoming the **youngest chess Grandmaster**, winning the Classic *Tetris* World Championship, living life as the ▶ **tallest teenager**... and even collecting lip balms!

Abhimanyu Mishra

AROUND THE WORLD
Jules Verne's classic novel *Around the World in Eighty Days* celebrates its 150th birthday in 2023, and to mark the occasion, we're taking you on a superlative tour of our planet. Don't worry – you won't need your passport: you can make this virtual trip without stepping outdoors!

SNAPSHOT
Tallest Snowman

AVIATION PIONEER
Wally Funk

HALL OF FAME
Eight more of the most inspirational, high-achieving Guinness World Records heroes are celebrated in the 2023 Hall of Fame. Among the inductees we salute this year are Paralympian Ellie Simmonds, Rubik's Cube champion Max Park, soccer legend Cristiano Ronaldo, multiple Grammy-winner Beyoncé and astronaut Wally Funk.

SNAPSHOT
In this feature, we picture a record holder out of context to show just how amazing it is. For example, we took the **tallest snowman** to Greece, where it towers above the Parthenon temple in Athens.

CONTINUE YOUR JOURNEY ONLINE
Whenever you see the play-button symbol, visit **guinnessworldrecords.com/2023** for free video content. Our digital team has curated a selection of clips from the world's most awe-inspiring record holders, so don't miss the opportunity to see the superlatives truly come to life. Plus, look out for QR codes that take you to more bonus material.

Editor's Letter

Welcome to the new edition of the world's best-selling annual book. This year, we processed 38,991 applications, and over the next 250 pages we've curated our favourites from the 4,964 titles that made it through the approvals process.

Being the proud owner of an official Guinness World Records certificate continues to be high on the bucket list for many thousands of people around the world. We hear this every day as our Records Managers process the tens of thousands of applications that cross their desks annually. The recent easing of COVID-19 restrictions and the return to some kind of "normality" has only fuelled this. And while it *is* a lot of work to sift through these applications, it does mean we get to witness superlative achievements across an ever-wider spectrum of record breaking, from an ever more diverse pool of record breakers.

Indeed, what I hope you'll realize when reading *Guinness World Records 2023* is that we strive to celebrate record breaking in its widest, most diverse form. No matter your age,

nationality, sex, race, religion, gender, sexuality or ability, there will be a superlative to suit you. To this end, in 2022 we initiated our Kids' Records project to formulate challenges specifically targeted at the under-16s (pp.8–9). Work also began on the GWR Impairment Initiative, to create even more record-breaking opportunities for those with physical and mental challenges by expanding the definition of our record categories (pp.10–11). We're also proud to have partnered this year with the likes of the Dwarf Sports Association and the Royal National Institute for the Blind to bring record breaking to an ever-widening circle of people.

MOST EFFERVESCENT TABLET ROCKETS LAUNCHED SIMULTANEOUSLY
We were back on *Live with Kelly and Ryan* on 23 Sep 2021, as "Science Bob" Pflugfelder sent 5,025 pressurized-gas rockets skywards. Kelly Ripa, Ryan Seacrest and the WABC-TV Props Department (all USA) joined in the fizz-fest. The props team spent nearly 10 hours setting up the explosive event!

MOST DOUBLE AROUND-THE-WORLD BALL-CONTROL TRICKS IN ONE MINUTE
On 13 Oct 2021, Laura Biondo (VEN) helped us celebrate GWR Day by performing 24 of these fleet-footed tricks in 60 sec. In fact, the prolific freestyler racked up another record that day, executing the **most sit-down football crossovers in 30 seconds (female)** – 62.

HEAVIEST VEHICLE-PULL OVER 100 FEET
Renowned Canadian strongman Rev. Kevin Fast thinks nothing of propelling cars, sleighs and even aircraft using only his bare hands. To honour his country's 150th anniversary, he hauled three fire trucks weighing a combined 99,060 kg (218,389 lb) over a distance of 100 ft (30.4 m).

MOST PEOPLE BACKFLIPPED OVER ON ICE SKATES
Former international figure skater Elladj Baldé (CAN) proved that he's not lost his edge by backflipping across three people in Los Angeles, California, USA, on 15 Apr 2022. Elladj regularly posts videos of his daring stunts on social media, hoping to encourage more Black and indigenous youngsters to take up ice skating.

The past 12 months has even seen a marked increase in interest from applicants wishing to break records beyond the bounds of our planet. This is why we kick things off this year with a chapter – or indeed Mission, as we're calling them – dedicated to space. The starting pistol has been fired on a new type of space race, one that sees civilians jostling to become the first, the highest, the oldest or the youngest to make their mark at the final frontier, fuelled by the commercialization of space travel. Admittedly, this kind

WITH BONUS CONTENT

BEYOND THE BOOK
We've got so much record-breaking news to share with you this year that we've added a whole constellation of bonus content online. Wherever you see our two astronauts bearing QR codes, just whip out your phone's camera, scan the square and you'll be directed to GWR TikTok videos, Facebook posts, Instagram stories and web articles. You'll also find guidelines on how you too can get your hands on a GWR certificate!

The ▶ button indicates that a record comes with a video from our YouTube channel. To find these quickly, scan the QR code on the right – you'll be taken straight there.

And if you're a Snapchat user, you can unlock even more video content by scanning the Snapcodes dotted throughout the book. Just open the app and point the camera at the Ghostface Chillah in adjudicator garb!

MOST PENCILS IN THE BEARD
On 21 Sep 2021, Joel Strasser (USA) broke his own record by inserting 456 pencils into his facial fuzz on the set of *Live with Kelly and Ryan* in New York City. It took him around 1 hr 10 min to place them all in his beard, but less than 10 sec to shake them out at the conclusion of the attempt!

of record breaking might not be open to the average person, but it is undeniably inspiring the human race to push the boundaries of what's possible.

We're back down on *terra firma* for the rest of the regular Missions: Life on Earth, Human Body, Extraordinary Exploits, Epic Engineering, Entertainment, Modern World and Sport. As ever, each section has been curated with the help of our global team of knowledgeable consultants and advisers (see pp.252-53). We're honoured to welcome some new names to the GWR roster, including

TALLEST POPSICLE-STICK STRUCTURE
There's no end to the possibilities for how to achieve a GWR title. Eric Klabel (USA) did it with popsicle sticks – gluing 1,750 of them together to create a 6.15-m-tall (20-ft 2-in) tower. The 12-year-old teamed up with his father, Brian, to construct the vertiginous structure, in a feat that will take some licking...

YOUNGEST OPERA SINGER
Golden-throated Victory Brinker (USA, b. 4 Feb 2012) was 7 years 314 days old when she performed at the Pittsburgh Public Theater's *Lights & Legends* show in Pennsylvania, USA, on 15 Dec 2019. This was Victory's fourth public recital, which qualified her as a professional singer, as set out in the GWR guidelines.

Editor's Letter

the IRONMAN Group, the World Jigsaw Puzzle Federation, AbleGamers and the International Surfing Association's World Para Surfing Championship. And thanks to the new individual recruits who've joined the team too, among them palaeontologist Dr Steven Zhang, political scientist Professor Erica Chenoweth, visual-effects guru Ian Failes, climbing enthusiast Michael Levy and fashion historian Cassidy Zachary.

New consultants also mean new topics, so look out for themes such as bird-spotting (pp.42–43), animal heroes (pp.50–51), political activism (pp.200–01) and even cryptocurrencies and NFTs (pp.202–03).

AROUND THE WORLD

In addition to the regular Missions, you'll also find a feature chapter inspired by the publication – 150 years ago – of Jules Verne's best-selling novel *Around the World In Eighty Days*. In "Around the World in 300 Records" (pp.114–47), we honour the author's sense of adventure by embarking on a global tour of our own, taking in 300 superlative cultural highlights along the way. If you've missed the opportunity to travel over the past couple of years, this section will hopefully remind you about our planet's myriad wonders.

SUPER BOWL 2022

As usual, there's a wealth of pulse-quickening Stateside sports in this year's *GWR*. You'll find the Super Bowl and World Series featured on pp.224–25. And flip to pp.226–27 for a must-know round-up of the latest US sports action. Shown here, from left, are two of the 2022 Super Bowl-winning LA Rams – Andrew Whitworth and wide receiver Cooper Kupp. The game made record holders out of both Kupp and the Rams' coach Sean McVay (see below).

Super Bowl 2022 highlights

Title	Record	Holder
Youngest Super Bowl-winning coach	36 years 20 days	Sean McVay (LA Rams)
Most sacks in a Super Bowl (team)	7	Pittsburgh Steelers (1976), Chicago Bears (1986), Denver Broncos (2016) and LA Rams (2022)
Most receptions in one postseason	33	Cooper Kupp
Youngest combined age for Super Bowl head coaches	74 years 299 days	Sean McVay (LA Rams) and Zac Taylor (Cincinnati Bengals)

All record holders USA

MOST PEOPLE IN AN ONLINE WEATHER-REPORTING VIDEO RELAY

On 21 Jun 2021, Al Roker (USA) and friends strung together a 63-person online weather-reporting relay on NBC's *Today* in New York City. A total of 63 NBC affiliate stations were involved in the relay across the United States, which spanned multiple time zones.

FASTEST 100 MILES ULTRA DISTANCE (FEMALE)

Endurance athlete Camille Herron (USA) ran 100 mi (160 km) in just 12 hr 41 min 11 sec, completing her epic trek in Henderson, Nevada, on 18 Feb 2022. She bettered her own record by 1 min 29 sec, in a race that was her first as a Master (i.e., in the aged 40-44 class).

Making a very welcome return this year are the "Young Achievers" – those record holders aged 15 or under who are already making an impact on the world. Among those selected this time around are a *Tetris* world champion, a chess Grandmaster, two breakdancers and an eight-year-old with an amazing aptitude for arithmetic.

HALL OF FAME

Equally worthy of praise are the eight new inductees to the GWR Hall of Fame. Each year, we identify individuals who we feel embody the spirit of record breaking and strive to inspire others. Look out for an octogenarian astronaut (pp.34–35), a tech-minded teen who changes lives with LEGO® (pp.148–49), and a tour-de-force of music, film and entrepreneurship (pp.164–65).

We're also revisiting our Snapshots. These poster-like pages show the immensity of a record by placing the holder somewhere more recognizable. How big is a blue whale, the world's **largest ever animal**? How tall is the new **largest Ferris wheel**? And how much meat does the **largest producer of beef** actually produce? To answer these questions, our artists at 55 Design have dropped the whale into a busy London street (pp.52–53), relocated the Ferris wheel next to Egypt's Great Pyramid (pp.160–61) and skewered a humongous hamburger on to the Washington Monument (pp.212–13). You'll make more of these mind-blowing discoveries as you flick through this year's book.

ALL-TIME BEST GAMING RECORDS

One more feature you shouldn't miss is the Top 25 videogaming records, which starts on p.184. The Editors and Records Managers have collaborated with our gaming consultants to vote for the GWR record titles that they feel encapsulate the greatest gaming records of all time – so, not necessarily the best games (although they are all pretty amazing titles!) but the most significant superlatives. These range from technical developments and individual achievements to the best-selling franchises and most critically acclaimed series.

OLDEST PERSON TO RELEASE AN ALBUM OF NEW MATERIAL
Veteran crooner Tony Bennett (USA, b. 3 Aug 1926) was aged 95 years 58 days when *Love for Sale*, his second collaborative album with vocalist Lady Gaga, was released on 30 Sep 2021. The set pays affectionate tribute to the composer Cole Porter.

Breaking a record – or even just reading about them or watching them via social media – is a mind-expanding experience. It broadens your horizons and opens you up to the possibilities out there. It doesn't matter how ambitious you are – whether you're weightlifting on a unicycle (p.81), summitting Everest (p.96) or rocketing off to the *International Space Station* (p.20) – the key is to set yourself goals, strive for them and, most important of all, enjoy the journey!

Craig Glenday
Craig Glenday
Editor-in-Chief

MOST DECADES ON THE US HOT COUNTRY SONGS CHART (FEMALE)
Dolly Parton (USA) has scored hits on *Billboard*'s Hot Country Songs chart for an astonishing seven consecutive decades (1960s–2020s). She extended her existing six-decade run when "Cuddle Up, Cozy Down Christmas" – a duet with Michael Bublé – debuted at No.48 on 2 Jan 2021.

THE HARLEM GLOBETROTTERS
On 6 Dec 2021, world-famous US basketball exhibition team the Harlem Globetrotters slam-dunked an astonishing 18 GWR titles! They included the **farthest bounce shot** – 28.56 m (93 ft 8.4 in) – by Corey "Thunder" Law (second from right) – and **most underhanded half-court shots in one minute** – seven – by Rock "Wham" Middleton (centre, with ball).

Kids Only!

Youngsters of the world assemble! We've heard your complaints that grown-ups have been hogging all the fun records for too long. But no more: now there are some exclusively for you!

There are loads of GWR challenges that are perfect for kids looking to achieve records, but adults (who *should* know better!) keep on breaking them and making them really difficult to beat. So, to give under-16s the chance to make a name for themselves, we've created a series of record titles that the old folk can't touch!

On these pages, you'll find four examples from the Kids' Records project, so you can get practising straight away. There are a whole lot more on the GWR Kids website – including a selection of videogame challenges – so whatever you're good at, you'll find a record to suit your skills. And who knows, maybe this time next year you'll find your name listed in the *GWR* book! Good luck!

Scan the QR code to access the full GWR guidelines for all the kids' records listed here. You'll also find a few more categories to challenge you. Just follow the on-screen instructions to register your attempt. Let's find out if you're Officially Amazing!

MOST SOFT TOYS CAUGHT BLINDFOLDED BY A TEAM OF TWO IN ONE MINUTE

For this sporting challenge, you'll need to grab as many plushies and cuddly toys as you can get your hands on.

1. This is a record for two people: one person throwing the toys and the other catching.
2. The toys must be commercially available (i.e., sold in shops) and no bigger than 19 cm (7.5 in) at the longest dimension.
3. A distance of 3 m (9 ft 10 in) must be measured on the floor and marked out with a line at both ends. The thrower must be behind one line and the catcher behind the other.
4. The catcher must be blindfolded.
5. The toys can only be caught with the hands, arms and upper body.
6. Once a toy is caught, it can be dropped.

Current record: apply now!

FASTEST TIME TO STACK A 20-BRICK RIGHT-ANGLE LEGO® TOWER

For this record, you just need a stopwatch and 20 LEGO bricks (and we advise using a base plate if you've got one).

1. This is a record for one person.
2. Only 2 x 4 LEGO bricks can be used. A LEGO base plate is optional (but highly recommended!).
3. Start with both of your hands flat on a table, and the bricks disconnected and not touching the base plate.
4. Once the timer starts, you can only use one hand to pick up one brick. You must then alternate the hand used – so left then right, or vice versa.
5. Each brick must be placed at right angles (90°) to the brick below, and aligned to create a straight tower (see left).
6. The timer stops when the 20th brick is placed. The finished tower must then stand for 5 seconds for the record to be valid.

Current record: 21.70 sec, by William Liu (USA) on 13 Nov 2021.

Do Try This At Home! The records shown here use objects commonly found around the home. You'll need a stopwatch and/or tape measure too, depending on the record. If gaming is more your thing, we've also created challenges using some of the most popular titles.

Stacking LEGO bricks

Building a block tower

Sorting the alphabet

Catching soft toys

Sticking notes on face

Sorting recyclables

Wearing socks

Stacking books

Hanging candy canes

Stacking cans

Matching emojis

MOST SOCKS PUT ON ONE FOOT IN 30 SECONDS

Don't put your foot in it when attempting this record! No, wait... DO put your foot in it – that's the whole point!

1. This is a record for one person.
2. The socks you use must be commercially available.
3. Once the timer starts, place one sock at a time over your chosen foot.
4. The socks must be pulled up above the ankle joint to count towards the record.
5. Any socks that rip during the record attempt will not be counted.

Current record: 15, by Alberto Ugolini (ITA) on 25 Feb 2022.

MOST TIMES TO HIT A TARGET WITH A PAPER AIRCRAFT IN THREE MINUTES

This should be *plane* sailing – all you need to do is throw some paper aircraft into a bucket. Easy! Right?!

1. This is a record for one person.
2. Before the attempt starts, make a LOT of paper aeroplanes. You must use A4 paper (210 x 297 mm) and your planes must have two recognizable wings.
3. The bucket you use as the target can be no wider at the top than 30 cm (11.8 in).
4. You must be standing at least 3 m (9 ft 10 in) from the centre of the bucket, so measure it out and mark it on the ground.
5. Lob as many planes as you can into the bucket – one at a time. If any bounce out, they won't count.

Current record: apply now!

Remember to re-use or recycle the paper at the end of your record attempts!

Throwing baubles

Throwing paper planes

MINECRAFT

HOT WHEELS UNLEASHED

BONUS: GAMING CHALLENGES!

Sorting candies

Packing a school bag

EA SPORTS FIFA 22

FORTNITE

BREAK THE RECORD
JULY 22

BREAK THE RECORD ON YOUTUBE

Our two volunteers helping us to introduce the Kids' Records project are Mia and Harry, both of whom featured in the GWR YouTube Originals series *Break the Record*.

In this show, kids were coached by some well-known record breakers before finally making a formal record attempt in front of an official GWR adjudicator. Harry bagged himself a certificate for the ▶ **farthest mini tennis hit from an elevated platform**, sending a ball flying 31.7 m (104 ft) while standing on a 10-m-high (32-ft 9-in) podium at the Crystal Palace National Sports Centre in London, UK. To see Harry in action, and watch more kids' content, scan the QR code below.

YouTube Originals
BREAK THE RECORD
START

Kidoodle tv™

GO ONLINE FOR MORE

GWR's own Kids website is packed with all the latest stunts and tricks, as well as some crazy collectors, astonishing animals and peculiar pastimes. Plus, you'll find games and puzzles inspired by your favourite record holders.

You'll also find all kinds of record-breaking action on Kidoodle.TV. This safe-streaming platform has content that's been hand-picked for a mind-blowing, eye-popping experience. Check out more than 100 videos featuring the likes of the **highest-jumping llama**, the **shortest woman** and the world's **fastest Rubik's Cubers**, plus how-to tutorials from some of the most successful record breakers.

Impairment Initiative

Inspired by the classifications in para sports, GWR is working with specialists in this field to introduce a range of categories for applicants with impairments. We will be announcing further classifications over the coming year.

GWR has always been determined to make record breaking accessible to everyone, irrespective of their physical limitations. Indeed, you can see some incredible examples of people overcoming adversity in "No Limits" on pp.98–99. And while we've always ratified records from para athletes (see pp.232–33), a new project is underway at GWR to extend record breaking beyond purely federated sports.

The aim of the initiative is to open record categories for applicants who face physical and intellectual challenges. We've sought advice from various sporting organizations and disability charities, and established a classification system that we hope will offer the widest range of superlatives to the widest range of applicants.

Opposite is a diagram that outlines the first of a number of classifications aimed at claimants with impairments, which is defined as "a loss or abnormality of an organ or body mechanism". The system is arranged into six sections – Sight (S), Intellectual (I), Muscle (M), Coordination (C), Amputation (A) and Stature (S) – with each further subdivided to encompass a range of impairments.

The initiative has already started to bear fruit, and on this page you can meet some of the applicants to have their records approved. If you're inspired by these remarkable individuals to make an application of your own, register your request at **guinnessworldrecords.com/apply** and tell us about the record(s) you want to attempt. This is your chance to be Officially Amazing!

FASTEST 100 MILES ON A TREADMILL (LA2)

Amy Palmiero-Winters (USA) took 21 hr 43 min 29 sec to complete 100 mi (160 km) on a treadmill in New York City, USA, on 10–11 Jul 2021. She changed over her prosthetic legs during the run to ensure that she stayed comfortable and safe throughout the attempt. You can discover more of Amy's amazing achievements on pp.98–99.

GREATEST VERTICAL UPHILL DISTANCE ON FOOT IN 24 HOURS (LA2)

On 17 Aug 2021, Jon Hilton (UK) climbed 1,345 m (4,412 ft) up Ben Nevis – the highest mountain in the British Isles. Jon had his leg amputated in Nov 2020 owing to damage caused by a blood clot. He attempted this record to prove that his disability does not define or limit him – and to raise over £13,000 ($18,000) for various charities. He's shown with his children (left to right) Ryan, Lauren and Joshua.

LONGEST 50-50 GRIND ON A SKATEBOARD (IS2)

Dan Mancina (USA) pulled off a 6.85-m (22-ft 5-in) grind in Royal Oak, Michigan, USA, on 15 Jan 2022. After losing his sight, Dan managed to remaster his skating skills by using sounds and cracks – along with a guide stick – to help orientate himself when he is on his board.

FASTEST ACCUMULATIVE TIME TO CROSS THE UK BY TANDEM BICYCLE (IS1)

Tim and Andy Caldwell (both UK) cycled across the UK from St David's in Pembrokeshire to Lowestoft in Suffolk in 24 hr 43 min 47 sec from 2 to 5 Jun 2021. Tim suffered a cardiac arrest in 2013, which caused him to lose his sight. The trauma also affected his ability to talk and walk. Andy, his cousin, began taking Tim out on the tandem to restore his physical and mental health – and the pair wound up setting this new GWR title!

You'll find para athletes – such as Daniel Dias (BRA), holder of the **most Summer Paralympics swimming medals (male)** – throughout the sports chapter (pp.218–45). We also have a dedicated para sports feature on pp.232–33.

Guinness World Records
IMPAIRMENT CLASSIFICATIONS

II
Intellectual impairment
An ongoing substantial limitation to learning or adaptive behaviour; needs help with everyday tasks. Participants must be medically diagnosed with a cognitive disability that significantly affects physical performance.

MP1
Muscle power impairment – arms
Inability to generate full force for movement through the arms and shoulders; limited functionality of the arms and shoulders but no trunk or leg function.

MP2
Muscle power impairment – trunk
Inability to generate full force for movement through the trunk; full ability to generate power using the arms, limited trunk function but no leg function.

CIM1
Coordination impairment – monoplegic arm*
Loss or lack of smooth body movements in a single arm (either limb).

CID1
Coordination impairment – diplegic arms*
Loss or lack of smooth body movements in corresponding parts of the body on both sides (both arms).

CI1
Coordination impairment – quadriplegic*
Loss or lack of smooth body movements in all four limbs (arms and legs).

CIH
Coordination impairment – hemiplegia*
Loss or lack of smooth body movements in either side of the body (right or left side).

CIM2
Coordination impairment – monoplegic leg*
Loss or lack of smooth body movements in a single leg (either limb).

CID2
Coordination impairment – diplegic legs*
Loss or lack of smooth body movements in corresponding parts of the body on both sides (both legs).

MP3
Muscle power impairment – legs
Inability to generate full force for movement through the legs; full ability to generate power using the arms, limited to full trunk function but limited leg function.

*Includes hypertonia, ataxia and athetosis conditions
†Unilateral: affects one limb; bilateral: affects both limbs

IS1
Impaired sight 1
Visual acuity range from (and including) LogMAR 0.5 to 1.48; and/or visual field constricted to a diameter of <40°.

IS2
Impaired sight 2
Visual acuity range from (and including) LogMAR 1.5 to 2.58; and/or visual field constricted to a diameter of <10°.

IS3
Impaired sight 3
Visual acuity over LogMAR 2.60.

IS4
Impaired sight 4
Visual field constricted to a diameter of <10°.

AA1
Unilateral above-elbow (transhumeral) amputation†
Absence of a single arm from above the elbow joint or through the shoulder joint (disarticulation); the elbow joint must not be present.

AA3
Bilateral above-elbow (transhumeral) amputation†
Absence of both arms from above the elbow joint or through the shoulder joint (disarticulation); the elbow joints must not be present.

AA2
Unilateral below-elbow (transradial/ulnar) amputation
Absence of a single arm from below the elbow; the elbow joint must be present, but the wrist joint must not.

AA4
Bilateral below-elbow (transradial/ulnar) amputation
Absence of both the arms from below the elbow; the elbow joints must be present, but the wrist joints must not.

LA1
Unilateral above-knee (transfemoral) amputation
Absence of the leg from above or through the knee joint.

LA3
Bilateral above-knee (transfemoral) amputation
Absence of both legs from above or through the knee joint.

LA2
Unilateral below-knee (transtibial) amputation
Absence of the lower leg; the knee joint must be present, but the ankle joint must not be present.

LA4
Bilateral below-knee (transtibial) amputation
Absence of both lower legs; the knee joints must be present, but the ankle joints must not be present.

SS
Short stature
For the purpose of this record, short stature refers to participants over the age of 18 who are less than 4 ft 10 in (147.32 cm) tall.

Each year, thousands of people around the globe take on an array of challenges in celebration of Guinness World Records Day. The 18th GWR Day took place on 17 Nov 2021, and after the COVID-enforced remote adjudications in 2020, our international community of record breakers were eager to get out and put on a show. And what a jaw-dropping variety of talent we witnessed!

━━━━━ = Location of record attempt

GWR Day 2021: record-breaking around the globe

	Title	Record	Holder
1	Most consecutive axe-juggling catches	2,919	David Rush (USA)
2	Most consecutive cars jumped over on a pogo stick	5	TPhil, aka Tyler Phillips (USA)
3	Most pool trick shots completed in one hour	58	Florian Kohler (FRA)
4	Farthest distance lache cat leap (bar to wall)	4.90 m (16 ft 1 in)	Najee Richardson (USA)
5	Fastest 1 km on crutches (one leg)	6 min 12.88 sec	Christian Roberto López Rodríguez (ESP)
6	Most double "around the world" ball-control tricks in one minute (female)	24	Laura Biondo (VEN)
7	Fastest time to flip three water bottles	1.20 sec	Rocco Mercurio (ITA)
8	Longest duration spinning five hula hoops using the bum and arms	4 min 6 sec	Andrea M (UK, b. USA)
9	Farthest backflip between horizontal bars	6.00 m (19 ft 8 in)	Ashley Watson (UK)
10	Most rope crossovers skipping on one leg blindfolded in 30 seconds	57	Cristian Sabba (ITA)

GWR Day 2021: record-breaking around the globe

	Title	Record	Holder
11	Most single-leg backward somersaults in 30 seconds	12	Ayoub Touabe (MAR)
12	Most thumbtacks inserted into a cork board in one minute	140	André Ortolf (DEU)
13	Most apples crushed by hand in one minute	21	Naseem Uddin (PAK)
14	Most magic tricks performed blindfolded in one minute	30	Avery Chin (MYS)
15	Most BMX Stick-B spins in 30 seconds	37	Takahiro Ikeda (JPN)
16	Fastest time to pull a car 50 m walking on hands	1 min 13.27 sec	Zhang Shuang (CHN)
17	Fastest 20 m by a three-person tower	11.20 sec	Jordan Steffens, Shani Stephens and Josh Strachan (all AUS)
18	Most chopsticks thrown blindfolded at a target in one minute	17	Anthony Kelly (AUS)

GWR Day 2021 also saw a pair of young breakdancers rip up the record books – turn to p.104 for more…

LARGEST SPACE STATION

As of 22 Dec 2021, following the addition of the *Nauka* module and the *Prichal* docking node, the *International Space Station* (*ISS*) had a mass of 418,190 kg (921,951 lb) – or 459,025 kg (1,011,976 lb) including docked spacecraft. It is also the **longest-lasting space station**, having been continuously occupied for more than 21 years.

This picture was taken by astronaut Thomas Marshburn, looking down on the *ISS* during a spacewalk in Dec 2021. Opposite is a view of the station from one of the SpaceX Crew Dragon spacecraft that delivered new personnel to the *ISS* in Nov 2021.

Space

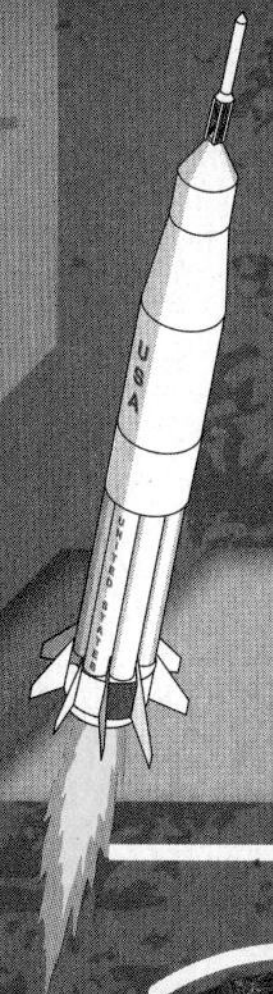

EXPLORATION

DISCOVERY

RESEARCH

2023

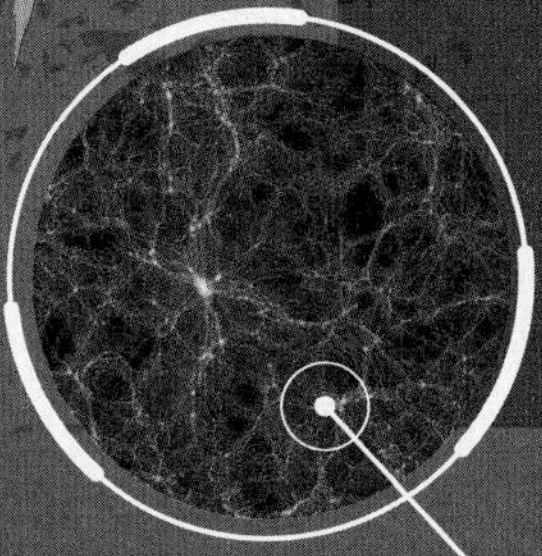

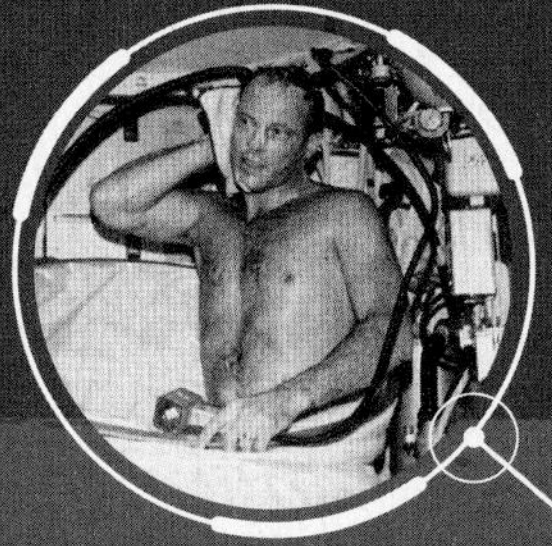

Nauka and *Prichal*

European Space Agency astronaut Matthias Maurer

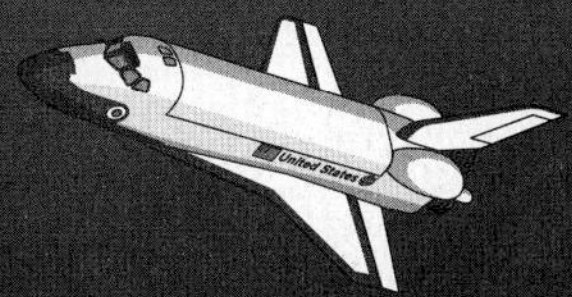

The station is crammed with gadgets, including more than 100 laptops and several free-flying robots.

Astrobee robot assistant

Rockets

Most successful launches (single rocket model)

Between its debut on 18 May 1973 and its retirement on 22 Feb 2017, Soviet/Russian Soyuz-U rockets (**10**; see opposite) reached orbit 765 times. This tally includes the **most successful launches in a single year** – 47, set in 1979. Even then, when the factory was sending a new rocket to the launchpad every eight days, the Soyuz-U suffered only two failures. Over the course of its decades-long career, only 22 Soyuz-U launches failed to reach the planned orbit, giving it a phenomenal success rate of 97.2%.

Largest reusable spacecraft

NASA's Space Transportation System (**8**) was built around the Space Shuttle orbiter, which had a mass of 78,200 kg (172,400 lb), measured 37.2 m (122 ft) from nose to tail and had a wingspan of 23.8 m (78 ft). On launch, the shuttle's engines provided a third of the system's thrust – drawing fuel from its distinctive orange external tank – while two solid-rocket boosters provided the rest.

The closest rival to the Space Shuttle was the Soviet Union's short-lived Energia rocket (**6**) and its Buran orbiter. The orbiter was 36.3 m (119 ft) long, had a wingspan of 23.9 m (78 ft 4 in) and a mass of around 62,000 kg (136,700 lb). It only flew once – uncrewed – on 15 Nov 1988 before the project was cancelled.

FIRST LIQUID-FUELLED ROCKET LAUNCH

On 16 Mar 1926, Dr Robert Hutchings Goddard (USA) fired off a rocket powered by gasoline and liquid oxygen in his Aunt Effie's cabbage patch in Auburn, Massachusetts, USA. His invention reached an altitude of 41 ft (12.5 m), flew at an average speed of around 60 mph (96.5 km/h) and travelled 184 ft (56 m). The total flight time was a shade over 2 seconds.

FIRST USE OF ROCKETS

In the late 12th century, Chinese chemists developed small, self-propelled fireworks known as *ti lao shu* ("ground rats") using gunpowder packed into short lengths of bamboo. It is likely that more substantial and stable rockets – attached to arrow-like shafts – appeared during the same period. By the time of the 14th-century military treatise known as the *Huo Lung Ching* ("Fire Drake Manual", above), a wide range of technically advanced rockets were known to Chinese military engineers.

Most powerful rocket by lift capacity

First launched on 6 Feb 2018, the SpaceX Falcon Heavy can lift a payload (the term for a rocket's cargo) of up to 63,800 kg (140,660 lb) into low Earth orbit. Falcon Heavy consists of a Falcon 9 rocket with an extra first-stage booster attached on either side, giving the vehicle a total of 27 rocket motors and 22,800 kN (kiloNewtons), or 5.1 million lbf (pounds-force), of thrust.

Of course, mass isn't everything – for some missions, the more important factor is the physical size of the payload. For oversize loads such as the James Webb Space Telescope (see pp.30–31), you need the **widest payload fairing** – the 5.4-m-diameter (17-ft 8-in) nose cone of the European Space Agency's Ariane 5 (**12**).

Most powerful liquid-propellant rocket

The Soviet/Russian RD-171M rocket engine, which first flew as the powerplant for the Zenit launch vehicle on 13 Apr 1985, generates 7,256 kN (1.6 million lbf) of thrust at sea level. The RD-171M has a central pump system that feeds a mixture of fuel and liquid oxygen to its four seperate combustion chambers at a rate of 2.5 tonnes (5,500 lb) per second.

Smallest orbital rocket

The SS-520-5 (**13**) stands just 9.54 m (31 ft 3 in) tall, with a diameter of 0.52 m (1 ft 8 in), and weighs 2,600 kg (5,732 lb), making it approximately 30 times lighter than the Space Shuttle *Columbia*. It was developed by the Japan Aerospace Exploration Agency (JAXA) to carry small satellites and scientific instruments into low orbits, and first flew on 3 Feb 2018. JAXA's primary launch vehicle is the much larger Mitsubishi H-IIA (**9**).

Most orbital launches by a country (current year)

In recent years, China has dominated the field when it comes to launch rates. Over the course of 2021, Chinese-made rockets made 53 successful orbital flights. The workhorse of China's space programme is the Long March 3 series (**7**), which has made 128 successful launches since its debut in 1984. The China National Space Administration plans to replace the Long March 2, 3 and 4 series rockets in the next few years, as they are some of only a few active launch vehicles that still use hydrazine – the **most toxic rocket propellant** – for their first-stage boosters. Ingesting or inhaling as little as 4 g (0.1 oz) of hydrazine is enough to kill an adult human.

MOST POWERFUL ROCKET STAGE

Initially fired on 21 Feb 1969, the Block A first stage of the Soviet N1 Moon rocket (**3**) generated around 45,250 kN (10.1 million lbf) of thrust at sea level. By comparison, the American Saturn V rocket generated 31,100 kN (7.8 million lbf). The N1 was designed by the OKB-1 design bureau (today known as RSC Energia) and was only launched four times. None of the attempts reached orbit and the programme was eventually shut down in 1974.

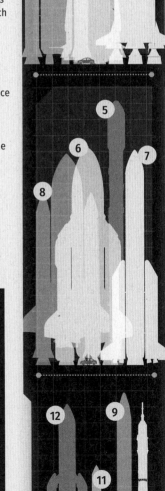

Each grid square = 4.2 m (13 ft 9 in)

MOST POWERFUL SINGLE-CHAMBER ROCKET
The Rocketdyne F-1 was built for the first stage of NASA's Saturn V rocket. This gigantic motor – which stood 18 ft 6 in (5.6 m) tall and weighed 18,500 lb (8,400 kg) – generated 1.5 million lbf (6,770 kN) of thrust at sea level. It first flew on an uncrewed test of the Saturn V rocket on 9 Nov 1967.

FIRST REUSABLE ORBITAL SPACECRAFT
NASA's Space Shuttle orbiters were the first spacecraft capable of repeated take-offs and landings. *Columbia* made the first flight on 12 Apr 1981 and was the first to be reflown, on 12 Nov the same year.

OLDEST ORBITAL ROCKET FAMILY
Rockets are often grouped into "families", which represent various different configurations and upgrades of the same basic design. Iterations of the Soviet/Russian R-7 series have included the rockets that launched the **first artificial satellite** in 1957 (**11**) and landers to Venus in the 1970s, as well as the Soyuz rockets (pictured) that carry crews to the *International Space Station*.

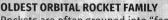

LARGEST SOLID-FUEL ROCKET BOOSTER
NASA's Space Launch System (SLS) Five-Segment Booster was built by Northrop Grumman (USA) for the SLS super-heavy rocket (**4**). Each one of these boosters, which will be used in pairs as part of the SLS, generates 14,590 kN (3.2 million lbf) at sea level, which also makes them the **most powerful rocket motors** ever made. Each Five-Segment Booster produces some 25% more thrust than the Space Shuttle's solid-rocket boosters.

MOST MISSIONS FLOWN BY A ROCKET FIRST STAGE
SpaceX Falcon 9 (**5**) booster B1051 flew 12 missions between 2 Mar 2019 and 19 Mar 2022. It made its first flight carrying the Crew Dragon Demo-1 mission for NASA, and has since launched a set of Canadian radar satellites, a SiriusXM broadcast satellite and 522 Starlink satellites (over nine flights). These fiery launch and re-entry cycles have transformed its original gleaming white paintwork to a sooty grey.

LARGEST ROCKET
The Saturn V (**2**), developed as part of NASA's Apollo programme, remains the largest rocket ever built. It stood 110.6 m (363 ft) tall on the launchpad and weighed as much as 3,268 tons (2,965 tonnes) when fuelled and ready to launch. From 1967 to 1973, Saturn V rockets carried out seven Moon-landing missions and launched the *Skylab 1* space station (see p.21) into orbit. It will be superseded by the 120-m-tall (394-ft) SpaceX Starship (**1**), if this launches in late 2022 as planned.

Edge of Space

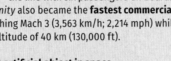

SpaceShipOne
A Paul G. Allen Project

N328KF

FIRST PRIVATELY FUNDED CREWED SPACEFLIGHT
On 21 Jun 2004, *SpaceShipOne* – which was built and operated by US aerospace company Scaled Composites – was flown to an altitude of 100.12 km (328,490 ft), crossing the Kármán Line on a suborbital trajectory over California's Mojave Desert. Its pilot, Mike Melvill (USA, b. ZAF), later received the **first commercial astronaut wings** issued by the US Federal Aviation Administration (FAA).

Where does space start? This is a hard question to answer because there is no natural boundary with air on one side and the vacuum of space on the other. The thin wisps of the upper atmosphere extend beyond the orbits of many satellites, and even the International Space Station. *This means we have to find somewhere to draw a line lower down. Today, the most widely accepted boundary, known as the Kármán Line, lies at 100 km (328,000 ft), but other transition points have been suggested.*

Highest "equivalent altitude" exposure survived
At around 19 km (62,500 ft) lies the first major boundary, known as the Armstrong Limit. At this point, air pressure is low enough that water boils at body temperature. Only a few people have been exposed to such low pressures and survived; the luckiest was NASA volunteer Jim LeBlanc (USA), who briefly experienced the equivalent of an altitude of 36.5 km (120,000 ft) when a spacesuit failed during vacuum-chamber tests on 14 Dec 1966.

Highest altitude by aircraft using aerodynamic lift
In the 1950s, Hungarian-born scientist Theodore von Kármán proposed a definition of space based on the physics of high-altitude flight. He calculated that there would be an altitude at which the speed required to maintain aerodynamic lift would be greater than the speed required to achieve orbit. He suggested

it would be located at 80–100 km (262,000–328,000 ft) but never devoted any time to working this out in detail. In a paper published in 2018, GWR spaceflight consultant Jonathan McDowell recalculated von Kármán's equations with modern data to establish what he calls the "Effective Kármán Line", a boundary that falls between 77 and 86 km (252,000–282,000 ft).

These calculations, however, rely on a hypothetical perfect aircraft. In reality, the highest altitude reached by a plane using aerodynamic lift is much lower, just 37.65 km (123,523 ft). This record was set on 31 Aug 1977 by Soviet test pilot Alexandr Fedotov in a modified MiG-25 "Foxbat" called the Ye-266M.

Highest flight in a commercial passenger aircraft
The US Air Force and NASA both use an atmospheric boundary called the mesopause, which lies at around 80 km (262,000 ft), to mark the line between air and space. On 11 Jul 2021, the Virgin Galactic rocket-plane *Unity* (see below) flew to 86 km (282,152 ft), crossing the line with six passengers on board. On the way up, *Unity* also became the **fastest commercial passenger aircraft**, reaching Mach 3 (3,563 km/h; 2,214 mph) while climbing through an altitude of 40 km (130,000 ft).

First artificial object in space
The German *Aggregat* 4 rocket (the prototype for the V-2 ballistic missile; see opposite) was the first human-made object to cross the 100-km Kármán Line. It is not clear exactly when this took place, but the record-setting flight most likely happened in the summer of 1944, when a series of secret vertical launches – reportedly to altitudes of up to 120 km (393,000 ft) – were carried out from an island in the Baltic Sea called the Griefswalder Oie.

After World War II, many of the Allied powers experimented with captured V-2 rockets. In addition to the **first photos from space** (see opposite), the V-2 was also used to fly the **first dogs in space**: two Moscow strays called Dezik and Tsygan, who were launched to 110 km (360,000 ft) by Soviet scientists on 22 Jul 1951.

Lowest quasi-circular orbit
The highest of the proposed boundaries of space is the minimum stable orbit. Achieving orbit requires an object to travel fast enough that the curve of Earth's surface is sloping away at the same rate that the object is falling towards it. The lower an object's altitude, the more the atmosphere slows it down, pulling it out of orbit. Satellites in quasi-circular orbits (with perigees and apogees – nearest and farthest points from Earth's centre – that differ by only a small amount) can't go below about 120 km (393,000 ft).

On 16 Aug 2016, China's *Lixing-1* research satellite was lowered into an orbit with a perigee and apogee of 124 km and 133 km (406,000 and 436,000 ft) respectively. It remained in this orbit for three days before re-entry on 19 Aug.

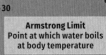

FIRST COMMERCIAL PASSENGER ROCKET PLANE
On 11 Jul 2021, the Virgin Galactic SpaceShipTwo *Unity* reached an altitude of 86 km (282,152 ft) and a top speed of Mach 3 (3,700 km/h; 2,300 mph). The crew of six comprised two pilots and four passengers, including Virgin founder Richard Branson (top right). Even at supersonic speeds, *Unity* is flown using manual controls only, with no computers to assist the pilots.

VIRGINGALACTIC aabar

N202VG

WHERE DOES SPACE START?

500 km
480
460
440
420
400
380
360
340
320
300
280
260
240
220
200
190
180
170
160
150
140
130
120
110
100
90
80
70
60
50
40
30
20
10

Thermopause
Edge of Earth's atmosphere

Minimum orbit
Lowest possible stable orbit

Kármán Line
FAI definition of the edge of space

Thermosphere

Mesopause
USAF "astronaut wings" line

Effective Kármán Line
New proposed boundary of space

Mesosphere

Armstrong Limit
Point at which water boils at body temperature

Stratosphere

Troposphere

FASTEST ROCKET-POWERED AIRCRAFT

An X-15A-2 aircraft attained a speed of Mach 6.7 (7,274 km/h; 4,520 mph) at an altitude of 31.12 km (102,100 ft) over California, USA, on 3 Oct 1967. A total of 199 flights were made as part of the X-15 programme, the highest of which reached 107.8 km (353,000 ft). Eight of the 12 pilots who flew the X-15 were awarded astronaut wings.

FIRST IMAGE OF EARTH FROM SPACE

On 24 Oct 1946, a German-made V-2 rocket was launched from New Mexico, USA, with a camera in place of the original explosive warhead. The camera recorded images showing the curvature of Earth and the blackness of space from an altitude of around 104.6 km (343,000 ft).

HIGHEST CREWED BALLOON FLIGHT

On 24 Oct 2014, Alan Eustace (USA) performed a stratospheric skydive from 41.42 km (135,898 ft) above New Mexico. He had risen by balloon, suspended beneath the envelope in a pressure suit, rather than in a capsule or gondola. Eustace was a senior executive at Google at the time of the jump, which was carried out in secret.

FIRST SUBORBITAL MISSION TO CARRY PAYING CUSTOMERS

Built and operated by US aerospace company Blue Origin, the New Shepard rocket made its first crewed launch from Van Horn, Texas, on 20 Jul 2021. The NS4 booster (an upgraded version of the vehicle that made the **first controlled landing by a suborbital rocket** on 23 Nov 2015) lifted the crew capsule to 107 km (351,000 ft).

All four of the passengers on the rocket became record holders that day. Blue Origin founder Jeff Bezos and his brother Mark (both USA; below left, on the left and right respectively) became the **first siblings in space at the same time**; paying customer Oliver Daemen (NLD, b. 20 Aug 2002; above left) became the **youngest person in space** at 18 years 334 days old; and veteran aviator Wally Funk (b. 1 Feb 1939) became the **oldest** (see p.34). Funk's record was broken on a subsequent Blue Origin flight by *Star Trek* actor William Shatner (CAN; b. 22 Mar 1931), who was 90 years 205 days old when he flew on 13 Oct 2021, but she remains the **oldest woman**.

Life in Orbit

FIRST PRIVATE-CITIZEN ORBITAL MISSION
On 16 Sep 2021, the Inspiration4 civilian spaceflight mission launched on a SpaceX Falcon 9 from Kennedy Space Center, Florida. On board were (left to right) mission organizer Jared Isaacman, medic Hayley Arceneaux, flight engineer Chris Sembroski and pilot Sian Proctor (all USA). Isaacman contracted SpaceX to fly a Crew Dragon spacecraft for the mission, which raised more than $200 m (£144 m) for the St Jude children's cancer charity.

First person to eat in space
During his historic 108-min Vostok 1 mission (the **first crewed spaceflight**) on 12 Apr 1961, Soviet cosmonaut Yuri Gagarin ate a meal of beef and liver paste from an aluminium tube. This was followed up with a dessert of chocolate spread.

First person to vomit in space
Space sickness is a form of kinetosis (motion sickness) caused by the disorientation that comes with weightlessness. The earliest victim was Soviet cosmonaut Gherman Titov, who experienced nausea and vomiting during the course of his Vostok 2 flight on 6 Aug 1961. Some form of space sickness is felt by around half of all people who fly in space, but symptoms usually disappear after the first day or two in orbit.

First musical performance in space
The dual-spacecraft Vostok 3/4 mission saw cosmonauts Andriyan Nikolayev and Pavel Popovich launched into space 24 hr apart on 11 and 12 Aug 1962, respectively. They were in direct radio communication for much of their flight and took advantage of this instant link to sing songs for the benefit of ground control.

The **first musical instruments in space** were a Hohner "Little Lady" harmonica and a set of small sleigh bells. They were smuggled on board the Gemini VI mission

by a pair of NASA astronauts – Walter "Wally" Schirra and Tom Stafford. On 16 Dec 1965, the duo surprised mission control and the crew of Gemini VII, who were also in orbit, with a performance of the Christmas carol "Jingle Bells".

First food grown in space
During their 61-day stay on the Salyut 4 space station in 1975, cosmonauts Pyotr Klimuk and Vitaly Sevastyanov used the Oasis-1M greenhouse to grow a crop of small spring onions, which they then ate with Sevastyanov's 40th-birthday dinner on 8 Jul.

On 26 Sep 2019, bovine cells harvested by food-tech start-up Aleph Farms (ISR) cultivated the **first lab-grown meat in space** on the International Space Station (ISS).

First people to vote in space
While on board the Mir space station, cosmonauts Yuri Onufriyenko and Yury Usachov (both RUS) voted in the Russian presidential election on 16 Jun 1996 via proxies on Earth.

In 1997, Texas legislature changed the law on absentee voting, allowing David Wolf (USA) to vote in a local US election from Mir, making him the first US astronaut to do so from space.

First fire on a space station
On 23 Feb 1997, a fire broke out on Mir when lithium perchlorate "candles" – which are heated in order to release oxygen – malfunctioned. Although it was extinguished, the crew came close to abandoning the space station in their Soyuz "lifeboat".

Most accumulated time on spacewalks
Cosmonaut Anatoly Solovyev (RUS) accrued a total of 82 hr 22 min in open space between 1988 and 1998, all while working on Mir. His 16 spacewalks included seven emergency repair missions conducted during Mir Expedition 24, following a collision with a resupply ship (see p.23).

The **female** spacewalk record is held by NASA astronaut Peggy Whitson (USA), who spent 60 hr 21 min working on the exterior of the ISS between 2002 and 2017. Over the course of her career, Whitson spent 665 days 22 hr 22 min in orbit, the **most accumulated time in space (female)**.

Most expensive toilet system
The Space Shuttle Endeavour launched in Jan 1993 with a new unisex toilet. Housed on the Shuttle's mid deck, the $30-m (£19.4-m) facility was described by NASA as a "complete sewage collection and treatment plant… contained in a space one half the size of a telephone booth". The toilet, which had 4,000 parts, included foot holds to keep the user in place.

LARGEST MENU IN SPACE
Space food has come a long way since Yuri Gagarin's tube of meat paste (see above left). As of 16 Nov 2021, the menu available to US astronauts comprises 200 standard items plus many more occasional treats that are sent up from time to time. The Russian crew have a menu that is reportedly even larger, including some 300 items.

INTERNATIONAL SPACE-CATION

In 2019, NASA announced that it would be opening the ISS to space tourists, thereby creating the world's most high-tech self-catering rental. A spot in this Space-BnB costs a suitably skyscraping $1.1 m (£815,200) a night, but what do you get for your money?

Internet and office

WiFi
Available throughout the station

Workspaces
Around 100 tablets and laptops

Laboratory equipment
Fume hoods, glove boxes, freezers

Kitchen and dining

Galley
Food-package hydrator, extensive menu

Table
With handles to hold on to

Coffee maker
The Italian-made "ISSpresso"

Facilities and services

Free parking on premises
Eight docking or berthing ports

Long-term stays allowed
Up to 437 days

Weightless environment
In a state of continuous freefall

Secluded
The neighbours are 408 km (253 mi) below

Gym
Treadmill, exercise bike, weight machines

Not included

Bath/shower

Patio or balcony

Washing machine

Oven

LARGEST ROOM IN SPACE

Launched on 14 May 1973, NASA's *Skylab* was the USA's first space station and the largest single habitable volume launched into space. Its main body consisted of a converted third-stage booster from a Saturn V rocket launcher. This cylindrical space station had a total internal volume of 238.3 m³ (8,419 cu ft), giving a habitable volume of 173 m³ (6,112 cu ft).

FIRST MUSIC VIDEO FILMED IN SPACE

On 12 May 2013, during his last mission on the *ISS*, Commander Chris Hadfield (CAN) posted a video to YouTube of himself singing David Bowie's "Space Oddity". Bowie later told Hadfield it was the most poignant cover of the song ever performed.

FASTEST TIME TO COMPLETE A MARATHON IN ORBIT (MALE)

Tim Peake (UK) ran a 3-hr 35-min 21-sec marathon on a treadmill inside the *ISS* on 24 Apr 2016.

On 16 Apr 2007, NASA astronaut Sunita Williams (USA) achieved the **female** record – 4 hr 24 min – as an official entrant of the 111th Boston Marathon.

MOST PEOPLE IN SPACE AT THE SAME TIME

For a few minutes on 11 Dec 2021, the human population of space numbered 19. It comprised six people in a Blue Origin New Shepard capsule, three in the Chinese *Tiangong* space station (pictured) and 10 in the *ISS*. This beats the previous record space population of 14, set on 20 Jul 2021 (during the first Blue Origin flight, see p.19), and equalled between 15 and 17 Sep during the Inspiration4 mission (see opposite).

LONGEST SINGLE SPACEFLIGHT

Russian doctor Valeriy Poliyakov (below) spent 437 days 17 hr 58 min 31 sec in space. He was launched to the *Mir* space station on board Soyuz TM18 on 8 Jan 1994, and returned to Earth on 22 Mar 1995.

The **longest single spaceflight by a woman** is 328 days 13 hr 58 min 12 sec, set by NASA astronaut Christina Koch (USA) between 14 Mar 2019 and 6 Feb 2020. Remarkably, this was Koch's debut mission.

FIRST SHOWER IN SPACE

Skylab's comparatively large interior volume (see above left) could accommodate a space shower. Users stood inside a ring on the floor and lifted a circular curtain attached to the ceiling. A hose would then spray 2.8 litres (6 pints) of water per use. This was collected afterwards using a vacuum system.

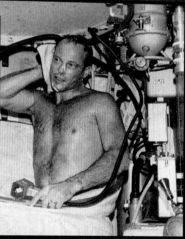

MOST TOILETS IN A SPACE STATION

With the arrival of Russia's *Nauka* module on 29 Jul 2021, the *ISS* boasted three toilets. In 2020, the toilet in the US section was replaced by the Universal Waste Management System. This unit was designed to be quieter, more hygienic and – most importantly – easier for female astronauts and cosmonauts to use.

Space Junk

FIRST PERSON HIT BY SPACE JUNK

On 22 Jan 1997, Lottie Williams (USA) was walking in Turley – a suburb of Tulsa, Oklahoma, USA – when she spotted what she took to be a shooting star. Shortly afterwards, she was struck a glancing blow on the shoulder by a 5-in (12.7-cm) piece of blackened fibreglass. She'd been hit by part of the second stage of a US-made Delta II rocket, whose re-entry she had witnessed earlier.

As of Jan 2022, the **largest pieces of debris (mass)** in orbit are 22 spent upper stages from the Soviet/Russian Zenit-2 rocket, active from 1985 to 2004. Each of these has a dry mass – i.e., with no fuel – of 8,900 kg (19,621 lb), but all have at least some fuel on board, so their actual mass is higher.

Most common type of space junk

The remnants of on-orbit explosions and collisions are known as "fragmentation debris". According to figures published by the NASA Orbital Debris Program Office in 2018, these bits of space shrapnel represent 52.6% of all tracked objects in Earth orbit. There are about 12 "on-orbit fragmentation events" (i.e., satellites or rocket bodies exploding in space) every year.

Excluding weapons tests (see opposite), the most significant fragmentation event was the **first collision between two satellites**. On 10 Feb 2009, the active communications satellite *Iridium 33* was struck by the derelict Russian military satellite *Kosmos-2251*, creating 2,296 pieces of trackable fragmentation debris.

The orbital environment high above our heads is becoming increasingly crowded. Just 65 years since the **first artificial satellite** launched (it later became the **first piece of space junk** – see opposite), there are 4,304 active satellites in Earth orbit and 19,167 items of trackable debris. Space junk makes operating satellites harder – and its levels are rising.

Most active satellites in orbit (country)

According to figures compiled by AstriaGraph on 15 Feb 2022, there are 2,453 active satellites belonging to the United States government or US-based private companies. More than 1,000 of these objects were launched over the course of the previous year, mostly as part of SpaceX's Starlink constellation.

As of 15 Feb 2022, there are 7,343 tracked pieces of orbital debris registered to the Commonwealth of Independent States (CIS) – some 40% of all space junk – making it the **largest contributor to space debris (country)**. The CIS comprises the Russian Federation and several countries of the former Soviet Union. This total includes 959 discarded rocket bodies and 1,287 inactive satellites.

Largest piece of orbital debris (dimensions)

Launched on 25 Mar 2000 and decommissioned on 18 Dec 2005, the *IMAGE* research satellite has a main body measuring 2.25 m (7 ft 4 in) along its longest axis and a mass of 494 kg (1,089 lb). Extending from its body, however, are four 250-m-long (820-ft) tether-like radial antennas, meaning that for collision avoidance, *IMAGE* is regarded as 502 m (1,646 ft) wide.

FIRST UNCREWED ON-ORBIT SATELLITE SERVICING

Most satellites are single-use equipment, abandoned in orbit as space junk when they reach the end of their lifespan. One possible solution to this problem is refuelling them in space, or "on-orbit servicing". The **first on-orbit satellite maintenance** was carried out by astronauts on the Space Shuttle *Challenger* in 1984, but crewed missions were soon found to be too costly.

This is where technologies like the Northrop Grumman *Mission Extension Vehicle* (MEV-1) come in. *MEV-1* is a "space-tug" which attached itself to *Intelsat 901* on 25 Feb 2020 using an extendable grapple (inset). *MEV-1* then used its attitude-control systems to return the conjoined spacecraft to active service on 2 Apr 2020.

LARGEST INACTIVE SATELLITE (MASS)

Envisat is an Earth observation research satellite with a dry mass of 7,911 kg (17,440 lb) and measuring 26 m (85 ft) along its longest axis. It was launched by the European Space Agency on 1 Mar 2002, but contact was lost on 8 Apr 2012. *Envisat* worries those monitoring space debris because of its size and proximity to other space junk. Its orbit brings it within 200 m (656 ft) of two other catalogued objects each year. Shown is a model of *Envisat* at an air show in 1999.

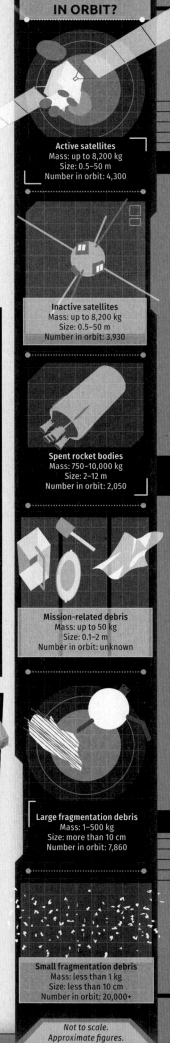

WHAT IS IN ORBIT?

Active satellites
Mass: up to 8,200 kg
Size: 0.5–50 m
Number in orbit: 4,300

Inactive satellites
Mass: up to 8,200 kg
Size: 0.5–50 m
Number in orbit: 3,930

Spent rocket bodies
Mass: 750–10,000 kg
Size: 2–12 m
Number in orbit: 2,050

Mission-related debris
Mass: up to 50 kg
Size: 0.1–2 m
Number in orbit: unknown

Large fragmentation debris
Mass: 1–500 kg
Size: more than 10 cm
Number in orbit: 7,860

Small fragmentation debris
Mass: less than 1 kg
Size: less than 10 cm
Number in orbit: 20,000+

Not to scale.
Approximate figures.

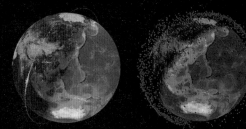

LARGEST SATELLITE FRAGMENTATION EVENT

On 11 Jan 2007, the Chinese military intentionally destroyed weather satellite *Fengyun 1C* (aka object 1999-025A) as part of a test. Its destruction created 3,430 pieces of trackable orbital debris – fragments measuring at least 10 cm (4 in) across – and an estimated 150,000 smaller pieces. The two pictures above show the debris cloud shortly after impact (left) and after one year in orbit (right).

LARGEST SPACECRAFT COLLISION

On 25 Jun 1997, an uncrewed 7-tonne (15,000-lb) Progress supply vehicle struck Russia's 130-tonne (286,600-lb) *Mir* space station. Cosmonauts Vasily Tsibliev and Alexander Lazutkin on board *Mir* had to quickly seal a breach in the hull of its *Spektr* module, whose solar arrays were also damaged (inset), while US astronaut Michael Foale prepared *Mir's Soyuz* capsule for possible evacuation. The station was left dangerously low on power and oxygen and temporarily tumbling out of control.

LARGEST OBJECT LOST ON A SPACEWALK

An 18-kg (39-lb) tool bag came loose from the equipment of astronaut Heidemarie Stefanyshyn-Piper (USA) during a spacewalk on the *International Space Station* on 18 Nov 2008. It was tracked as object 2008-059B. Its orbit decayed naturally without it posing any threat to the station, and it burned up on re-entry on 3 Aug 2009.

FIRST PIECE OF SPACE JUNK

The R-7 rocket transported the Soviet Union's *Sputnik 1* satellite into orbit on 4 Oct 1957. After separating from the satellite, the R-7's spent core remained in orbit for just under two months, performing 882 orbits before re-entering Earth's atmosphere on 1 Dec.

LARGEST PIECE OF ORBITAL DEBRIS TO MAKE AN UNCONTROLLED RE-ENTRY

The *Skylab* space station had a mass of 75.7 tonnes (166,890 lb) when it re-entered Earth's atmosphere on 11 Jul 1979. NASA had shifted its orientation to increase its chances of burning up, but had little control over where or when it would land.

   Skylab came down over Western Australia, scattering debris over an area roughly 150 km (93 mi) wide. The Shire of Esperance later issued NASA with a tongue-in-cheek $400 penalty – the **first fine for littering from space**.

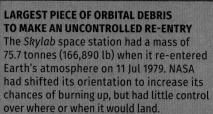

OLDEST SPACE JUNK STILL IN ORBIT

A US-made Vanguard rocket placed the *Vanguard 1* satellite in orbit on 17 Mar 1958. After separating from the grapefruit-sized satellite, the Vanguard third-stage booster settled into an orbit with a perigee, or lowest point, of 651 km (404 mi) and an apogee, or highest point, of 4,226 km (2,625 mi). It remains in orbit to this day, tracked as object 1958-002A.

Robotic Exploration

CLOSEST APPROACH TO THE SUN

The *Parker Solar Probe* came within around 8,542,000 km (5.3 million mi) of the Sun at 21:25:24 on 20 Nov 2021. The probe's latest perihelion (the closest point in its elliptical orbit around the Sun) followed a gravity assist from a Venus fly-by on 16 Oct 2021. It achieved the **fastest spacecraft speed** – 586,800 km/h (364,620 mph) – at the same time.

FIRST INTERPLANETARY SPACECRAFT TO LAND ON WHEELS

NASA's *Curiosity* rover touched down on Mars wheels-first on 6 Aug 2012 at 05:17. Previous rovers landed inside a stationary carrier, but *Curiosity* was too big for this. After descending through the Martian atmosphere under a parachute, it fired up a rocket-powered backpack and reeled itself down to the surface. This technique was repeated by the *Perseverance* rover (see below opposite).

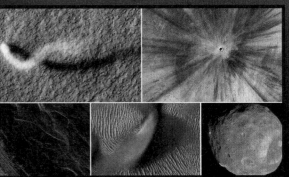

MOST DATA RETURNED FROM ANOTHER PLANET

NASA's *Mars Reconnaissance Orbiter* had sent 422 terabits of data back to Earth as of 1 Jan 2022 – the equivalent of 154 Earth days of 4K video streaming. This included high-resolution photos, subsurface radar soundings and spectral measurements. The multipurpose spacecraft has been orbiting the Red Planet since 10 Mar 2006.

MOST DISTANT EXPLORATION OF A SOLAR-SYSTEM OBJECT

On 1 Jan 2019 at 05:33, NASA's *New Horizons* probe flew within 3,538 km (2,198 mi) of 486958 Arrokoth in the Kuiper belt, a billion miles beyond Pluto. It discovered that Arrokoth was a "contact binary", made of two connected squashed spheres.

FARTHEST-TRAVELLED PLANETARY ROVERS

Lunokhod 1 (1970–71): 10.5 km

Spirit (2004–10): 7.7 km

Perseverance (2021–): 6.58 km

Yutu-2 (2018–): 1.1 km

MOST ACTIVE SPACECRAFT ORBITING ANOTHER PLANET

The arrival of China's *Tianwen-1* orbiter on 10 Feb 2021 took the number of operational spacecraft looking down on Mars to eight. On 1 Jan 2022, dramatic photos were released of *Tianwen-1* in orbit, taken by a remote camera released from the craft and showing the planet's ice-covered north pole below it.

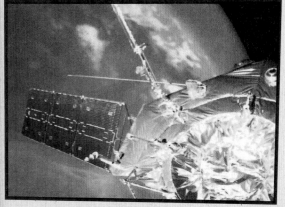

First planetary rover

The Soviet Union's *Lunokhod 1* soft-landed on the Moon on 17 Nov 1970. This solar-powered robotic rover was originally scheduled to operate for around 90 days, but survived for a total of 321 days, travelling 10,540 m (34,580 ft).

First spacecraft to visit Mercury

NASA's *Mariner 10* robotic probe made its first fly-by of Mercury on 29 Mar 1974. It would go on to make two further passes close to the planet before powering down. *Mariner 10* remains in orbit around the Sun to this day.

Longest survival on Venus by a spacecraft

After touching down on the surface of Venus at 03:57 on 1 Mar 1982, the Soviet lander *Venera 13* was able to transmit data until 06:04 – a total of 127 min. This was four times as long as mission scientists had predicted, given Venus's hurricane-force winds, crushing pressure and ambient temperature of 457°C (854°F).

First image taken on the surface of a comet

On 12 Nov 2014, the *Philae* lander alighted on comet 67P/Churyumov-Gerasimenko. An image released the next day was a mosaic from two of *Philae*'s cameras, showing the cliff face it had landed next to, as well as part of the lander itself.

The **first image taken on the surface of an asteroid** was snapped by the Japanese *HIBOU* rover at 02:44 on 22 Sep 2018, on the rocky surface of asteroid 162173 Ryugu.

Closest orbit of an asteroid

On 6 Oct 2020, NASA's *OSIRIS-REx* tightened its orbit around 101955 Bennu, closing to within 374 m (1,227 ft) of the surface. Two weeks later, *OSIRIS-REx* descended from this transfer orbit to Bennu's surface and used an extendable arm to collect a sample. The probe is now on its way back to Earth, and will return its cargo in Sep 2023.

With a diameter of just 510 m (1,673 ft) from pole to pole, Bennu is the **smallest object orbited by a spacecraft**.

LONGEST-OPERATING LUNAR ROVER

China's *Yutu-2* had been operational on the Moon for 40 lunar days as of 9 Mar 2022. (A lunar day lasts for around 28 Earth days.) *Yutu-2* arrived on board the *Chang'e 4* probe, which made the **first landing on the far side of the Moon** on 3 Jan 2019.

MOST POWERFUL ION ENGINE USED IN SPACE

Launched on 24 Nov 2021 to explore the Trojan asteroids, *Lucy* flies with NASA's Evolutionary Xenon Thruster-Commercial engines operating at up to 3.5 kW (4.6 hp). Ion engines generate thrust by using electricity to accelerate heavy ionized atoms to incredibly high speeds.

Rover drives took place in the afternoon, so the Sun could heat the motors to optimal temperatures.

LAND-SPEED RECORD ON MARS

The twin Mars Exploration Rovers *Spirit* and *Opportunity* reached a straight-line top speed of 3.7 cm/sec (1.4 in/sec). The wheels could spin at up to 5 cm/sec, but engineers never commanded straight-line drives at that speed. *Spirit* and *Opportunity* landed on Mars in Jan 2004, with the latter active until 2018.

FARTHEST FLIGHT ON MARS

NASA's autonomous helicopter *Ingenuity* covered a distance of 625 m (2,051 ft) on its ninth flight on the Red Planet on 5 Jul 2021. *Ingenuity* crossed an area of loose, wind-blown sand called Séítah in the Jezero Crater, bypassing an obstacle that the *Perseverance* rover (below) was having to navigate around.

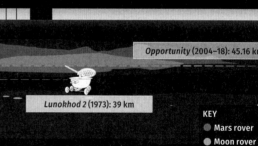

Opportunity (2004–18): 45.16 km

Curiosity (2012–): 27.44 km

Lunokhod 2 (1973): 39 km

KEY
- Mars rover
- Moon rover

Smallest interplanetary spacecraft

Launched on 5 May 2018 along with the *InSight* Mars lander, the twin spacecraft of the Mars Cube One (MarCO mission) each fitted into a box weighing 13.5 kg (29 lb 12 oz) and measuring 30 x 20 x 10 cm (11 x 7 x 3 in). The satellites – nicknamed *WALL-E* and *EVE* – travelled to Mars independently and were designed to perform radio relay between *InSight* and Earth.

Most probed planet

As of 24 Jan 2022, a total of 26 at least partially successful missions had been launched to Mars. These missions have sent five fly-by craft past the planet, placed 14 spacecraft in orbit and made 11 successful landings. An additional 23 had failed before returning any science data.

Most planets visited by one spacecraft

NASA's *Voyager 2* passed by all four of the outer gas giants – Jupiter, Saturn, Uranus and Neptune – between 1979 and 1989. It conducted the **first fly-by of Uranus** (closest approach: 24 Jan 1986) and **Neptune** (25 Aug 1989). *Voyager 2* was one of two NASA probes (see below) launched in 1977, each able to perform a gravitational slingshot from one planet to the next thanks to a special alignment of the outer planets that occurs only once every 176 years.

Most remote human-made object

On 20 Jan 2022, *Voyager 1* was 23.298 billion km (14.476 billion mi) away from Earth – roughly 156 times the distance between our planet and the Sun. A decade has passed since *Voyager 1* became the **first probe to leave the Solar System**, on 25 Aug 2012, but it continues to periodically phone home, earning it the record for the **longest communications distance**. Assuming it survives, *Voyager 1* will reach a distance of 23.836 billion km (14.811 billion mi) from Earth by 20 Jan 2023. It is expected to run out of power by 2025.

FARTHEST DISTANCE DRIVEN IN ONE MARTIAN DAY (SOL)

The *Perseverance* rover drove 319.786 m (1,049 ft 2 in) on its 351st Martian day; a single sol lasts for 24 hr 39 min 35 sec. The NASA rover was set to "AutoNav" – meaning that it received only general instructions from ground control and used its own software to avoid obstacles.

The Solar System

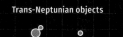

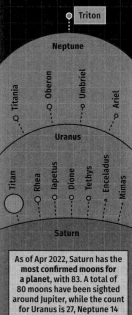

EARTH'S NEIGHBOURHOOD

FIRST INTERSTELLAR OBJECT
'Oumuamua ("scout" in Hawaiian) is a 400-m-long (1,300-ft) comet that originated from a different stellar system. It was discovered on 19 Oct 2017 by Canadian astronomer Robert Weryk. Passing beyond Neptune's orbit in 2022, 'Oumuamua will leave the Solar System in about 20,000 years.

Youngest Moon rocks
For the 2020 *Chang'e 5* sample-return mission, the China National Space Agency targeted an area of the Moon called the Oceanus Procellarum. This is one of the dark "mares" – plains of volcanic rock – that are clearly visible from Earth. As these areas are less heavily cratered than the light-coloured "highlands", it was thought they probably formed more recently. After the spacecraft returned with 1.7 kg (3 lb 12 oz) of samples on 16 Dec 2020, it was found that the rocks were only 1.96 billion years old, making this the youngest sample of lunar rock by more than one billion years.

Deepest crater
The South Pole-Aitken basin on the far side of the Moon is 2,250 km (1,400 mi) in diameter and has an average depth of 12 km (7 mi), measured from the rim of the crater.

Largest moon
With a mean diameter of 5,262.4 km (3,269.9 mi), Jupiter's Ganymede is the ninth-largest object in the Solar System. It is bigger than the planet Mercury and more than twice the mass of Earth's Moon.

Most distant moon from a planet
Neso orbits Neptune at an average distance of 50.18 million km (31.18 million mi) from the planet's centre, taking 9,631.9 Earth days (26.37 years) to complete one orbit. Its retrograde or "backwards" orbit around the planet indicates that Neso is likely a captured object that was once an icy world beyond Neptune.

The **largest retrograde moon** is Triton, another of Neptune's satellites. It measures 2,706 km (1,681 mi) across.

Smallest round world
Methone is a tiny, egg-shaped moon of Saturn that measures 3.88 x 2.58 x 2.42 km (2.41 x 1.60 x 1.50 mi). Its surface appears almost perfectly smooth, making it a true space oddity. Methone's shape suggests that it is likely covered with a deep layer of very fine dust that has no inherent strength.

Shortest-period asteroid
The fastest-orbiting asteroid is 2021 PH27, which circles the Sun every 114.7 days. It crosses the orbit of Mercury but passes nearer to the Sun. The 2-km-diameter (1.2-mi) asteroid was discovered on 13 Aug 2021 by Scott Sheppard, using the DECam imager at Cerro Tololo Inter-American Observatory in Chile.

Comets, which are distinguished by their icy composition, orbit much farther out. The **shortest-period comet** is 311P/PanSTARRS, which orbits in the main asteroid belt. Unlike most comets, whose orbits are measured in decades or centuries, 311P completes an orbit of the Sun every 3 years 88 days.

Longest river system on another world
Saturn's moon Titan has a network of rivers, lakes and seas beneath its dense cloud layer (see below left). However, because Titan is so cold (-176°C; -284°F) the fluid that flows through these channels is methane rather than water. The longest of Titan's rivers is the 412-km (256-mi) Vid Flumina, which flows through a network of deep canyons to a sea called Ligeia Mare. It was first spotted in radar scans of Titan's surface taken by the *Cassini* spacecraft on 26 Sep 2012.

Superlative planets
· **Largest**: Jupiter has an equatorial diameter of 143,884 km (89,405 mi). Its volume is more than 1,000 times greater than that of Earth.
· **Densest**: Earth has an average density of 5,513 kg per m³ (344 lb per cu ft). This compares with 687 kg per m³ (42 lb per cu ft) for Saturn, the **least dense planet**.
· **Hottest**: Venus has an average surface temperature of 473°C (883°F).
· **Largest tilt**: Uranus spins on an axis that is slanted 97.77° relative to its orbital plane. It has been theorized that this is the consequence of a collision with an Earth-sized planet that knocked Uranus over on its side.
· **Most eccentric**: Mercury's orbit brings it to within 46 million km (28.58 million mi) of the Sun at its closest point (perihelion) and out as far as 69.81 million km (43.37 million mi) at its most distant (aphelion).

Trans-Neptunian objects

Eris & Dysnomia

Gonggong

Pluto & Charon

Haumea

Makemake

Triton

Neptune

Titania | Oberon | Umbriel | Ariel

Uranus

Titan | Rhea | Iapetus | Dione | Tethys | Enceladus | Minas

Saturn

As of Apr 2022, Saturn has the most confirmed moons for a planet, with 83. A total of 80 moons have been sighted around Jupiter, while the count for Uranus is 27, Neptune 14 and Mars two.

Ganymede | Callisto | Io | Europa

Jupiter

Minor planets of the asteroid belt

Vesta | Ceres | Pallas

This infographic shows the bodies of the Solar System to scale, with each of the eight planets, as well as all the minor planets and moons (connected by dotted line to their parent planet) that are large enough to be visible at this size. The Sun is cropped out because it is 1.4 m (4 ft 7 in) wide.

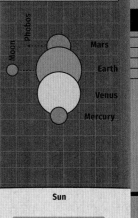

Phobos

Moon

Mars

Earth

Venus

Mercury

Sun

LARGEST EXTRATERRESTRIAL LAKES
Around 75 lakes measuring up to 110 km (68 mi) across were discovered by the NASA/ESA *Cassini* mission on the surface of Saturn's largest moon, Titan. The bodies are composed of liquid methane and ethane, and are clustered near the moon's poles.

LONGEST-LASTING LIGHTNING STORM
A lightning storm on Saturn observed by the *Cassini* orbiter lasted 333 days from 14 Jan to 13 Dec 2009. The gas giant is subject to periodic weather disturbances known as "Great White Spots" (pictured), which can be large enough to be viewed from telescopes on Earth.

TALLEST MOUNTAIN
The summit of Olympus Mons on Mars is 21,287 m (69,839 ft) above the datum (the Martian equivalent of sea level). It is a volcano with a diameter of 624 km (387 mi), roughly the size of France and more than two-and-a-half times higher than Everest.

LARGEST ANTICYCLONE
The Great Red Spot is a storm located in Jupiter's southern hemisphere. Although still larger than Earth, this 350-year-old anticyclone is shrinking: it was roughly 25,000 km (15,500 mi) wide when observed by the *Voyager* probes in 1979, but Hubble Space Telescope images from 4 Sep 2021 show it is now only 14,893 km (9,254 mi) wide.

LARGEST DUST STORMS
Mars experiences irregular dust storms that cover the entirety of the planet's surface and can last for months. These dramatic climatic events pose real problems for engineers designing equipment for the Red Planet, particularly with dust impacting on the amount of energy that solar panels can create.

LARGEST RING SYSTEM
Saturn's rings extend from 7,000 km (4,300 mi) above the planet's equator to 15 million km (9.3 million mi) away, where the outer edge of the almost imperceptibly fine Phoebe Ring is located (pictured). These discs of ice and debris have a combined mass of around 1.54×10^{16} tonnes (1.69×10^{16} tons).

LARGEST KUIPER BELT OBJECT
The dwarf planet Pluto has a diameter of 2,376 km (1,476 mi), as measured by the *New Horizons* probe during its fly-by on 14 Jul 2015. Pluto is the biggest of the icy bodies in the Kuiper Belt, which lies beyond Neptune's orbit, but it does not have the **highest mass**: that title is held by its neighbour Eris at 1.66×10^{19} tonnes (1.82×10^{19} tons).

LARGEST M-TYPE ASTEROID
16 Psyche has an average diameter of 226 km (140 mi) and an estimated mass of 2.28×10^{16} tonnes (2.51×10^{16} tons). It orbits the Sun between Mars and Jupiter and, like all M-type asteroids, is thought to contain a high quantity of metal. NASA's *Psyche* spacecraft, scheduled to launch in Aug 2022, will be the first spacecraft to visit an object of this type.

MOST SPACECRAFT TO OBSERVE A COMET
When comet C/2013 A1 (Siding Spring) passed within 141,000 km (87,600 mi) of Mars on 19 Oct 2014, all seven active spacecraft around the planet attempted observations. Of these, three orbiters and the *Opportunity* and *Spirit* rovers on the surface were able to detect it.

Astronomy

WOH G64
Largest star
2.14 billion km wide

MOST PLANETS IN ANOTHER SOLAR SYSTEM

Kepler-90 is a star in the constellation Draco that has eight confirmed planets – the same number as our own Solar System. The Kepler-90 planets are grouped within 1 AU of their host star, i.e., about the same distance as Earth and the Sun. Located 2,840 light years from Earth, the planetary system was discovered by NASA's Kepler Space Telescope.

*Astronomers use a system called apparent magnitude to describe the brightness of objects in the night sky. The higher the number, the dimmer an object appears to observers on Earth. The zero point on this scale is the brightness of the star Vega, meaning that some exceptionally luminous objects can have negative magnitudes. The **brightest star viewed from Earth**, Sirius A (or alpha Canis Majoris), for example, has an apparent magnitude of -1.46.*

Most luminous star

Situated in the Tarantula Nebula of the Large Magellanic Cloud (see right), RMC 136a1 shines 6,170,000 times more brightly than the Sun. Although the star is extremely luminous, its distance from Earth – 160,000 light years – means that it has an apparent magnitude of only 12.23.

Fastest star in the galaxy

S4714 reaches a speed of 24,000 km (15,000 mi) per sec as it orbits around Sagittarius A*, the supermassive black hole at the centre of the Milky Way. At this speed, S4714 could travel from the Sun to Mars in 2 hr 45 min. For comparison, our Solar System orbits the centre of the Milky Way at only around 220 km (137 mi) per sec.

Lowest mass for an exoplanet

An exoplanet is a planet that orbits a star other than the Sun. They can be detected by careful examination of the light emitted by the stars they orbit. The **first confirmed exoplanets** were Poltergeist and Phobetor, which were spotted in orbit around the pulsar PSR B1257+12 (aka Lich) in 1992. In Apr 2020, astronomers studying Lich discovered another planet, which they called Draugr, that has a mass of just 0.02% of Earth.

Closest black hole to Earth

Astronomers studying the red giant V723 Monocerotis, located 1,500 light years from Earth, deduced the presence of an unseen black hole exerting a pull on the star, distorting its shape and causing its light intensity to change periodically. The black hole

Sirius A
Brightest star
2.38 million km wide

was dubbed "The Unicorn" and is believed to have a mass just three times that of the Sun, making it one of the lowest-mass black holes in the known universe.

Shortest orbital period for a planet

K2-137b orbits its host star at a distance of just 0.005 AU, giving it a solar year of just 4 hr 18 min. It has a mass about 89% of Earth's, but its orbit makes it a highly unlikely candidate for life. For context, Mercury, the sun-scorched planet that lies closest to the Sun, orbits at a distance of 0.38 AU.

Closest exoplanet to Earth

In Apr 2020, a third planet was discovered in orbit around Proxima Centauri – the **nearest star** excluding the Sun, at a distance of 4.2 light years. Named Proxima Centauri c, it has a more distant orbit than Proxima Centauri b; this means that, for some of its 1,928-day year, it is Earth's nearest exoplanet neighbour.

Most distant confirmed galaxy

Discovered using the Spitzer Space Telescope and a number of ground-based telescopes in Apr 2022, HD1 is located 33.4 billion light years away. The galaxy is observed as it existed 13.5 billion years ago, just 300 million years after the Big Bang, making it also the **oldest galaxy**. HD1 may contain the universe's most primitive stars – so-called "Population III" stars – and so will likely be an early target for the James Webb Space Telescope (see pp.30–31).

The Sun
Closest star
1.39 million km wide

Most distant object visible to the naked eye

The Triangulum Galaxy is located about 3 million light years from Earth and shines with a magnitude of 5.7. Light pollution means that such a faint object is today only visible in extremely isolated areas. The most distant object visible under common conditions is the Andromeda Galaxy, which is 2.5 million light years away and has a magnitude of 3.44.

The **most distant object visible to the naked eye ever** was an explosion known as GRB 080319B. At 6:12 a.m. UTC on 19 Mar 2008, NASA's *Swift* satellite detected a gamma-ray burst (GRB) from a galaxy some 7.5 billion light years away. The explosion reached a peak brightness of magnitude 5.8 and would have been visible to the naked eye for around 30 sec. GRBs are produced during supernovas, when stars implode to form neutron stars or black holes.

Proxima Centauri
Closest star
excluding the Sun
214,553 km wide

EBLM J0555-57Ab
Smallest star
116,464 km wide

MOST MASSIVE BLACK HOLE

Located 10.8 billion light years from Earth, TON 618 has an estimated mass 66 billion times that of the Sun. It is a hyperluminous "radio-loud" quasar that produces powerful jets emitting at radio wavelengths. Measuring ~2,600 AU from one side of its event horizon to the other, TON 618 is big enough to swallow our entire Solar System 40 times over.

RMC 136a1
Most luminous star
56 million km wide

1 light year = 9.461 trillion km (5.878 trillion mi)
1 astronomical unit (AU) = 149.6 million km (92.96 million mi)

BRIGHTEST SUPERNOVA
The stellar explosion SN 1006 appeared in Apr 1006 CE, flaring for two years and reaching a magnitude of -7.5. Although it took place around 7,000 light years away, near the star Beta Lupi, the supernova was brilliant enough to be seen even during the day, and was noted in contemporary records from Europe to East Asia.

LARGEST VOID
Also known as the "Local Hole", the KBC Void is an immense region of space with an abnormally low density of galaxies. It is approximately 2 billion light years in diameter and is boundaried by "filaments" (computer model pictured) – thread-like formations of densely packed galaxy clusters. The Milky Way is located at the heart of the Local Hole.

LARGEST SATELLITE GALAXY
Lying 160,000 light years from the centre of the Milky Way galaxy, the Large Magellanic Cloud measures around 20,000 light years across and has the mass of 10 billion suns. This dwarf irregular galaxy is the largest and brightest of the 59 satellite galaxies that have been discovered orbiting our home galaxy. It takes its name from the explorer Ferdinand Magellan, who sighted it on his 1519 expedition to the East Indies.

LARGEST STAR
Due to the difficulties in directly measuring the size of a distant star, the identity of the largest star is a matter for debate among astronomers. The most likely candidate is WOH G64, a red supergiant in the Large Magellanic Cloud that was discovered in 1981. It has a diameter of 2.14 billion km (1.32 billion mi) – 1,400 times that of the Sun. If WOH G64 replaced the Sun in our Solar System, it would extend beyond the orbit of Jupiter.

COLDEST PLACE IN THE UNIVERSE
The Boomerang Nebula – a cloud of dust and gases 5,000 light years from Earth – has a temperature of -272°C (-457.6°F). Colder temperatures have been produced in laboratories, but this is the lowest recorded natural temperature, being just above absolute zero. It is caused by the rapid outflow of expanding gas from the nebula.

SMALLEST STAR
EBLM J0555-57Ab has a mass just 8.1% that of the Sun, and is roughly the size of the planet Saturn (right). It is located in a triple-star system around 600 light years from Earth. A star has to have a minimum mass in order to sustain the fusion of hydrogen into helium in its core and shine – below this amount, it is called a brown dwarf.

James Webb Space Telescope

The Houston Rockets are NASA's local basketball team in Texas – their name inspired by the nearby Johnson Space Center. The Rockets are used to astronauts making courtside appearances, but this latest guest is causing problems! With a sunshield that covers most of the court and a 6.5-m (21-ft 3-in) primary mirror, the James Webb Space Telescope (JWST) is the **largest space telescope** and the new flagship of NASA's astronomy programme.

Launched on 25 Dec 2021, the JWST is not only the largest telescope in space but also arguably the most technologically complex spacecraft ever constructed.

Fitting such a powerful telescope into a package small and light enough to go to space was a huge engineering challenge. The JWST had to launch folded up into a fairing just 4.57 m (15 ft) wide, and then unfurl itself during the month-long voyage to its new home. A total of 344 deployments had to go flawlessly – the failure of just one would break the telescope.

Everything about the JWST has been planned with the goal of filtering out as much of the "noise" of our Solar System as possible, so that the telescope can detect the faint infrared glow of the most distant – and ancient – objects in the universe. While the Hubble Space Telescope sits in low Earth orbit, the JWST is located at a spot in space called Earth-Sun Lagrange Point 2. This allows it to orbit in unison with Earth, but far enough away (1.6 million km; 1 million mi) that the sunshield can block the Sun's light.

Factor in the novel technologies invented specifically for the JWST project and it's little wonder that it's also the single **most expensive spacecraft** ever made. In 2005 the project was given a budget of $3.5 bn (then £2 bn), but by the time of its (long-delayed) launch, the cost to design and build the telescope had risen to $9.5 bn (£7 bn). Despite its high price tag, NASA is confident it will soon prove it was worth every cent.

FOCUSING THE PRIMARY MIRROR
In this test picture, published on 19 Mar 2022, dozens of distant galaxies are visible behind the nearby star chosen as the JWST's calibration target. Each of the primary mirror's 18 segments must be aligned to an accuracy of within 50 nanometres for optimal focus, enabling them to work as one huge mirror.

The mirror is coated with a microscopic layer of gold to optimize its ability to reflect infrared light.

Round-Up

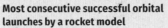

Most consecutive successful orbital launches by a rocket model

Between 14 Jan 2017 and 21 Apr 2022, the SpaceX (USA) Falcon 9 rocket executed 120 orbital launches – including six crewed missions – without a total or partial failure. The most recent loss of a Falcon 9 took place on 1 Sep 2016, when a rocket that was due to launch Israel's *AMOS-6* satellite exploded, along with its payload, during pre-launch testing.

Farthest distance driven on Mars by an individual

Martian rovers from NASA's Jet Propulsion Laboratory had travelled 17.2 km (10.6 mi) under the control of Paolo Bellutta (ITA/USA), as of his retirement from remotely driving rovers in Jul 2019. This total combines the distance covered by the twin rovers *Spirit* and *Opportunity* (13 km; 8 mi), and the *Curiosity* rover (4.2 km; 2.6 mi).

Longest-functioning Mars orbiter

NASA's *2001 Mars Odyssey* had been circling the Red Planet for 20 years 178 days as of 20 Apr 2022. The spacecraft was launched on 7 Apr 2001, and since reaching its destination on 24 Oct that year has gathered a vast quantity of data on the chemical and mineralogical composition of Mars.

LONGEST-FUNCTIONING SPACE OBSERVATORY

The Hubble Space Telescope was launched on 24 Apr 1990 and was still active as of 24 Apr 2022 – a mission duration of 32 years. Hubble's long lifespan is largely a consequence of the five servicing missions that it underwent between 1993 and 2009.

Most data collected by a rover

NASA's *Curiosity* rover, which landed on Mars on 6 Aug 2012, had returned 2,096 gigabits of data to Earth as of 1 Jan 2022. Planetary landers are generally smaller than planetary orbiters, so have less power for radio transmission and much smaller antennas. *Curiosity* has returned virtually all of its science data through a UHF antenna that communicates with orbiters passing overhead – mostly via the *2001 Mars Odyssey* and the *Mars Reconnaissance Orbiter*. (See also p.24.)

Largest solar array in space

With the deployment of the second IROSA (*ISS* Roll-Out Solar Array) on 28 Jun 2021, the total area of the solar panels on the *ISS* reached 3,244 m² (34,918 sq ft), generating around 120 kilowatts of electrical power for the space station. The flexible IROSA panels (one of which can be seen behind spacewalker Thomas Pesquet, left) were added as part of a series of power-system upgrades.

Shortest crewed spaceflight

New Shepard NS-20 was a sub-orbital mission by US company Blue Origin on 31 Mar 2022. The rocket took off from a facility in Van Horn, Texas, USA, at 08:57 a.m. local time (13:57 Universal Time Coordinated) and its components – booster and

TALLEST LAUNCH TOWER

The Starbase Integration Tower rises 146 m (479 ft) above the SpaceX facility in Boca Chica, Texas, USA – making it taller than the Great Pyramid of Giza (see pp.160–61). It was built to support the development of SpaceX's 120-m-tall (393-ft) Starship/Super Heavy launch vehicle (see p.16) and was first used to stack the latter's two stages on 10 Feb 2022.

MOST SPACEWALKS FROM A SPACE STATION

There had been 246 extra-vehicular activities from the *International Space Station* (*ISS*) by 18 Apr 2022. The year 2021 was unusually busy, with 13 spacewalks, including three related to the arrival of the *Nauka* module, and others to upgrade *ISS* power systems.

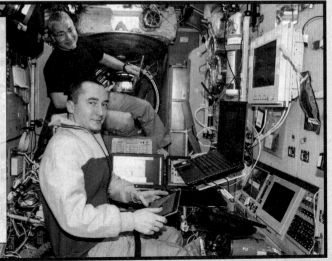

LONGEST STAY ON THE *ISS*

The *International Space Station* was home to Mark Vande Hei (USA, top) and Pyotr Dubrov (RUS) for 354 days 14 hr 56 min. The pair arrived on 9 Apr 2021 and departed on 30 Mar 2022. Only four people have remained in space for longer periods than this duo, all of whom served on the Soviet/Russian *Mir* space station (1986–2001). For the **longest single spaceflight** outright, turn to p.21.

MOST DISTANT STAR

WHL0137-LS (aka Earendel) is located 12.9 billion light years from Earth. The star was discovered by an international team of researchers coordinated by Brian Welch and Dan Coe, who published their findings in *Nature* on 30 Mar 2022. The team looked through Hubble Space Telescope imagery for examples of "gravitational lensing". This phenomenon occurs when the extreme mass of a relatively close galaxy warps the light from objects beyond it, creating narrow strips of magnified objects otherwise too distant to see.

capsule – returned to Earth 9 min 57 sec later. (For more on commercial and privately funded spaceflights, see pp.18–19.)

Most comets discovered using spacecraft images

Amateur astronomer Worachate Boonplod (THA) was credited with having discovered 780 comets as of 1 Jan 2022. Boonplod works with images taken by ESA and NASA's Solar and Heliospheric Observatory. As of the same date, a total of 4,343 comets had been found using this space observatory – the **most comets discovered by a spacecraft**. For the **youngest comet hunter**, see p.110.

Largest satellite constellation

As of 29 Apr 2022, SpaceX's Starlink constellation comprised some 2,146 operational satellites. The company's ultimate aim is to utilize 12,000 of these 260-kg (573-lb) satellites in orbits of 550 km (342 mi) or below to provide global high-speed internet coverage.

Largest Oort Cloud comet

On 10 Apr 2022, the results of the Hubble Space Telescope's examination of the comet C/2014 UN271 (Bernardinelli-Bernstein)

Crawler-Transporter 2 is 131 ft long and 114 ft wide (39.9 x 34.7 m) – about the size of a baseball infield.

were published in *The Astrophysical Journal Letters*, confirming that this comet has a nucleus 119 km (73.9 mi) in diameter. It is the largest comet in the distant region of our Solar System known as the Oort Cloud (where most comets form).

The **largest comet** overall is 95P/Chiron, an enormous 182-km-wide (113-mi) rocky body that orbits between the planets Saturn and Uranus. However, its unusually close orbit around the Sun means that it has lost most of its ice and therefore bears little resemblance to classical comets like Bernardinelli-Bernstein.

Most exoplanets discovered by a single telescope

As of 24 Jan 2022, a total of 3,184 exoplanets had been identified and confirmed on the basis of observations made by the *Kepler* space telescope. This

HIGHEST-RESOLUTION FULL-DISC IMAGE OF THE SUN

On 7 Mar 2022, a 9,148 x 9,112-pixel mosaic picture of our star was taken by the Extreme Ultraviolet Imager on the European Space Agency's *Solar Orbiter* probe. It captured the image from a distance of 75 million km (46.6 million mi) – about halfway between Earth and the Sun. The definition was 10 times sharper than that of a 4K TV screen.

represents 64.9% of the 4,903 exoplanets known to astronomers. More than 3,000 candidate exoplanets await follow-up and confirmation.

First Black woman to serve on an extended mission on the *ISS*

On 27 Apr 2022, NASA astronaut Jessica Watkins (USA) launched to the *ISS* on a SpaceX Crew Dragon. Watkins is scheduled to remain on the station until Sep 2022, forming part of the Expedition 67/68 crew. Two Black women astronauts, Stephanie Wilson and Joan Higginbotham, were involved in the station's construction in the 2000s but were not long-term crew.

HEAVIEST SELF-POWERED VEHICLE

Weighing in at 3,106 tonnes (3,423 tons), Crawler-Transporter 2 is operated by NASA's Exploration Ground Systems Program at the Kennedy Space Center in Florida, USA. It generates its own power using locomotive diesel engines and is designed to transport rockets and their mobile platforms to the launchpad. It is pictured here carrying NASA's Space Launch System (SLS) rocket, which along with the SpaceX Starship/Super Heavy (see opposite) is one of two gigantic rockets scheduled to make their first launch in 2022.

Wally Funk

HALL OF FAME

This octogenarian aviator is living proof that dreams can come true. But in Wally's case, gender discrimination meant that she had to wait 60 years before they could be fulfilled.

Wally became fascinated by flight at a young age. She idolized pioneering aviator Amelia Earhart and persuaded her parents to let her take flying lessons. She earned her pilot's licence at the age of just 17 and racked up thousands of hours' flying time at university.

In 1961, when Wally was 21, she joined the Mercury 13 programme, a privately funded initiative to prove that women could be astronauts. Candidates took the same gruelling physical and mental tests as the Mercury 7 astronauts – NASA's first spaceflight recruits – and not only met the requirements but sometimes surpassed their male counterparts.

The project was shelved in 1962, but Wally remained determined to carve out a career in aviation. Neither commercial airlines nor the US Air Force accepted female pilots, however, so she had to find other roles – first as a civilian flight instructor, then as an FAA inspector and air-safety investigator.

It was not until the age of 82 years 169 days that Wally finally fulfilled her goal. On 20 Jul 2021, she joined the crew of the Blue Origin NS-16 mission and became the **oldest woman in space**. "No one has waited longer," said Blue Origin founder Jeff Bezos. "It's time."

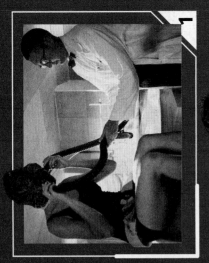

1

2

3

W. FUNK

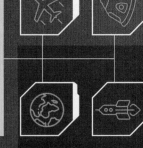

VITAL STATISTICS

Name	Wally Funk
Birthplace	Las Vegas, New Mexico, USA
Date of birth	1 Feb 1939
Current GWR title	**Oldest woman in space**
Professional achievements	First female FAA* inspector. First female NTSB† air-safety investigator

*Federal Aviation Administration
†National Transportation Safety Board

7

Find out more about Wally in the Hall of Fame section at www. guinnessworldrecords.com/2023

1. Wally during the Mercury 13 trials, preparing for a test at the Lovelace Clinic in New Mexico. No one knew then what qualities would be important for astronauts, so the tests were wide-ranging and, by today's standards, sometimes quite strange!

2. Wally in the cockpit of an AT-6 training plane in 1961. That year, she signed up to undergo astronaut training and became one of the Mercury 13.

3. Aged 20, Wally embarked on her first job as a civilian flight instructor at Fort Sill, Oklahoma, USA. There, she taught male Air Force recruits how to fly, despite not being allowed to join the Air Force herself.

4. In 1995, several Mercury 13 candidates, including Wally, were invited to the launch of the Space Shuttle *Discovery* for mission STS-63, which featured the **first female Shuttle pilot**, Eileen Collins. They referred to themselves as FLATS (First Lady Astronaut Trainees).

5. Wally chats at home with Jeff Bezos, the founder of Blue Origin and her fellow crew member on the NS-16 mission (see p.19). Later, he praised both her unflappable demeanour and her eagerness to blast off into space.

6. Blue Origin's quartet greet the press after their record-breaking flight. Left to right: Oliver Daemen (the **youngest person in space**), Jeff Bezos, Wally Funk and Mark Bezos. "I want to go again," Wally told the crowd. "Fast."

7. Wally receives her astronaut's wings from former Space Shuttle commander Jeff Ashby, who is now part of the Blue Origin team.

5

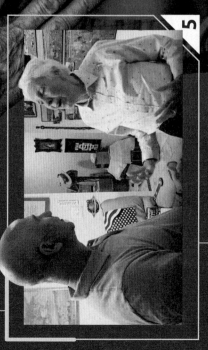

6

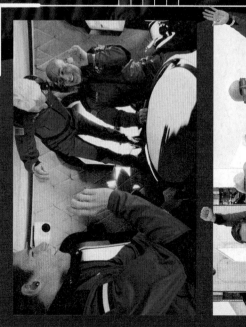

LARGEST HORN SPREAD ON A GOAT
From tip to tip, the curlicued horns of Albino measure a straight-line distance of 1.44 m (4 ft 8.6 in) – about as long as a broom handle – as verified in Naters, Switzerland, on 23 Jun 2020. Owned by Swiss farmer Roland Fercher (opposite), Albino is a Sempione goat, a rare breed originating from the mountainous Swiss-Italian border region. From May to October, he grazes with 10 other billy goats of various breeds, and owing to his prodigious protuberances, he naturally assumes the role of group leader.

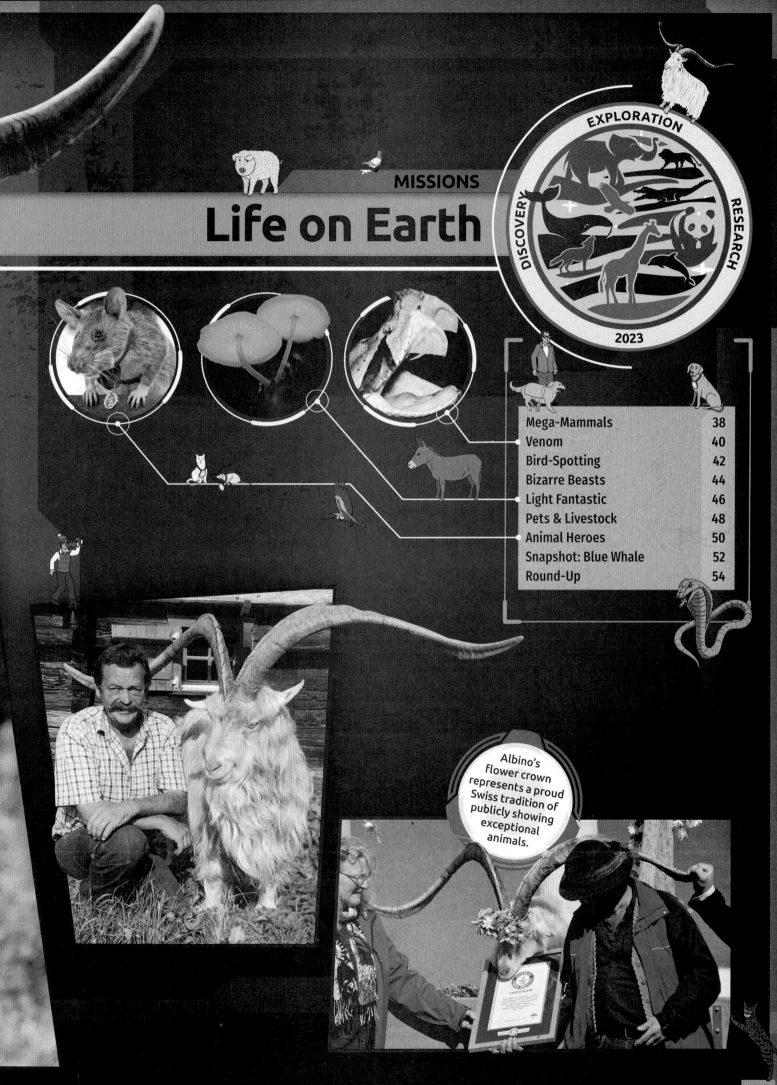

Life on Earth

EXPLORATION

DISCOVERY

RESEARCH

2023

Albino's flower crown represents a proud Swiss tradition of publicly showing exceptional animals.

Mega-Mammals

While the **largest animal ever** still swims in Earth's oceans today (see pp.52–53), much magnificent megafauna has been lost to history. Giant reptiles, such as dinosaurs, hog the limelight when it comes to behemoth beasts, but the ancestors of our own kind – the mammals – also reached epic proportions...

Land mammal

The crown for biggest terrestrial mammal of all time could go to several contenders. The frontrunner is *Paraceratherium* (**1**), a type of gigantic rhino with an elongated neck that lived 23–34 million years ago (MYA). It stood at least 4.8 m (15 ft 9 in) at the shoulder and weighed c. 18.5 tonnes (40,785 lb). Its monstrous mass exceeds more than *three* adult African elephants (*Loxodonta africana*) – the **largest land animal** of our age.

A close rival, however, is the straight-tusked elephant (*Palaeoloxodon*, **2**). It reached up to 4.5 m (14 ft 9 in) at the shoulder, and estimates of its mass vary between 15 and 22 tonnes (33,070–48,500 lb).

Also in the running is Borson's mastodon (*Mammut borsoni*), which may have hit 16 tonnes (35,275 lb) and risen to 4.1 m (13 ft 5 in) at the shoulder.

Mammoth

The largest mammoths were the southern mammoth (*Mammuthus meridionalis*) and its descendant, the steppe mammoth (*M. trogontherii*, **3**). Both species regularly attained a shoulder height of 4 m (13 ft 1 in) and could exceed 14 tonnes (30,865 lb). The **last population of mammoths** – a dwarf variety of woolly mammoth (*M. primigenius*) – lived on Wrangel Island off Siberia as "recently" as c. 4,000 years ago.

Sloth

The distant relatives of today's tree sloths were giant ground-dwellers native to the Americas.

Palaeoloxodon tusks could grow 1 m (3 ft 3 in) longer than those of modern African elephants!

Both *Eremotherium* (**4**) and *Megatherium* tipped the scales at 4 tonnes (8,820 lb) and, when standing on two legs, could tower to more than 3.5 m (11 ft 6 in). By comparison, a modern three-toed tree sloth (*Bradypus*) has a body length of 45 cm (1 ft 6 in) and weighs 1,000 times less than its extinct cousins!

Deer

The broad-fronted stag moose (*Cervalces latifrons*, **5**) roamed northern Eurasia 0.21–1.5 MYA during the Pleistocene epoch. Its upper foot bone alone, which is about 25% more massive than that of an Alaska moose (*Alces alces gigas*, today's **largest deer**), supported an animal that could exceed 2.5 m (8 ft 2 in) at the shoulder and weigh between 900 and 1,200 kg (1,985–2,645 lb). Overall, it was around the size of an American bison (*Bison bison*). Despite its superior scale, its tip-to-tip antler span of 2.5 m was, in fact, surpassed by another deer (see right).

Primate

Estimates from cheek teeth and jawbones suggest that *Gigantopithecus* (**6**) stood up to 3.7 m (12 ft) tall on its hind legs and weighed 300 kg (660 lb), though more conservative palaeobiologists favour 2.5–3 m (8 ft 2 in–9 ft 10 in) and 200–300 kg (440–660 lb), respectively. Related to orangutans (*Pongo*) of Indonesia, this huge ape inhabited what is now southern China from 2.15 MYA to 300,000 years ago. A full-grown male eastern lowland gorilla (*Gorilla beringei graueri*) – today's **largest primate** – usually stands 1.75 m (5 ft 9 in) bipedally and weighs under 210 kg (463 lb).

Marsupial

A rhino-sized cousin of modern wombats (Vombatidae), *Diprotodon optatum* (**7**) lived in Australia until *c.* 44,000 years ago. Research by Dr Stephen Wroe on a full skeleton of this megaherbivore – over 3.7 m (12 ft 2 in) long from nose to tail – posited a mass of 2.8 tonnes (6,173 lb) for an average adult. This is more than 30 times the weight of even the biggest male specimens of today's **largest marsupial**: the red kangaroo (*Osphranter rufus*).

LARGEST ANTLERS EVER

Skeletal remains and cave paintings reveal that males of the giant deer (*Megaloceros giganteus*) bore enormous palmated (open-hand-like) antlers spanning up to 3.6 m (11 ft 9 in) between the tips. Despite its common name of "Irish elk", evidence of this cervid has been found across northern Eurasia.

Rodent

Josephoartigasia monesi (**8**) inhabited South America *c.* 2.6 MYA. Based on a 53-cm-long (1-ft 9-in) skull, a body mass of 1–2 tonnes (2,205–4,410 lb) has been proposed for this guinea-pig-like animal. The average capybara (*Hydrochoerus hydrochaeris*, the **largest rodent** now) has a 24-cm (9.4-in) skull and weighs *c.* 55 kg (121 lb 4 oz). *J. monesi*'s closest living relative, however, is the smaller pacarana (*Dinomys branickii*).

Sabre-toothed cat

The current **largest wild cat** is the Siberian tiger (*Panthera tigris altaica*); it can exceed 1 m (3 ft 3 in) at the withers (ridge between shoulders) and 300 kg (660 lb). But some of its former feline cousins grew even more hefty. *Smilodon populator* (**9**) – a sabre-toothed cat, or machairodontine – could reach 1.2 m (3 ft 11 in) at the shoulder, making it one of the largest felids of all time. A recent exceptionally large skull unearthed in Uruguay may have belonged to a 436-kg (961-lb) individual – more than twice the weight of a male lion (*P. leo*). *Smilodon*'s formidable serrated teeth grew to the size of carving knives!

Canid

Nature's top dog (excluding domestic breeds, see p.49) was *Epicyon haydeni* (**10**), which lived across North America 7–10 MYA. Fossil remains indicate a predator that measured 95 cm (3 ft 1 in) at the shoulder and 75 kg (165 lb), rivalling a black bear (*Ursus americanus*) in size. *Epicyon* (which translates as "more than a dog") was a borophagine, a now completely extinct group. Today's **largest wild canid** – grey wolves (*Canis lupus*) – average 73 cm (2 ft 4 in) to the withers, with a wide weight range of 16–80 kg (35–176 lb).

Venom

MOST VENOMOUS FROG
By "head-butting" predators, the Bruno's casque-headed frog (*Aparasphenodon brunoi*) can inject venom via small subdermal spines on its skull. With an LD_{50} of 0.16–0.24 mg/kg of body weight, just 1 g (0.04 oz) of its toxin is sufficient to kill 80 adult humans, or 300,000 mice.

100%

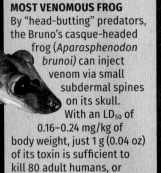

100%

LONGEST SNAKE FANGS
The teeth of the gaboon viper (*Bitis gabonica*) of sub-Saharan Africa can grow to 50 mm (2 in). It produces more poison than any other venomous snake and uses its phenomenal fangs to ensure deep penetration. A single adult male may possess enough venom to inject lethal doses into 30 people.

MOST VENOMOUS SPIDERS
There are two contenders for this title. The wandering spiders (*Phoneutria*, right) of South and Central America cause more severe envenomations than any other spider, with a human LD_{50} as low as 7.5 micrograms (μg) of venom per kg. Male specimens of Australian funnel-web spiders (*Atrax*, left) have a similar toxicity but bite fewer people. Humans are particularly susceptible to their bites, however, as funnel-web venom has peptides that send our nervous system into overdrive, sometimes with fatal results.

THE SCHMIDT STING PAIN INDEX

In 1983, US entomologist Justin O Schmidt published a detailed pain index of insect stings. Using first-hand experience, he rated the stings of many ants, bees and wasps on a 1–4 scale. He also included a short précis to describe the sensation, a few examples of which are given here...

Slender twig ant (*Tetraponera* spp.) "A skinny bully's punch. It's too weak to hurt, but you suspect a cheap trick might be coming."

1

Giant sweat bee (*Dieunomia heteropoda*) "Size matters but isn't everything. A silver tablespoon drops squarely on to your big toenail, sending you hopping."

1.5

2

Bumblebee (*Bombus* spp.) "Colourful flames. Fireworks land on your arm."

MOST VENOMOUS SCORPIONS
Venom from the deathstalker (*Leiurus quinquestriatus*, pictured) delivered under the skin of mice had an LD_{50} of 0.25 mg/kg. The fat-tailed scorpions (*Androctonus*) of North Africa have only slightly less toxic venom, but are responsible for far more human fatalities.

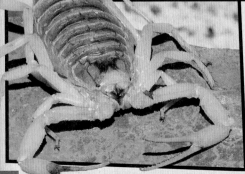

Venom is actively injected via stings or bites; by contrast, poison is passively ingested or absorbed when a toxic animal is eaten or touched. Venom potency is commonly assessed using the median lethal dose (LD_{50}) system, which calculates the amount of venom required to kill 50% of test subjects (e.g., mice). It is typically expressed as milli- or micrograms of venom per kilogram of the victim's body weight (mg/kg or μg/kg).

First venomous frogs
Poisonous frogs that secrete toxins have long been known to science, including the golden poison-dart frog (*Phyllobates terribilis*) of Colombia – the **most poisonous frog**, with an LD_{50} of 0.2 μg/kg for its batrachotoxin. But the first confirmation of *venomous* frogs came as late as 2015. The new-found species were both from Brazil: Bruno's casque-headed frog (*A. brunoi*, see above) and Greening's frog (*Corythomantis greeningi*). The venom of both is more toxic than that of fer-de-lance pit vipers (*Bothrops*).

First venomous salamander
A 2010 study confirmed the Iberian ribbed newt (*Pleurodeles waltl*), aka *gallipato*, of Spain, Portugal and Morocco as venomous. Under threat, it can reorient its ribs so that they puncture its own body to form a line of bony barbs. Combined with a toxic milky secretion, these spikes are an effective deterrent.

First venomous crustacean
Formally described in 1987, *Xibalbanus tulumensis* is a blind remipede, a centipede-like marine crustacean. It dwells in the underwater caves of Mexico's Yucatán Peninsula. To hunt, its front claws inject prey with a toxin akin to rattlesnake venom that breaks down the victim's inner tissues until they can be slurped out!

Most toxic insect venom
The venom of Maricopa harvester ants (*Pogonomyrmex maricopa*) has an LD_{50} value of 0.12 mg/kg of body weight. This is around 20 times more potent than honeybee venom. Just 12 stings from these ants – native to Arizona, USA – can dispatch a rat.

MOST VENOMOUS CEPHALOPOD

The blue-ringed octopuses *Hapalochlaena maculosa* and *H. lunulata* are equipped with a neurotoxic venom called tetrodotoxin (TTX). A bite imparting just 0.87 mg can prove fatal to humans. TTX is the same deadly agent that is found in pufferfish (Tetraodontidae) – the **most poisonous fish**.

Australia has the **most venomous snake species** – more than 100 terrestrial species out of a global total of *c.* 600.

MOST VENOMOUS LAND SNAKE

A mere 1 mg of venom from an inland taipan (*Oxyuranus microlepidotus*) could kill a human, though it has no documented fatalities. It is native to Queensland, Australia. Unlike most snakes, it mainly hunts mammals such as rats, which explains why its venom has evolved to be so potent as it must subdue prey quickly.

MOST PAINFUL INSECT STING

The bullet ant (*Paraponera clavata*) registers 4+ on the Schmidt index (see below). Some victims have likened the pain of its sting to being shot – hence its common name. The ant is native to Nicaragua and southwards to Paraguay.

MOST VENOMOUS FISH

Stonefish (*Synanceia*) possess up to 15 dorsal spines, each with two sacs housing 5–10 mg of venom. *S. horrida* venom has an intravenous LD_{50} as low as 0.4 µg/kg in mice, meaning that a lethal human dose can be delivered by one or two spines. Stonefish are all the more dangerous owing to their artful camouflage.

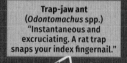

Trap-jaw ant (*Odontomachus* spp.) "Instantaneous and excruciating. A rat trap snaps your index fingernail." — **2.5**

Florida harvester ant (*Pogonomyrmex badius*) "Bold and unrelenting. Somebody is using a power drill to excavate your ingrown toenail."

Warrior wasp (*Synoeca septentrionalis*) "Torture. You are chained in the flow of an active volcano. Why did I start this list?" — **3**

4

4+

Bullet ant (*Paraponera clavata*, see above) "Pure, intense, brilliant pain. Like walking over flaming charcoal with a three-inch nail embedded in your heel."

Most snakebite fatalities by country

Estimates from medical data indicate that 1.2 million people in India died from snakebites between 2000 and 2019. Equating to an average of 58,000 deaths per annum, this represents around half of all global snakebite deaths. Among reports that named the species, the most common culprit was the Russell's viper (*Daboia russelii*). Fatality rates are high in India owing to frequent encounters with snakes that have come to favour built-up areas and farmland, as well as limited antivenom in remote regions.

Largest venomous land animal

An adult male Komodo dragon (*Varanus komodoensis*) – also the **largest lizard** – averages 2.59 m (8 ft 6 in) long and weighs 79–91 kg (174–200 lb). Scientists long assumed that its saliva contained deadly bacteria, but in 2009 it was shown to have two venom glands in its lower jaw. It is therefore a venomous bite, rather than bacterial infection, that immobilizes its prey, such as deer and pigs. Dr Bryan G Fry (see right, with a Komodo dragon) helped to make this discovery.

Q&A: DR BRYAN G FRY

The "Venom Doc" heads up the Venom Evolution Lab at the University of Queensland, Australia.

What question are you most often asked?
"Have you ever been bitten?" which is like asking Lewis Hamilton if he has ever wrecked a car! With any extreme activity accidents happen, but we always have contingency plans. If we go *really* remote, that will involve bringing a doctor and antivenom with us.

Why does Australia have so much toxic wildlife?
It's largely down to the blazing-hot climate, which makes Australia the land of the reptiles and the only continent to have more venomous species of snake than non-venomous ones. Among them is the inland taipan [see above], whose venom is superlatively potent; it both rapidly clots blood [which then blocks blood vessels] and physically destroys nerve endings. This one-two punch is particularly devastating.

Which animal are people most shocked to learn is venomous?
Komodo dragons. There have been decades of misinformation about them, particularly the wildly incorrect idea that they use pathogenic bacteria as a weapon. They have less bacteria in their mouth than a lion, or the average five-year-old kid who chewed on a classmate's ankle!

Bird-Spotting

MOST BIRD SPECIES (COUNTRY)

According to BirdLife International, Colombia boasted 1,884 bird species as of 2020 – 16.9% of the worldwide total. Natives include the rare turquoise dacnis (*Dacnis hartlaubi*, left). Peru and Brazil follow after Colombia, so it's little wonder that South America has the **most bird species (continent)** – 3,445, almost one-third of global species.

MOST EXPENSIVE NATURAL-HISTORY BOOK SOLD AT AUCTION

Far from *cheep*, a copy of John James Audubon's *Birds of America* fetched £7.3 m ($11.4 m) on 7 Dec 2010. The book contains 1,000 life-size illustrations of 435 birds drawn by the Haitian-born artist and pioneering ornithologist between 1827 and 1838. Only 120 complete editions are thought to exist.

FIRST BIRDWATCHING ARCHITECTURAL STUDIO

Founded in Nov 2010 by architect and naturalist Tormod Amundsen, Biotope (NOR) specializes in structures geared towards wildlife watching, such as hides/blinds, towers and wind breaks. The firm is based in Vardø, Norway. Many of its designs are inspired by "gapahuks" – small ad hoc shelters built in the wilderness using natural materials.

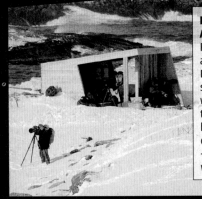

FIRST BIRDWATCHING FIELD GUIDE

Birds Through an Opera-Glass was an 1889 compilation of articles by Florence A Merriam (USA), widely known as the "First Lady of Ornithology". Including hand-drawn sketches, it was the earliest guidebook to promote observing birds for pleasure, as opposed to hunting.

ABUNDANT AVIANS

Train your field glasses on the three most spotted birds per region, as registered on the *eBird* app (see opposite) by 1 Dec 2021, since it launched in 2002.

AFRICA
1. Common bulbul (*Pycnonotus barbatus*) = 151,357
2. Laughing dove = 104,745
3. Red-eyed dove = 98,231

ASIA
1. Common myna (*Acridotheres tristis*) = 1,016,833
2. Rock pigeon = 896,052
3. Spotted dove = 819,547

AUSTRALIA
1. Australian magpie (*Gymnorhina tibicen*) = 812,893
2. Magpie-lark = 657,076
3. Rainbow lorikeet = 545,434

CENTRAL AMERICA
1. American black vulture (*Coragyps atratus*) = 500,862
2. Clay-coloured thrush = 472,662
3. Great-tailed grackle = 443,750

LONGEST-RUNNING BIRD CENSUS

The National Audubon Society's annual Christmas Bird Count (CBC) was begun in 1900 by Frank M Chapman (USA) as an alternative to the tradition of wild bird shoots on Christmas Day. Today, more than 3,000 CBC events are held throughout the Americas each year, spying out birds such as the northern cardinal (*Cardinalis cardinalis*, inset).

First use of the term "birding"

In Scene 5, Act 3 of William Shakespeare's *The Merry Wives of Windsor* (1602), Mistress Quickly tells Falstaff that Mistress Ford's husband "goes this morning a-birding". This most likely would have referred to hunting birds. The first reference to imply bird*watching* was the 1896 travelogue *A-Birding on a Bronco* by Florence A Merriam (USA, see also above).

Birders often refer to the difficult-to-define overall impression of a bird – based on characteristics such as shape, colour and flight profile – as its "giss" (aka "jizz"). The **first use** of this birding expression in print was by the British naturalist Thomas Alfred Coward in his "Country Diary" column for *The Manchester Guardian* on 6 Dec 1921.

First leg-ringed wild bird

A grey heron (*Ardea cinerea*) banded in the early 1700s in Turkey was identified in Germany in 1710. Leg rings were likely used on domestic falcons even earlier.

First species split based on birdsong

In his seminal 1789 work *The Natural History and Antiquities of Selborne*, Reverend Gilbert White (UK) recognized that the common English "willow wren" actually comprised three different species – based purely upon the calls of these otherwise near-identical birds. They are now known as the willow warbler (*Phylloscopus trochilus*), wood warbler (*P. sibilatrix*) and chiffchaff (*P. collybita*).

Longest-running ornithological journal

The *Journal of Ornithology* (formerly *Journal für Ornithologie*) began in 1853. The official periodical of the German Ornithologists' Society, it was established by Jean Louis Cabanis (DEU).

The **first ornithological popular magazine** was *The Audubon Magazine*, launched by George Bird Grinnell (USA) in Feb 1887. It was discontinued after only two years owing to a lack of resources. In its wake, Frank M Chapman launched *Bird Lore* in 1899; this re-adopted the title of *Audubon Magazine* in 1941, following the establishment of the National Audubon Society.

MOST BIRD SPECIES (NATIONAL PARK)

A total of 1,009 bird species have been documented inside Peru's Manú National Park since its foundation in 1973. Avian denizens of this UNESCO World Heritage Site include the Andean cock-of-the-rock (*Rupicola peruvianus*, pictured), the national bird of Peru.

YOUNGEST PERSON TO BIRDWATCH ON ALL CONTINENTS

Ornithologist Mya-Rose Craig (UK, b. 7 May 2002) was 13 years 234 days old when she completed her global birding tour. On 27 Dec 2015, she visited her seventh continent, Antarctica, logging snow petrels (*Pagodroma nivea*) and emperor penguins (*Aptenodytes forsteri*).

In 2020, Mya-Rose staged the most northerly climate protest in the Arctic; she saw several birds en route!

MOST BIRDS SPOTTED IN ONE YEAR (INDIVIDUAL)

Arjan Dwarshuis (NLD, centre) observed 6,852 wild bird species in 40 countries in 2016 – about two-thirds of the then global total. Using the IOC World Bird List as his checklist, Dwarshuis beat the previous "Big Year" record by 699 species. His trip also raised funds for BirdLife International.

LARGEST BIRD COUNT IN 24 HOURS (TEAM)

On 8 Oct 2015, four professional guides – left to right: Rudy Gelis (NLD), Mitch Lysinger (USA), Tuomas Seimola (FIN) and Dušan Brinkhuizen (NLD) – documented 431 bird species in Ecuador. Among them was the chestnut-breasted chlorophonia (*C. pyrrhophrys*, right).

EUROPE	NORTH AMERICA	SOUTH AMERICA	ANTARCTICA/ SUBANTARCTIC
1. Eurasian blackbird (*Turdus merula*) = 1,629,309	1. American crow (*Corvus brachyrhynchos*) = 17,877,617	1. House wren (*Troglodytes aedon*) = 605,384	1. Wilson's storm petrel (*Oceanites oceanicus*) = 5,746
2. Common wood pigeon = 1,375,646	2. American robin = 17,824,243	2. Rufous-collared sparrow = 581,085	2. Southern giant petrel = 5,365
3. Great tit = 1,250,389	3. Mourning dove = 17,008,253	3. Great kiskadee = 579,485	3. Gentoo penguin = 5,035

Oldest bird-conservation charity

The origins of the UK-based Royal Society for the Protection of Birds (RSPB) date to 1889, when philanthropists Emily Williamson and Eliza Phillips set up protest groups decrying the killing of wild birds for feathers used in fashion. In 1891, they joined forces to found the Society for the Protection of Birds, which acquired Royal Charter status in 1904. Today, the RSPB has more than 1 million members.

First bestowed in 1908, the RSPB Medal is the charity's highest accolade. Past winners include Dame Georgina Mace, Bill Oddie OBE and Sir David Attenborough. The **youngest RSPB Medal winner** to date is Dara McAnulty (UK, b. 31 Mar 2004), author of the award-winning book *Diary of a Young Naturalist*. The teen conservationist from Northern Ireland received the prize in 2019, aged 15 years 209 days.

First photo-illustrated nature book

Produced by British brothers Richard and Cherry Kearton in 1895, *British Birds' Nests: How, Where, and When to Find and Identify Them* was an A–Z guide for amateur birders and oologists (egg collectors) illustrated exclusively with photographs. In their quest to snap wild birds, the Keartons devised some novel hides including a hollow taxidermy ox, inside which they could conceal themselves!

Largest bird count in 24 hours (worldwide)

In birding, "Big Days" are contests where teams or individuals attempt to identify as many bird species as possible in one day. Counts are, by necessity, largely based on an honour system. On 8 May 2021, the Global Big Day event tallied 7,234 species, logged by 51,816 bird-spotters in 192 countries.

The day was orchestrated by *eBird*, the **largest citizen-science birdwatching project**. The website/app was set up for amateur birders by the Cornell Lab of Ornithology (USA), based in Ithaca, New York, in 2002. By Dec 2021, *eBird* had archived more than 1.1 billion species observations and 81 million birding checklists.

MOST BIRDS SPOTTED (LIFETIME)

Claes-Göran Cederlund (SWE, 1948–2020) logged 9,761 avian species in the field. His passion took him to 135 countries, including French Polynesia – below, with a Tuamotu sandpiper (*Prosobonia parvirostris*). His favourite bird was the common swift (*Apus apus*).

Bizarre Beasts

LONGEST HORN ON A BIRD

The horned screamer (*Anhima cornuta*), aka unicorn bird, has a cartilage protrusion between its eyes that can grow to 15 cm (6 in). These cornified quills are fragile and easily snap off, so seem to be purely for display. The screamer's not defenceless, though, wielding a spiky bone spur in the middle of each wing.

HEAVIEST BONY FISH

Disc-shaped sunfish (*Mola*), most commonly observed sunbathing near the ocean surface, weigh around 1 tonne (2,200 lb) on average. An exceptional bump-head sunfish (*M. alexandrini*) found off Japan in 1996 tipped the scales at 2.3 tonnes (5,070 lb). Sunfish are also the **most fertile fish**. The ovaries of one female held 300 million eggs, each measuring 1.27 mm (0.05 in) across, akin to grains of sand.

LARGEST GENOME

A genome is a full set of genetic instructions for any living organism. The genome of the axolotl (*Ambystoma mexicanum*) comprises 32 billion base pairs (the building blocks of DNA) – at least 10 times more than a human. This amphibious oddball from Mexico spends its entire life in its neotenic (juvenile) form.

LONGEST-LIVED RODENT

Their odd appearance is *not* the most unusual characteristic of East Africa's naked mole rat (*Heterocephalus glaber*). They live in colonies like bees and ants (making them the **most eusocial mammals**), are resistant to diseases such as cancer, and live up to 31 years.

WEIRD WEAPONS

Whether it's to catch their next meal, or to stop themselves becoming one, animals have evolved some cunning, and frankly disgusting, tactics. In some cases, their predatory and defensive adaptations also break records...

4.5 m

Striped skunks (*Mephitis mephitis*) are the smelliest mammals. Their sulphuric secretions can be fired 4.5 m (15 ft) from their rear ends and whiffed at a concentration of just 10 parts per billion!

Turkey vultures (*Cathartes aura*) vomit undigested food over those that harrass them. They are the most widespread New World vulture, found from Canada to South America.

The giant palm salamander (*Bolitoglossa dofleini*) can extend its tongue to more than half its body length in just 7 milliseconds. At 50 times faster than the blink of an eye, it is the fastest tongue.

Most eyes on a fish

The most visually endowed fish is the six-eyed spookfish (*Bathylychnops exilis*), which inhabits depths of up to 900 m (3,000 ft) in the north-east Pacific, and was only formally discovered in 1958. Beneath its principal eyes are two that are known as "secondary globes" with their own retinas and lenses, which look downwards. Behind these sit a third set of eyes, which although lacking retinas, are thought to help divert limited light to the primary eyeballs.

Longest primate nose

Aptly named proboscis monkeys (*Nasalis larvatus*), endemic to Borneo, have pendulous noses reaching up to 17.5 cm (6.8 in) long in elderly males. The nose becomes red and swollen when the simian is alarmed or excited, and also serves as a resonator, helping to amplify its distinctive honking warning call.

Most teeth for a crocodilian

Found exclusively in the Indian subcontinent, gharials (*Gavialis gangeticus*) are distinguished from other

FASTEST FORAGER (MAMMAL)

On average, the star-nosed mole (*Condylura cristata*) can identify, apprehend and consume its prey – e.g., worms – in 230 milliseconds (ms). In one case, a time of 120 ms was logged; that's a quarter of the time it takes us to blink. Covered with 25,000 mechanoreceptors known as "Eimer's organs", its incredible snout is the **most sensitive animal organ**.

MOST DIGITS FOR A PRIMATE

A 2019 study revealed that the gremlin-like aye-aye (*Daubentonia madagascariensis*) has six digits on each hand, rather than five. A tiny nub on each wrist was determined to be a "pseudo-thumb". This is in addition to an unusually spindly middle finger, perfect for winkling out bugs from holes in trees.

GREATEST EYE SPAN (RELATIVE TO BODY)

Cyrtodiopsis whitei – a Malayan stalk-eyed fly – can be 7.5 mm (0.29 in) long and yet have a gap of 10.5 mm (0.41 in) between its peepers. Based on that ratio, a 6-ft-tall (1.8-m) human would have eyes spaced more than 8 ft (2.4 m) apart!

LONGEST EARS ON A BAT (RELATIVE TO BODY)

The spotted bat (*Euderma maculatum*), native to south-western Canada, the western USA and northern Mexico, has a head-and-body length of around 7 cm (2.8 in), yet its ears can reach 5 cm (2 in). Scaled to adult human size, that would equate to us having 1.2-m-long (4-ft) lobes! Most bats rely on echolocation to catch their prey, so such big audio receivers can only be an evolutionary advantage.

At rest, the spotted bat's ears roll up around its head. When hunting, they fill with blood and unfurl.

Mangrove-dwelling archerfish (*Toxotes jaculatrix*) are sharp shooters. They're able to spit a pellet of water to dislodge a bug as far as 1.5 m (5 ft) away.

Several fish generate their own electricity to stun prey. Top of the shocks, though, are electric eels (*Electrophorus*). With discharges of up to 860 volts, they are the **most electric animals.**

Horned lizards or horntoads (*Phrynosoma*) of North America have pressurized sinuses in their eye sockets. If threatened, they can be ruptured to squirt blood at their attacker up to 1.2 m (4 ft) away.

1.2 m

As well as having super vision (below), mantis shrimp also throw a killer punch. Swinging a club-like leg at speeds of 23 m (75 ft)/sec delivers the **strongest self-powered strike.**

---

members of the crocodilian fraternity by their extremely slender snouts, which feature as many as 110 razor-sharp, interlocking teeth. While their jaws are exceptionally narrow compared with crocodiles and alligators, they are perfectly adapted to catching small, fast-moving fish – the gharial's main food.

Greatest mimic

Nature's foremost impersonator is the mimic octopus (*Thaumoctopus mimicus*), which inhabits Indo-Pacific waters. By altering its body shape, colouration and even the way it moves and behaves, this species can masquerade as at least 16 different animals. These range from sea snakes, lionfish, jellyfish and cuttlefish to stingrays and even hermit crabs.

Largest litter for a wild mammal

Resembling a cross between a shrew and a hedgehog, tenrecs are insectivores endemic to Madagascar and nearby islands. The largest of their family, the tailless tenrec (*Tenrec ecaudatus*), has been documented giving birth to 31 babies (30 of which survived).

First "exploding" ants

Colobopsis cylindrica are a group of tree-dwelling carpenter ants from south-east Asia that go to extreme lengths to protect their colony. If their nest is being raided, workers can sacrifice themselves by rupturing their own bodies, covering rival insects with a sticky, toxic goo that stops them in their tracks.

MOST COMPLEX EYES

Mantis shrimp (Stomatopoda), found mostly in reefs and warm coastal waters, boast the most sophisticated eyes of any animal. Made up of thousands of repeating units called "ommatidia", the compound eyes contain as many as 16 different photoreceptors, compared to three in the human eye. Twelve receptors are dedicated to colour analysis (enabling them to see deep ultraviolet through to far infrared), while the remaining four can detect polarized light.

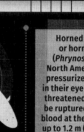

Light Fantastic

MOST DIVERSE BIOLUMINESCENT ANIMALS ON LAND
More than 3,000 types of beetle (Coleoptera) across several families have the ability to generate their own light. Most are fireflies (below), but they also include click beetles, railroad worms (see opposite) and some glowworms. The **brightest bioluminescence** is produced by the fire beetle (*Pyrophorus noctilucus*, inset) with an intensity of 45 millilamberts, or 143.2 candela/m^2, which is as bright as a single-LED torch.

100%

MOST FLUORESCENT CARNIVOROUS PLANT
In a 2013 study of meat-eating plants, the Khasi Hills pitcher plant (*Nepenthes khasiana*), native to India, outshone all its rivals. When scanned with a 366-nm UV light, the peristome (lip) of its traps fluoresced blue at 430–480 nm. Scientists suspect that this serves to draw in bugs, unwittingly to their death.

FIRST FLUORESCENT MONOTREME
In 2020, the platypus (*Ornithorhynchus anatinus*, below) became the first known egg-laying mammal to fluoresce. The fur of this Australian species usually appears brown, but when 200–400-nm UV light was shone on three museum specimens, it glowed green/cyan at 500–600 nm.
  This research inspired further study that led to the discovery of the **largest fluorescent mammal** to date: the 1.3-m-long (4-ft 3-in) common wombat (*Vombatus ursinus*).

HEAVIEST SCORPION
All scorpions glow in the dark under ultraviolet (UV) light, including the hefty emperor scorpion (*Pandinus imperator*), which weighs up to 60 g (2 oz). Fluorescent exoskeletons may serve to confuse prey, provide protection from sunlight, or help scorpions detect ambient UV levels, allowing them to better hide at night.

GOING WITH THE GLOW

Thousands of organisms flash and glow to survive; most of them dwell in the ocean, where natural light is scarce. The uses for this ability extend far beyond just illuminating their surroundings. Dr Steven Haddock of the Monterey Bay Aquarium Research Institute, who specializes in bioluminescence, has identified 12 key functions – a few spotlighted here...

Some animals, such as anglerfish and dragonfish (see opposite), use light as a lure. Prey is drawn to the light, only to be gobbled up before they realize it's a trap!

Light can also be used more proactively as a weapon by stunning or confusing victims into a stupor – a technique employed by giant squid.

In the bioluminescence arms race, prey too can use light, to evade enemies. Take counterillumination: fish lighten their bellies to stay hidden from predators below.

Bioluminescence is a light-producing chemical reaction that takes place within a living organism. Photons are emitted when two chemicals mix: luciferin with either luciferase or photoprotein. Some animals can produce all the components themselves, some absorb them in their diet, and others still work symbiotically with bioluminescent micro-organisms, e.g., bacteria live inside anglerfish lures. *Fluorescence* (or biofluorescence) occurs when one type of light is absorbed and another wavelength on the visible light spectrum is sent back out, often with a different hue; light wavelength is quantified in nanometres (nm).

Oldest bioluminescent beetles
Beetles are the most diverse light-emitting terrestrial animals (see above) and also among the most ancient. A notable example is *Cretophengodes azari*, dating back some 99 million years to the mid-Cretaceous. This elateroid beetle is known from a single specimen discovered fossilized in amber from Myanmar. Studies of its abdominal bioluminescent organ suggest that its light may have been a defence mechanism.

MOST VISITED GLOWWORM CAVES
Since 1889, tourists have flocked to the Waitomo Caves on New Zealand's North Island to witness the stunning displays put on by the larvae of *Arachnocampa luminosa* fungus gnats. In a typical year, the caverns draw 450,000–500,000 people. These glowworms emit blue-green light to trick moths into flying up towards what *looks* like the starry night sky, only to become snared in a web of sticky, mucus-coated silk.

LARGEST "MILKY SEA"

Milky seas are a natural event during which vast colonies of bioluminescent bacteria light up the ocean at night. Between 25 Jul and 9 Aug 2019, a milky sea covering more than 100,000 km² (38,610 sq mi) – about the size of Iceland – was spotted near Java, Indonesia, by satellite, as shown in this colour-enhanced composite.

MOST DIVERSE BIOLUMINESCENT FUNGUS

Of the 81 known species of fungi to exhibit the ability to bioluminesce, at least 68 belong to the genus *Mycena* (bonnet mushrooms) – a proportion of 84%. Still relatively unstudied, glowing fungi have been noted for millennia; Greek philosopher Aristotle (384–322 BCE) likened their eerie light to "a cold fire".

GREATEST RANGE OF BIOLUMINESCENCE (FISH)

Thousands of marine fish – including all deep-sea dragonfish (example above) – can generate light, typically in the blue-green spectrum (450–550 nm). However, three genera of dragonfish (*Aristostomias*, *Malacosteus* and *Pachystomias*; inset below is *P. microdon*) have also evolved to emit – and see – far-red light (>700 nm). It means that they are able to see their prey but their prey can't see them.

Sharks may bioluminesce to help them locate prey, attract mates, or to conceal themselves.

LARGEST BIOLUMINESCENT VERTEBRATE

Several sharks possess the ability to bioluminesce. The largest species to exhibit this trait – and indeed the largest among all animals with a backbone – is the kitefin shark (*Dalatias licha*), which can reach 1.8 m (5 ft 11 in) from nose to tail. It is pictured here both in daylight and in darkness, glowing blue. Found globally at depths of up to 1,800 m (5,905 ft), this deep-sea dweller's bioluminescent biology only came to light in 2020.

Red photophore (light-emitting organ)

Under attack, some animals, e.g. squid, jellyfish and crustaceans, can release a cloud of glowing material. The smokescreen buys them vital time to escape.

Resigned to being on the menu, certain sea cucumbers and jellies light up a body part that they can live without – what is known as a "sacrificial tag".

As the saying goes, there is safety in numbers. Group organisms like tiny dinoflagellates can set off a silent alarm by flashing to warn their neighbours of an impending threat.

It's not all about attack and defence: in a dark world, bioluminescence can also be pivotal to romance. Many sea creatures use light to both find and communicate with prospective mates.

Largest bioluminescent organism

The largest glowing life-form, and the **largest organism** overall, is a single *Armillaria ostoyae* honey mushroom in Oregon's Malheur National Forest, USA. The "humongous fungus" covers 890 ha (2,200 acres), or 740 Trafalgar Squares. Unlike other glow-in-the-dark fungi (see above), only the root-like mycelia – not the fruiting bodies – produce light. Research in 2015 revealed that fungi glow when oxygen interacts with luciferin, producing oxyluciferin, perhaps as a means to attract insects that spread their spores.

Longest bioluminescent animal

Measuring up to 50 m (164 ft) – the same as an Olympic swimming pool – the giant siphonophore (*Praya dubia*) is a near-transparent species of marine invertebrate related to the jellyfish-like Portuguese man o' war. Technically, siphonophores are not singular animals but "super-organisms" made up of thousands of tiny individual creatures called zooids, each responsible for its own function. This species emits a bluish light to lure passing prey into its stinging tentillae.

First land animal to emit red light

Blue-green light is the most common emitted by bioluminescent animals, but not exclusively. Railroad worms (*Phrixothrix*), a type of glowworm, dazzle with two shades. They owe their nickname to the fact that the worms' larvae and adult females resemble train carriages, owing to 11 pairs of green light organs that run along their sides. What sets them apart, though, are their two ruby-red-coloured "head lights", with a wavelength of 620–638 nm.

Darkest animals

While some animals create light, others do all they can to suppress it. The most extreme examples are *Oneirodes* anglerfish, with a reflectance as low as 0.044% at 480 nm. Put another way, their ultra-black skin absorbs 99.95% of all light hitting it. This helps to conceal them in the gloomy ocean depths, not from sunlight but rather the bioluminescent light cast by their prey!

BRIGHTEST BIOLUMINESCENT BAY

Mosquito Bay on the island of Vieques in Puerto Rico, USA, contains up to 700,000 tiny dinoflagellates per gallon (4.5 l) of seawater. When agitated, these micro-organisms (*Pyrodinium bahamense*, aka "whirling fire") react by flashing blue-green light for about one-tenth of a second. The concentration is particularly high here owing to the bay's narrow mouth and plentiful food.

Pets & Livestock

SU-*PURR*-LATIVE FELINE DYNASTY

The **tallest domestic cat** is Fenrir Antares Powers (left), who measures 47.83 cm (1 ft 6.83 in), as verified in Farmington Hills, Michigan, USA, on 29 Jan 2021. (The height is taken from the base of the front paws to the top of the withers – the ridge that runs between the shoulder blades.) Fenrir, a Savannah cat, assumed the record on the death of his brother, Arcturus Aldebaran Powers. The latter is still a GWR title holder, though: his height of 48.40 cm (1 ft 7.05 in) – as ratified on 3 Nov 2016 – makes him the **tallest domestic cat ever**.

These statuesque cats were raised by William Powers (USA; pictured left, with Fenrir), as were another pair of record-breaking siblings. Altair Cygnus Powers, a silver Maine Coon (above), has the **longest tail on a domestic cat** – measuring 40.83 cm (1 ft 4.07 in) – as verified on 25 Oct 2021. Altair was brother to Cygnus Regulus Powers, who held this record until his passing. But Cygnus retains the title for the **longest tail on a domestic cat ever** – 44.66 cm (1 ft 5.58 in), when assessed on 28 Aug 2016.

The names of the cat quartet derive from folklore and cosmology; e.g., Fenrir was a mighty wolf in Norse mythology.

MOST EXPENSIVE PAINTING BY AN ANIMAL

Wild and Free by Pigcasso sold for 430,000 ZAR ($26,898; £20,276) on 13 Dec 2021. The porcine painter from South Africa is owned by Joanne Lefson and has created more than 400 artworks. She paints with non-toxic (o)ink and signs pieces with her snout.

FASTEST TIME FOR A DOG TO RUN ALL BASEBALL BASES

Jack Russell Macho flew around the diamond in 21.06 sec at Dodger Stadium in Los Angeles, California, USA, on 24 Sep 2021. Macho and his owner, Lori Signs, trained for more than a year to take on this challenge, organized by pet-food producer Lucy Pet.

CATCH THEM IF YOU CAN!

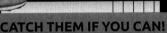

Fastest 30 m on a bicycle by a dog: 55.41 sec, by Norman (USA)

Fastest 30 m on a scooter by a dog: 20.77 sec, by Norman

Longest wave surfed by a dog (open water): 107.2 m (351 ft 8 in), by Abbie Girl (USA)

Most legs travelled through on a skateboard by a dog: 33, by Dai-chan (JPN)

Most legs travelled through on a skateboard by a cat: 13, by Boomer (AUS)

Fastest time to complete five jumps by a rabbit

Under the guidance of her owner Nicole Barrett, a plush lop bunny named Penelope leapt five hurdles in 4.816 sec on 18 Jan 2020. The venue was the Bradford Premier Small Animal Show in South Yorkshire, UK. Rabbit showjumping began in Sweden in the 1970s.

Highest platform jump by a guinea pig

Fizz executed a 32-cm (1-ft 0.6-in) standing jump on to a platform in Bellevue, Switzerland, on 10 Mar 2021. He is owned by nine-year-old Gabriele Nava Mambretti.

LARGEST RIDDEN PARADE OF MULES

A procession of 50 mules and their riders passed through Warrensburg, Missouri, USA, on 23 Oct 2021. The event was overseen by the University of Central Missouri and formed part of its sesquicentennial (150-year) celebrations. The mule is both the university's mascot and Missouri's state animal.

OCT. 23, 2021 WARRENSBURG, MISSOURI
WORLD RECORD LARGEST RIDDEN
PARADE OF MULES
CENTRAL MISSOURI

Highest jump by a pig

Kotetsu – a pot-bellied pig trained by Makoto Ieki – cleared a 70-cm-high (2-ft 3.5-in) bar at the Mokumoku Tezukuri Farm in Mie, Japan, on 22 Aug 2004.

Most basketball slamdunks by a...

• **Guinea pig in 30 seconds**: On 16 Nov 2021, Molly the guinea pig put away four slamdunks in half a minute in Dombóvár, Hungary. Her owner is Emma Müller.
• **Dog in one minute**: Three-year-old border collie Leonard Lee netted 14 basketballs in 60 sec in River Rouge, Michigan, USA, on 28 Oct 2021. He is owned and trained by Teresa Hanula.

Most clothes retrieved from a washing line by a dog in one minute

Guided by Jennifer Fraser, blue-merle Australian shepherd Daiquiri collected 18 items from a clothes line in Strathmore, Alberta, Canada, on 28 Feb 2021. The pair's other GWR feats include the **most toys retrieved in one minute** – 15 – and the **most weaves through a person's legs in 30 seconds** – 37.

FASTEST 5 M ON A SCOOTER BY A PARROT

On 15 Feb 2022, a Triton cockatoo named Chico rolled 5 m (16 ft 4 in) in 14.58 sec on the set of *Lo Show dei Record* in Milan, Italy. In doing so, he shaved nearly 3 sec off his own record, set just five days earlier. Chico's owner is bird trainer Kaloyan Yavashev from Bulgaria.

TALLEST DOG

Zeus, a two-year-old Great Dane, stood 1.046 m (3 ft 5.1 in) to the withers on 22 Mar 2022. He is owned by Brittany Davis of Bedford in Texas, USA. Inset, he is on hind legs with Brittany's 15-year-old son, Jamison. Confusingly, the **tallest dog ever** was also a Great Dane called Zeus: he stood 1.118 m (3 ft 8 in) on 4 Oct 2011 and belonged to the Doorlag family of Michigan, USA.

FASTEST 5 M ON HIND LEGS BY A HORSE

On 27 Feb 2022, a Shetland pony named Alvin covered 5 m on two legs in 16.70 sec in Klippan, Skåne, Sweden. Alvin is trained by Paulina Tufvesson. "In his mind, he's as big and powerful as any other horse," she reveals. "He hates being babied – he's a super diva!"

Farthest skateboard ride by a goat: 36 m (118 ft), by Happie (USA)

Fastest five hurdles jumped while on a skateboard by a dog: 2.46 sec, by Lenny the Batdog (FRA)

Farthest SUP ride on a river bore by a dog/human pair: 1.69 km (1 mi), by Bono & Ivan Moreira (both BRA)

Longest dive by a pig: 3.31 m (10 ft 10 in), by Miss Piggy (AUS)

Fastest tightrope crossing by a dog: 18.22 sec, by Ozzy (UK)

Daiquiri and Jennifer formerly also held the record for **most consecutive items caught by a dog**, with 11 treats. The record now stands at 23 catches without a drop, set by Molly and owner Oscar Lynagh in Melbourne, Victoria, Australia, on 20 Jun 2021.

Oldest pig ever

Baby Jane (b. 1 Feb 1998) was 23 years 221 days old when she passed away on 10 Sep 2021. Her owners were Patrick Cunningham and Stanley Coffman of Mundelein, Illinois, USA. Remembered by them as "extremely affectionate and empathetic", Baby Jane regularly travelled around the country with the couple. She apparently loved being at the beach and one of her favourite places was Key West in Florida – the continental USA's most southerly point.

Oldest cat siblings

Twin black-and-white domestic shorthairs Pika and Zippo (b. 1 Mar 2000) celebrated their 22nd birthday in 2022, giving them a combined age of 44 years. The sisters live with the Teece family in London, UK.

Largest horn spread on a steer

Poncho Via, a Texas longhorn, had a 3.23-m (10-ft 7-in) distance between the tips of his horns, as confirmed in Goodwater, Alabama, USA, on 8 May 2019. That's around three times the width of a bowling lane! He lives on a ranch with the Pope family.

The **largest horn spread on a cow** is 2.65 m (8 ft 8 in), belonging to 3S Danica, as verified in Lawton, Oklahoma, USA, on 4 Oct 2019. Also a Texas longhorn, she is owned by Mike Davis.

Most expensive sheep

At an auction in Lanark, UK, on 27 Aug 2020, a pedigree Texel ram lamb named Sportsmans Double Diamond sold for 350,000 guineas (£367,500; $483,960) to a consortium of farmers. He was bred by Charlie Boden.

Tallest donkey

Romulus, an American Mammoth Jackstock, stood 17 hands (172.7 cm; 5 ft 8 in) on 8 Feb 2013. Aged 18 in 2022, he lives on a farm in Texas, USA, with his brother – Remus – and owners Cara and Phil Yellott.

MOST TRICKS BY A CAT IN ONE MINUTE

Working with her owner Anika Moritz, Alexis put on a 60-sec show that included 26 different tricks in Bruck an der Leitha, Niederösterreich, Austria, on 10 Jun 2020. Anika has owned Alexis since she was 11 and started teaching her using positive reinforcement just a few weeks after she arrived.

Animal Heroes

AMERICA'S FIRST ANIMAL BRAVERY AWARD

On 14 Nov 2019, the charity Animals in War & Peace awarded eight animals (see table) the debut Medal of Bravery – six posthumously – in Washington, DC, USA. Each had displayed "gallantry and acts of valor within the performance of their duties". A second ceremony – on 9 Mar 2022 – saw three more dogs honoured; a new Distinguished Service Medal for acts that go beyond the call of duty was also bestowed on three other dogs: Hurricane, Smoky and Feco.

First recipients of the Medal of Bravery

Name	Animal	Service
Chips	Dog	Scout stationed in North Africa in WWII
Stormy	Dog	Marine scout in the Vietnam War
Lucca	Dog	Specialized search agent with US Marine Corps deployed in Iraq and Afghanistan
Bucca (top centre)	Dog	Fire-scene investigation animal in New York City
Bass (top left)	Dog	Multipurpose canine with the Marine Corps Special Ops in Afghanistan and East Africa
Cher Ami (top right)	Pigeon	Delivered vital messages during WWI
GI Joe	Pigeon	Helped avert a friendly-fire attack in WWII
SSgt Reckless (left)	Horse	Mare that attained Staff Sergeant's rank; supplied ammo and retrieved wounded in the Korean War

First animal gallantry medal

The Blue Cross Medal* for heroic animals debuted in 1940, with a daring dog named La Cloche (FRA) its **first recipient**. He was on the SS *Meknes* on 24 Jul 1940 when it was torpedoed off Dorset, UK, and jumped into the sea to save his owner, who could not swim.

The **most Blue Cross Medals won by an animal** is two, for Juliana, a Great Dane owned by Mr W T Britton (UK). Her first medal was for reportedly extinguishing an incendiary device, dropped in the Blitz in 1941, by urinating on it. The second was for alerting her owners to a fire in 1944.

The **first feline recipient of the Blue Cross Medal** was a British cat called Jim, owned by Mr and Mrs Coffey. In 1942, he awoke the couple during a night-time house fire, enabling them to escape.

Most medical conditions detected by dogs

In 2008–22, Medical Detection Dogs (UK) trained dogs to recognize 28 conditions by odour alone, including malaria, Parkinson's, cancer and COVID-19. As well as "bio-detection" dogs that diagnose ailments, the charity also teaches medical alert assistance dogs; these super-sniffers can sense tiny changes in their owners' bodies and warn them of an imminent health emergency.

Highest-ranking...

· **Camel**: Bert – made Reserve Deputy Sheriff for the LA County Sheriff's Department in San Dimas, USA, in 2003.
· **Penguin**: Brigadier Sir Nils Olav of the Norwegian Royal Guards since 2016; he was knighted by King Harald V of Norway in 2008.
· **Horse**: Major Perseus of the Household Cavalry Blues and Royals Regiment, the British Army's most senior animal since 2017.

Q&A: ROBIN HUTTON

The founder of Animals in War & Peace has also authored two books on unsung animal heroes during wartime.

What led to your current role as an animal ambassador?
When I was researching my two books, I developed a deeper respect for animals. I wanted to honour them in the way they deserved – the way the PDSA has been doing in Great Britain since WWII with their Dickin Medal [see right]. In 2016, I nominated Staff Sergeant Reckless for the PDSA Dickin Medal. At the ceremony, I asked the director of the PDSA, "Why doesn't America have a medal like this? *We* need something like this." And that was it.

How do you decide which heroic animals make the list?
We have a five-member Nominating Board and a 10-member Advisory Board. We reach out to the public, branches of the military and first responders, asking them to nominate. Our board also nominates animals.

Can the public put forward nominees?
Yes, it's very important that they do! Just click on the "Medals" tab at **animalsinwarandpeace.org**.

Some argue that animals shouldn't be used in human conflicts. What's your take?
The animals that have gone to war that I've seen are very well cared for by their handler and unit because everyone knows how valuable they are to the team. They are "force multipliers", bringing skills to the team that their human counterparts just don't have.

SGT. RECKLESS
AMERICA'S WAR HORSE

WAR ANIMALS
THE UNSUNG HEROES OF WORLD WAR II
ROBIN HUTTON

▶ SHORTEST HORSE (MALE)

Bombel stands just 5.5 hands (56.7 cm; 1 ft 10 in) to the shoulders, as verified in Łódź, Poland, on 24 Apr 2018. The miniature Appaloosa often works as a therapy animal in local children's hospitals alongside his owner, Katarzyna Zielińska.

The **first use of the term "pet therapy"** appeared in the journal *Mental Hygiene* in Apr 1964, in a paper by psychologist Dr Boris Levinson (LTU, b. RUS).

*The Blue Cross issued an Order of Merit (not a medal) in 1918 to all military horses involved in WWI

PDSA PLAUDITS

Introduced in 1943 by Maria Dickin – the founder of the UK-based People's Dispensary for Sick Animals (PDSA) – the PDSA Dickin Medal is the animal equivalent of the British Victoria Cross for human valour. The first Dickin Medals were handed out on 2 Dec 1943 (to three pigeons) and, as of 1 Apr 2022, it has had 71 more recipients, 37 of which have been dogs. The charity has also since added two further accolades.

Dickin Medal (est. 1943)
The earliest PDSA award for animal heroism, celebrating bravery or devotion to duty during military conflict.

Gold Medal (est. 2002)
The Dickin Medal's civilian counterpart, likened to the George Cross. Salutes courage and dedication outside war.

Magawa (see right)

Order of Merit (est. 2014)
The latest award – equivalent to an OBE – is for acts of extreme loyalty and service that goes above and beyond.

MOST LANDMINES DETECTED BY A RAT

Magawa, an African giant pouched rat from Tanzania trained and deployed by Belgian non-profit APOPO, sniffed out 71 mines during his career. He uncovered the explosives in Cambodia between Jan 2017 and May 2021 when, aged seven, he was retired from duty. Magawa was awarded the PDSA Gold Medal (see left) for his valiant efforts. He passed away peacefully in 2022.

FIRST DONKEY TO RECEIVE THE RSPCA PURPLE CROSS

On 19 May 1997, an Australian Army donkey named Murphy was posthumously issued the RSPCA Australia Purple Cross for animal bravery. During an abortive WWI offensive in Gallipoli, Turkey, in 1915–16, Murphy bore the wounded from the front on a perilous journey to field hospitals with his trainer, John Simpson Kirkpatrick. Together, they rescued some 300 injured soldiers.

FIRST CAT TO RECEIVE THE PDSA DICKIN MEDAL

Simon was ship's cat on board Britain's HMS *Amethyst* when it came under bombardment during the Yangtse Incident in 1949. He was bestowed this medal "for disposing of many rats though wounded by shell blast". His actions helped sustain the ship's dwindling food supplies.

HIGHEST-RANKING BEAR

A polar bear named Juno, a resident at Toronto Zoo in Ontario, Canada, was made the Canadian Army's official live mascot and an Honorary Private on 27 Feb 2016 (International Polar Bear Day). On her first birthday (11 Nov 2016), she became Honorary Corporal. On turning five in 2020, Juno was promoted again, to Honorary Master Corporal. One of her primary duties is to raise awareness about Arctic climate change.

MOST THERAPY ANIMALS AT AN AIRPORT

Devised to help de-stress nervous travellers, the Canine Airport Therapy Squad (CATS) at Denver International Airport in Colorado, USA, is the biggest programme of its kind. It comprised 87 volunteer owner-pet pairs as of Dec 2021. Dog breeds range from a toy fox terrier to an Irish wolfhound. Despite its name, CATS currently has only one feline member: Xeli.

CAUTION
Guide dog
in training

MOST GUIDE DOGS TRAINED

As of 31 Dec 2021, the UK's Guide Dogs for the Blind Association (Guide Dogs for short) had taught 36,670 dogs to provide mobility assistance to blind or partially sighted people. In 2021, the charity marked its 90th anniversary, having begun in 1931 under Muriel Crooke and Rosamund Bond, who trained the first four British guide dogs from a lock-up garage.

FIRST SKYDIVING ANTI-POACHING DOG

On 17 Sep 2016, German shepherd Arrow and his handler, Henry Holsthyzen (ZAF), jumped from a helicopter flying 6,000 ft (1,828 m) above Air Force Base Waterkloof near Pretoria, South Africa, to demonstrate their aerial interception skills. While Arrow isn't the first dog to tandem-skydive, he was the first to make the leap as part of a pioneering programme to apprehend wildlife poachers from the sky.

Blue Whale

At an average of 25 m (82 ft) long and 160 tonnes (176 tons), blue whales (*Balaenoptera musculus*) are not just the **largest mammals**, but the **largest animals** ever to live on our planet. The biggest specimen on record, measured in 1909 at a whaling station in the South Atlantic, came in at a whopping 33.57 m (110 ft 1.6 in). That's about the same length as three London double-decker buses.

Blue whales are an inventory of superlatives, from their extraordinary size to their bottomless appetites. Not surprisingly, given their magnitude, they have the **largest heart**. One example, extracted from a 24-m (78-ft) carcass that washed up in 2014, weighed in at 440 lb (199.5 kg) – about the same as an upright piano – and was 5 ft (1.5 m) from top to bottom.

Recent research suggests that as a blue whale dives, its heartbeat drops to just twice a minute – the **slowest heart rate in a mammal**. It rises to nearer 40 beats at the ocean surface, but "that's about as fast as that heart can physically beat," according to Stanford University's Dr Jeremy Goldbogen.

Blue whales can remain underwater for an hour, primarily thanks to possessing the **largest lungs**. They have a combined capacity of 5,000 litres (1,320 gal) of air – enough to fill around 450 party balloons using a single breath! Not only are these organs massive, but they are extremely efficient: up to 90% of the air intake is transferred to the bloodstream.

GREATEST SIZE DIFFERENCE BETWEEN PREDATOR AND PREY
Krill are shrimp-like crustaceans that grow to about 50 mm (2 in) long, making them nearly 500 times smaller than the blue whales that consume them. In Nov 2021, researchers at Stanford University revealed that baleen whales (among which blues are the biggest) eat up to three times more krill than was thought – an average of 16 tons (14.5 tonnes) daily during the summer season. To trap them, a whale gulps in vast amounts of krill-filled seawater, then presses the **largest tongue** (typically 4 tonnes, or 4.4 tons) to the roof of its mouth, expelling the water. Hair-like baleen then sieves out the krill for consumption.

100%

Krill amass in such large numbers in the Southern Ocean that their swarms can be seen from space!

THE NEED TO FEED
The blue whale's daily diet makes for a hugely calorific intake. Indeed, just one mouthful of krill represents around 457,000 calories, or the equivalent of 830 Big Mac burgers. But the whale needs such a rich diet in order to sustain its massive bulk, and that mouthful typically gives it almost 200 times the energy that it expends while capturing its food.

Round-Up

NEWEST CARNIVOROUS PLANT GENUS
A 2021 study revealed that false asphodels (*Triantha*) derive some of their nourishment from eating meat. Native to marshes and wet meadows (mainly in North America), the plants capture small flies using sticky hair-like appendages (trichomes) on their flower stalks, then absorb the nutrients.

Oldest guts
Preserved internal organs of 550-million-year-old fossils unearthed in the Wood Canyon Formation of Nevada, USA, were reported in Jan 2020. The rudimentary digestive tracts were found inside the tubular shells of cloudinids, a primitive group of marine animals dating back to the late Ediacaran period – some 300 million years before the emergence of the dinosaurs. Cloudinids measured no more than 15 cm (6 in) long and are among the earliest shell-based life forms to have ever existed on Earth.

Largest arthropod ever
Arthropleura armata was a gigantic millipede measuring up to 2.6 m (8 ft 6 in) long – about the same as a polar bear – and more than 0.45 m (1 ft 5 in) wide. Tipping the scales at around 50 kg (110 lb), its segmented body was heavily plated and had between 32 and 64 legs in all – a long way short of its more diminutive descendant (see below). *Arthropleura* lived from *c.* 345 to 295 million years ago. At that time, oxygen levels in the atmosphere were considerably higher than today, enhancing the insect's respiratory efficiency and enabling it to grow so huge.

Most legs
Eumillipes persephone, a new-found species of millipede from the Goldfields region of Western Australia, possesses 1,306 legs (653 pairs) – more than any other animal, living or extinct. It measures just 95.7 mm (3.8 in) long and

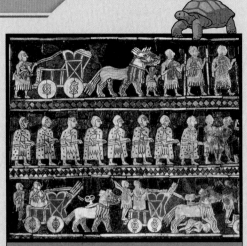

FIRST HUMAN-MADE HYBRID ANIMAL
Remains of the now-extinct kunga – a stocky equid once used to pull war wagons and royal chariots – have been found in the Middle East dating back *c.* 4,500 years. DNA analysis of kunga bones published in Jan 2022 revealed that the animal was the progeny of female domestic donkeys (*Equus africanus asinus*) and male Syrian wild asses (*E. hemionus hemippus*), the latter of which also no longer exists.

0.95 mm (0.04 in) wide, and has two pairs of limbs for almost every one of its 330 major body segments. Discovered some 60 m (200 ft) below ground in a drill hole created for mineral exploration, *Eumillipes* has neither pigmentation nor eyes, and explores its surroundings by touch with the aid of a pair of relatively enormous antennae. This remarkable new thread-like species was discovered in Aug 2020 and formally described and named in Dec 2021 in the journal *Scientific Reports*.

OLDEST DOG
Chihuahua TobyKeith (b. 9 Jan 2001) was confirmed to be the oldest living pooch on 16 Mar 2022, aged 21 years 66 days. He lives with Gisela Shore (USA) and his "sisters" Luna (an American bulldog) and Lala (a Chinese crested) in Greenacres, Florida, USA. Gisela describes TobyKeith as "a blessing. He's sweet, gentle, loving... and my little bodyguard."

OLDEST LAND ANIMAL
A Seychelles giant tortoise (*Aldabrachelys gigantea hololissa*) named Jonathan is believed to have been born no later than 1832, meaning that he celebrated his 190th birthday in 2022. He lives on the South Atlantic island of St Helena and was said to be "fully mature" (hence at least 50 years old) when he arrived there in 1882.

The **largest shark ever** is only surpassed in mass by one other marine animal: the blue whale (see pp.52–53).

LARGEST FISH EVER
The extinct megalodon (*Otodus megalodon*; formerly *Carcharodon megalodon*) is now believed to have reached up to 20 m (65 ft) long – three times the size of a great white shark (*C. carcharias*). A new method of extrapolating body length from tooth width (inset, alongside a great-white tooth) is behind the slightly increased size estimate for the "meg".

DARKEST BUTTERFLIES

In a study of dark-coloured butterflies published in Mar 2020, three species of the subfamily Biblidinae – *Eunica chlorochroa*, *Catonephele antinoe* and *C. numilia* males (above) – recorded a light reflectance as low as 0.06%. This compares to readings of 1–3% for butterflies with black (but not *ultra*-black) wings. For the **darkest animal** overall, see p.47.

Deepest squid

A bigfin squid (*Magnapinna*) was recorded close to the seafloor at a depth of 6,212 m (20,381 ft) in the Philippine Trench in the western Pacific Ocean. The observations, published in *Marine Biology* on 2 Dec 2021, extend the bathymetric range of this genus by 1,477 m (4,846 ft). This is the first squid known to inhabit the hadal zone, the deepest region of the ocean starting at 6,000 m (19,685 ft) below the surface.

Largest fish colony

A breeding ground of Jonah's icefish (*Neopagetopsis ionah*) located under an ice shelf in the southern Weddell Sea off Antarctica is estimated to comprise more than 60 million active nests. This means that the site could contain as many as 100 billion eggs. The 240-km² (93-sq-mi) mega-colony – roughly the same size as Scotland's capital city, Edinburgh – is believed to have formed over several decades.

FIRST ANIMAL WITH OPPOSABLE THUMBS

The prehistoric flying reptile *Kunpengopterus antipollicatus* has been called "Monkeydactyl" owing to an ability to touch its thumbs to the tips of its other digits – a trademark of most primates, including humans. This may have helped it to climb trees. The creature lived in north-east China *c.* 160 million years ago and was described in *Current Biology* in Apr 2021.

Largest insect hotel

Highland Titles Nature Reserve in Duror, Argyll and Bute, UK, constructed a 199.9-m³ (7,059-cu-ft) minibeast mansion, as verified on 28 Mar 2022. It took seven people half a year to construct the bug B&B, which was made from felled non-native Sitka spruce, bamboo canes, masonry bricks, forest bark and wood chippings. The aim is to increase biodiversity and also attract more visitors to the park.

Oldest captive...

· **Leopard**: A melanistic (all-black) leopard (*Panthera pardus*) named Raven (b. 15 Jul 1997) was 24 years 26 days old as of 10 Aug 2021. She is the most elderly exotic cat at the Center for Animal Research and Education (CARE) in Bridgeport, Texas, USA.

· **Koala**: Midori (b. Feb 1997) was at least 25 years old as of 1 Mar 2022 – far beyond the average lifespan of 15–16 years for a koala (*Phascolarctos cinereus*). This also makes her the **oldest captive koala ever**. Midori was sent to Japan in 2003 as a gift from Western Australia's state government and since has resided at Awaji Farm Park England Hill in Hyogo.

· **Wombat**: Wain, a common wombat (*Vombatus ursinus*), was rescued from the wild and is thought to have been born *c.* Jan 1989. He lives at Satsukiyama Zoo in Ikeda, Osaka, Japan, and was at least 32 years old on 31 Jan 2022.

· **Snake**: A green anaconda (*Eunectes murinus*) – the world's **heaviest snake species** – born on 1 Jul 1983 was 37 years 317 days old on 14 May 2021. Named Annie, she was owned by Paul Swires until 2004, when he donated her to Montecasino Bird Gardens in Johannesburg, South Africa.

· **Sloth**: Jan, a Linne's two-toed sloth (*Choloepus didactylus*), was estimated to have been aged six months when found in the wild in May 1970, meaning he will turn 52 years old in 2022. A resident at Krefeld Zoo in Germany since 1986, in Jan 2022 the quinquagenarian became a father for the 20th time, to a son (Kalle).

LARGEST *TRICERATOPS* SKELETON

The mounted skeleton of "Big John", a *Triceratops horridus* dating to the late Cretaceous period, measures 7.15 m (23 ft 5 in) long and stands 2.7 m (8 ft 10 in) at the hips. Discovered in 2014 in South Dakota, USA, the fossil (inset with Iacopo Briano, a natural-history auction expert) was bought for $7.7 m (£5.6 m) in Oct 2021.

LONGEST INSECT TONGUE

Wallace's sphinx moth (*Xanthopan praedicta*) of Madagascar has a proboscis that can unravel to 28.5 cm (11.2 in) – more than four times its body length! Only its titanic tongue can reach the nectar deep inside the star-shaped flowers of Darwin's orchid, so the two species' fates are now irrevocably intertwined.

LONGEST JOURNEY BY A LAGOMORPH

In 2019, a tagged Arctic hare (*Lepus arcticus*) known as "BBYY" hopped 388 km (241 mi) in 49 days across Ellesmere Island in Nunavut, Canada. This epic trek is of scientific importance as lagomorphs (i.e., hares, rabbits and pikas) were previously thought largely to confine themselves to familiar territory where food is plentiful.

Rumeysa Gelgi

VITAL STATISTICS

Name	Rumeysa Gelgi
Birthplace	Safranbolu, Turkey
Date of birth	1 Jan 1997
Current GWR titles	**Tallest woman** (215.16 cm; 7 ft 0.7 in) **Longest finger*** (11.2 cm; 4.4 in) **Largest hands*** (24.93 cm; 9.8 in) **Longest back*** (59.90 cm; 1 ft 11 in)
*female	
Hobbies	Swimming, reading

Rumeysa Gelgi (TUR) turns heads wherever she goes. With a standing height of over 215 cm (7 ft), she is the world's tallest living woman.

Rumeysa owes her astonishing stature to an extremely rare condition called Weaver syndrome, which causes accelerated growth and skeletal deformities. Hers was only the 27th case ever diagnosed, and the first in Turkey. Rumeysa uses a wheelchair and can only stand using a walker. While her condition does not make life easy, Rumeysa says that being so tall makes her feel special.

In 2014, she was named as the world's **tallest female teenager**, and used this as a platform for advocacy on behalf of others with Weaver syndrome and scoliosis. Rumeysa refuses to let these physical challenges hold her back: she was home-schooled and now works as a qualified web designer.

On 23 May 2021, Rumeysa's height was re-measured at 215.16 cm (7 ft 0.7 in), confirming her as the ❷ **tallest woman**. She is yet to meet the **tallest man** – fellow Turk Sultan Kösen (see p.72) – but would like to. "Being a record holder is a very amazing thing," Rumeysa says. "I know that only the special people can make it, and I know I'm one of them now."

2

3

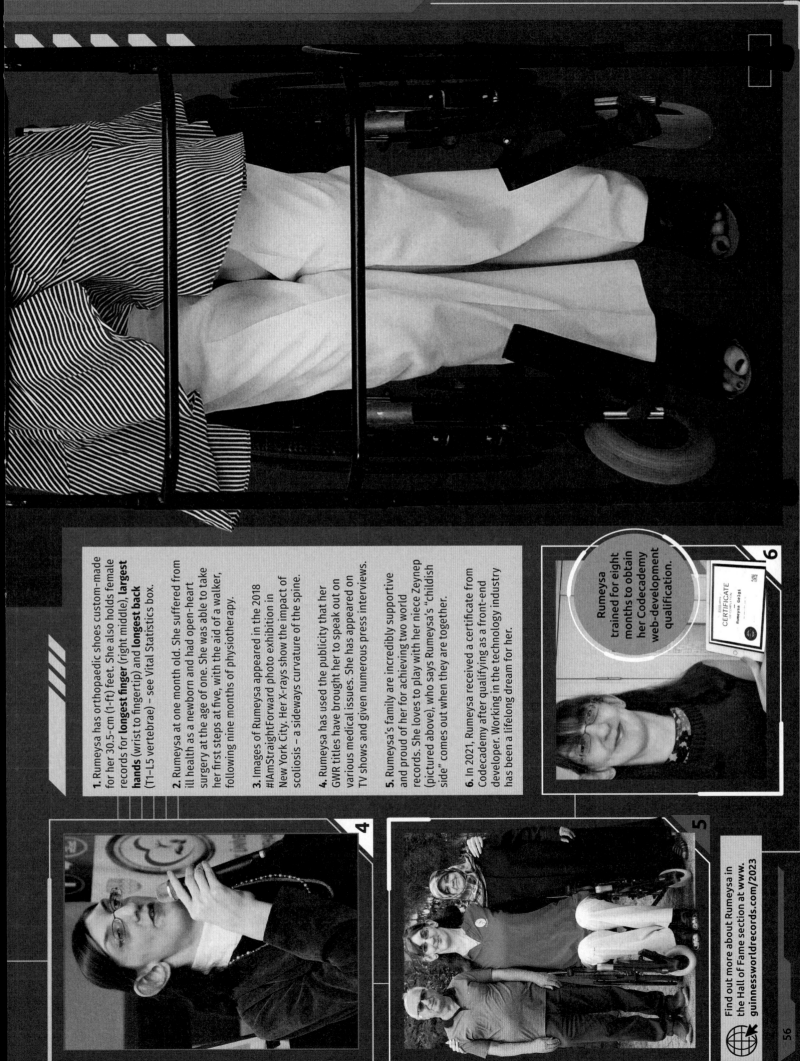

1. Rumeysa has orthopaedic shoes custom-made for her 30.5-cm (1-ft) feet. She also holds female records for **longest finger** (right middle), **largest hands** (wrist to fingertip) and **longest back** (T1–L5 vertebrae) – see Vital Statistics box.

2. Rumeysa at one month old. She suffered from ill health as a newborn and had open-heart surgery at the age of one. She was able to take her first steps at five, with the aid of a walker, following nine months of physiotherapy.

3. Images of Rumeysa appeared in the 2018 #IAmStraightForward photo exhibition in New York City. Her X-rays show the impact of scoliosis – a sideways curvature of the spine.

4. Rumeysa has used the publicity that her GWR titles have brought her to speak out on various medical issues. She has appeared on TV shows and given numerous press interviews.

5. Rumeysa's family are incredibly supportive and proud of her for achieving two world records. She loves to play with her niece Zeynep (pictured above), who says Rumeysa's "childish side" comes out when they are together.

6. In 2021, Rumeysa received a certificate from Codecademy after qualifying as a front-end developer. Working in the technology industry has been a lifelong dream for her.

Rumeysa trained for eight months to obtain her Codecademy web-development qualification.

CERTIFICATE
OF COMPLETION
Rumeysa Gelgi

Find out more about Rumeysa in the Hall of Fame section at www.guinnessworldrecords.com/2023

LARGEST MOUTH GAPE (FEMALE)
Samantha Ramsdell of Norwalk, Connecticut, USA, can open her jaw and separate her upper and lower incisors by an impressive 6.52 cm (2.56 in), as confirmed on 15 Jul 2021. Her cavernous maw – which also stretches to 10 cm (4 in) in width – can comfortably accommodate an entire large portion of french fries. "No, it's not a filter," says TikTok sensation Samantha, "it's just my face!" For her male counterpart, turn to p.62.

Human Body

EXPLORATION

DISCOVERY

RESEARCH

2023

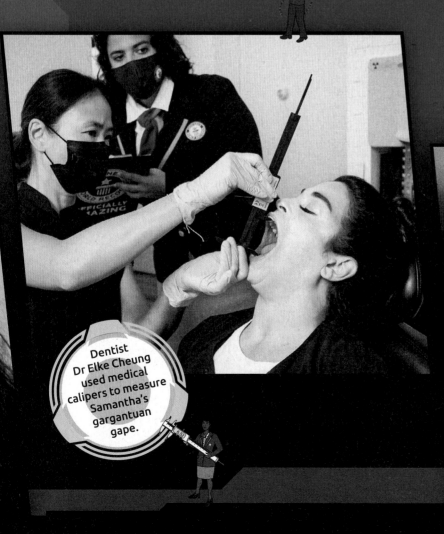

Dentist Dr Elke Cheung used medical calipers to measure Samantha's gargantuan gape.

Oldest...

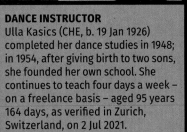

PERSON TO RELEASE AN ALBUM OF NEW MATERIAL
Tony Bennett (USA, b. 3 Aug 1926) was aged 95 years 58 days when *Love for Sale*, his second collaborative album with vocalist Lady Gaga, was released on 30 Sep 2021. Billed as his 61st and final studio album, the set pays homage to the American composer Cole Porter.

LONGEST CAREER IN THE SAME COMPANY
Sales manager Walter Orthmann (BRA, b. 1922) had worked at textile company RenauxView in Brusque, Santa Catarina, Brazil, for 84 years 9 days as of 26 Jan 2022. He started out as a shipping assistant on 17 Jan 1938, when the firm was known as Industrias Renaux S.A.

PERSON TO ROW ACROSS THE ATLANTIC
On 5 Feb 2021, Frank Rothwell (UK, b. 9 Jul 1950) completed his journey from San Sebastián on La Gomera in the Canary Íslands to Nelson's Dockyard on the Caribbean island of Antigua aged 70 years 212 days. His 3,000-mi (4,828-km) solo and unassisted row raised £1 m ($1.3 m) for dementia research.

DANCE INSTRUCTOR
Ulla Kasics (CHE, b. 19 Jan 1926) completed her dance studies in 1948; in 1954, after giving birth to two sons, she founded her own school. She continues to teach four days a week – on a freelance basis – aged 95 years 164 days, as verified in Zurich, Switzerland, on 2 Jul 2021.

AGE IS JUST A NUMBER

Surgery patient: 116; Chiyo Miyako (JPN, b. 2 May 1901)

Aircraft passenger: 115; Charlotte Hughes (UK, b. 1 Aug 1877)

Hot-air balloon passenger: 109; Emma Carrol (USA, b. 18 May 1895)

Barber: 107; Anthony Mancinelli (USA, b. ITA, 2 Mar 1911)

Oldest circumnavigator by public transport: 106; Saburō Shōchi (JPN, b. 16 Aug 1906)

OLDEST PROFESSIONAL ACTOR TO PLAY HAMLET
Ian McKellen (UK, b. 25 May 1939) was 82 years 28 days old on the opening night of *Hamlet* at the Theatre Royal Windsor, UK, on 21 Jun 2021. The 2021 production was notable for being age-, colour- and gender-blind.

On 19 Apr 2022, GWR was sad to hear of the passing of ▶ Kane Tanaka (JPN, b. 2 Jan 1903, right). Having reached the age of 119 years 107 days, she was the second-oldest verified human on record, behind Jeanne Calment (FRA, 21 Feb 1875–4 Aug 1997), who lived for 122 years 164 days.

Top 10 oldest living people

	Name	Born	Age
1	Lucile Randon (FRA)	11 Feb 1904	118 years 90 days
2	Tekla Juniewicz (POL, b. UKR)	10 Jun 1906	115 years 336 days
3	María Branyas Morera (ESP, b. USA)	4 Mar 1907	115 years 69 days
4	Casilda Benegas-Gallego (ARG, b. PRY)	8 Apr 1907	115 years 34 days
5	Fusa Tatsumi (JPN)	25 Apr 1907	115 years 17 days
6	Sofía Rojas (COL)	13 Aug 1907	114 years 272 days
7	Bessie Hendricks (USA)	7 Nov 1907	114 years 186 days
8	Mila Mangold (USA)	14 Nov 1907	114 years 179 days
9	Edie Ceccarelli (USA)	5 Feb 1908	114 years 96 days
10	Kahoru Furuya (JPN)	18 Feb 1908	114 years 83 days

Source: Gerontology Research Group; correct as of 12 May 2022

IDENTICAL TWINS EVER
Japanese sisters Umeno Sumiyama (right) and Koume Kodama were born on 5 Nov 1913 in the village of Nouma in Kagawa Prefecture – the third and fourth of 11 siblings. At the time of Koume's passing on 3 Feb 2022, the pair had reached a record age for monozygotic twins of 108 years 90 days.

HIGHEST COMBINED AGE FOR FOUR LIVING SIBLINGS
The USA's Goebel siblings – Geraldine (b. 3 Apr 1921), Marjorie (b. 19 May 1924), Robert (b. 2 Aug 1928) and Richard (b. 17 Oct 1929), born to Walter and Anne Goebel – had a combined age of 383 years 147 days as of 8 Nov 2021.

▶ PERSON
Sister André, aka Lucile Randon (FRA, b. 11 Feb 1904), was aged 118 years 73 days when she acceded to the title of **oldest living woman** and **person**. Also the **oldest nun** – and **oldest survivor of COVID-19** – the former governess and teacher now resides in a nursing home in Toulon, France.

MAN
As of 4 Feb 2022, Juan Vicente Mora (VEN, b. 27 May 1909) was 112 years 253 days old, as ratified in San José de Bolívar, Venezuela. For context, the year he was born, construction began on the RMS *Titanic*. To date, the man nicknamed "El Tío" ("The Uncle") has 18 grandchildren, 41 great-grandchildren and 12 great-great-grandchildren!

Zip-wire rider: 106; Jack Reynolds (UK, b. 6 Apr 1912)

Bridesmaid: 105; Edith Gulliford (UK, b. 12 Oct 1901)

Judge: 105; Albert R Alexander (USA, b. 8 Nov 1859)

Competitive sprinter: 105; Hidekichi Miyazaki (JPN, b. 22 Sep 1910)

Pilot: 105; Cole Kugel (USA, b. 14 Mar 1902)

Person to climb K2 (female)
Vanessa O'Brien (UK/USA, b. 2 Dec 1964) topped K2 (8,611 m; 28,251 ft) – the world's second-highest mountain – on 28 Jul 2017, aged 52 years 238 days.

Person to walk from John o' Groats to Land's End
Allan Knight (UK, b. 11 Jun 1945) completed his trek between the two extremes of Great Britain at the age of 76 years 144 days on 2 Nov 2021. He was supported by his wife Christina during the epic walk, which he completed in just under two months.

Kite surfer
As of 28 Jul 2021, Susan Frieder (USA, b. 21 Jan 1944) was still regularly kite surfing off the coast of Hawaii, USA, at the age of 77 years 188 days.

Competitive rope skipper
On 25 Jul 2021, Annie Judis (USA, b. 23 Nov 1943) took part in the American Jump Rope Virtual Championship in Beverly Hills, California, USA, at the age of 77 years 244 days.

Competitive speed skater
Iichi Marumo (JPN, b. 1 Apr 1929) was 92 years 314 days old when he competed in the Japan Masters Championships in Koriyama, Fukushima, on 9 Jan 2022. He raced over two sprint distances, clocking times of 2 min 28.47 sec in the 500 m and 6 min 22.94 sec in the 1,000 m.

Heliskier
On 5 Apr 2021, Junior Bounous (USA, b. 24 Aug 1925) dropped from a helicopter on to the ski run at Snowbird in Utah, USA, aged 95 years 224 days. He became an instructor in 1947, first heliskied in 1961 and was inducted into the National Ski Hall of Fame in 1996.

Reigning queen
Elizabeth II (b. 21 Apr 1926), Queen of the UK and Commonwealth, celebrated her 96th birthday in 2022. Her Majesty succeeded to the throne on 6 Feb 1952, and as of 22 Apr 2022 had reigned without interruption for 70 years 75 days, making her also the **longest-reigning living monarch**.

OLDEST PERSON IN SPACE
Star Trek legend William Shatner (CAN, b. 22 Mar 1931) was 90 years 205 days old when he took part in a sub-orbital spaceflight on 13 Oct 2021. Shatner was part of the crew of Blue Origin's New Shepard NS-18 mission, which launched from Van Horn, Texas, USA. For the **female** record holder, see p.34.

Amazing Anatomy

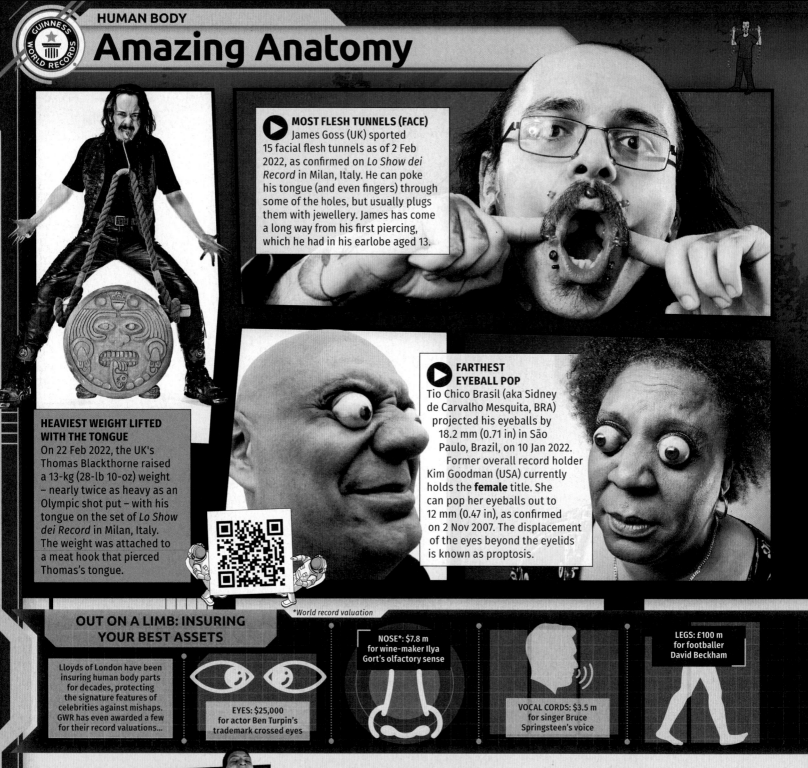

MOST FLESH TUNNELS (FACE)
James Goss (UK) sported 15 facial flesh tunnels as of 2 Feb 2022, as confirmed on *Lo Show dei Record* in Milan, Italy. He can poke his tongue (and even fingers) through some of the holes, but usually plugs them with jewellery. James has come a long way from his first piercing, which he had in his earlobe aged 13.

HEAVIEST WEIGHT LIFTED WITH THE TONGUE
On 22 Feb 2022, the UK's Thomas Blackthorne raised a 13-kg (28-lb 10-oz) weight – nearly twice as heavy as an Olympic shot put – with his tongue on the set of *Lo Show dei Record* in Milan, Italy. The weight was attached to a meat hook that pierced Thomas's tongue.

FARTHEST EYEBALL POP
Tio Chico Brasil (aka Sidney de Carvalho Mesquita, BRA) projected his eyeballs by 18.2 mm (0.71 in) in São Paulo, Brazil, on 10 Jan 2022. Former overall record holder Kim Goodman (USA) currently holds the **female** title. She can pop her eyeballs out to 12 mm (0.47 in), as confirmed on 2 Nov 2007. The displacement of the eyes beyond the eyelids is known as proptosis.

OUT ON A LIMB: INSURING YOUR BEST ASSETS

*World record valuation

Lloyds of London have been insuring human body parts for decades, protecting the signature features of celebrities against mishaps. GWR has even awarded a few for their record valuations...

EYES: $25,000 for actor Ben Turpin's trademark crossed eyes

NOSE*: $7.8 m for wine-maker Ilya Gort's olfactory sense

VOCAL CORDS: $3.5 m for singer Bruce Springsteen's voice

LEGS: £100 m for footballer David Beckham

WIDEST ARM SPAN
Mohamed Shehata (EGY) can stretch his arms 250.3 cm (8 ft 2.5 in) apart – about the same length as a smart car. His reach – which was verified in Cairo, Egypt, on 27 Apr 2021 – is related to his lofty stature: Mohamed stands 213.8 cm (7 ft) tall. He also boasted the **widest hand span** – 31.3 cm (1 ft 0.32 in) – as of the same date.

Most continuous cracking of different joints
On 23 Jun 2021, Sebastian Qval Wold (SWE) audibly popped 36 joints in his fingers, toes, neck, back, ankles, wrists, elbows and knees. This cracking display – medically known as crepitus – was documented in Varberg, Halland, Sweden.

Widest tongue
At its broadest, Brian Thompson's (USA) tongue measures 8.88 cm (3.49 in), as ratified in La Cañada, California, USA, on 30 Jul 2018. That makes his licker wider than the diameter of a baseball!

The **female** record – 7.33 cm (2.89 in) – is held by fellow American Emily Schlenker (USA) and was confirmed in Syracuse, New York, USA, on 2 Nov 2014.

Loudest tongue click
On 6 Aug 2003, Kunal Jain (CAN) generated a peak sound level of 114.2 dBA – louder than a chainsaw at a distance of 3 ft (0.9 m) – by clicking his tongue in Richmond Hill, Ontario, Canada.

The **loudest snoring** – 93 dBA – was registered by Kåre Walkert (SWE) while asleep at the Örebro Regional Hospital, Sweden, on 24 May 1993. That's similar to the sound levels you'd experience inside a moving subway train. Kåre's sonorous snorts were exacerbated by apnea, a breathing disorder.

Strongest human bite
In Aug 1986, Richard Hofmann (USA) achieved a bite force of at least 975 lbf (pound-force; 4,337 Newtons) for c. 2 sec in research at the College of Dentistry, University of Florida, USA. This is more than six times greater than the human average. Our powerful biting strength comes from the paired masseter on each side of the mouth – the **strongest muscle** in the human body.

Largest muscular chest measurement
On 20 May 1993, Isaac Nesser (USA) was confirmed to have a chest size of 188 cm (74 in) in Greensburg, Pennsylvania, USA. Isaac owed his prodigious muscularity to weightlifting, which he devotedly

LARGEST MOUTH GAPE
On 22 Feb 2022, the gap between Isaac Johnson's (USA) upper and lower incisors was measured at 10.19 cm (4.01 in). How big is that? Big enough to accommodate anything from a couple of satsumas to a soda can or even a baseball!

LARGEST TONGUE CIRCUMFERENCE
Dante Barnes (USA) has won more than 16 million likes for his TikTok videos, in which he inflates his tongue, balloon-like, to around three times its original size. Dante can manipulate his muscles such that his tongue measures 12.19 cm (4.80 in) around, as confirmed in Battle Creek, Michigan, USA, on 24 Dec 2021. It can grow to some 4.2 cm tall and 4 cm wide (1.65 x 1.57 in).

HANDS: $1.6 m
for The Rolling Stones'
guitarist Keith Richards

TEETH: $4 m
for comedian
Ken Dodd

SMILE: $10 m
for actress America
Ferrera's lips

TONGUE*: $14 m for coffee
taster Gennaro Pelliccia

HAIR*: $1 m for NFL player
Troy Polamalu's lengthy locks

practised twice a day in two-hour shifts. His programme included bench-pressing 254 kg (560 lb) and curling 136-kg (300-lb) barbells.

Most tongue piercings
As of 5 Jan 2017, Francesco Vacca (USA) had 20 tongue piercings. The count was confirmed at the Invisibleself piercing studio in Lyndhurst, New Jersey, USA.

Most insect tattoos
From bees and beetles to millipedes and moths, Michael Amoia (USA) has 864 bugs inked on his body, as verified on 28 Oct 2021 in New York City, USA.

Most body modifications
Rolf Buchholz (DEU) has had 516 body alterations, as verified on 16 Dec 2012 in Dortmund, Germany. They include 481 piercings, two subdermal horn implants and magnets in every fingertip of his right hand. His most painful procedure was a palm tattoo.

Maria José Cristerna (MEX) has the **female** record, with 49 body mods. She has major tattoo coverage, various transdermal implants on her forehead, chest and arms, and multiple piercings in her eyebrows, lips, nose, tongue, earlobes, belly button and nipples.

The ⊘ **most body modifications for a married couple** is 84, held by Victor Hugo Peralta (URY) and his wife Gabriela Peralta (ARG), as counted in Milan, Italy, on 7 Jul 2014. Their adaptations comprise 50 piercings, eight microdermals, 14 body implants, five dental implants, four ear expanders, two ear bolts and a forked tongue (Victor's). They also each have 50%-plus tattoo coverage.

LARGEST FLESH TUNNEL
Kalawelo Kaiwi (USA) has a 10.5-cm (4.13-in) flesh tunnel in each stretched earlobe, as verified on 14 Apr 2014 in Hawaii, USA. Both are large enough for him to pass a hand through. His other body mods include a split tongue, silicon horn implants and spikes set into bolt holes across his skull.

Fingernails

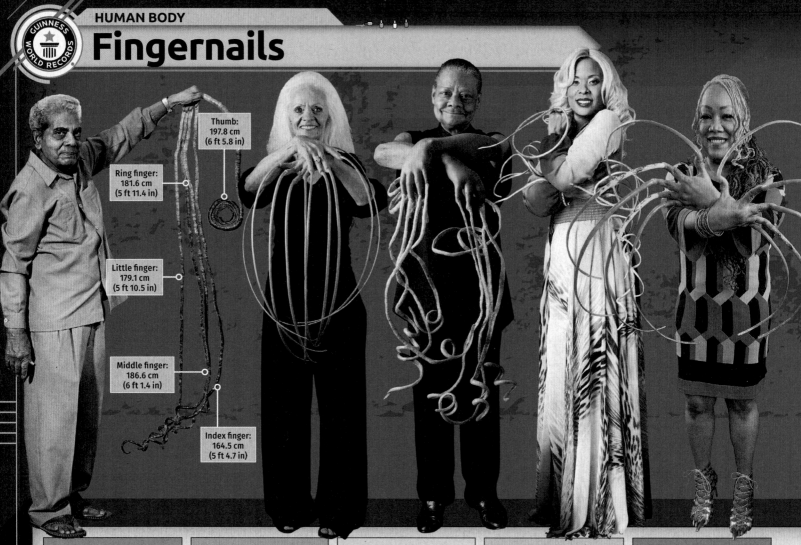

Thumb:
197.8 cm
(6 ft 5.8 in)

Ring finger:
181.6 cm
(5 ft 11.4 in)

Little finger:
179.1 cm
(5 ft 10.5 in)

Middle finger:
186.6 cm
(6 ft 1.4 in)

Index finger:
164.5 cm
(5 ft 4.7 in)

1980: Shridhar Chillal
Stopped trimming the nails of his left hand in 1952; reached 909.6 cm (29 ft 10 in) before they were cut off using a power tool in 2018.

1999: Lee Redmond
Last cut in 1979; nails bathed regularly in warm olive oil, and reached 865 cm (28 ft 4 in) before they snapped off in a car crash in early 2009.

2009: Melvin Boothe
Measured on 30 May 2009 and found to be 985 cm (32 ft 3 in) – longer than a London double-decker bus; Melvin sadly died later that year.

2011: Chris Walton
"The Dutchess", a Las Vegas club singer, began her nail odyssey in 1990, growing them to 731.4 cm (23 ft 11 in) before trimming them in 2016.

2017: Ayanna Williams
"My nails are 50% of who I am," said Ayanna after inheriting the record; by 2021, they'd reached 733.5 cm (24 ft 0.7 in) before she had them cut.

WHAT IS A FINGERNAIL?
Like skin and hair, our nails are mostly composed of a fibrous protein known as keratin. Nails are produced by living cells in the finger. As new cells form in the matrix, they push out older cells, which then compact and harden, forming our fingernails.

Free edge of nail

Nail bed, containing matrix

Nail plate

Bone

Lunula

Tendon

Guinness World Records first opened a nail file in 1960, to recognize an unnamed Chinese priest with fingernails reaching 57.79 cm (1 ft 10.75 in). Today, with the recent discovery of a new claimant from Minnesota, USA, the record stands at over 13 m – or nearly 43 ft – an increase over the intervening years of more than 2,200%!

The story of that Shanghai priest, who reportedly didn't cut his nails for 27 years, dates from 1910 but wasn't recognized by GWR until the eighth edition (1960). Since then, the various **longest fingernail** categories – which include male, female, one-hand, two-hand and all-time records – have appeared in every *GWR* book and become some of the most iconic and widely discussed records.

A surprisingly competitive category, the record has changed hands multiple times over the years. Shown above is a line-up of some of the most recent holders.

The newest incumbent – Diana Armstrong (USA, right) – emerged in 2022 after 24 years of untrimmed growth. Her brightly painted nails, measured in her home city of Minneapolis, broke both the absolute **living** and **all-time** records for a pair of hands, stretching to a staggering 1,306.58 cm (42 ft 10.4 in). Her right thumb alone, the longest of her nails, reached 138.94 cm (4 ft 6.7 in)...

Q&A: DIANE ARMSTRONG, NAIL GODDESS

Why did you stop cutting your nails?
I went through something when my daughter Latisha passed away in 1997. She died of an asthma attack in her sleep at just 16 years old. The day before, she'd spent time polishing and filing my nails, so after that, I just couldn't cut my nails off. And I didn't tell anyone why. Even my kids never knew why, because I kept it to myself for years.

What's the most difficult part of having long nails?
Zipping up my pants or jacket! I can pop open a can of soda but I need a knife. I drove a car but had to stick my hand out the window, so I don't drive any more. And in public restrooms, I need to use the biggest stall – my nails are usually longer than the regular-sized stalls!

Are your nails a challenge to maintain?
I haven't been to a nail salon for about 22 years – they don't want to deal with them – so my grandchildren take care of them. Each nail takes about 10 hours to file and polish. To file them, I need to use a Dremel woodwork tool. I get them done every four to five years, and get through between 15 and 20 bottles of polish. I painted them last week and it took four days!

2022: Diana Armstrong
Nails on both hands measured on 13 Mar 2022 and found to be 1,306.58 cm (42 ft 10.4 in). Last trimmed in 1997 and maintained as a living tribute to her late daughter Latisha. "My nails are a part of me, so I can't ever imagine cutting them off."

Hair

FIRST SUIT MADE FROM MOUSTACHE HAIR
Pam Kleemann-Passi, POLITIX and Nico from Germanicos Bespoke Tailors (all AUS) created a "mo-hair" suit in Nov 2021. It was part of the annual Movember campaign – an event that encourages moustache growth to raise awareness of men's health issues. The hair was sourced from the Sustainable Salons network in Australia and from collaborators whose lives have been affected by such concerns.

Thickest strand of human hair
A single hair 772 micrometres (0.03 in) thick was plucked from the beard of Muhammad Umair Khan (PAK) in Lahore, Pakistan, as verified on 3 Mar 2021. This is some four times the average maximum thickness for a human hair.

▶ Longest hair on a teenager ever
On 29 Jul 2020, Nilanshi Patel's (IND) tresses measured 2 m (6 ft 6.7 in) in Modasa, Gujarat, India. Dubbed the "real-life Rapunzel", she decided to have her luxurious locks cut for the first time in 12 years. She donated them to a museum.

▶ Largest afro
Aevin Dugas (USA) has cultivated a natural coiffure that grows up to 25 cm (9.8 in), giving a circumference of 1.57 m (5 ft), as confirmed in Gonzales, Louisiana, USA, on 4 Feb 2021.

Longest hair extension
Nikola Kulezic (SRB) applied a hair extension measuring 820.29 m (2,691 ft 3 in) to model Ivana Knežević in Šabac, Serbia, on 26 Jun 2013. Kulezic used synthetic hair of various colours and shades, which he knotted, knitted, singed and bonded together to form an extension some 7.5 times longer than an American football field.

TRAN VAN HAY
It's said that this Vietnamese septuagenarian's outsized lock had grown to 6.8 m (22 ft 3 in) by the time he died in Feb 2020. Does this make him a contender for the **longest hair ever**, then? Unfortunately not. We didn't have the opportunity to measure it before he passed away, so he never became an official GWR title holder.

Longest beard
Sarwan Singh (CAN) had a 2.49-m-long (8-ft 2-in) beard, as verified on 8 Sep 2011 in Surrey, British Columbia, Canada. As a devoted Sikh, Singh strictly adheres to the articles of faith known as the "Five Ks", one of which – "Kesh" – forbids the cutting of hair.

The **female** record – 25.5 cm (10.04 in) – is held by Vivian Wheeler (USA), as verified on the set of *Lo Show dei Record* in Milan, Italy, on 8 Apr 2011.

Longest beard locks ever
Hans N Langseth (NOR) grew a beard – knotted into a lock-like coil – that measured 5.33 m (17 ft 6 in) at the time of his death in 1927. He wanted it to be preserved for posterity, so his son duly donated it to the USA's Smithsonian Institution in 1967.

Largest beard and moustache championships
On 1 Sep 2017, a total of 738 well-groomed participants attended the World Beard and Moustache Championships, hosted by Austin Facial Hair Club (USA) in Texas.

At the same event, Rose Geil (USA) became the championships' **first female competitor in a "full beard" category**. She came a highly creditable sixth out of 107 entrants, with a score of 48.0. Geil puts her hirsute growth down to a mixture of polycystic ovary syndrome and genetics.

Karl-Heinz Hille (DEU) has enjoyed the **most wins** in the contest, securing his eighth victory in 2011.

Largest donation of hair (individual)
On 26 Aug 2021, Zahab Kamal Khan (USA) gifted 155 cm (5 ft 1 in) of her hair to be turned into wigs for the charity Children with Hair Loss. It was her first haircut in 17 years, and took place in McLean, Virginia, USA.

Human hair grows by about 1.2 cm (0.5 in) a month. If left uncut, it will usually grow to 60–90 cm (2–3 ft).

▶ LONGEST HEAD HAIR
China's Xie Qiuping combed out her hair to 5.627 m (18 ft 5.5 in) on 8 May 2004. She had last had her tresses cut in 1973, when she was 13. "It's no trouble at all," she assured GWR. "But you need patience and you need to hold yourself straight."

There is currently a vacancy for the **male** record. Swami Pandarasannadhi, a monk in Madras, India, in the 1940s, reportedly had 26-ft-long (7.92-m) hair but it was matted, perhaps the result of a scalp condition called plica neuropathica. For the absolute record, the hair must be untangled.

LONGEST HAIRS

Visualized here are the longest body hairs, reproduced at actual size. To qualify for the record, a hair must still be attached to the claimant; the average of three wet measurements determines the final length.

- **Chest:** 28.2 cm; Vittorio Lullo (ITA)
- **Leg:** 22.46 cm; Jason Allen (USA)
- **Arm:** 21.7 cm; David Reed (USA)
- **Eyebrow:** 19.1 cm; Zheng Shusen (CHN)
- **Nipple:** 17 cm; Daniele Tuveri (ITA)
- **Abdomen:** 16.77 cm; Elaine Martin (USA)
- **Back:** 13 cm; Craig Bedford (UK)

100%

▶ LONGEST EYELASH

You Jianxia (CHN) has extravagantly lengthy lashes – those on her left upper lid measured 20.5 cm (8 in) in Shanghai, China, on 20 May 2021. While the cause of the follicular phenomenon is a mystery, it has unexpected benefits: "Thanks to my naturally long eyelashes, I don't need to wear eyeshadow or eyeliner," she told GWR.

LARGEST FROZEN HAIR COMPETITION

On 1 Apr 2020, the Takhini Hot Springs Hair Freezing Contest (CAN) welcomed 288 participants to Whitehorse in Yukon, Canada. Entrants visit the facility when the temperature is below -20°C (-4°F), dip their head into the water then style their wet hair, letting it freeze into extraordinary shapes.

LONGEST EAR HAIR

Anthony Victor (IND) had hair sprouting from the centre of his outer ears (the middle of the pinna) that measured 18.1 cm (7.12 in) at its maximum as of 26 Aug 2007. A retired headmaster, Victor was jokingly dubbed the "ear-haired teacher" by his pupils.

LONGEST LOCKS

Asha Mandela (USA) has 5.96-m-long (19-ft 6.6-in) locks, as confirmed on 11 Nov 2009 on CBS's *The Early Show* in New York City, USA. Her hair weighs in at 19 kg (42 lb) – about three times heavier than a bowling ball – and it takes Asha a full two days to wash and dry it. She prefers to lie out in the sun with her tresses fanned around her, so they can dry naturally.

LONGEST LOCKS (MALE)

Sudesh Muthu (CAN) had 1.91-m-long (6-ft 3-in) locks on 6 Aug 2010, when measured at the Guinness World Records office in London, UK.

▶ TALLEST MOHICAN

Joseph Grisamore (USA) sported a Mohawk hairstyle that stood 108.2 cm (3 ft 6.5 in) proud on 20 Sep 2019, as confirmed in Park Rapids, Minnesota, USA. On the day itself, Grisamore's standout spike was prepared by hair stylist Kay Jettman, assisted by Joseph's wife (Laura), mother (Kay) and half a can of got2b Glued Blasting hairspray.

▶ HEAVIEST BALL OF HUMAN HAIR

Hair stylist Steve Warden (USA) began crafting a bumper ball of hair cuttings – dubbed "Hoss" – at his salon Blockers in Cambridge, Ohio, USA. But after Hoss went on display at the Ripley's Believe It or Not! museum in Orlando, Florida, visitors began contributing their own clippings, and donations also arrived by post. As of 13 Dec 2021, Hoss weighed 102.12 kg (225 lb 2 oz).

ADAM KAY'S CASEBOOK!

Adam Kay is a former doctor who gave it all up to become a writer and comedian. His first-hand experience at the messy end of the operating table resulted in a series of best-selling books that reveal all you need to know about how our bodies work... and what happens when they don't! Here, the funny physician rummages through the GWR medical files and picks out some of the weirdest, grossest and most stomach-churning human-body records.

MOST CONTAGIOUS DISEASE

If you've had measles then congratulations – you've survived the world's most contagious known disease! It's caused by a virus (*Measles morbillivirus*) that's so infectious that one sick person will – on average – spread the disease to 15 other people if they're not vaccinated. Eek!

LONGEST TONGUE

No one has a lengthier licker than Nick Stoeberl from California, USA. He can poke his tongue out so far that the tip is a whopping 10.1 cm (3.97 in) from his lip. What do you do with such a mighty muscle? Well, Nick wraps his in cling film and paints with it! Offithially Amathing!

LONGEST TIME HOLDING BREATH

How long can you hold your breath? A few seconds? Maybe a minute or so? Bet you've got a long way to go to beat Budimir Šobat of Croatia. On 27 Mar 2021, this 56-year-old freediver held his breath for a lung-bursting 24 min 37.36 sec. That's longer than an episode of *The Simpsons*!! And to prove he wasn't cheating, he did it underwater, in a swimming pool! Gasp!

LARGEST COLLECTION OF HUMAN TEETH

Maybe you collect pencil erasers. Or squishies. Or stamps. But not Giovanni Battista Orsenigo of Italy. Oh, no... he collected teeth. HUMAN teeth! This determined dentist kept every molar, canine and incisor he'd ever extracted and ended up with drawers full of them – 2,000,744 to be precise!

LONGEST BOUT OF HICCUPS

In 1922, while trying to weigh a hog, American farmer Charles Osborne experienced an attack of singultus... which is doctor-speak for hiccuping. And he didn't stop hiccuping for ages. In fact, not until 1990! That's about 430 million non-stop, teeth-rattling hics over 68 years! Hic!

WORST OUTBREAK OF DANCING MANIA

Imagine not being able to stop dancing! That's the main symptom of a medical condition called "tarantism", or dancing mania. The most widespread case reported occurred in Aachen, Germany, in Jul 1374, when thousands of people are said to have broken into a frenzied jig. The boogying would last for hours – or even days! – until the dancers collapsed from sheer exhaustion. It was once thought to be caused by a spider bite, but this has never been confirmed.

HIGHEST FALL DOWN AN ELEVATOR SHAFT

Construction worker Stuart Jones (NZ) plummeted 70 m (229 ft) – that's 23 storeys! – down a lift shaft he was working on at the Midland Park building in Wellington, New Zealand, in May 1998. He shattered his ribs, hips, legs and kneecaps, but amazingly the ultimate fall guy lived to tell the tale!

LOUDEST BURP

Australia's Neville Sharp can let rip with an eardrum-busting belch – or eructation, if you're being polite – of 112.4 dB. That's a "repeat performance" about as loud as a trombone blast in your ear hole (just a whole lot smellier!).

MOST BEE STINGS SURVIVED

The average adult could probably survive about 1,000 bee stings, which makes Johannes Relleke (ZWE) anything but average. Back in Jan 1962, Jonannes was attacked by an angry swarm at the Kamativi tin mine in Zimbabwe. Despite diving into a crocodile-infested river to escape, Johannes was stung repeatedly. Afterwards, doctors removed a record 2,443 barbs!

HEAVIEST HUMAN BRAIN

In 1899, a lump of grey matter removed from the skull of a 21-year-old patient (he was already dead, in case you were wondering!) tipped the scales at a whopping 2,850 g (6 lb 4 oz) – about the same weight as four basketballs, or heavier than a Chihuahua dog! By comparison, the average adult human brain is about 1,350 g (3 lb) – so, more like a pineapple and less like a family pet!

HIGHEST BODY TEMPERATURE

It's a bad sign when the mercury in your thermometer goes off the scale, as it did for Willie Jones (USA). On 10 Jul 1980, heat stroke sent his temperature soaring to a barely believable 46.5°C (115.7°F) – and that's AFTER doctors had packed him in ice for 15 min! Remarkably, Willie survived. He emerged from Atlanta's Grady Memorial Hospital 24 days later, with a nickname bestowed on him by incredulous staff: the "Human Torch".

STRANGEST DIET

France's Monsieur Mangetout ("Mr Eat-All"), aka Michel Lotito, had unusual taste in food. Between 1966 and 2007, he consumed a total of 18 bicycles, 15 shopping carts, numerous televisions (back when TVs were bigger!) and an entire Cessna 150 light aircraft! His odd meals were the result of a disorder called pica – a strong appetite for things that aren't food!

LONGEST BOUT OF YAWNING

In 1888, American doctor Edward W Lee reported on the unusual case of a 15-year-old girl who began yawning after having a tooth removed. And kept on – for five weeks, continuously! Even doses of the poison belladonna and chloroform (chloroform!) couldn't stop her. The moral? Look after your teeth – you never know...

LARGEST FOREIGN OBJECT LEFT IN A PATIENT

Leaving hospital? Always check you haven't left anything there – and that the doctors haven't left anything in YOU! Meena Purohit (IND) had surgery on 1 Jul 1989, but absent-minded surgeons left a pair of 33-cm-long (1-ft 1-in) artery forceps in her abdomen!

LOUDEST SCREAM

Jill Drake (UK) let rip with a banshee-like 129-dBA screech at the Halloween festivities in London's Millennium Dome in 2000. How do you hone a scream that borders on the pain threshold? Jill believes her jaw-dropping yowl stems from her time working as a classroom assistant... *NOW QUIET AT THE BACK!!*

LONGEST NOSE

Mehmet Özyürek (TUR) has a nose not to be sniffed at: his prodigious proboscis is 8.8 cm (3.46 in) long. "I am very happy with my nose and I don't have any intention to change it," he told GWR. "I always had a feeling I was going to go places and be someone because of my nose." His super schnoz has given him a whiff of opportunity – and he's not going to blow it.

HIGHEST-INSURED NOSE

A good sense of smell can be heaven *scent*. Take Ilja Gort (NLD): in Mar 2008, he insured his nose for €5 m (£3.9 m; $7.8 m). As owner of the Château de La Garde vineyard in Bordeaux, France, and producer of Tulipe wines, Ilja had to ensure he could stay *au fait* with booze bouquet. (For more insured body parts, turn to pp.62–63.)

LONGEST NOSE EVER

Mehmet's snout may be peerless today, but history suggests that there was one more than twice as long. Thomas Wedders reportedly had a 19-cm (7.5-in) hooter, which he exhibited as part of a travelling circus in England during the 1770s.

Largest Feet

As a small boy, Jeison Rodríguez (VEN) walked to school barefoot because he couldn't get big enough shoes. Now, the owner of the ● **largest feet** has travelled the world on account of his astonishing attributes. We've pictured Jeison's right shoe on the Hollywood Walk of Fame, just outside the GWR Museum on Hollywood Boulevard – how do your own feet measure up?

Jeison's US size 26 shoe is shown next to his nephew's kids size 10½, by way of comparison.

At 220 cm (7 ft 2.61 in) tall, Jeison Orlando Rodríguez Hernández has always stood out from the crowd. But it's the Venezuelan's phenomenal feet that have caught the world's attention.

Jeison owes his supersized stature to an overactive pituitary gland. He realized aged nine that his feet were bigger than his friends' – a rapid growth spurt saw his shoe size increase from a 5½ to an 11 in a single year! But his eye-catching extremities didn't make life easy for him. He was bullied and couldn't find shoes that fitted. Instead, Jeison had to wear sandals fashioned from fabric scraps, and often ended up going barefoot to school.

Robert Wadlow (USA, 1918–40), the **tallest man ever**, wore US size 37AA shoes (UK size 36 or approximately a European size 75), equivalent to a length of 47 cm (18.5 in) long. But Jeison believed he had the **largest feet** for a living person, and in 2014 contacted GWR. He was duly awarded the title later that year, but he was still growing. In 2018, he flew to Europe for measurements in the French city of Beauvais, and it was found that his left foot had grown to 40.47 cm (1 ft 3.93 in) and right foot to 40.55 cm (1 ft 3.96 in).

Jeison dreams of becoming a pastry chef, but he also wants to help other people who have the same condition as him. He's talked about the challenges he faces on international TV shows, and now has his shoes made by hand, thanks to German cordwainer Georg Wessels (above right). Indeed, Jeison's original sandals now take pride of place in Georg's museum.

He may never see his name immortalized on the Hollywood Walk of Fame, but to GWR, Jeison will always be a superstar who's a step above the rest.

100%

Round-Up

Newest human species

The most recently discovered species of human is *Homo longi* ("Dragon Man"), which was described for the first time in the journal *The Innovation* on 25 Jun 2021. A fossil cranium was unearthed in 1933 in Harbin City in China, but only recently dated – to at least 146,000 years ago, in the Middle Pleistocene era. Huge and heavily browed, the hominin had a broad but modern-looking face. This species may be the closest kin of *H. sapiens*, ahead of Neanderthals, who currently hold that position.

Deadliest coronavirus outbreak

As of 31 Mar 2022, COVID-19 (Coronavirus Disease 2019) had claimed 6,132,461 lives and was confirmed to have infected 483,556,595 people, according to the World Health Organization (WHO).

It also represents the **first coronavirus pandemic**, having been classed as a global outbreak by the WHO on 11 Mar 2020. COVID-19 was first detected in Wuhan, China, towards the end of 2019.

Longest-lived quadriplegic

Donald Clarence James (CAN, b. 12 Aug 1933) had been paralysed for 69 years 192 days, as of 19 Feb 2021. His courage and determination not to be limited by his condition have become an inspiration to everyone who knows him – not least his nephew Brent, who applied to GWR on his uncle's behalf.

Longest-working pacemaker

As of 7 Jun 2021, Stephen Peech's (UK) pacemaker had been functioning for 37 years 251 days. He was then aged 75 years old.

Longest survivor of a single artificial heart valve replacement

On 4 Dec 1972, Annabella Bell (UK) received an artificial mitral valve replacement for her heart. She has had the implant for 49 years 60 days, as verified in Falkirk, UK, on 2 Feb 2022.

The **longest survivor of a double artificial heart valve replacement** is Seth Wharton (USA). His aortic and mitral valve replacements were fitted on 2 Oct 1990 and were still working well 31 years 207 days later, as confirmed in LaVale, Maryland, USA, on 27 Apr 2022.

TALLEST FAMILY
Savanna Trapp-Blanchfield, Scott Trapp, Kristine Trapp, Molly Steede and Adam Trapp (all USA) have an average height of 203.29 cm (6 ft 8.03 in), as verified in Duluth, Minnesota, USA, on 6 Dec 2020. "We have always been proud of our height and want to represent height in a positive way."

SHORTEST MAN
Edward "Niño" Hernández (COL) measured 72.1 cm (2 ft 4.38 in) tall, as of 29 Feb 2020 in Bogotá, Colombia. His stature is the result of hypothyroidism, in which the thyroid gland doesn't produce enough hormones. Edward, who turned 35 in 2022, is an enthusiastic reggaeton and vallenato dancer.

SHORTEST TEENAGER (MALE)
On 23 Mar 2022, Nepal's Dor Bahadur Khapangi measured an average of 73.43 cm (2 ft 4.9 in) tall in Lainchaur, Kathmandu. The 17-year-old weighs 10 kg (22 lb) and was introduced to GWR by fellow Nepali Thaneswar Guragai, who holds multiple world records, among them the **most times to pass through a tennis racket in one minute** (38).

WHEN SULTAN MET JYOTI
In 2018, the world's **tallest man** and **shortest woman** were invited to meet at the foot of the Great Pyramid in Giza, Egypt. Sultan Kösen (TUR) measures 251 cm (8 ft 2.8 in) tall, while the diminutive Jyoti Amge (IND) stands 62.8 cm (2 ft 0.7 in). In 2014, Jyoti joined the cast of the hit US show *American Horror Story* as Ma Petite, making her the world's **shortest actress**.

SHORTEST WOMAN (NON-MOBILE)
Wildine Aumoithe (USA) measured 72 cm (2 ft 4.3 in) in North Miami Beach, Florida, USA, on 13 Oct 2021. Wildine was born with SADDAN dysplasia – a rare bone-growth disorder – but does not let that stop her from living a full life. She says that even though the world is not designed for her, she can conquer it and hopes to be an inspiration to other little people.

LIGHTEST BIRTH
Kwek Yu Xuan (SGP) weighed just 212 g (7.48 oz) – lighter than a can of soup – when born by emergency Caesarean at the National University Hospital, Singapore, on 9 Jun 2020. Her gestational age of 24 weeks 6 days meant that she was four months premature. Her parents, Kwek Wee Liang and Wong Mei Ling, were finally able to take her home in Aug 2021.

Oldest embryo used in a successful pregnancy
In Feb 2020, Tina and Ben Gibson of Tennessee, USA, "adopted" an embryo that had been frozen on 14 Oct 1992. Tina was implanted with the embryo and, on 26 Oct 2021, gave birth to daughter Molly Gibson. Molly's birth, 29 years 12 days after being frozen, broke the record set by her sister Emma, who was born in 2018 – 14 years after her embryo was frozen.

▶ Longest interval between births of triplets
Cian DeShane was born at 10:40 a.m. on 28 Dec 2019 in Burlington, Vermont, USA. His identical twin brother Declan and sister Rowan didn't follow until 2 Jan 2020, however, with Rowan's birth (at 11:14 p.m.) a full 5 days 12 hr 34 min after Cian's. This means that the triplets were born in different decades.

▶ Longest legs (female)
When measured on 21 Feb 2020, Maci Currin of Cedar Park, Texas, USA, had a left leg of 135.2 cm (4 ft 5.2 in) and a right leg of 134.3 cm (4 ft 4.8 in).

Largest spleen
The spleen is an organ of the lymphatic system that aids with immune defence. In adults, it averages 5 in (12.7 cm) long, but during her splenectomy on 14 Sep 2020, Megan Compton of Richmond, Virginia, USA, was divested of a spleen measuring 2 ft 5 in (73.66 cm). It is one of the organs the body can still function without.

MOST CHILDREN DELIVERED AT A SINGLE BIRTH TO SURVIVE
On 6 May 2021, Associated Press announced the delivery of nine children born to Halima Cissé (MAL) at the Ain Borja clinic in Casablanca, Morocco. This is the **first known incidence of nonuplets** surviving birth.

Doctors initially thought that Cissé was carrying seven children, so she was flown to Casablanca for specialist care. There, on 4 May, she actually gave birth to nine babies, prematurely – at 30 weeks – via Caesarean section. Each of the five girls and four boys weighed between 500 g and 1 kg (1.1 and 2.2 lb). Pictured are Cissé and husband Kader Arby in Oct 2021, with five-month-old girls Adama, Oumou, Hawa, Kadidia and Fatouma, and boys Oumar, Elhadji, Bah and Mohammed VI.

▶ MOST PREMATURE BABY
Curtis Zy-Keith Means (USA) was born to Michelle Butler on 5 Jul 2020 in Birmingham, Alabama, USA, at a gestational age of 21 weeks 1 day, making him 132 days premature. The usual gestational period for a full-term baby is 40 weeks. Doctors put his chances of survival at less than 1%, but he defied the odds and was able to leave hospital in Apr 2021, aged nine months.

▶ GREATEST HEIGHT DIFFERENCE FOR A COUPLE
Taller female: A height disparity of 56.8 cm (1 ft 10 in) proved no barrier to James and Chloe Lusted (both UK, right). She stands 166.1 cm (5 ft 5.4 in) tall, while he comes in at 109.3 cm (3 ft 7 in), as confirmed in Rhyl, Clwyd, UK, on 2 Jun 2021. The couple married in 2016 and have a daughter, Olivia.

Taller male: On 14 Apr 1990, a difference of 94.5 cm (3 ft 1.2 in) was recorded between French couple Fabien Pretou (188.5 cm; 6 ft 2.2 in) and Natalie Lucius (94 cm; 3 ft 1 in).

Same sex: Applications are now open for height differences in same-sex couples.

▶ MOST SIBLINGS WITH ALBINISM
Six British brothers and sisters all have albinism, as verified in Coventry, UK, on 14 May 2021. This lack of the skin pigment melanin results in pale complexions, light hair and poor eyesight. They are (clockwise from left) Ghulam Ali, Muqadas Bibi, Haider Ali, Mohammed Rafi, Naseem Akhtar and Musarat Begum. Their parents, Aslam Parvez and Shameem Akhtar, have the same condition.

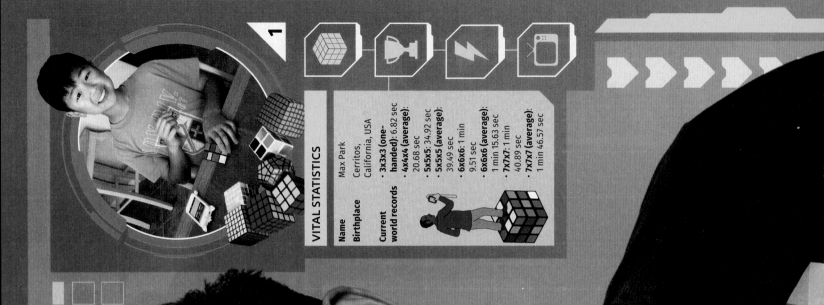

VITAL STATISTICS

Name	Max Park
Birthplace	Cerritos, California, USA
Current world records	• **3x3x3 (one-handed):** 6.82 sec • **4x4x4 (average):** 20.68 sec • **5x5x5:** 34.92 sec • **5x5x5 (average):** 39.49 sec • **6x6x6:** 1 min 9.51 sec • **6x6x6 (average):** 1 min 15.63 sec • **7x7x7:** 1 min 40.89 sec • **7x7x7 (average):** 1 min 46.57 sec

SPEEDCUBER

Max Park

HALL OF FAME

Max Park can solve a rotating puzzle cube in the blink of an eye. He has set **47 speedcubing world records, earned 314 gold medals and become a world champion. But not all of his triumphs have been on the clock.**

When Max was diagnosed with autism at the age of two, his parents, Schwan and Miki, were told he would need assistance for the rest of his life. Max struggled with social and fine motor skills, which affect the coordination of muscles in the fingers and hand. Puzzle cubes offered a way to address both issues, and Max quickly showed he was a natural. Aged 10, he won only his second cubing event, defeating college graduates. These competitions offered Max more than just the chance of victory: they also introduced him to a community with a strong shared interest, one that helped him develop social skills that people with autism can find challenging.

Max's rise to the top was confirmed in Jul 2017, when he claimed the prestigious 3x3x3 title at the World Rubik's Cube Championship in Paris, recording an average time over five solves of just 6.85 sec. And he continues to push the boundaries of cubing. On 22 Jan 2022, Max improved his record for the **fastest 4x4x4 solve (average),** in a lightning-quick time of 20.68 sec.

Max
has helped
popularize the
average
"a100" – the average
time of 100 solves
of a puzzle cube
in a row.

1. Max's parents hoped that puzzle cubes would help improve his motor skills – but had no idea Max would go on to become a world champion and record holder!

2. Through speedcubing, Max met filmmaker Chris Olson, who made a short documentary profile on him. Chris also produced the documentary *Why We Cube* and worked on *The Speed Cubers* (see #4).

3. Max and two-time 3x3x3 world champion Feliks Zemdegs doing promotional work in 2018. Regarded as one of the greatest speedcubers in history, Feliks was the first person that Max ever asked for an autograph.

4. The 2020 Netflix documentary *The Speed Cubers* focused on Max and Feliks in the run-up to the 2019 WCA World Championship in Melbourne. Although Max has surpassed many of Feliks's records and the two are constantly pitted against one another in competition, their friendship transcends any rivalry.

5. Max in competition during the 3x3x3 final at the 2019 World Championship. Although he was disappointed to finish fourth, with Germany's Philipp Weyer taking the title, Max won an incredible five other events at the championship, confirming his status as cubing's leading star. His motto is "Don't think, just solve."

Find out more about Max in the
Hall of Fame section at www.
guinnessworldrecords.com/2023

A NETFLIX ORIGINAL DOCUMENTARY

PARK

THE SPEED
CUBERS

NETFLIX | JULY 29

HIGHEST SLACKLINE WALK

On 2 Dec 2021, Rafael Zugno Bridi (BRA) took a walk in the clouds along a 2.5-cm-wide (1-in) slackline between two hot-air balloons 1,901 m (6,236 ft) above Praia Grande in Santa Catarina, Brazil. Bridi crossed the 18-m (59-ft) gap barefoot. His feat was verified by the International Slackline Association. In 2020, Bridi and Alexander Schulz (DEU) made headlines when they both completed the ❍ **longest slackline walk over an active volcano** – 261 m (856 ft) – above Mount Yasur in Vanuatu (opposite).

Another absolute slacklining record was beaten in 2021: the **longest slackline walk** (far right). On 4–6 Jul, a team of 15 slackliners attempted to cross a span of 2,130 m (6,988 ft) over Sweden's Lapporten valley. Only four, however, made the 600-m-high (1,968-ft) walk without falling: Quirin Herterich (pictured), Lukas Irmler, Ruben Langer and Friedi Kühne (all DEU). The above records were all verified by the International Slackline Association.

Extraordinary Exploits

DISCOVERY · EXPLORATION · RESEARCH

2023

The "LavaLine" team battled acid rain, red-hot lava fountains and toxic fumes to cross Mount Yasur.

Safety rope/leash for protection

Keep it in the Family

THE PIONEERING PICCARDS

Bertrand Piccard (CHE), a third-generation adventurer, followed in his family's trailblazing footsteps when he and co-pilot Brian Jones (UK) completed the **first circumnavigation by balloon**. On 21 Mar 1999, their *Breitling Orbiter 3* touched down in the Egyptian desert, 19 days 21 hr after taking off from Château d'Oex in Switzerland – a total distance of 40,814 km (25,361 mi). See right for more on the Piccards.

The record-breaking Piccard family starts with two Swiss brothers, Auguste and Jean-Felix:
• **1931**: Auguste sets the record for the **highest altitude flight** (51,775 ft; 15,781 m) and becomes the **first person to reach the stratosphere**.
• **1934**: Jean-Felix's wife, Jeannette Ridlon, makes the then **highest altitude flight by a woman** (57,579 ft; 17,550 m).
• **1937**: Jean-Felix takes to the air to complete the **first flight in a cluster balloon**.
• **1948**: Auguste and his son Jacques turn their attention to the sea, building the **first bathyscaphe** (a submersible called the *FNRS-2*).
• **1960**: Jacques makes the **first dive to the Challenger Deep by a crewed vessel**.
• **1963**: Jacques' cousin Don – who had stuck with ballooning – makes the **first hot-air balloon crossing of the English Channel**.
• **1999**: Jacques' son Bertrand (left, with his father and grandfather) achieves the **first circumnavigation by balloon** (see left).
• **2016**: Bertrand completes the **first circumnavigation in a solar-powered aeroplane** on board *Solar Impulse*.

The Kehaiovi Troupe

The Kehaiovi circus family of Bulgaria claimed their first record on 21 Jul 1976, when they used springboards to create the **tallest human perch-pole tower** (six people high). They would go one better in 1986, with family patriarch, George Kehaiov, supporting six acrobats on his shoulders to form a seven-level tower.

Two of George's daughters, Dessi and Getti, would go on to earn GWR titles of their own. Dessi broke the record for the **most hula hoops spun** three times between 1987 and 1989, raising the bar from 65 to 97 (today held by Marawa Ibrahim, with 200). Getti, meanwhile, holds the women's record for the **largest hula hoop spun**, which she set with a 17-ft (5.18-m) hoop on 2 Nov 2018.

The Lauenburger dog whisperers

The dog-training skills of Wolfgang Lauenburger and his daughter, Alexa, have earned the German duo multiple GWR titles, as well as spots on TV talent shows and circus tours worldwide. Guided by Wolfgang, dog Emma completed the **fastest 10 m on hind legs** (3.05 sec), while another of his pooches, Maya, has executed the

THE HYPER-ACTIVE HICKSONS

Eamonn Hickson (IRL; far left) has broken five records, including the **fastest 100 m crawling** (55.4 sec) on 25 Jul 2019. Since attaining his first title in 2014, his whole family have been bitten by the record bug. His sister Sandra (centre) has three GWR titles including the **fastest mile wearing handcuffs (female)**, which she ran in 6 min 37 sec on 18 May 2018, and his brother Jason (centre right) has four, including **most rugby conversions in one minute** (12, set on 9 Dec 2018). Sandra's partner, Nathan Missin (far right), started his own tally on 12 Dec 2020 with the **fastest mile carrying a 60-lb pack**, logging a time of 6 min 54 sec.

most spins by a dog in 30 seconds (49). On 8 Feb 2022, Alexa also teamed up with Maya, this time to perform the **most skips by a dog and person in one minute** (62), before going on to lead nine choreographed canines in the **longest dog conga line**.

The balancing Brauns

On 30 Jul 2005, young mother and fitness fanatic Cricket Braun (USA) achieved the **longest duration on a balance board**, keeping herself steady for 1 hr 30 min 38 sec in Salt Lake City, Utah, USA.

Almost a decade later, after Cricket's record had been broken several times by noted record-breakers such as Ashrita Furman and Silvio Sabba (see opposite), her 17-year-old daughter Tatum reclaimed the title for the Braun family with a time of 7 hr 25 min 30 sec on 10 Jul 2015. This new mark stood until Tatum's record was beaten by none other than her own big sister, Cally, who pushed it to 8 hr 2 min 2 sec on 29 Jun 2019.

The Connors collection

Lily and Rhianna Connors of Swansea, UK, share a passion for collecting. On 20 Jun 2016, then-12-year-old Lily was confirmed as the owner of the **largest collection of *Doctor Who* memorabilia**, with 6,641 items. Three years later, on 24 Sep 2019, little sister Rhianna came to us with the **largest collection of Shopkins toys**, an impressive 2,271 items.

Lily and Rhianna's brother Thomas has carved out a very different record-breaking path. On 28 Oct 2012, he achieved the **most backward free throws in one minute** (nine), breaking a basketball record originally set by NBA mascot Harry the Hawk. He has since increased it to 13. Also, on 25 Sep 2014, Thomas claimed the **most backward half-court shots in one minute**, netting six despite facing the wrong way.

The soaring Smiths

For many years, David "Cannonball" Smith (USA) was known as the world's greatest human cannonball. Using a giant launcher of his own design, he smashed the record for the **farthest human cannonball flight** on 13 Aug 1995, travelling 180 ft (54.9 m). All seven of David's children were launched out of a cannon as soon as they were old enough, and one of them – David "Bullet" Smith Jr – went into the human cannonball business full-time. Since his father's retirement, David Jr has broken the distance record another four times, most recently with a 195-ft (59.4-m) flight on 13 Mar 2018.

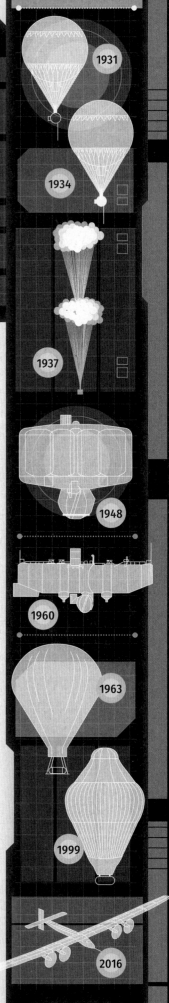

PICCARD TIMELINE

1931

1934

1937

1948

1960

1963

1999

2016

THE FLYING WALLENDAS
In 1922, German-born tightrope performer Karl Wallenda put together an act with his future wife, Helen Kreis, and his brother Herman. Over the following decades, the growing Wallenda clan became famous for their high-wire antics, including the **tallest human pyramid on a tightrope**, which currently stands at four levels, a record set on 4 Aug 2001. Today, the family's record-breaker-in-chief is Karl's great-grandson Nik, who holds 11 GWR titles, including the **first tightrope walk at the base of Niagara Falls**, achieved on 15 Jun 2012.

THE SUPERLATIVE SABBAS
Since he earned his first GWR title in 2011, Italy's Silvio Sabba has gone on to become one of our most prolific record-breakers. He had 223 titles to his name as of 20 Oct 2021. Silvio's son Cristian has also been getting in on the action, starting in 2019 with the **fastest time to set up and topple a set of dominoes (team of four)**. He now has eight GWR titles – not bad for a 12-year-old!

The current touring line-up of The Flying Wallendas includes six of Nik's cousins, led by his uncle Tino.

THE FIRST FAMILY OF DRAG RACING
In his 43 years of NHRA drag racing, John Force (USA) has won 154 events (**most career wins**) and 16 Funny Car championships (**most championship wins**). His three daughters have all driven for his team, and Brittany (pictured) is a record holder in her own right. On 1 Nov 2019, she achieved the **fastest speed in a Top Fuel race** (below), hitting 338.17 mph (544.23 km/h) in Las Vegas, Nevada.

BUBBLES & SONS
On 13 Apr 2016, performer Ray Bubbles (aka Umar Shoaib) and his son Rayhaan achieved the **longest bubble rally** (10 hits) in Rungis, France. This record has since been broken (by fellow father-and-son team Eran and Lucian Backler, with 17 hits). However, Rayhaan's brother Farhaan still retains the solo version: on 23 Sep 2018, at the Bubble Daze festival in Caernarfon, UK, Farhaan completed the **most bounces of a soap bubble on a soap film** (113 hits).

Multi-Taskers

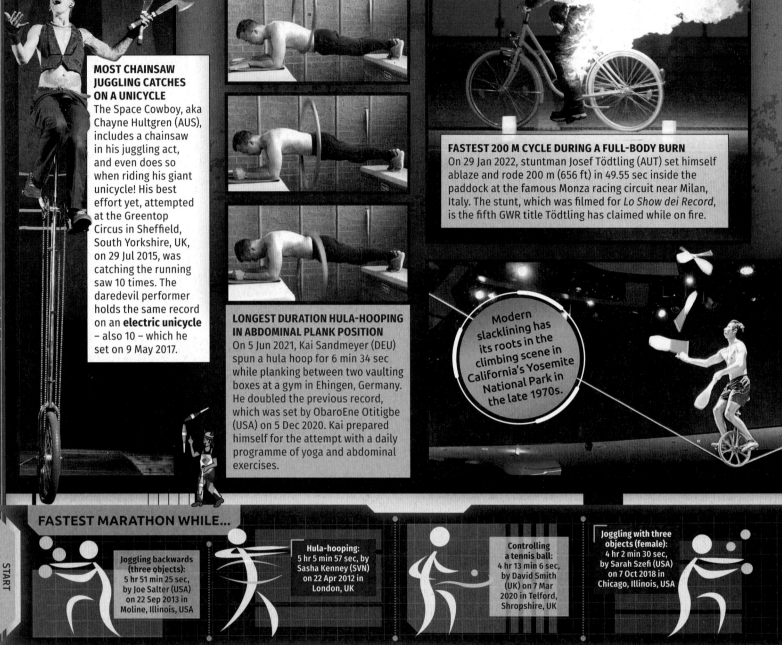

MOST CHAINSAW JUGGLING CATCHES ON A UNICYCLE

The Space Cowboy, aka Chayne Hultgren (AUS), includes a chainsaw in his juggling act, and even does so when riding his giant unicycle! His best effort yet, attempted at the Greentop Circus in Sheffield, South Yorkshire, UK, on 29 Jul 2015, was catching the running saw 10 times. The daredevil performer holds the same record on an **electric unicycle** – also 10 – which he set on 9 May 2017.

LONGEST DURATION HULA-HOOPING IN ABDOMINAL PLANK POSITION

On 5 Jun 2021, Kai Sandmeyer (DEU) spun a hula hoop for 6 min 34 sec while planking between two vaulting boxes at a gym in Ehingen, Germany. He doubled the previous record, which was set by ObaroEne Otitigbe (USA) on 5 Dec 2020. Kai prepared himself for the attempt with a daily programme of yoga and abdominal exercises.

FASTEST 200 M CYCLE DURING A FULL-BODY BURN

On 29 Jan 2022, stuntman Josef Tödtling (AUT) set himself ablaze and rode 200 m (656 ft) in 49.55 sec inside the paddock at the famous Monza racing circuit near Milan, Italy. The stunt, which was filmed for *Lo Show dei Record*, is the fifth GWR title Tödtling has claimed while on fire.

> Modern slacklining has its roots in the climbing scene in California's Yosemite National Park in the late 1970s.

FASTEST MARATHON WHILE...

Joggling backwards (three objects): 5 hr 51 min 25 sec, by Joe Salter (USA) on 22 Sep 2013 in Moline, Illinois, USA

Hula-hooping: 5 hr 5 min 57 sec, by Sasha Kenney (SVN) on 22 Apr 2012 in London, UK

Controlling a tennis ball: 4 hr 13 min 6 sec, by David Smith (UK) on 7 Mar 2020 in Telford, Shropshire, UK

Joggling with three objects (female): 4 hr 2 min 30 sec, by Sarah Szefi (USA) on 7 Oct 2018 in Chicago, Illinois, USA

START

FASTEST ESCAPE FROM A STRAITJACKET WHILE SWORD-SWALLOWING

Frankie Stiletto, aka Rachael Williams (USA), freed herself from a Posey straitjacket in 47.94 sec while swallowing a 38-cm (1-ft 3-in) blade on 2 Apr 2016 in Dallas, Texas, USA. The neuroscience-student-turned-sideshow-artiste perfected the art of sword-swallowing in just 18 months.

Farthest distance skied while juggling three objects

Tommy Tropic, aka Thomas Petrie (USA), covered 1.6 km (1 mi) while "skuggling" in Boyne Falls, Michigan, USA, on 6 Jan 2021. He teamed up with powerlifter Lillii Armstrong (USA) on the same day to set the **farthest distance skied while passing six objects between two jugglers**: 400 m (1,312 ft). Tropic also set the **farthest distance travelled on skates while juggling three objects** – 5 km (3.1 mi).

Fastest 100 m hula-hooping

On 18 May 2019, Thomas Gallant (USA) marked his final year of high school by covering 100 m (328 ft) in 15.97 sec while hula-hooping in Saint Johns, Florida, USA.

Longest duration skipping while hula-hooping

Zhang Jiqing (CHN) celebrated GWR Day 2018 by jumping rope for 1 min 32.65 sec while hula-hooping in Beijing, China. He was aged 63.

Fastest time to solve a puzzle cube on a hoverboard

On 7 Mar 2021, Samuel Smookler (USA) combined his two favourite hobbies – speedcubing and hoverboarding – to record-breaking effect, clocking 15.86 sec in Altadena, California, USA. He was aged just 13. Here are some other lightning-quick 3x3x3 cube solves performed under unusual circumstances:
- **On a pogo stick**: 9.61 sec, by Xia Yan (CHN) in Xi'an, Shaanxi, on 7 Jan 2021.
- **While hula-hooping**: 9.87 sec, by Josiah Plett (CAN) in Victoria, British Columbia, Canada, on 14 Feb 2021.
- **On a bike**: 14.95 sec, by Ramanathan Venkatachalam (IND) in Chennai, India, on 18 Nov 2020.
- **◉ While in freefall**: 30.14 sec, by Nitin Subramanian (USA) in Waialua, Hawaii, USA, on 19 Mar 2021.

Most fire-whip cracks with two whips in 30 seconds (full-body burn)

Red-hot performance artist Aaron Bonk (USA) made 92 cracks of a fire whip – i.e., a whip on fire! – while himself engulfed in flames from ankles to shoulders on 26 Jul 2018 in Brunswick, Ohio, USA.

MOST PINE BOARDS BROKEN IN FREEFALL

Ernie Torres (USA) smashed through 12 pine boards while skydiving over Eloy in Arizona, USA, on 23 May 2013. He had just 70 sec to break the previous record of seven, set by *Power Rangers* actor Jason David Frank. Ernie, a first-degree black belt in Tang Soo Do, was raising money for wounded US servicemen.

MOST JUGGLING CATCHES ON A UNICYCLE WHILE BALANCING ON A SLACKWIRE (FIVE OBJECTS)

On 18 Jan 2020, Raul Cañas Zamora (MEX) completed 10 juggling catches while riding a slackwire on a unicycle in Dubai, UAE. The record attempt took place on board the MSC *Bellissima* cruise ship, where Raul was working with Cirque du Soleil. He also holds the equivalent GWR title for **three objects**, with an incredible 203 catches.

HEAVIEST WEIGHT LIFTED BY BARBELL OVERHEAD PRESS ON A UNICYCLE

On 5 Apr 2021, Jason Auld (UK) raised 68 kg (149 lb) above his head while riding a single-wheeler in Edinburgh, UK. Jason had the perfect skill set for this record, having been a professional unicyclist for 14 years and also a *Ninja Warrior* coach. He is a founder member of the Team Voodoo extreme unicycling team.

Dribbling two basketballs: 3 hr 50 min 26 sec, by Kev Howarth (UK) on 6 Oct 2019 in Katowice, Poland

Skipping a rope: 3 hr 29 min 54 sec, by Volkan Yıldız (TUR) on 4 Mar 2018 in Antalya, Turkey

Dribbling a football: 3 hr 27 min 16 sec, by Alistair Kealty (AUS) in Antalya, Turkey, on 3 Mar 2019

Joggling with three objects: 2 hr 50 min 12 sec, by Michal Kapral (CAN) on 30 Sep 2007 in Toronto, Ontario, Canada

FINISH

Most consecutive jumping jacks (full-body burn)

On 13 Aug 2015, Sean Kinney (USA) of Los Angeles, California, decided to celebrate turning 45 by making himself into a birthday candle. He performed 30 jumping jacks in 30 seconds – an impressive feat considering he was holding his breath the whole time.

Longest duration controlling a soccer ball on a slackline

On 14 Jan 2016, freestyle footballer extraordinaire John Farnworth (UK) combined a flair for slacklining and freestyle football by keeping a ball aloft for 29.82 sec in Preston, Lancashire, UK.

Most bounce-forward somersaults on an exercise ball while riding a bicycle in one minute

On 16 Sep 2021, trials rider Matthew Turner (UK) completed 11 forward somersaults on a trials bike with the help of a carefully placed exercise ball. He first performed a half-somersault on to the ball, then bounced up to continue the somersault back on to two wheels. The attempt took place on CBBC's *Blue Peter*.

Most consecutive skips on a tightrope

Juan Pedro Carrillo (USA) jumped a skipping rope 1,323 times while balanced on a tightrope at the Big Apple Circus Big Top in Boston, Massachusetts, USA, on 26 Apr 2004.

The **one minute** record is 211, by Henry Ayala (VEN) on 30 Sep 2003 at Billy Smart's Circus in Bristol, UK. The wire was set at a height of 8.1 m (26 ft 6 in).

The **most skips on a unicycle in one minute** is 237, by Peter Nestler (USA) on 20 Feb 2013 at Moorhead Junior High School in Conroe, Texas, USA.

Lowest death-dive escape

Magician Robert Gallup (AUS) took multi-tasking to terrifying extremes for his 1997 stunt, "The Challenge of the Death Dive". He was leg-manacled, handcuffed, chained, tied into a mail bag and then locked in a cage before being thrown out of a plane at 18,000 ft (5,485 m) above the Mojave Desert in California, USA. With less than a minute before impact and travelling at 240 km/h (150 mph), he escaped to reach his parachute secured on the outside of the cage.

HEAVIEST WEIGHT LIFTED WHILE HANGING BY THE TEETH

Leonardo Costache (ROM) lifted 101.3 kg (223 lb 5 oz) – the weight of almost 15 bowling balls – in Bucharest, Romania, on 16 Aug 2020. The steel-jawed strongman has also recorded the **most juggling catches in one minute while hanging by the teeth (three objects)** – 195, in Gilleleje, Denmark, on 4 Jul 2019.

Superlative Skills

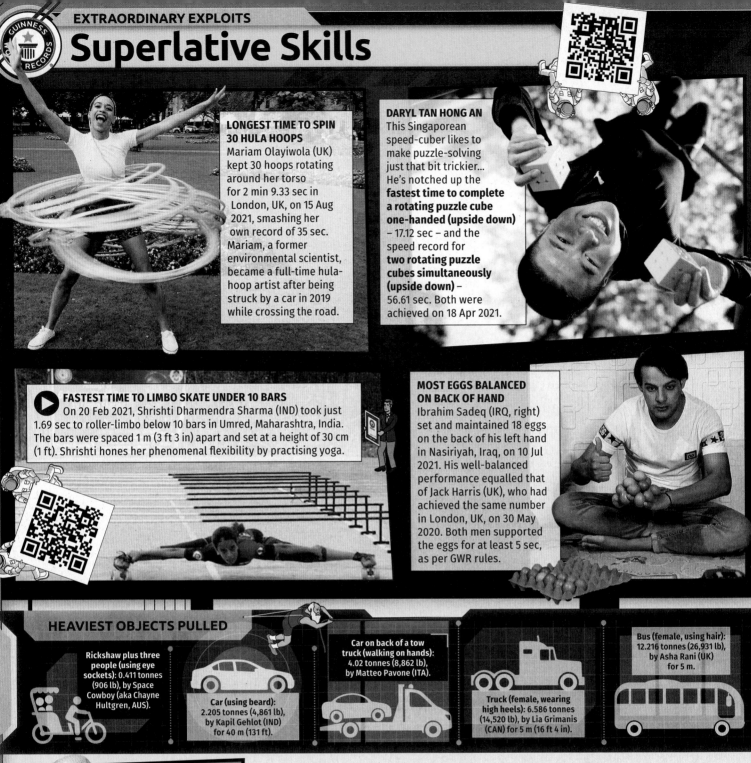

LONGEST TIME TO SPIN 30 HULA HOOPS

Mariam Olayiwola (UK) kept 30 hoops rotating around her torso for 2 min 9.33 sec in London, UK, on 15 Aug 2021, smashing her own record of 35 sec. Mariam, a former environmental scientist, became a full-time hula-hoop artist after being struck by a car in 2019 while crossing the road.

DARYL TAN HONG AN

This Singaporean speed-cuber likes to make puzzle-solving just that bit trickier… He's notched up the **fastest time to complete a rotating puzzle cube one-handed (upside down)** – 17.12 sec – and the speed record for **two rotating puzzle cubes simultaneously (upside down)** – 56.61 sec. Both were achieved on 18 Apr 2021.

FASTEST TIME TO LIMBO SKATE UNDER 10 BARS

On 20 Feb 2021, Shrishti Dharmendra Sharma (IND) took just 1.69 sec to roller-limbo below 10 bars in Umred, Maharashtra, India. The bars were spaced 1 m (3 ft 3 in) apart and set at a height of 30 cm (1 ft). Shrishti hones her phenomenal flexibility by practising yoga.

MOST EGGS BALANCED ON BACK OF HAND

Ibrahim Sadeq (IRQ, right) set and maintained 18 eggs on the back of his left hand in Nasiriyah, Iraq, on 10 Jul 2021. His well-balanced performance equalled that of Jack Harris (UK), who had achieved the same number in London, UK, on 30 May 2020. Both men supported the eggs for at least 5 sec, as per GWR rules.

HEAVIEST OBJECTS PULLED

Rickshaw plus three people (using eye sockets): 0.411 tonnes (906 lb), by Space Cowboy (aka Chayne Hultgren, AUS).

Car (using beard): 2.205 tonnes (4,861 lb), by Kapil Gehlot (IND) for 40 m (131 ft).

Car on back of a tow truck (walking on hands): 4.02 tonnes (8,862 lb), by Matteo Pavone (ITA).

Truck (female, wearing high heels): 6.586 tonnes (14,520 lb), by Lia Grimanis (CAN) for 5 m (16 ft 4 in).

Bus (female, using hair): 12.216 tonnes (26,931 lb), by Asha Rani (UK) for 5 m.

FASTEST 20 M IN A CONTORTION ROLL

To prove that "strength and power can be combined with flexibility", Sofia Tepla (UKR) contorted her body into a circular shape – by lying face down and lifting her legs over her head – and rolled 20 m (65 ft 7 in) in just 10.49 sec. The 13-year-old achieved the record in Milan, Italy, on 10 Feb 2022.

Fastest time to eat a banana (no hands)

British gastronaut and social-media star Leah Shutkever downed a banana in 20.33 sec on 24 Oct 2021. She also racked up the **hot dog (no hands)** record – 18.15 sec – on 11 Apr that year. Her many eating feats include in-a-minute records for the most **tomatoes** (8), **sausages** (10), **mini gherkins** (23) and **almonds** (40).

Fastest 100 m on all fours (female)

Julie Holland (USA) took just 22.99 sec to scuttle down a 100-m (328-ft) course in Vernon, British Columbia, Canada, on 9 Aug 2021. She modelled her running stance on that of a horse.

Tallest stack of chairs

On 22 Apr 2021, Jay Ehsan (UK) erected a 5.2-m (17-ft) tower of chairs in Manchester, UK, in about 45 minutes. With the help of a stepladder, he stacked 31 chairs.

LONGEST DURATION...

Juggling three fire balls: 2 min 25.2 sec, by Michael Francis (CAN) in Kitchener, Canada, on 5 Jun 2021.

Habanero pepper kiss: 3 min 36.86 sec, by Lance Rich and Matthew Burnham (both USA) in Shreveport, Louisiana, USA, on 8 May 2021.

Spinning a basketball on a pencil tip: 1 hr 11 min, by Ryosuke Kanaoka (JPN) in Osaka, Japan, on 2 Jul 2021.

Surfing a wave (female): 8 hr, by wake-surfer Lori Keeton (USA) in Rockville, Indiana, USA, on 8 Jun 2021.

MOST...

High and low high-fives by a pair in a skydive: Emily Aucutt and Josh Carratt (both UK) exchanged 32 hand slaps during a 63-sec freefall above Langar Airfield in Nottingham, UK, on 9 Jul 2021. The attempt was organized by the hand-sanitizer brand Carex.

Flames blown in 30 seconds: Christopher Campbell (CAN) "breathed fire" 55 times from a single mouthful of fuel in London, Ontario, Canada, on 26 Jan 2021. Appropriately enough, the attempt took place during a hot-wings eating contest titled "An Evening of Heat".

▶ MOST CHAIN LINKS CARVED FROM A PENCIL LEAD

Koppineedi Vijaya Mohan (IND) carved out 246 chain links from a single unbroken piece of graphite in Narasapuram, Andhra Pradesh, India, on 1 Jul 2021. His intricate creation was 37 cm (1 ft 2.5 in) long. Mohan hopes to further hone his creative skills and make his mark in the field of miniature art.

100%

▶ MOST SKYSURFING HELICOPTER SPINS

On 1 Nov 2021, Keith "KĒBĒ" Edward Snyder (USA) pulled off 160 helicopter spins (i.e., inverted 360° rotations) while skysurfing. He beat the existing record by nearly 100 spins! The dizzying feat took place above the Giza Plateau in Cairo, Egypt.

SMALLEST VACUUM CLEANER

Miniaturization specialist Ahsan Qayyum (PAK) – a former holder of the pencil-carving record above – created a functioning vacuum cleaner just 1.3 cm (0.51 in) long. Carved from a hollowed-out pencil, it is electrically operated.

100%

▶ LARGEST NERF GUN

From micro to macro... Michael Pick of Huntsville, Alabama, USA, crafted a 3.81-m-long (12-ft 6-in) version of the Nerf N-Strike Elite Longshot CS-6, scaling it up 300%. The 30-cm (1-ft) darts that it fires can smash through watermelons and even concrete!

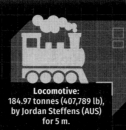
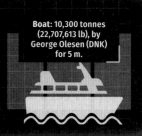

Sleigh (on a flatbed truck): 16.5 tonnes (36,376 lb), by Kevin Fast (CAN) for 5 m.

House (on wheels): 35.9 tonnes (79,145 lb), by Kevin Fast for 11.95 m (39 ft 2 in).

Locomotive: 184.97 tonnes (407,789 lb), by Jordan Steffens (AUS) for 5 m.

Aircraft: 188.83 tonnes (416,299 lb), by Kevin Fast for 8.8 m (28 ft 10 in).

Boat: 10,300 tonnes (22,707,613 lb), by George Olesen (DNK) for 5 m.

Lit candles in the mouth: On 25 Jun 2021, Garrett James (USA) held 105 flaming candles in his mouth for nearly 40 sec in Charlotte, North Carolina, USA.

Rotating puzzle cubes solved while upside down: An inverted Li Zhihao (CHN) completed 195 puzzle cubes in Shangluo, Shaanxi, China, on 23 Jan 2021. The **most rotating puzzle cubes solved while hula hooping** is 1,015, by Josiah Plett (CAN) in Victoria, British Columbia, Canada, on 13 Feb 2021.

Consecutive juggling catches of five tennis racquets: On 28 May 2021, Lauri Koskinen (FIN) made 501 catches of five racquets in Masala, Uusimaa, Finland. The versatile and multiple record holder has also recorded the **most headers of a Swiss ball in 30 seconds** (88) and **most consecutive pirouettes while juggling a chainsaw and two balls** (9).

Sandwiches assembled in three minutes: Elmwood School rustled up 1,334 sandwiches in Rockcliffe Park, Ontario, Canada, on 5 Oct 2021.

MOST IN A MINUTE

Shoes sorted: 18, by Joshua Block (USA) in Paramus, New Jersey, USA, on 6 Jun 2021.

Concrete blocks broken by axe kicks: 37, by N Narayanan (IND) in Madurai, India, on 6 Apr 2021.

Magic tricks: 37, by Avery Chin (MYS) in Kuala Lumpur, Malaysia, on 31 Aug 2021.

One-handed claps: 468, by Cory Macellaro (USA) in Wading River, New York, USA, on 15 Aug 2021.

Baseball bats broken with hands: 68, by Muhamed Kahrimanovic (DEU, b. BIH) in Milan, Italy, on 14 Feb 2022.

FIRST PAY-PER-VIEW PILLOW FIGHT

On 29 Jan 2022, a playful knockabout became a pay-per-view pro sport with *Pillow Fight Championship: Pound Down* in Miami, Florida, USA. Combatants fought with specialized pillows and mandatory mouthpieces, and could be watched for $12.99 (£9.69) on FITE.TV. Hauley Tillman topped the men's bracket, while UFC strawweight Istela Nunes (right) won an eight-fight battle to become the first PFC women's champion.

Collections

BE@RBRICK BEARS
As of 20 Dec 2020, Gao Ke (CHN) had acquired 1,008 Be@rbrick figurines in Beijing, China. Produced by Medicom Toy of Japan, these ursine collectables are styled on icons from the history of pop culture. How many can you identify here?

▶ STUDIO GHIBLI MEMORABILIA
Eloïse Jéglot (FRA) has had a soft spot for this famed Japanese anime studio since she was six, when her mother bought her the DVD of *Princess Mononoke* (1997). By 7 Oct 2021, Eloïse had collected 1,304 items of licensed Studio Ghibli merchandise at her home in Paris, France. She also pays tribute with her colourful display of tattoos inspired by Ghibli productions.

ROTATING PUZZLES
Florian Kastenmeier (DEU) had amassed 1,519 rotating puzzles in Mindelheim, Bavaria, Germany, as of 28 Feb 2022. His prize possession is a 1977 Rubik's Cube from the first production line in Hungary. Top of Florian's wish list is the original wooden prototype made in 1974 by inventor Ernő Rubik.

OUTSTANDING COLLECTIONS

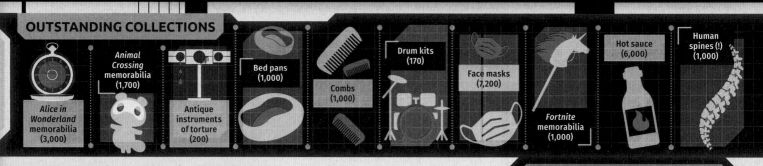

- *Alice in Wonderland* memorabilia (3,000)
- *Animal Crossing* memorabilia (1,700)
- Antique instruments of torture (200)
- Bed pans (1,000)
- Combs (1,000)
- Drum kits (170)
- Face masks (7,200)
- *Fortnite* memorabilia (1,000)
- Hot sauce (6,000)
- Human spines (!) (1,000)

▶ CHRISTMAS BAUBLES
To celebrate Christmas 2021, Sylvia Pope (UK) decorated her home in Swansea, UK, with 1,760 festive trinkets. Affectionately dubbed "Nana Baubles", Sylvia now has so many ornaments that she has to start festooning her ceiling with them in September, to be ready in time for Christmas!

Six-leaf clovers
László Hegedűs (HUN) had collected 27 ultra-rare six-leaf clovers as of 23 Sep 2021. They are reputed to bring a sextet of advantages: faith, hope, love, luck, money and longevity.

Salt and pepper sachets
Seasoned hoarder Salacnib "Sonny" Molina (USA) has a store of 395 paired condiment packs in Woodstock, Illinois, USA. His eclectic taste also extends to collections for **Pringles tubes** (256), **skull drinkware** (307) and **finger puppets** (497).

Socks
As of 30 Sep 2020, Ashan Fernando (USA) had collected 660 unique pairs of socks in Berkley, Massachusetts, USA.

Manny Pacquiao memorabilia
The Filipino boxing champion inspired a passion for collecting in Marc Anthony Eser (PHL), who owns 705 items of Pacquiao ephemera. His cache was counted in Calamba, Laguna, Philippines, on 20 Apr 2021. Pacquiao himself holds several GWR titles, including the **most boxing world titles in different weight divisions** – eight.

Paper cups
Rafael Levin (USA) owns 800 paper cups, as ratified on 4 Aug 2021 in Woodmere, New York, USA. His record application was motivated by the chance to show his younger sister that "anything is possible".

Hotel keycards
As a memento of his extensive travels, Kamalesh Kumar Maheshwari of Nashik in Maharashtra, India, began to keep hotel door cards. He now owns 922 examples.

The 20 GWR record categories shown above are currently open and awaiting applications. We've added the minimum requirement for each in brackets. So, if your bathroom is knee-deep in combs, or you can't sit down in the kitchen because of all those torture instruments, register at www.guinnessworldrecords.com/apply

POWER RANGERS MEMORABILIA

Michael Nilsen of Gilbert, Arizona, USA, has been sourcing *Power Rangers* toys and ephemera since 1993, and had 9,364 items as of 2 Jan 2021. As a nine-year-old, Michael was captivated by the show's shape-shifting Megazord robots; once he realized that he could buy and transform these "Mighty Morphin" toys himself, he started collecting in earnest.

▶ HARRY POTTER MEMORABILIA

J. K. Rowling's boy wizard has cast such a spell over Tracey Nicol-Lewis (UK) that she now owns 5,284 *Harry Potter* collectables. Tracey, from Bargoed in Mid-Glamorgan, Wales, has incorporated them into an even larger collection of **Wizarding World memorabilia** that ran to 5,434 items as of her last count in Apr 2021.

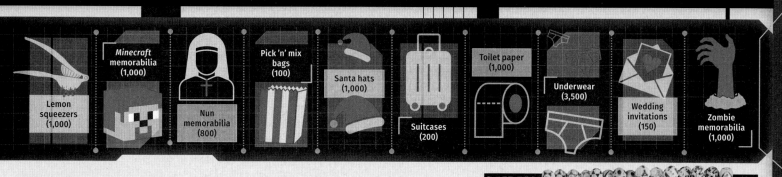

Lemon squeezers (1,000)

Minecraft memorabilia (1,000)

Nun memorabilia (800)

Pick 'n' mix bags (100)

Santa hats (1,000)

Suitcases (200)

Toilet paper (1,000)

Underwear (3,500)

Wedding invitations (150)

Zombie memorabilia (1,000)

Wind-up toys

A mechanical ski bunny bought on impulse more than 30 years ago kick-started Marla Mogul's (USA) passion for clockwork toys. As of 30 Mar 2021, she had acquired 1,258 of them in Los Angeles, California, USA.

Casino chips

By 21 Jan 2022, Gregg Fisher (USA) owned 2,222 unique casino chips and gaming tokens. Fittingly, they're kept in the gambling nirvana of Las Vegas, Nevada, USA.

Chopsticks

Benny Vervaeck (BEL) has 2,529 unique pairs of eating utensils in Humbeek, Brabant, Belgium. His best-loved set was made in Bali to mark the birth of his daughter.

Nutcrackers

As ratified on 23 Jul 2021, Arnas Jurskis (LTU) houses 10,000 nutcrackers in a dedicated museum in Vilnius, Lithuania. His favourite pieces are 16–17th-century French crackers that are elaborately adorned with crowns, coats of arms and fleurs-de-lis.

Horseshoes

Petru Costin (MDA) has had the good fortune to collect 13,855 horseshoes, as verified in Chişinău, Moldova, on 4 Jul 2021. He also collects military berets.

One Piece memorabilia

Lam Siu Fung (CHN) owns 20,125 objects inspired by Eiichiro Oda's manga series, as verified in Hong Kong, China, on 11 Apr 2021. His pride and joy is the *Portrait of Pirates* figurine series.

Soccer memorabilia

The Museum of Michel Platini in Mosfiloti, Cyprus, featured 40,669 football-related items as of 30 Jun 2017. The gallery, which doubles as a kebab shop, was founded by superfan Philippos Stavrou Platini (CYP), who appended his name in tribute to the legendary French midfielder.

▶ SOCCER BALLS

On a trip to the 2006 FIFA World Cup in Germany, Rodrigo Rafael Romero Saldívar (MEX) bought a football for a kickabout with a friend. The purchase inspired a passion: as of 21 May 2020, his collection in San Andrés Cholula, Puebla, Mexico, had grown to 1,230 balls. He cherishes the one from the 2012 Olympic Games, at which Mexico took the men's soccer gold medal.

Garden Giants

HEAVIEST MANGO

Germán Barrera and Reina María Marroquín (both COL) cultivated a 4.25-kg (9-lb 5-oz) mango, as verified in Guayatá, Boyacá, Colombia, on 25 Jul 2020. "It's a recognition of dedication to the Guayatuno countryside, and the love for nature that our parents passed down to us," Germán said.

Highest-scoring Master Gardener (GPC)*

Since 2009, the Great Pumpkin Commonwealth (GPC) has bestowed the title of "Master Gardener" on a grower with an all-round talent for cultivating giant produce. Allowing eight categories, each grower's top five entries of the year are scored based on size. Of the 54 entrants in 2021, teacher Cindy Tobeck (USA) won with an all-time-high tally of 265.72 points. Cindy's bumper crop comprised: a 2,030-lb (920.8-kg) squash, 1,738-lb (788.3-kg) giant pumpkin, 7-lb 3-oz (3.26-kg) tomato, 152-lb 8-oz (69.2-kg) marrow and a 10-ft 9.75-in (3.29-m) long gourd.

HEAVIEST...

Strawberry

A 289-g (10.19-oz) Elan strawberry was grown by Chahi Ariel (ISR), as ratified in Kadima-Zoran, Israel, on 12 Feb 2021. Unusually cold weather may have contributed to its size.

Plum

Yoshiyuki Tomiyama (JPN) from Niigata, Japan, produced a Kiyo-variety plum that registered a weight of 354.3 g (12.5 oz) on 14 Aug 2021. The fruit had a circumference of 27.6 cm (10.9 in), making it bigger than a baseball.

Tomato*

A tomato grown by Dan Sutherland (USA) weighed 10 lb 12 oz (4.8 kg) when measured in Walla Walla, Washington, USA, on 15 Jul 2020.

Gourd*

The heaviest fruit specimen from the *Lagenaria* genus (as recognized by the GPC) is a bushel gourd weighing 470 lb 8 oz (213.41 kg). Cultivated by Steve Connolly (USA), it was assessed on 10 Oct 2020.

▶ HEAVIEST BROAD-BEAN POD†

On 23 Sep 2021, Joe Atherton (see above) submitted a 106-g (3.7-oz) broad-bean pod – more than twice the weight of a golf ball – for consideration at the CANNA UK National Giant Vegetables Championship. The contest is held annually in Malvern, Worcestershire, UK. Broad beans are also known as fava or faba beans.

▶ INTRODUCING THE ROOT MASTER

Joe Atherton (UK) is a multiple GWR title holder. Prior to the CANNA UK National Giant Vegetables Championship in Sep 2021, he already held six records for record-breaking root vegetables: **turnip**, **salsify**, **carrot**, **parsnip**, **radish** and **beetroot** (see right). At the latest event, he registered the **longest leek** (left), at 1.36 m (4 ft 5.5 in). "When you lift the 'longs', it is very stressful!" Joe revealed. "The hardest bit is cleaning all the compost off."

TALLEST/LONGEST...

Coriander plant

As verified on 12 Nov 2020, Dalbir Maan's (AUS) coriander plant stood 2.25 m (7 ft 4 in) high in Melbourne, Victoria, Australia. Dalbir used cow manure to ensure a rich nutrient supply.

Scallion

At the 18th Zhangqiu Scallion Culture Tourism Festival held on 15 Nov 2020, a 2.53-m-long (8-ft 3.6-in) green onion stole the show. It was presented by the Agriculture and Rural Affairs Bureau of Zhangqiu District (CHN) in Jinan City, Shandong, China.

Sunflower

Hans-Peter Schiffer (DEU) grew a sunflower standing 9.17 m (30 ft 1 in) tall, as verified on 28 Aug 2014 in Kaarst, Nordrhein-Westfalen, Germany. He is a four-time holder of this GWR title.

Papaya tree

On 2 Sep 2021, a 14.55-m (47-ft 8.8-in) papaya tree was verified in Cafelândia, Paraná, Brazil. The record is shared by former farm owner Gilberto Franz and current owner Tarcísio Foltz (both BRA).

Tomato plant

Nutriculture (UK) unveiled a 19.8-m (65-ft) tomato plant – more than three times the height of an adult giraffe – in Mawdesley, Lancashire, UK, on 11 May 2000.

The **most tomatoes from one truss/flowering stem** is 1,269, harvested by Douglas Smith (UK) in Stanstead Abbotts, Hertfordshire, UK, on 27 Sep 2021. He beat his own record of 839.

HEAVIEST CHERRY

Italian brothers Alberto and Giuseppe Rosso produced a 33.05-g (1.16-oz) Carmen cherry, as verified on 22 Jun 2021 in Pecetto Torinese, Turin, Italy. The Rosso family have cultivated cherries for more than a century and now grow more than 70 varieties on their farm. Cherries from this region are known for their sweetness.

100%

JOE'S RECORD ROOT VEG†

Turnip: 4.06 m, 2019

Salsify: 5.57 m, 2020

Carrot: 6.24 m, 2016

Parsnip: 6.55 m, 2017

Radish: 6.70 m, 2017

Beetroot: 8.56 m, 2020

Ratified by the: *Great Pumpkin Commonwealth; †CANNA UK National Giant Vegetables Championship

HEAVIEST SQUASH*
Todd and Donna Skinner (both USA) had a 2,164-lb (981.57-kg) squash authenticated on 10 Oct 2021 in Dublin, Ohio, USA. They spend upwards of 50 hours per week in peak season tending to their plants. Squashes and pumpkins are from the same family and are distinguished only by the colour of their fruit.

▶ HEAVIEST AUBERGINE†
Peter Glazebrook (UK) presented a 3.12-kg (6-lb 14-oz) eggplant in Sep 2021. A legend in the field of competitive veg growing, Peter has grown a plethora of prodigious produce over the decades, including the current **heaviest cauliflower** (27.48 kg; 60 lb 9.3 oz) and **heaviest potato**† (4.98 kg; 10 lb 15 oz).

HEAVIEST BUTTERNUT SQUASH*
Nineteen-year-old Henry Swenson (USA) unveiled a 65-lb 8-oz (29.7-kg) butternut squash at a weigh-off at Frerichs Farm in Warren, Rhode Island, USA, on 9 Oct 2021. Grown from a "55.5 Brown" seed derived from the former record holder, this behemoth butternut was 20 times heavier than a typical example.

HEAVIEST PUMPKIN*
As confirmed at a contest in Peccioli, Italy, on 26 Sep 2021, Stefano Cutrupi (ITA) grew an Atlantic Giant pumpkin tipping the scales at 1,226 kg (2,702 lb 13 oz). This beat the mark of 1,190.49 kg (2,624 lb 9 oz) that had stood since 2016. Stefano had a phenomenal season, also claiming second and third place.

How long have you been growing pumpkins?
I started in 2008 and have focused on cultivating Atlantic Giants ever since.

How did you feel when it was confirmed that you'd broken the world record?
I had my back to the weigh-in screen. When my friends saw the weight, they swept me up in celebration. I screamed until I lost my voice!

What's the secret to growing giant pumpkins?
There are no secrets. As in any other field, it's about pursuing the goal with technique and perseverance.

Could you grow an even heavier pumpkin?
Everything is possible. Records are made to be broken. I'll try next year!

LARGEST JACK O'LANTERN BY CIRCUMFERENCE*
This XXL Halloween decoration was carved from a pumpkin measuring 19 ft 4 in (5.91 m) around, from stem to blossom, grown by Travis Gienger (USA, above). It was ratified on 12 Oct 2020, then taken to Travis's hometown of Anoka, Minnesota (the "Halloween Capital of the World"), for the festivities on 31 Oct. With a pre-carved weight of 2,350 lb (1,065.9 kg), it's also the **heaviest jack o'lantern***.

Inspired by Netflix's Tiger King, artist Mike Rudolph remodelled the giant gourd for an All Hallows' Eve parade.

▶ HEAVIEST MARROW†
Vincent Sjodin (UK) grew a monster marrow weighing 116.4 kg (256 lb 9 oz) – about the same as 17 bowling balls! He attributes his success to the inclusion of fish guts and heads in his compost.

Season's Greetings!

OLDEST CHRISTMAS TREE
Paul Parker (UK) owns an artificial Christmas tree that has been in his family since 1886. It stands 30 cm (1 ft) tall in an ornate pot and was originally bought for his great-great Aunt Lou, possibly from Woolworths. It was bequeathed to Paul by his mother in 2008, continuing the 136-year tradition.

Religious celebrations and festivals – such as Diwali, Ramadan, Passover and Día de los Muertos – often inspire some awe-inspiring record breaking. But no other holiday generates as many applications to GWR as Christmas...

▶ LARGEST COLLECTION OF CHRISTMAS BROOCHES
Adam Wide (UK) owns 7,929 bejewelled festive pins, as ratified on 2 Dec 2021 in Berlin, Germany. His oldest brooch dates from the 1920s, while his most precious item is an Art Nouveau-inspired piece incorporating platinum and precious jewels.

First printed Christmas card
Mass-produced festive greetings cards were first printed and sold in the UK in 1843. The lithographed design depicts a family enjoying a Christmas dinner, flanked by charitable scenes. Only 12 of the original 1,000 cards remain. One, sent by businessman Sir Arthur Cole to his mother, sold for £20,000 ($28,146) at auction on 24 Nov 2001, becoming the **most expensive Christmas card** ever.

Tallest cut Christmas tree
In Dec 1950, a 64.6-m (212-ft) Douglas fir (*Pseudotsuga menziesii*) was erected and dressed at Northgate Mall in Seattle, Washington, USA. The mall had only opened in April that year, and the tree was intended to attract media attention and shoppers.

The **tallest artificial tree** was made from steel pipes, concrete, chicken wire and wood – and painted and hung with decorations – by Arjuna Ranatunga Social Services in Colombo, Sri Lanka. It stood 72.1 m (236 ft 6 in) tall when measured on 24 Dec 2016.

Longest wish list to Santa
Beijing Hyundai and the Mohe Tourism Bureau (both CHN) collected 124,969 festive wishes written to Father Christmas. The list was presented to the big man himself at Santa Village in Mohe, Heilongjiang, China, on 28 Dec 2017.

Longest Christmas-cracker-pulling chain
A total of 1,081 individuals lined up to crack open traditional table decorations on 10 Dec 2015, in an event arranged by The Harrodian School in Barnes, London, UK.

Most people wearing Christmas jumpers
On 19 Dec 2015, Kansas Athletics (USA) brought together 3,473 participants bedecked in kitsch seasonal sweaters. The bad-taste bonanza took place at the basketball game against Montana in Lawrence, Kansas, USA.

Largest group of carol singers
The Godswill Akpabio Unity Choir (NGA) united 25,272 choristers at the Uyo Township Stadium in Akwa Ibom, Nigeria, on 13 Dec 2014.

Most Brussels sprouts eaten in one minute
Linus Urbanec (SWE) downed 31 of these love-them-or-loathe-them veggies in 60 sec in Rottne, Sweden, on 26 Nov 2008.

Another festive favourite is stollen, the German cake-like bread flavoured with fruit, nuts, spices and marzipan. The **most stollen eaten in one minute** is 336 g (11.8 oz), by André Ortolf (DEU) in Krumbach, Germany, on 5 Oct 2018.

Even André would have struggled with the **longest stollen**. Created by Lidl (NLD), it was 72.1 m (236 ft 6 in) long, as ratified at Haarlem railway station, Netherlands, on 10 Dec 2010.

LARGEST COLLECTION OF SANTA CLAUS MEMORABILIA
Jean-Guy Laquerre (CAN) owned 25,104 different Father Christmas-themed objects as of the most recent count. His hoard included 2,360 figurines, 2,846 cards and postcards from 33 countries, 1,312 serviettes, and 241 pins and brooches.

The **largest collection of snowmen** belongs to Karen Schmidt (USA, inset) and consisted of 5,127 items as of 19 Mar 2013. Her favourite items are a red bird making a snowman and a pink snowman that sings "Santa Baby".

FULSOME FESTIVE FARE

Christmas cake
9 x 6 m (29 ft x 19 ft), weighing 3,825 kg (8,432 lb 10 oz). Created by Just Bake (IND).

Christmas pudding
c. 1.5 m (4 ft 11 in) wide, weighing 3,280 kg (7,231 lb). Made by the villagers of Aughton in Lancashire, UK.

Gingerbread house
18.28 m long x 3.07 m at apex (60 x 10 ft); volume of 1,110.1 m³ (39,202 cu ft). Made by Traditions Club (USA).

Gingerbread man
c. 3.7 m tall x 2.9 m wide (12 x 9 ft 6 in), weighing 651 kg (1,435 lb). Prepared by IKEA Furuset (NOR).

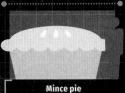

Mince pie
6.1 x 1.5 m (20 x 5 ft), weighing 1,025 kg (2,260 lb). Made in Burton upon Trent, Staffordshire, UK, by Messrs L and W Radford Ltd.

Mulled wine
2,034.7 litres (537.5 gal). Made by Alessandro De Dea and Fabrizio Vigilante (both ITA).

Average human (165 cm; 5 ft 4 in)

FASTEST TIME TO DRESS IN A SANTA COSTUME

Theo Toksvig-Stewart (UK) donned Santa's red-and-white garb in 28.91 sec during filming of the *QI* (BBC) Christmas episode on 17 Aug 2020. The attempt was earmarked for the programme's ho-ho-host, Sandi Toksvig, but she allowed her son Theo to take her place.

MOST CHRISTMAS CRACKERS PULLED BY AN INDIVIDUAL IN 30 SECONDS

On 12 Dec 2021, DJ Joel Corry (UK) pulled 41 crackers in quick succession at radio station Capital FM's Jingle Bell Ball. The feat took place behind the scenes of the event, which was staged at the O2 Arena in London, UK.

LARGEST CHRISTMAS BAUBLE

The Dubai Mall (Emaar Malls) presented a colourful festive decoration with a 4.68-m (15-ft 4-in) diameter in Dubai, UAE, on 19 Dec 2018. Suspended from the roof of the shopping arcade, the outsized ornament weighed 1,100 kg (2,425 lb), making it almost as heavy as a MINI Cooper car. For a big bauble collection, turn to p.84.

MOST PEOPLE DRESSED AS SNOWMEN

On 8 Dec 2017, a 489-strong group assembled by Centro Social e Cultural da Atalhada (PRT) dressed up as snowmen in Lagoa, Azores, Portugal. The seasonal get-together took place at a pop-up Christmas village to raise funds for the local community.

▶ LONGEST-RUNNING SANTA SCHOOL

The Charles W Howard Santa Claus School was established in Oct 1937 in Albion, New York, USA, and is due to celebrate its 85th anniversary in 2022. Its founder, a former farmer and in-store Santa, started the school at his home before expanding to a larger site in Midland, Michigan. Graduates were originally conferred with a BSC – Bachelor of Santa Claus.

HIGHEST-GROSSING CHRISTMAS MOVIE

Dr. Seuss' The Grinch (USA, 2018) earned $513,537,178 (£376.9 m) on its various releases between 8 Nov 2018 and 21 Jan 2022. The animated fantasy is based on the 1957 book *How the Grinch Stole Christmas!* by Dr Seuss (aka Theodor Seuss Geisel) and features the voice of Benedict Cumberbatch as the mean, green Grinch.

BEST-SELLING CHRISTMAS SINGLE

First recorded in 1942, "White Christmas" by Bing Crosby has sold more than 50 million copies worldwide on vinyl, cassette and CD. This makes it not just a festive record breaker but also the **best-selling single** of all time. Crosby's version of the song has been reissued annually, and continues to chart in the 21st century; its latest UK appearance was at No.48 in Jan 2022.

WHITE CHRISTMAS
BING CROSBY

Fitness Fanatics

As a result of the COVID-19 pandemic, GWR saw a huge increase in claims for fitness challenges, as wannabe record holders looked to stay healthy and capitalize on being stuck at home. Meet the incredible athletes pushing their bodies to the limit in order to redefine what's physically possible.

Darine has overcome a leg amputation and a fractured hip to become a physical trainer and life coach.

Aaron Greally

Marcus Winship

Jake Palmer

Samuel Stafford

"IN A MINUTE" WORKOUTS

LUNGES
Male: 75, by Christian Roberto López Rodríguez (ESP) on 13 Aug 2020
Female: 80, by Sandra Hickson (IRL) on 25 Jul 2019

JUMPING JACKS
Male: 132, by Fares Mohamed Shaban (EGY) on 15 Mar 2021
Female: 132, by Melanie Bemis (USA) on 7 May 2021

BURPEES
Male: 48, by Wesley Prado (BRA) on 23 Jul 2020
Female: 40, by Leigh Scott (UK) on 23 May 2018

JUMP SQUATS
Male: 80, by Ali Mounir (EGY) on 23 Mar 2020
Female: 67, by Areej Al Hammadi (UAE) on 24 Jun 2021

MOST TIMES TO SQUAT LIFT ONE'S OWN BODY WEIGHT IN ONE MINUTE (FEMALE)

Karenjeet Kaur Bains (UK) completed 42 squat lifts of 67.5 kg (148 lb 13 oz) in Warwick, UK, on 7 Mar 2022. A teenage sprinter, Karenjeet took up powerlifting aged 17 and is the first Sikh woman to represent Great Britain in the sport.

1. Longest Samson's chair (female, LA1)

Darine Barbar (LBN) maintained a static wall-sit for 2 min 8.24 sec on 4 Jun 2021 in Dubai, UAE. Her record attempt marked the launch of the GWR Impairment Initiative (see pp.10–11). Darine, who lost her left leg to bone cancer at the age of 15, was classified in the LA1 category (unilateral above-knee amputation).

2. Most chest-to-ground burpees in one hour (female)

On 8 Aug 2021, Issy Watson (CAN) completed 829 chest-to-ground burpees in 60 min in Victoria, British Columbia, Canada. Between repetitions, she had to place both arms out at right angles away from her body while lying on the floor.

3. Most skips over a human skipping rope in one minute

Acrobatic gymnastic team Acropolis (UK) managed 57 human skipping-rope jumps in 60 sec on 15 Feb 2022. They competed in a head-to-head battle for the record with Italy's Wildcats Cheerteam on *Lo Show dei Record* in Milan, beating the previous best by nine.

4. Farthest lache (bar-to-bar swing)

On 10 Nov 2020, The Flying Phoenix, aka Najee Richardson (USA), flung himself 5.56 m (18 ft 3 in) from one bar to another in Hainesport, New Jersey, USA. The lord of the lache has also achieved the **highest lache** – 2.28 m (7 ft 6 in) – and the **farthest lache cat leap (bar to wall)** – 4.90 m (16 ft 1 in).

5. Longest triathlon

On 8 May 2021, Adrian Bennett (UK) completed a 189-day triathlon around the island of Singapore that covered a total distance of 7,519.67 km (4,672.50 mi). The design teacher exceeded his goal of swimming 225 km (139.8 mi), cycling 5,820 km (3,616.3 mi) and running 1,450 km (900.9 mi) by nearly 20 km (12.4 mi).

6. Longest L-sit bar hang with one arm (female)

Stefanie Millinger (AUT) toughed out a one-armed L-sit bar hang for 1 min 38.05 sec in Salzburg, Austria,

> Mohammad set his push-up record wearing a 40-lb pack – about the same as two-and-a-half bowling balls.

> The "yoga wheel" pose is a deep backbend that's also known as a "bridge" in the field of acrobatics.

PULL-UPS	PISTOL SQUATS	KNUCKLE PUSH-UPS	WEIGHT DEADLIFTED
Male: 74, by Hong Zhongtao (CHN) on 30 Oct 2020 Female: 36, by Amanda Stacey (USA) on 19 Aug 2021	Male: 52, by William Rauhaus (DEU) on 27 Jul 2016 Female: 42, by Kara Webb (AUS) on 1 Feb 2017	Male: 113, by Jagdishram B Midle (IND) on 3 Mar 2019 Female: 70, by Eva Clarke (AUS) on 9 Jan 2015	Male: 5,834.8 kg, by Viacheslav Pavlichuk (UKR) on 15 Apr 2021 Female: 3,160.5 kg, by Katie Carlisle (AUS) on 17 Jul 2021

on 13 Aug 2021. An acrobat and handstand artist who trains for up to 10 hours a day, Stefanie holds multiple GWR titles. These include the **longest time in an L-sit (female)** – 10 min 15 sec – and the **longest time balancing on the hands** – 59 min 6 sec.

7. Most knuckle push-ups carrying a 40-lb pack in three minutes (male)
On 1 Oct 2021, Mohammad Abdul Kader Feido (SYR) completed 148 push-ups on his knuckles in 180 sec in Latakia, Syria. He also holds records for the **most push-ups on the back of the hands carrying a 40-lb pack in one minute** (65) and the **most archer push-ups in one minute** (122).

8. Most consecutive ring muscle-ups
Gymnast Simen Solberg Uriansrud (NOR) executed 20 muscle-ups in a row on 13 Jun 2021 in Oslo, Norway. He had to perform each pull-up on the rings until he was supporting his body on straight, extended arms. Simen beat the previous record by a single muscle-up.

9. Longest handstand on a rotating platform (male)
On 16 Mar 2022, Nicolas Montes de Oca (MEX) stayed in a handstand for 25.78 sec while revolving at high speed in Amatlán, Morelos, Mexico. Nine days later, he added the **longest one-arm handstand (male)** – 1 min 11.82 sec – to his growing roster of records.

10. Most aerial silk front saltos in one minute
On 13 Dec 2021, Celeste Dixon (AUS) performed 23 forward rotations in 60 sec while wrapped around a length of suspended silk in Adelaide, Australia. An Olympic-standard gymnast, Celeste is a five-time contestant on *Australian Ninja Warrior*. She holds GWR titles for the **most backward somersault burpees in 30 seconds** – eight – and the **fastest 10 m walking on hands while holding a 10-kg medicine ball between the legs (female)** – 10.55 sec.

11. Longest time to hold the yoga wheel pose
Sanjeevi Suresh (IND) maintained a Chakrasana – pushing up from the ground with an arched back and hands and feet planted on the ground – for 22 min 52.5 sec on 22 Jul 2021 in Thoothukudi, Tamil Nadu, India. The 18-year-old had been practising yoga for five years.

MOST ONE-ARM FINGERTIP PUSH-UPS IN ONE MINUTE
Mahmoud Mohamed Ayoub (EGY) completed 72 one-arm push-ups on his fingertips in 60 sec in El Kharga, Egypt, on 10 May 2021. He is the holder of numerous GWR sporting and fitness records.

Ball Skills

TARUN KUMAR CHEDDY (MUS)
Tarun honed his skills on the island of Mauritius and has earned GWR freestyle titles using basketballs, footballs and rugby balls. His records include the **most basketball neck catches in one minute** (48) and the **most rugby-ball neck throw and catches in 30 seconds** (22).

ZAILA AVANT-GARDE (USA)
Basketball prospect Zaila is also a juggler, unicyclist and winner of the 2021 Scripps National Spelling Bee. On 2 Nov 2020, she completed the **most bounce juggles of four basketballs in one minute** (255), and has set or equalled three other GWR titles.

ASH RANDALL (UK)
Ash's freestyle talents have taken him around the world, and seen him showcase his skills alongside stars such as One Direction and Bollywood legend Shah Rukh Khan. Among Ash's many GWR titles are the **most football step-overs in one minute** – both **forward** (127) and **backward** (99).

JUNJI NAKASONE (JPN)
When it comes to basketball freestyling tricks, Japan's "JJ" is king of the court. His records include the **most arm rolls in one minute with three basketballs** (49), the **highest throw and catch of a spinning basketball** (6.2 m; 20 ft 4 in) and the **longest time spinning four basketballs** (21.65 sec).

TAMÁS FELFÖLDI (HUN)
A member of the Face Team Acrobatic Sports Theatre, Tamás equalled the record for the **most one-arm "around the world" basketball tricks in one minute** (28) on 20 Aug 2020. He matched the total set by Drew Hoops (UK) on 27 Jun 2014.

MOST FOOTBALL TOUCHES IN ONE MINUTE

High-speed football juggling demands both lightning-fast reflexes and concentration. Pro freestylers can touch the ball several times a second – sometimes with the most unlikely of body parts!

Head: Gao Chong (CHN) 341

Knee: Konok Karmakar (BGD) 162

Heel: Sinan Öztürk (DEU) 157

Lips: Daniel Cutting (UK) 153

BEN NUTTALL (UK)
Professional freestyler Ben learned his gravity-defying skills on the streets of his hometown of Birmingham. He has earned GWR certificates for the **most football knee catches in 30 seconds** (31) and the **most consecutive rugby ball touches with the feet** (187).

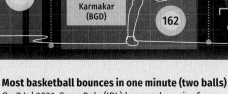

Most basketball bounces in one minute (two balls)
On 7 Jul 2021, Sean Daly (IRL) bounced a pair of basketballs a total of 729 times in 60 sec in Cork, Ireland. Crouching down on the court, he averaged an incredible 12 bounces every second.

Fastest mile balancing a football on the head
Yee Ming Low (MYS) covered one mile (1.6 km) in 8 min 35 sec with a ball balanced on his forehead at MPSJ athletics stadium in Selangor, Malaysia, on 20 Mar 2010. Although the record guidelines stated that he could lose control of the ball and restart from the same place, Yee Ming Low completed the entire distance without once letting the ball fall.

Fastest marathon juggling a football
Abraham Muñoz (MEX) ran 26.2 mi (42.1 km) while juggling a soccer ball in 5 hr 41 min 52 sec at the Mexico City Marathon on 28 Aug 2016. He only lost control of the ball four times in the entire race, with the first occasion occurring four hours in.

Abraham also holds the GWR titles for the **fastest 100 m** (17.53 sec) and **fastest mile** (8 min 17.28 sec) while doing keepy-ups. And on 31 Jul 2017, he completed the **most football touches in one hour (male)** – 11,901 – in New York City, USA.

Greatest height to flick and control a football with the neck
On 11 Oct 2019, pro freestyler Daniel Cutting (UK) overcame wind and rain at the Stantonbury athletics field in Milton Keynes, UK, to flick a ball 6 m (19 ft 8 in) into the air and catch it on the nape of his neck.

Greatest height to control a football
Former England international Jamie Redknapp kicked a ball 18.6 m (61 ft) into the air before controlling it with three touches on 9 Jul 2015 in London, UK. Jamie took on the challenge for the sports panel show *A League of Their Own* (CPL, UK).
On 7 Jul 2017, Jamie teamed up with Spanish World Cup-winner Cesc Fàbregas to complete the **most football volley passes in 30 seconds by a pair** – 15.

JOHN FARNWORTH (UK)
Whether juggling footballs up the Himalayas or across the Sahara Desert, John is always looking for new freestyle challenges. Among his GWR titles, he counts the **longest duration controlling a football on an elevated slackline** (29.82 sec) and the **most full-volley rebounds in 30 seconds** (28).

John has performed everywhere from Broadway theatres to the FIFA World Cup finals.

KONOK KARMAKAR (BGD)
Freestyler Konok has inspired other Bangladeshi record breakers with his haul of GWR titles, which include the **most football touches with the knee in one minute** (162) and the **most football "hotstepper" tricks in 30 seconds** (49) and **one minute** (90).

CHINONSO ECHE (NGA)
"Amazing Kid Eche" didn't get his nickname for nothing. The teenage prodigy has already earned four GWR certificates, including the ❍ **most consecutive football touches in one minute while balancing a football on the head** (111) and the **most football headers in a prone position in one minute** (233).

Shin: Leon Walraven (NLD) — 267

Shoulders: Yuuki Yoshinaga (JPN) — 230

Soles: Yuuki Yoshinaga — 402

Toes: John Farnworth (UK) — 109

Most football touches in one hour
On 22 Sep 2020, Maya Fung (USA) took a total of 13,300 touches as she juggled a football for 60 min in Prosper, Texas, USA – averaging more than three touches every second! A street freestyler and futsal player, Maya had spent three years practising for her record attempt, which beat the **male** record (see opposite) by 1,399. The ball didn't touch the floor once in the course of the hour.

Most football touches in one minute
Chloe Hegland (CAN) racked up 339 touches in 60 sec of football juggling in Beijing, China, on 3 Nov 2007. She also holds the **30-second** record – 163 – which she set on 23 Feb 2008 in Madrid, Spain.

Longest time heading a football between two people
On 8 Apr 2021, Kosovans Agim Agushi and Bujar Ajeti headed a ball back and forth for 34 min 1 sec in Pristina, Kosovo. It was the third time that Agim had claimed this GWR title.

Longest time continuously controlling a football...
• **Outright (male)**: 10 hr 7 min 29 sec, by Mark Jordan (USA) on 30 Nov 2018 in Stamford, Connecticut, USA.
• **Outright (female)**: 7 hr 5 min 25 sec, by Cláudia Martini (BRA) at Caxias do Sul in Brazil on 12 Jul 1996.
• **With the head**: 8 hr 32 min 3 sec, by Tomas Lundman (SWE) in Lidingö, Sweden, on 27 Feb 2004.
• **With the head while seated**: 4 hr 9 min 26 sec, by Tomas Lundman on 20 Apr 2007 in Stockholm, Sweden.
• **With the soles**: 28 min 47 sec, by Masaru Kitagawa (JPN) in Yokohama, Kanagawa, Japan, on 3 Jul 2016.
• **While lying down**: 11 min 9.97 sec, by Akinori Wase (JPN) on 14 Jan 2017 in Yangon, Myanmar.

Longest time to spin a basketball on one finger while dribbling
On 4 Aug 2020 in Buderim, Queensland, Australia, serial record breaker Brendan Kelbie (AUS) spent 1 min 14.40 sec dribbling a basketball while spinning another on his finger. On the same day, he also achieved the **longest time spinning a basketball on the nose** – 9.57 sec.

LAURA BIONDO (VEN)
A former Cirque du Soleil artist, Laura has gone on to become a freestyle world champion with a host of GWR titles. She added two more in celebration of GWR Day 2021 (see p.12), including the **most sit-down football crossovers in 30 seconds (female)** – 62.

Rock Climbing

The climbs on these pages are described using the Yosemite Decimal System, which was developed to grade the difficulty of hikes, scrambles and climbs. On this scale, rock climbing is covered by level five and its fifteen sub-levels, from 5 to 5.15. Above 5.9, additional letters are used for finer distinctions – 5.10c is more challenging than 5.10a, for example.

Hardest...
- **Free-solo route climbed**: "Panem et Circenses" ("Bread and Circuses") is a 5.14b climb near Arco in northern Italy. The 15-m (49-ft) route was completed free-solo by 52-year-old Alfredo Webber (ITA) in Mar 2021.
- **Route climbed by an amputee**: Urko Carmona Barandiaran (ESP), whose right leg was amputated above the knee after a car accident, has completed two routes graded 5.13c without a prosthetic. Both climbs were made at Spanish sites – "Ximpleta" in Margalef in 2012 and "Paideia" in Rodellar in 2015.
- **Flash ascent (male)**: On 10 Feb 2018, Adam Ondra (CZE; see opposite) scaled the 5.15a-graded "Supercrackinette" in Saint-Léger-du-Ventoux, France, in a "flash ascent" (i.e., on his first attempt). This is the only 5.15a flash ascent in history. As of 3 Feb 2022, Ondra also holds the record for the **most 5.15 routes climbed** – 70.
- **Flash ascent (female)**: Janja Garnbret (SVN) climbed the 5.14b route "Fish Eye" in Oliana, Spain, on 1 Nov 2021. On the same trip, Garnbret also flashed a second 5.14b route known as "American Hustle".

First paraplegic ascent of El Capitan
Mark Wellman (USA) lost the use of his legs after a fall in 1982. Despite this, on 26 Jul 1989 he scaled El Capitan. Over eight days, with his friend Mike Corbett leading, Wellman performed some 7,000 pull-ups, using his arms and core strength alone to scale the cliff via the "Shield" route.

Fastest climb of "The Naked Edge"
On 22 May 2020, John Ebers and Ben Wilbur (both USA) took just 24 min 14 sec to complete "The Naked Edge" – a 5.11b multi-pitch challenge in Eldorado Canyon, Colorado, USA. The accepted route

Other elite climbers might take four days to top El Capitan, not least because of the gear and supplies they carry.

FIRST FREE CLIMB OF THE EL CAPITAN "NOSE" ROUTE
One of the world's most challenging rock-climbing locations, El Capitan is a 900-m (3,000-ft) granite monolith in Yosemite National Park, California, USA. The most famous route to the top is a tough 5.13c climb called "The Nose". It was not climbed free until 16 Sep 1993, when Lynn Hill (USA) figured out how to get past the crux (hardest point) of the climb, a spot called "Changing Corners".

for speed climbers here comprises climbing from the bridge at the base of the canyon, scaling the 500-ft (150-m) vertical ascent itself and returning to the bridge again.

Most ascents of the same climbing route
On 26 Feb 2012, at the age of 63, Ken Nichols (USA) completed his 10,000th climb of "Dol Guldur" – a 5.11 route at East Peak in Connecticut, USA. He first climbed the route in 1975 and likes it for its sustained and consistent level of difficulty.

Longest climbing route
The world's lengthiest rock climbs go sideways, not upwards. Known as "girdle traverses", they cross large cliffs from one side to the other. The longest such route that is continuous (meaning that climbers never have to walk between disjointed cliff bands) is the 14,000-ft-long (4,267-m) "El Capitan Girdle Traverse", rising from the lower right side to the upper left side of the Yosemite National Park monolith. It was established by US climbers Chris McNamara and Mark Melvin in Apr 1998 and has never been repeated.

Longest roof climb
The "Great Rift" is a 2,500-ft-long (762-m) traverse that runs along the underside of the M5 motorway bridge near Exeter in Devon, UK. This gruelling 5.13 "crack climb" (i.e., following natural cracks in the surface) was discovered by Tom Randall and Pete Whittaker (both UK), who tackled the route over four days in Nov 2021. The "Great Rift" has no handholds aside from the narrow expansion gap between the two decks, which Randall and Whittaker also used to support the portaledge they slept on each night.

FIRST FREE-SOLO CLIMB OF EL CAPITAN
On 3 Jun 2017, Alex Honnold (USA) ascended Yosemite National Park's revered monolith without ropes, harnesses or other protective gear (see inset) in 3 hr 56 min.

With the use of ropes, Honnold and Tommy Caldwell (USA) also executed the **fastest climb of El Capitan** – 1 hr 58 min 7 sec – on 6 Jun 2018. They were the first climbers to do so in less than 2 hr.

On 14 Jan 2015, Caldwell and Kevin Jorgeson (USA) completed the **first free climb of El Capitan's "Dawn Wall"**. It took the pair 19 days to complete all 32 pitches (rope lengths).

CLIMBING STYLES

Aid
Supporting yourself, and ascending, using ropes and anchors driven into the rock

Free solo
No ropes, anchors or fall protection of any kind

Traditional
The lead climber (top) places removable anchors in the rock as they ascend, while the belayer (bottom) provides fall protection and collects used hardware as they go

In all types of free climbing – including solo, traditional and sport – upward movement is achieved only through contact with the rock face and ropes are just for fall protection

Sport
The lead climber follows a pre-planned route with permanent fixed anchors drilled into the rock

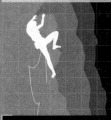

Bouldering
Climbers tackle intense technical challenges called "problems" close enough to the ground to not need fall protection

HARDEST ROUTE CLIMBED

"Silence" is a 45-m-long (147-ft) sport climb in the Hanshelleren Cave near Flatanger in Norway. It has a grade of 5.15d. No other climbs of this grade exist and only one person has ever climbed it: Adam Ondra (CZE), on 3 Sep 2017. Almost the entire route is inverted, running across the ceiling of the cave.

HARDEST TRADITIONAL CLIMB

"Tribe" near Cadarese, Italy, is a 30-m (98-ft) overhanging route estimated at 5.15a. The first trad climber to tackle the route was Jacopo Larcher (ITA, right), who reached the top on 22 Mar 2019.

The **female** traditional climb record was broken by Beth Rodden (USA) on 14 Feb 2008, when she completed the 5.14c route "Meltdown", a 22-m (72-ft) vertical seam in Yosemite National Park.

HARDEST ROUTE CLIMBED (FEMALE)

The most demanding ascents executed by female climbers are graded at 5.15b. Three women have so far achieved this feat. The first was Angela Eiter (AUT, below), who climbed "La Planta de Shiva" in Villanueva del Rosario, Spain, on 22 Oct 2017. Laura Rogora (ITA) and Julia Chanourdie (FRA) both matched her with 5.15b climbs in 2020.

FASTEST TIME TO CLIMB EL CAPITAN (FEMALE)

Mayan Smith-Gobat (NZ, above right and below) and Libby Sauter (USA, left) took just 4 hr 43 min to scale the "Nose" of El Cap on 31 Oct 2014. They knocked 19 min off the previous record, which they had set four days earlier.

HARDEST BOULDERING PROBLEM CLIMBED

"Burden of Dreams" – in Lappnor, Finland – and "Return of the Sleepwalker" – in Red Rock Canyon National Conservation Area, Nevada, USA – are both graded as V17, the highest difficulty rating. Each has only been climbed once: the former by Nalle Hukkataival (FIN) on 23 Oct 2016, and the latter by Daniel Woods (USA, above) on 30 Mar 2021.

FIRST BLIND PERSON TO LEAD A CLIMB OF THE OLD MAN OF HOY

On 4 Jun 2019, Jesse Dufton (UK) led an ascent of the 137-m-tall (449-ft) Old Man of Hoy sea stack in the Orkney Islands, UK. He was followed by his sighted partner, Molly Thompson, up six pitches of the east face, which has a climbing grade of 5.9.

HARDEST BOULDERING PROBLEM CLIMBED (FEMALE)

Three teenagers have achieved a bouldering grade of V15 (the third-highest). Ashima Shiraishi (USA, right) was 14 when she climbed "Horizon" on Mount Hiei in Japan on 22 Mar 2016; 18-year-old Kaddi Lehmann (DEU) climbed "Kryptos" near Balsthal in Switzerland in May 2018; and in May 2019, Mishka Ishi (JPN) ascended "Byaku-dou" on Mount Hōrai, Japan, aged just 13.

Epic Journeys

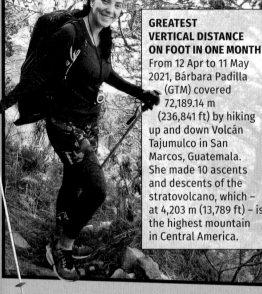

GREATEST VERTICAL DISTANCE ON FOOT IN ONE MONTH

From 12 Apr to 11 May 2021, Bárbara Padilla (GTM) covered 72,189.14 m (236,841 ft) by hiking up and down Volcán Tajumulco in San Marcos, Guatemala. She made 10 ascents and descents of the stratovolcano, which – at 4,203 m (13,789 ft) – is the highest mountain in Central America.

GREATEST DISTANCE CYCLED ON ROAD IN 24 HOURS BY A TEAM OF EIGHT (FEMALE)

The "Octowomen" – Meera Velankar, Zainab Shoaib, Preeti Maske, Tasneem Mohsin, Sowmya Chandran, Priya Narayan, Sushma Swamy and Anjana Sudeendra (all IND) – cycled a collective 660.11 km (410.17 mi) on 14 Nov 2021. The relay took place in Karnataka, India.

Greatest distance cycled on road in...

Time	Cyclist	Distance
6 hours (male)	Christoph Strasser (AUT)	270.85 km (168.30 mi)
6 hours (female)	Amanda Coker (USA)	221.89 km (137.88 mi)
12 hours (male)	Christoph Strasser	532.22 km (330.71 mi)
12 hours (female)	Amanda Coker	435.55 km (270.64 mi)
24 hours (male)	Christoph Strasser	1,026.22 km (637.66 mi)
24 hours (female)	Amanda Coker	824.79 km (512.50 mi)
One week (female)	Alexandra Meixner (AUT)	3,258.38 km (2,024.66 mi)
One week (male)	Arvis Sprude (LTV)	3,022.48 km (1,878.08 mi)
One month (female)	Alexandra Meixner	13,333.25 km (8,284.90 mi)

All records set on standard bicycles in 2021; approved by the World Ultracycling Association (WUCA)

First solo row from mainland Europe to mainland USA

British soldier Jack Jarvis rowed from Lagos, Portugal, to Sandsprit Park, Florida, USA, between 3 Dec 2021 and 24 Mar 2022. It took him 111 days 12 hr 22 min to make the 4,500-nautical-mile (8,334-km; 5,178.5-mi) voyage, which he undertook in memory of his grandfather; he also raised £60,000 ($79,380) for the charity *brainstrust*. En route, his boat was struck by a marlin and he received a video message from soccer star David Beckham.

Fastest solo transatlantic row (Trade Winds I route, female)

Victoria Evans (UK) concluded a 40-day 21-hr 1-min ocean odyssey between Tenerife, Spain, and Port St Charles, Barbados, on 24 Mar 2022. On the journey, she encountered sharks and bad weather, while also seeing in her 35th birthday. Evans's primary motivation was to raise funds for the charity Women in Sport. She also wanted to set an example to women and girls, and demonstrate that, with hard work and resilience, anything is possible.

Youngest person to climb Everest and Lhotse (male)

The youngest climber to top two of the world's five highest peaks is Arjun Vajpai (IND, b. 9 Jun 1993), who was 17 years 345 days old when he scaled the 8,516-m (27,939-ft) Lhotse on 20 May 2011. He had previously scaled Everest (8,848.8 m; 29,031 ft), aka Sagarmāthā or Chomolungma, on 22 May 2010, becoming the then-youngest Indian to summit Earth's **highest mountain**.

Farthest ocean swim

Extreme swimmer and multiple record holder Pablo Fernández Álvarez (ESP) covered 250 km (155.34 mi) off southern Florida, USA, on 19–20 Jul 2021, assisted by favourable currents in the Gulf Stream. In doing so, he also achieved the **farthest open-water swim in 24 hours** – 238 km (147.88 mi) – on 19 Jul.

Farthest ice swim

On 3 Apr 2022, Krzysztof Kubiak (POL) swam 4.70 km (2.92 mi) in Lake Ełckie in Poland – with an average water temperature of 3.87°C (39.96°F) – as verified by the International Ice Swimming Association. In all, he spent 1 hr 23 min 18 sec in the water.

Fastest circumnavigation by car

The record for the **first and fastest man and woman to have circumnavigated the Earth by car** covering six continents under the rules applicable in 1989 and 1991 embracing more than an equator's length of driving (24,901 road miles; 40,075 km), is held by Saloo Choudhury and his wife Neena Choudhury (both IND). The journey took 69 days 19 hours 5 minutes from 9 September to 17 November 1989. The couple drove a 1989 Hindustan "Contessa Classic" starting and finishing in Delhi, India.

Not to scale

Day 3
Distance: 9.6-km hike/climb
Vertical gain: 2,450 m to 4,207 m

Day 2
Distance: 60-km bicycle ride
Vertical gain: 0 m to 2,450 m

Day 1
Distance: 43-km row in an outrigger canoe (coxed by Chad Cabral)
Vertical gain: 0 m to 0 m

YOUNGEST PERSON TO CLIMB EARTH'S TWO HIGHEST MOUNTAINS

On 27 Jul 2021, aged 19 years 138 days, Shehroze Kashif (PAK, b. 11 Mar 2002) topped K2 (8,611 m; 28,251 ft) on the border between China and Pakistan, making him the **youngest person to climb K2**. He had summitted Everest just 77 days earlier. Kashif made his first climb aged 11, scaling Pakistan's 3,885-m (12,746-ft) Makra Peak.

On 1–3 Feb 2021, explorer Victor Vescovo and marine scientist Dr Clifford Kapono (both USA) became the **first people to scale Mauna Kea** in Hawaii, USA, from seabed to summit. Mauna Kea is the world's **tallest mountain**: from base to peak, it measures c. 10,200 m (33,465 ft), though more than half of it lies underwater. Everest reaches *higher* above sea level but is not as tall overall. Here, we track the pioneering 9,323-m (30,587-ft) ascent by deep-sea submersible, canoe, bicycle and foot.

Day 1
Distance: 5.1 km from seabed to surface in DSV *Limiting Factor*
Vertical gain: -5,116 m to 0 m

FIRST ASIAN WOMAN TO SKI SOLO TO THE SOUTH POLE

Setting out from Hercules Inlet on the Antarctic coast on 21 Nov 2021, British Army physio Preet Chandi (UK) reached the South Pole on 3 Jan 2022. Her time of 40 days 7 hr 3 min is the third-quickest by a woman. Johanna Davidsson (SWE) is the **fastest woman** to make this trek solo to date: 38 days 23 hr 5 min in 2016.

YOUNGEST PERSON TO CLIMB THE SEVEN VOLCANIC SUMMITS (MALE)

On 22 Dec 2021, at the age of 24 years 119 days, Yousef Al Refaie (b. 25 Aug 1997) of Kuwait topped his seventh volcanic peak: Mount Sidley in Antarctica. His mission to scale the highest volcano on each continent began with Mount Kilimanjaro in Tanzania on 30 Dec 2015. Here, he's waving the Kuwaiti flag at the top of Mount Elbrus in Russia.

MOST ENGLISH CHANNEL SWIMS

Chloë McCardel (AUS) swam between the UK and France for the 44th time in her marathon-swimming career on 13 Oct 2021, as ratified by the Channel Swimming Association. Her tally includes three double crossings and even one triple crossing. Her average time to traverse the 33-km-wide (20.5-mi) strait is just under 10 hr 25 min.

FIRST SOLO VOYAGE AROUND THE WORLD BY A DOUBLE AMPUTEE

Dustin Reynolds – aka the "Single-handed Sailor" – completed a seven-and-a-half-year, on-off sailing trip on 4 Dec 2021, returning to his native Hawaii, USA. His left arm and leg had to be amputated in 2008 after he was knocked off his motorcycle. Reynolds was inspired to take on this challenge – despite having no ocean-sailing experience! – after reading about other solo circumnavigations.

YOUNGEST PILOTS TO CIRCUMNAVIGATE THE WORLD SOLO BY AIRCRAFT

Male: Travis Ludlow (UK, b. 13 Feb 2003) was 18 years 149 days old on completing his round-the-world journey by air in Teuge, Netherlands, on 12 Jul 2021. He piloted a single-engine 2001 Cessna 172R.

Female: Zara Rutherford (BEL, b. 5 Jul 2002) was aged 19 years 199 days when she touched down in Kortrijk, Belgium, on 20 Jan 2022. This also makes her the **youngest person to circumnavigate the world solo by microlight**.

No Limits

McKeand, a former holder of the **fastest South Pole expedition (female)** record (see p.97). Starting from the Ronne-Filchner Ice Shelf, they covered 890 km (553 mi) on skis and sledges in 39 days.

Longest journey by wheelchair
Between 21 Mar 1985 and 22 May 1987, Rick Hansen (CAN) – who became paralysed from the waist down in 1973 – wheeled himself 40,075 km (24,901 mi) through four continents and 34 countries. He started and finished his journey in Vancouver, British Columbia, Canada. His epic trek raised $24 m (£14.3 m) for spinal-cord-injury research.

Fastest wheelchair crossing of Qatar
Ahmed Al-Shahrani (QAT) traversed Qatar south to north in 1 day 17 hr 55 min, ending in Al Ruwais on 3 Apr 2021. He sought to honour and encourage the participation of people with disabilities in sport.

Greatest vertical distance on a climbing wall using one hand in one hour (female)
Para climber Anoushé Husain (UK), who was born without a right forearm and lives with several health conditions, scaled an equivalent elevation of 374.85 m (1,229 ft 9 in) on an indoor rock wall at The Castle Climbing Centre in London, UK, on 5 Apr 2022.

Fastest marathon (LA2, female)
Below-the-knee amputee Amy Winters (USA) took just 3 hr 4 min 16 sec to run the Chicago Marathon in Illinois, USA, on 22 Oct 2006. On 16 Sep 2007, she also ran the **fastest half marathon (LA2, female)** – 1 hr 25 min 56 sec – in Philadelphia, Pennsylvania, USA. (For a full list of GWR impairment classifications, see p.11.)

In 2021, as Palmiero-Winters, she set the LA2 record for the **fastest 100 miles on a treadmill**, to help launch Guinness World Records' Impairment Initiative (see p.10). Discover another of this endurance athlete's gruelling endeavours opposite.

Most Deaflympics gold medals
· **Male**: Swimmer Terence Parkin (ZAF) accrued 29 golds at the Deaflympic Games between 1997 and 2009. With 33 podium finishes altogether – including a cycling road-race bronze at Taipei 2009 – Parkin has racked up the **most Deaflympics medals** overall.
· **Female**: Australian swimmer Cindy-Lu Bailey won 19 gold medals between 1981 and 1997. Her total tally of 29 medals is also a record, making her the **most decorated Deaflympian (female)**.

FIRST PERSON TO CROSS AN OCEAN IN A MOUTH-CONTROLLED BOAT
Natasha Lambert (UK), who has dyskinetic cerebral palsy, skippered a five-person team across the Atlantic in *Blown Away*, between Gran Canaria and Saint Lucia, from 22 Nov to 11 Dec 2020. Her father fitted the boat with a technology known as "sip and puff", which enables her to control the vessel using only her breath and tongue. The journey lasted 18 days 21 hr 39 min.

On 1 Jul 2013, Lambert – who lives on the Isle of Wight – became the **first person to cross the English Channel in a mouth-controlled boat**. Aged 16, she sailed from the French port of Boulogne to Dover, UK, in 4 hr 30 min.

First amputee to complete the Marathon des Sables
Established in 1986, this six-day ultramarathon across the Sahara Desert in southern Morocco covers 251 km (156 mi) – approximately the same as six regular marathons. In Apr 1996, former British Army Officer Chris Moon (UK) became the first amputee to finish the race. He had lost his right arm and leg during the clearing of a minefield just the previous year.

First expedition to the South Pole by an amputee
Double-amputee Paralympian Cato Zahl Pedersen (NOR), who lost his left arm and half his right arm in an accident aged 14, trekked from Berkner Island, in Antarctica's Ronne-Filchner Ice Shelf, to the South Pole from Nov to Dec 1994. He arrived at the pole on 28 Dec, with fellow Norwegians Odd Harald Hauge and Lars Ebbesen as part of the "Unarmed to the South Pole" expedition. They covered 1,400 km (870 mi) in 56 days.

Royal Navy Officer Alan Lock (UK) completed the **first South Pole expedition by a blind person** between 25 Nov 2011 and 3 Jan 2012. He ventured to the pole from the coast, accompanied by two sighted teammates – Andrew Jensen and Richard Smith – and guide Hannah

MOST INDIVIDUAL GOLD MEDALS WON AT THE ISA WORLD PARA SURFING CHAMPIONSHIP
Between 2015 and 2021, Bruno Hansen (DNK) claimed six golds at the World Para Surfing Championships in California, USA. Hansen has become a legend in the world of adaptive athletics. A car heist left him paralysed from the waist down at the age of 25 and he credits surfing with helping him rebuild his life, praising its physical, mental and spiritual benefits. (See table, right, for more record-setting para surfers.)

ISA WORLD PARA SURFING CHAMPIONS

Title	Record	Holder
Most individual gold medals (female)	3	Melissa Reid (UK, left) & Victoria Feige (CAN, right)
Most individual medals (male)	10	Davi Teixeira & Elias Figue Diel (both BRA)
Most individual medals (female)	6	Alana Nichols (USA)
Most team medals	5	Brazil & USA
Youngest champion	11 years 138 days	Davi Teixeira
Oldest champion	59 years 351 days	Mark "Mono" Stewart (AUS)

Source: International Surfing Association

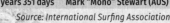

EVEREST AGAINST THE ODDS

First amputee
Tom Whittaker (USA, b. UK): 27 May 1998. Scaled **highest mountain** with a prosthetic foot.

First single-arm amputee
Gary Guller (USA): 23 May 2003. On second attempt, from south side in Nepal.

First female amputee
Arunima Sinha (IND): 21 May 2013. From south side with a below-knee prosthetic leg.

First double amputee (north side)
Mark Inglis (NZ): 15 May 2006. With two prosthetic legs.

First double amputee (south side)
Xia Boyu (CHN): 14 May 2018. With two prosthetic legs.

First blind person
Erik Weihenmayer (USA): 25 May 2001. Also first blind person to climb Seven Summits (2008).

First deaf person (IH2*)
Satoshi Tamura (JPN): 21 May 2016.
*>55 dB hearing loss

MOST HALF MARATHONS COMPLETED IN ONE MONTH

Stacey Kozel (USA) finished 23 half marathons in 18 US states from 18 Jun to 17 Jul 2019. She also walked the **most half marathons with crutches in one year** – 90 – in the 12 months to Feb 2020. Lupus – an autoimmune disease – has left Kozel paralysed from the waist down, but she refuses to let it keep her from her passion of hiking, with the aid of leg braces.

FIRST AMPUTEE TO ROW AN OCEAN SOLO

From 9 Jan to 11 Mar 2019, Lee "Frank" Spencer (UK) rowed the Atlantic from Portimão in Portugal to Cayenne in French Guiana in *Rowing Marine*. At 3,162 nautical mi (5,856 km; 3,639 mi), this is the **farthest rowed solo by an amputee**. His time of 60 days 16 hr 6 min is also the overall **fastest solo row from Europe to South America**.

▶ FARTHEST WHEELCHAIR RAMP JUMP

Wheelchair motocross star Aaron Fotheringham (USA) cleared a 21.35-m (70-ft) gap between ramps on 20 Jul 2018 in California, USA. On the same day, he set two more GWR wheelchair titles: the **tallest quarter-pipe drop-in** and the **highest hand plant** – both 8.4 m (27 ft 6 in).

FIRST DOUBLE-AMPUTEE SKATEBOARDER TO COMPLETE A LOOP THE LOOP

On 8 Oct 2019, Brazil's Felipe Nunes conquered "Tony Hawk's Loop of Death" in Vista, California, USA. His first skateboard was a gift from a neighbour. Its practicality quickly appealed to him and he was soon using a board to get around instead of a wheelchair.

HEAVIEST AIRCRAFT PULLED 100 M BY A WHEELCHAIR TEAM

On 23 Nov 2018, "Wheels4Wings" saw 98 wheelchair users haul a 127.6-tonne (281,310-lb) Boeing 787-9 Dreamliner. Heathrow Airport, British Airways and Aerobility (all UK) facilitated the collaborative feat of strength, which raised funds for disabled people to take part in aviation.

FIRST FEMALE AMPUTEE TO COMPLETE THE MARATHON DES SABLES

Amy Palmiero-Winters (see opposite) finished this demanding race in the Sahara Desert between 7 and 12 Apr 2019. Palmiero-Winters – who trained by doing burpees in a sauna – had her prosthetic leg covered in a heat-reflective paint and modified to house an air chamber for insulation.

FIRST FEMALE TETRAPLEGIC COMPETITIVE RACING DRIVER

On 2 May 2015, Nathalie McGloin (UK) drove on to the Brands Hatch circuit in Kent, UK, having been granted her racing licence just days before. She has since enjoyed a string of Top 10 Porsche Club Championship finishes, and also races in the Classic Sports Car Club, in both cases against able-bodied drivers. In 2016, McGloin co-founded the Spinal Track charity, which gives other disabled drivers the opportunity to race in modified cars.

McGloin's modified Porsche Cayman S enables her to both accelerate and brake using her hands.

Round-Up

First BMX triple flair
On 6 Jan 2022, professional BMXer Kieran Reilly (UK) executed three backflips followed by a 180° rotation at Asylum Skatepark in Sutton-in-Ashfield, Nottinghamshire, UK.

Farthest distance to throw a bull's-eye in darts
Paul Webber (NZ) hit the centre of a dartboard from 7 m (23 ft) in Auckland, New Zealand, on 17 Jul 2021.

Farthest American football field goal blindfolded
Daniel Schuhmacher (DEU) – a punter for Düsseldorf Rhein Fire – kicked a 50-yd (45.7-m) field goal in Cologne, Germany, on 25 Mar 2021. This is longer than five London double-decker buses!

Fastest time to build the LEGO® *Star Wars Millennium Falcon™* (#75192)
On 28 Aug 2021, Joshua LaFrance (USA) constructed Han Solo's iconic spacecraft in 21 hr 36 min 29 sec in Forest, Virginia, USA. At 7,541 pieces, this was formerly the **largest 3D LEGO set** – a record now held by the 135-cm-long (4-ft 5-in) *Titanic* (#10294) at 9,090 pieces.

Fastest time to solve a puzzle cube blindfolded
It took Tommy Cherry (USA) just 14.61 sec to complete a 3x3x3 Rubik's Cube unsighted. His dexterous deed was ratified at the Florida Big & Blind & Time competition in Orlando, USA, on 13 Mar 2022.

The **fastest time to solve three puzzle cubes while juggling** is 4 min 31.01 sec, by Angel Alvarado (COL) in Bogotá, Colombia, on 1 Apr 2022.

Longest time to balance a chainsaw on the forehead
Serial record breaker David Rush (USA) balanced a chainsaw on his brow for 31 min 25 sec in Boise, Idaho, USA, on 14 Dec 2021. The saw was not running at the time.

Longest time spinning three hula hoops while wearing high-heeled roller skates
On 16 Sep 2021, Symoné, aka Rachel Brown (UK), kept a trio of hula hoops spinning for 4 min 3 sec, while atop high-heeled roller skates, in London, UK.

Heaviest vehicle pushed over 100 ft
On 14 May 2021, Troy Conley-Magnusson (AUS) shunted an 11,770-kg (25,948-lb) truck for 100 ft (30.4 m) in Brisbane, Queensland, Australia. Troy's feat raised AUS$20,000 ($15,440; £10,990) for local charities and was dedicated to his mentor, Canada's Kevin Fast (see p.83), and a young leukaemia survivor named Ava.

FASTEST TIME TO DRINK ONE LITRE OF TOMATO SAUCE
On 9 Jul 2021, Mike Jack (CAN) downed one litre (0.26 gal) of pureed tomatoes – i.e., a cooking ingredient, not the condiment – in 1 min 32.54 sec in London, Ontario, Canada. (The **ketchup** record is one 14-oz or 396-g bottle in 17.53 sec by Germany's André Ortolf.) Mike is a vegan competitive eater who wants to use his GWR titles to prove you can be plant-based but still have fun with your food. See below for three more of his superlative scoffs.

Fastest time to eat a lettuce *(minimum weight 163 g; 5.7 oz)*	1 min 31.05 sec	6 Mar 2021
Fastest time to eat three Bhut Jolokia chillies	9.75 sec	26 Jan 2019
Most Bhut Jolokia chillies eaten in one minute	97 g (3.42 oz)	2 Mar 2019

MOST TAP-DANCE WINGS IN ONE MINUTE
Emmy-nominated choreographer Chloe Arnold (USA) executed 123 tap wings in Los Angeles, California, on 13 Apr 2022. In this move, the right leg moves in a clockwise circle as the left leg performs an anti-clockwise circle at the same time.

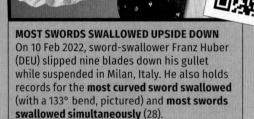

MOST SWORDS SWALLOWED UPSIDE DOWN
On 10 Feb 2022, sword-swallower Franz Huber (DEU) slipped nine blades down his gullet while suspended in Milan, Italy. He also holds records for the **most curved sword swallowed** (with a 133° bend, pictured) and **most swords swallowed simultaneously** (28).

MOST JUGGLING CATCHES OF SIX OBJECTS WITH THE HANDS AND FEET IN 30 SECONDS
On 9 Nov 2021, Kimberly Lester (UK) made 87 catches of half a dozen size-five soccer balls using her palms and soles in Benidorm, Spain. Kimberly is a renowned foot-juggling artist who performs around the world.

LONGEST ICE-HOCKEY MARATHON
The Chestermere Recreation Centre in Alberta, Canada, played host to an epic ice battle lasting 261 hr 15 sec between 30 Mar and 11 Apr 2022. Forty participants played almost a full NHL season's worth of ice time each to raise funds for the Alberta Children's Hospital Foundation.

Longest sports marathons in 2021

Footvolley	24 hr	D Neuhold, L Saurugger, J Hofmann-Wellenhof and K Hofmann-Wellenhof (all AUT)
Outdoor bowls (singles)	28 hr 23 min	Colin Haysham and Nicholas Third (both NZ)
Four square	30 hr 2 min	A Grence, Chris Hetzel, Cole Hetzel, G McElwee, A Harris, M Harris, M Jackman, J Blair, R Turnbill and D Grence (all USA)
Touch rugby	33 hr 33 min	Hoylake Rugby Club (UK)
Five-a-side soccer	75 hr	Permanent Staff, Catterick Garrison (UK)
Basketball	120 hr 2 min	Revelas Family Foundation (USA)

MOST CONSECUTIVE "DOUBLE UNDER TO FROG SKIPS"

Geraldo Alken (NLD) executed seven of these exhausting paired tricks in Papendrecht, Netherlands, on 3 Oct 2021. A "double under" is a jump in which the skipping rope is passed twice under the feet. For a "frog", the challenger then launches into a handstand before pushing back upright and passing the rope under the feet once more before landing.

MOST...

360° horizontal spins in a wind tunnel in one minute: 60, by Fuyuki Kono (JPN) in Koshigaya, Saitama, Japan, on 23 Jul 2021.

Spoons balanced on the body: 85, by Abolfazl Saber Mokhtari (IRN) in Karaj, Iran, on 24 Dec 2021.

Caber tosses in one hour: 161, by Jason Baines (CAN) at the Montreal Highland Games in Quebec, Canada, on 1 Aug 2021.

Consecutive ollies on a skateboard: 323, by David Tavernor (UK) in Norwich, Norfolk, UK, on 23 Aug 2021.

LONGEST SLACKLINE WALK... *

Between cable-cars

On 2 Sep 2021, Yannick Loerwald, Justin Kroppa and Thomas Spöttl (all AUT) each crossed a 65-m (213-ft) slackline between two gondolas suspended 200 m (656 ft) above the Brandnertal valley in Austria.

Between hot-air balloons

A barefoot Quirin Herterich (DEU) walked 88 m (288 ft) along a slackline connecting the tops of two balloons over Rottach-Egern in Tegernsee, Germany, on 10 Oct 2021. The crossing – on a 25-mm-wide (1-in) polyamide band – took 6 min 41 sec, after which Herterich made the return trip and then abseiled to the ground.

Blindfolded

Alexander Schulz (DEU) negotiated a 1,712-m-long (5,616-ft) slackline positioned at a height of 800 m (2,624 ft) above Cañón del Sumidero in Chiapas, Mexico, on 30 Dec 2021. The walk took an hour and a quarter, but the planning for the event lasted two years. The attempt doubled Schulz's personal best for a *non*-blindfolded walk!

*Ratified by the International Slackline Association (ISA)

FARTHEST WASHING-MACHINE THROW

Johan Espenkrona (SWE) hurled a washing machine (minimum weight: 45.3 kg; 99 lb 13 oz) a distance of 4.45 m (14 ft 7 in) in Milan, Italy, on 15 Feb 2022.

On the day, he out-flung Kelvin de Ruiter (NLD), but Kelvin holds multiple GWR titles including the **fastest time to flip a car five times** – 41.27 sec – and **fastest 20 m carrying a piano** – 15.80 sec – both also achieved in Feb 2022.

MOST DRINK CANS RIPPED IN HALF USING THE TEETH

Who needs ring pulls?! On 3 Feb 2022, René "Golem" Richter (CZE) tore open 36 soda cans with his teeth in 60 sec on the set of *Lo Show dei Record* in Milan, Italy. On the same TV programme 10 years earlier, he had achieved the **heaviest weight supported by the mouth**: a wooden bench seating six women and totalling 173.5 kg (382 lb 8 oz).

TALLEST STACK OF PLATFORMS BALANCED ON A ROLLA BOLLA

A rolla bolla – or rocker-roller board – is a piece of circus apparatus comprising a plank balanced on a cylinder. On 20 Sep 2021, Rubel Medini (ITA) erected an 11-layer rack of shelves on top of a single rolla-bolla tube in Benidorm, Spain, and then stood atop it for a minimum of 5 sec.

Tallest Snowman

Olympia is the world's loftiest snowman – well, technically snowwoman! – standing taller than Lady Liberty. This tower of snow briefly dominated the skyline of Bethel in Maine, USA, but we've pictured her here at an iconic location in the country that inspired her name.

The name "Olympia" means "from Olympus", the mountain in Greece that was considered to be the home of the gods. So, to visualize just how enormous our divine snowwoman was, we've relocated her to a rocky hill in the Greek capital of Athens and the ruins of a famous ancient temple: the Parthenon.

The town of Bethel in Oxford County, Maine, gets pummelled each year by three times the average snowfall in the USA. Back in 1999, the townsfolk put the snow to good use by erecting Angus, King of the Mountain, a record-breaking 10-storey-tall snowman that earned the town its first GWR certificate.

Fast-forward to 2008, and when the Bethel Area Chamber of Commerce was looking for ideas to attract tourists to the area, someone suggested revisiting the idea

of building a behemoth snowman and beating their own record...

Finished on 26 Feb that year, after a month's work, the record-breaking Bethel snowwoman soared to 37.21 m (122 ft 1 in), beating Angus by 2.58 m (8 ft 6 in). As giant carrots are rare (see p.86!), local children crafted her nose from wire and cheesecloth; they gave her a beguiling smile made from car tyres, and used skis to make her eyelashes.

The Greek gods may have been immortal, but not so Olympia: five months after her creation, she'd melted away.

The 11-storey Olympia was actually named after the US senator from Maine. Her name? Olympia Snowe!

Eyelashes: eight pairs of skis

Fleece hat: 48 ft (14.6 m) wide

Eyes: 4-ft-wide (1.2-m) wreaths and two tyres for pupils

Lips: five red car tyres

Nose: 8-ft-long (2.4-m) "carrot" of chicken wire and cheesecloth

Scarf: 130 ft (39.6 m) long

Body: 6,500 tons (5,890 tonnes) of snow

Pendant: 6-ft 6-in-wide (1.9-m) snowflake made from the mineral mica

Arms: two 30-ft-tall (9-m) spruce trees

Buttons: three 5-ft-wide (1.5-m) truck tyres

If she'd survived the heat of the Greek sun, Olympia would have stood 23.5 m (77 ft) taller than the Parthenon!

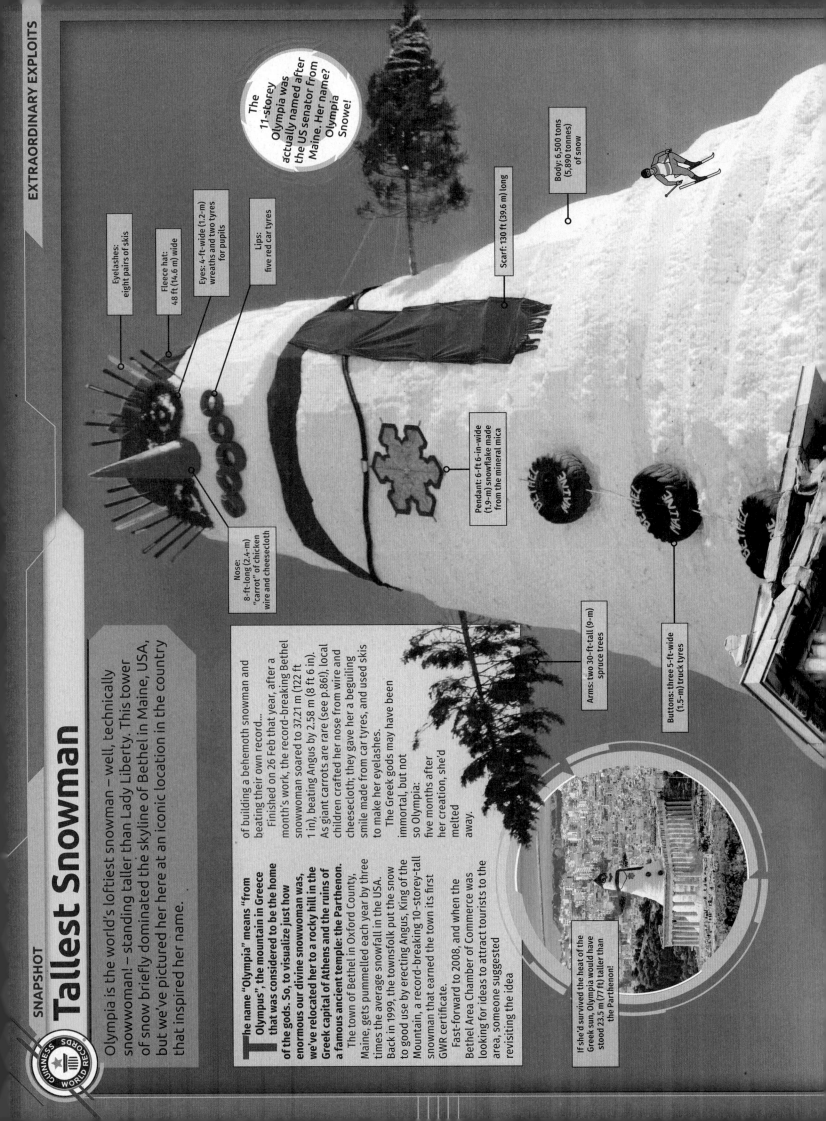

From her heel to the top of her cranium, Lady Liberty on Liberty Island in New York City, USA, stands 34 m (111 ft 1 in) tall – just a few metres shorter than Olympia (measured to the top of her hat).

Wang Guanwutong

A precocious pair of Chinese breakdancers marked GWR Day 2021 in the only way they knew how – by taking to the floor and showing off their skills.

Eleven-year-old Wang Guanwutong has been breakdancing for seven years and has displayed his b-boy moves on Chinese TV. He was five when he first tried air flares – an acrobatic move in which performers support themselves on alternating hands, while rotating their legs in the air. Guanwutong says he spent months falling over before he cracked it, but he loves a challenge and never gave up. On 29 Sep 2021, he performed the **most consecutive air flares (male)** – 94, setting the record on his second attempt.

Even younger is seven-year-old Qi Yufan, nicknamed Guoguo, who despite her tender age has had success in numerous breakdancing contests and already has her eyes set on the Olympics. She broke the **female** (and overall) record, with a dizzying 121 air flares in a row on 10 Oct 2021.

1. Guanwutong is a two-time GWR title holder, having also performed the **most air flares in one minute (male)** – 55 – on *Beyond Dreams* (Tianjin TV) on 30 Jan 2018.

2. No stranger to winning competitions, Guanwutong hopes to one day represent his country at the Olympic Games. Breakdancing will debut as an Olympic discipline at Paris 2024.

When did you first start breakdancing and what attracted you to this sport?
I've been learning breakdance since I was four years old. I saw it on TV and thought it was cool.

Any tips for beginners?
Make sure you do your basic training first, and start slowly with simple step-by-step actions. Breakdancing isn't something you can learn in a day or two. Persevere and never give up.

Who are your inspirations?
My father, who first took me to the dance studio, and my coach, Geng Bin.

What has been the highlight of your competitive breakdancing career?
Dancing with my idol, [French hip-hop dancer] Bouboo, in his final performance on *Street Dance of China Season III*. And achieving two Guinness World Records record titles!

How does it feel to have two records?
It's a pleasure and an honour. If you work hard, your dream will come true.

Do you foresee breakdancing being your long-term career?
The road ahead is long and unpredictable, but I'll continue to dance. It has become an integral part of my life. And in the future, I'm going to get a lot more people dancing!

Qi Yufan

When did you start breakdancing?
I got into breakdancing in Oct 2018, when I was four-and-a-half years old. I fell in love with it watching hip-hop reality shows with my dad.

How often do you train?
Every day – less on school days, but longer at weekends.

What's the best thing about breakdancing?
It brings me joy and has helped me make lots of friends.

Who inspires you in the world of breakdancing?
My dad. Although he isn't a dancer, he learns through videos and asks the teacher for advice.

What do your family and friends think about you being a record breaker?
They were very happy and proud of me. Though my mum told me I shouldn't become arrogant!

What are your future breakdancing ambitions?
I'll keep dancing. I want to put myself on the best stage – for example, the Olympics.

1. Yufan keeps her GWR certificate hanging on her bedroom wall. "I look at it every day," she says. "It's a reward and it keeps me going."

2. Even though she's taken part in many breakdancing competitions, Yufan admits that she still gets nervous. Her advice to beginners is to "listen to music and practise!"

Michael "Dog" Artiaga

When Michael Artiaga (USA, b. 20 Nov 2007) entered the 2020 Classic *Tetris* World Championship (CTWC), he had no idea that he'd make history – or that the final player standing between him and glory would be his own brother!

Michael – aka DogPlayingTetris, or Dog for short – has always been interested in electronics, and began coding at the age of five. But he only started playing *Tetris* on the NES in 2019, inspired by 16-year-old Joseph Saelee's victory at the 2018 CTWC.

In Dec 2020, Michael and his elder brother, Andy (aka PixelAndy), joined 300 qualifiers for that year's tournament and battled all the way to the final. The nail-biting showdown on 6 Dec went to a deciding fifth set, with both siblings reaching the kill screen; however, Michael scored a "max-out" (999,999 points) to clinch a blockbuster victory. Aged just 13 years 16 days, he had become the **youngest winner of the Classic *Tetris* World Championship**.

1. Michael and Andy with their parents – who were "super-excited" to watch their sons battle it out in the finals.

2. Michael received $3,000 (£2,265) in prize money, with which he bought a drum kit and a guitar, and also invested in cryptocurrency (see pp.202–03).

3. The 2020 CTWC event was held online, so each Artiaga brother was based in a different room of their house. Moments after Michael's victory in their head-to-head final (pictured), Andy came through to offer him a congratulatory high-five.

4. The Artiaga brothers with their trophies. Michael followed up his 2020 title with a second in 2021, beating Jacob Huff by three games to one; brother Andy finished fourth in 2021.

What was your introduction to *Tetris*?
I first played *Tetris* on an old Game Boy my dad owned, but I wasn't too into it. It was only after I watched the 2018 Joseph Saelee vs Jonas Neubauer finals video at the CTWC that I became hooked.

What is it about the game that appeals to you?
Tetris is different to other games that are played competitively, because of the amount of quick thinking and comprehension it requires.

What is "hypertapping"?
It's a technique where instead of holding down the buttons, you tap them more than 10 times per second. Before hypertapping, people simply held down the right and left buttons to move the pieces, which wasn't very fast.

Are you good at other videogames?
I'm pretty decent at *Super Mario Bros.* speedrunning. It's a game that actually has a lot of overlap with the *Tetris* community.

What was it like to compete against – and beat – your brother?
It was surreal. It was our first time competing in the world championship, so we weren't expecting to both get to the finals. When we competed, we were just hoping to play our best game. Finishing first and second was pretty awesome.

How does it feel to know that you're the best in the world at something?
It's pretty unbelievable when I think about it. When I started playing *Tetris*, I never expected to get anywhere close to the pros. It felt great when there were people congratulating me all around the world when I won. It's changed my life a lot.

What does it mean to be recognized by Guinness World Records?
It's a dream. I remember thumbing through *GWR* books at school and watching videos on YouTube. I never would have expected to be featured myself.

To discover more about record-breaking young achievers, visit **kids.guinnessworldrecords.com**

Abhimanyu Mishra

Imagine a "chess Grandmaster". Odds are you are picturing someone of, shall we say, more advanced years…? But Abhimanyu "Abhi" Mishra (b. 5 Feb 2009) from New Jersey, USA, is toppling preconceptions around age as deftly as he topples his adversaries' chess pieces.

While competing in Hungary on 30 Jun 2021, Abhi chalked up his third "Grandmaster norm" event win. This, in turn, pushed his Elo rating (a score by which chess players' skill level is quantified) over the 2,500-point threshold. Together, these achievements meant that not only could he claim the esteemed "GM" badge of honour but, aged 12 years 145 days, Abhi is the **youngest chess Grandmaster** in the game's history.

The chess prodigy isn't content to stop there, though. "Now that I'm a Grandmaster, the actual journey begins. There's so much to learn and execute and I want to be a Super Grandmaster [Elo rating of 2,700 points] by the age of 15. My ultimate goal is to be a World Champion one day."

What was your introduction to chess?
My father introduced me to chess when I was two-and-a-half years of age. I started playing the tournaments when I was five. My father inspired me as he was my first teacher.

At what stage did you realize you had a special affinity for the game?
Because I was introduced to chess very early on, it became part of my life. After I started playing in the tournaments, I realized that it's so much fun and started loving it even more.

What are the benefits of playing chess?
Chess helps you with your analytical skills and calculations. Chess is very close to real life. It helps in making informed decisions.

Did you ever see yourself becoming a Grandmaster?
I've always aspired to be the **youngest Grandmaster** since I started playing chess. On the way to achieving this record, I had to reach many other milestones, including becoming the **youngest International Master** [aged 10 years 276 days].

How many hours do you practise each day?
Since the pandemic, I've worked 10–12 hours a day, but generally, it's 7–8 hours of chess; that includes learning about game openings, middle and end games, doing tactics, and playing chess online.

If you could play anyone at chess, from any time in history, who would it be?
I'd have loved to play [World Chess Champion] Bobby Fischer. His love for the game was unparalleled. His devotion [was proven] by the fact he learned Russian, as all the chess literature at that time was in that language.

Where do you see yourself in 10 years' time?
I want to be the very best in the chess world and rule it like a king. I see myself competing in the World Chess Championship – or maybe I'll *be* the World Champion!

1. Abhimanyu has become a star in the chess community, particularly since becoming a Grandmaster. He has secured worldwide press coverage including a cover feature in *Chess Life* magazine.

2. For a break from the chess board, Abhi likes to read books and play videogames.

3. Abhi claimed his first-ever winner's trophy at a tournament when he was just five years old.

4. Current World Champion Magnus Carlsen is one of Abhi's heroes: "There are so many things we can all learn from him," he says.

5. The **youngest female Grandmaster** is Hou Yifan (CHN, b. 27 Feb 1994), who reached this level in 2008 aged 14 years 184 days.

To discover more about record-breaking young achievers, visit kids.guinnessworldrecords.com

Scarlett Cheng

If there's one thing Scarlett Cheng (CHN) knows, it's that you're never too young to start collecting. She has amassed the ◎ largest collection of lip balms – verified on 24 Apr 2021 at a gob-smacking 3,388 items – at the age of just seven!

Scarlett lives in Hong Kong, China, with her family and her trove of lip moisturizers. Pride of place is her very first balm, a present from her grandmother (see 3). From that humble beginning, Scarlett has built up an international collection, with examples from countries as far away as Israel, the USA and Sweden. She has lip balms that taste like her favourite candies – Skittles and M&Ms – and even some flavoured like breakfast cereals!

Scarlett is assisted in the curation of her collection by her elder sister, nine-year-old Kaylyn. The pair even like to make their own organic lip balms and distribute them among their family and friends. For Scarlett, collecting beautiful things brings a lot of "joy and fun".

Why did you start collecting lip balms?
We went to Japan during a winter break and the weather was so dry my lips were cracking. So we went to a pharmacy and there were so many cute lip balms and flavours to choose from – that's when I fell in love! We ended up buying the special ones and trying them all.

Where do you keep all of your lip balms?
I display some of my favourites in my room and store the rest of my collection in labelled boxes. Luckily, lip balms are relatively small items and don't take up too much space.

What are the rarest items in your collection?
The Sour Patch Kids lip balms were really hard to find in Hong Kong. I managed to track them down in the USA.

Are there any lip balms you don't have that you would like to own?
I wish I could have my own lip-balm brand, with my name and face on them!

What do your family and friends think of you being a world record holder?
Many of them were amazed, as they didn't know that I'd collected so many. Everyone is very excited for me and proud.

Tell us an interesting fact about lip balms.
Lip balms have been around since the 1800s. Isn't that incredible?!

1. Scarlett with her mum, Joyce. Her parents fully support their daughter's passion for lip moisturizers.

2. As big fans of the *Guinness World Records* books, Scarlett and her sister Kaylyn had even more reason to celebrate earning a place in GWR history. According to the family, achieving an official GWR title is an "unforgettable" feat.

3. Scarlett's first-ever lip balm is her favourite. A gift from her grandmother, it features the cat Marie from the Disney film *The Aristocats* (1970).

4. Scarlett and Kaylyn have also become experts at making their own DIY lip balms at home using wax and essential oils.

Olivier Rioux

Whether on the basketball court or just walking down the street, Olivier Rioux of Quebec, Canada, is used to standing out from the crowd. The 7-ft-tall teen is making the most of his superlative stature and is on track for sporting fame.

By the age of three, it was already clear that Olivier was growing at a far faster rate than other children. His parents were determined to make sure that he felt positive and proud of his stature, and they encouraged him to take up sports. At the age of five – when he was already 157 cm (5 ft 2 in)! – Olivier began playing basketball. Now he hopes to make it as a professional, and is currently part of the IMG Academy team in Bradenton, Florida, USA.

Applying for a Guinness World Records title was Olivier's own idea. He had been browsing a *GWR* book when he saw that he was bigger than the then ❍ **tallest teenager**. On 19 Dec 2020, aged 14, Olivier's height was verified at 226.9 cm (7 ft 5.3 in): the record was his.

Do you know why you are so tall?
The doctors investigated and think it can only be explained by our family's genes. My father is 203 cm [6 ft 8 in], my mom is 187 cm [6 ft 2 in] and my older brother is 205 cm [6 ft 9 in].

How do you feel about being the height you are?
I love it. I was always taller than the rest of my friends at school or my teammates. This is what nature planned for me. I learned to be peaceful and happy about it.

What's the best thing about being so tall?
I am noticed anywhere I go. I enjoy interacting with people that come to see me, because every reaction is special.

What do your opponents say when they see you at a basketball game?
I'd say that they are impressed to begin with, but that doesn't make them less physical in the game!

What hobbies or interests do you have outside basketball?
I like to do abstract drawing.

What's your plan for the future?
I'm aiming for a pro basketball career, and I plan to do all that it takes to achieve this. I also hope that I'll have the opportunity to impact my community through environmental action.

What does it mean to have a GWR certificate?
For me it's an achievement because I have been reading *GWR* books since I was a kid.

1. Regimes such as the Brookwood Elite summer programme in Quebec have helped Olivier hone his basketball skills. Coaches have praised his good hands and passing skills.

2. Olivier with his family: (from left) brother Émile, father Jean-François and mother Anne Gariepy.

3. Olivier says that the worst thing about his height is having to duck through doorways, as "sometimes I hit my head and it hurts".

4. One of Olivier's favourite characters is the tree-like alien Groot from *Guardians of the Galaxy*, because "he is tall, friendly and still growing".

Tyler Hainey

Scooter prodigy Tyler Hainey (UK) has been flipping head over heels for years. Having mastered the single and double backflip, he was ready for the next challenge: to break a record set a decade ago by one of his heroes.

From the moment he began to ride his first kick scooter, Tyler was a natural. In 2018, he landed his first backflip – at the age of just six! That same year, he became the under-eight UK champion, and he continued to put in the hours on the ramps. Not even the occasional crash could stop him, despite splitting his chin after one particularly nasty fall. In 2021, a video showing Tyler landing his first double backflip went viral, receiving more than 100 million views across social media.

But could Tyler take the record for **most kick-scooter backflips in one minute** from freestyle legend Dakota Schuetz? Kota's mark of 12 had stood since 2012, but on 15 Jan 2022 Tyler executed 15 backflips in 60 sec. And on 18 Feb 2022, Tyler also secured the **front flip** record – six in one minute – in Milan, Italy.

Why did you first start riding a scooter?
I saw a scooter in a toy shop one day and I'd seen the cool tricks you could do on YouTube videos, so I wanted to try it.

What about other street sports?
I actually rode a motocross bike at the age of three, and I can backflip a BMX as well!

How did it feel when you landed your first backflip in 2018?
It was the best feeling, as it was *soooo* scary but also cool, as I'd put lots of work into learning it.

...and how about pulling off the double backflip in 2021?
The day I did it was just amazing – my emotions showed how much it meant to me. I'd worked at it for more than three years and I never gave up. Even though I landed on my head once and it really, really hurt, I knew I could do it.

How much time do you spend training?
Three or four days a week – normally for a few hours, but sometimes the whole day.

What other things do you like to do?
I love going to the gym, kickboxing and also trampolining, as it helps with scooter tricks.

Do you think scooter riding might become an Olympic event one day?
I really hope so, as I'd love to take part in the Olympics on my scooter!

Any tips for other kids thinking of taking their scooter to the local skate park?
The best thing to do is get some pads and a helmet, and just start riding and getting comfortable. Then you can start on some small ramps. Riding with friends is really good for helping with nerves.

1. Tyler with his idol Ryan Williams, a scooter rider with Nitro Circus.

2. As part of the Scooter Boys, Tyler (second from right) wowed the judges of *Britain's Got Talent* with his daredevil riding in 2022.

3. Topping the podium at Scoot Jam in Oct 2018, with pals Sam Voke (second) and Helian González Piñeiro (third).

4. Tyler practises in his back garden on a home-made ramp constructed by his dad, Brian.

To discover more about record-breaking young achievers, visit kids.guinnessworldrecords.com

109

Rafał Biros

1

2

Rafał Biros (POL, b. 28 Apr 2008) is a cosmic citizen scientist, one of many amateurs who pore over images from space to find something noteworthy. In 2020, this stargazer became a star in his own right.

Inspired by his uncle (see **4**), he signed up to NASA's Sungrazer Project, giving him access to pictures taken by the *Solar and Heliospheric Observatory* (*SOHO*). On 13 Nov 2020, Rafał spotted a curious moving blob in the images. It later emerged that, at 12 years 199 days old, he had become the **youngest person to discover a comet** – a celestial snowball of rock and ice, in this case only 10 m (32 ft) wide at most. "I'm still shocked this actually happened," Rafał (pictured with his family, right) admitted to *Forbes*. "It's amazing to have achieved something like that."

Rafał's find proves that astronomy – like breaking records – is open to all, from schoolkids to OAPs. Anyone can look through *SOHO*'s image bank via their website (**sungrazer.nrl.navy.mil**). So, comet hunters: what are you waiting for?

3

4

5

How long have you been interested in astronomy?
I first became intrigued by the subject in kindergarten. I got back to it in May 2020, while distance-learning during the COVID lockdown. Then I started looking for comets.

Who are your inspirations?
I got to know about the Sungrazer Project thanks to my Uncle Szymon, who taught me comet hunting. I was also inspired by the Polish astronomer Michał Kusiak. It was a real pleasure to meet him in person (**2**).

Tell us about the moment you realized you may have found a comet.
When I reported the object, I was 99% sure it was a comet. I was shocked that I'd done it. Then I waited anxiously for confirmation of my first discovery!

Has your first comet received a name?
It was named SOHO-4094. In the Sungrazer Project, explorers don't name objects.

Have you discovered any more?
I'm currently the discoverer of 11 comets. Ten of them belong to the Kreutz group and one to the Meyer group.

What are your favourite cosmic phenomena?
My favourite objects in the sky are comets, of course. But also deep-sky objects such as nebulae and galaxies. Unfortunately, they're very difficult to observe.

What other hobbies do you have?
I'm also into genealogy and I'm making my own family tree. Finding my ancestors is a fascinating process as well.

How does it feel to be in the *Guinness World Records* book?
It's a great feeling! I feel really honoured and proud to be part of the GWR family.

1. Operated jointly by NASA and the ESA, *SOHO* has led to the detection of more than 4,300 comets to date.

2. Astronomer Michał Kusiak – discoverer of 160 comets and a fellow Pole – is one of Rafał's heroes.

3. The split-tailed comet NEOWISE – found in 2020 – and the Moon, photographed by Rafał and his Uncle Szymon.

4. Rafał caught the comet-hunting bug from his uncle – but he insists there's no rivalry between them!

5. Rafał in Olsztyn, Poland, paying homage to a statue of the 16th-century Polish astronomer Copernicus, who placed the Sun (not Earth) at the centre of the universe.

To discover more about record-breaking young achievers, visit
kids.guinnessworldrecords.com

Brooke Cressey

Take one extraordinary number-cruncher, add an innovative app designed to enhance mathematical performance, and what's the result? A new GWR title holder!

Times Tables Rock Stars (*TTRS*) is a daily programme of exercises used by many schools to hone number skills. One user who took to it immediately was Brooke Cressey (UK). In 2021, aged eight, she was competing against nearly 400,000 other mathematically minded youngsters in the *TTRS* England Rocks contest, a series of against-the-clock multiplication and division challenges. She won decisively, correctly answering 41,627 questions in under four hours – a rate of 173 per minute!

A month later on 3 Dec, she achieved the **highest score on *Times Tables Rock Stars* in one minute** – 210 – at home in Kent, UK. Her father, Mark, is in awe of his daughter's speedy calculations, revealing that she'll even stop blinking while on *TTRS*, as it breaks her rhythm! And Brooke's GWR journey has only just begun... she's already planning to better her own record.

BROOKE CRESSEY

ENGLAND ROCKS 2021

MOST VALUABLE PLAYER
In any school
ENGLAND ROCKS 2021
08.11.2021 - 11.11.2021

Position		Student score
1	HEATH FOX Scotney 2021/22	41,627
2	FLEA BLACK	38,747
3	ADAM ECHO	35,969
4	SERGEANT SANSONE	35,929
5	JESSE ROCKSON	35,775
6	TAV GREEN	35,078
7	JAKE BURNS	34,124
8	ROYAL STORM	33,146
9	BELLA REECE	33,102
10	AMAZON WILDDOG	32,77

Have you always enjoyed maths?
Well, I've always liked working through times tables. And when I discovered the *TT Rock Stars* app, I fell in love with it. I began using it sometime around the end of Sep 2020 and I still have a video of my first few goes at home!

Can you remember your first ever score?
I got 28.

How long did it take to build up to your current record-breaking speed?
It took me around six months. By May 2021, I was getting scores of more than 200.

Do you think you could improve on your total of 210 sums in a minute?
Yes, absolutely! The day after I did the world record, I got my best score of 211 in "Garage" mode, although that was unofficial.

Can you offer any expert tips for anyone looking to take on the *TTRS* challenge?
It takes lots of practice and determination. Plus, it's important not to feel any pressure.

What do your family and friends think of you setting a world record?
They're all very proud – although it's led to me gaining some new nicknames. Now they call me a robot and the Human Calculator!

You beat some 400,000 pupils at the *TTRS* England Rocks 2021 competition. Were you confident you could win?
To be quite honest... yes! I became convinced I could do it, but only after I started getting my high scores regularly.

Finally, what would you say to someone who thinks that maths is boring?
That's OK – we all have our own opinions. But maths can really be fun with things like *TT Rock Stars*! So why not try it for yourself?

GUINNESS WORLD RECORDS

CERTIFICATE

The highest score achieved on Times Tables Rock Stars in one minute is 210, and was achieved by Brooke Cressey (UK) in Sittingbourne, Kent, UK, on 3 December 2021

OFFICIALLY AMAZING

1. Brooke with dad Mark, mum Shelley and sister Paige. Her parents openly admit there's no precedent in the family for Brooke's skill with numbers.

2. The maths marvel puts in around 30 minutes of practice on *TTRS* every morning. She can answer three multiplication questions per second!

3. Brooke proudly shows off the spoils of her success: trophies and *TTRS* merch.

4. Her triumph at *TTRS* England Rocks 2021 – under the pseudonym "Heath Fox" – saw Brooke correctly answer a remarkable 2,880 questions more than her closest rival. Naturally, she was the MVP.

GARAGE

ALL TRAINING LEVELS PASSED

NO MORE GIGS

Lucky Diamond Rich

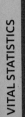

VITAL STATISTICS

Name	Lucky Diamond Rich (b. Gregory McLaren)
Birthplace	New Zealand
Current GWR title	**Most tattooed man**
Skills	Unicycling, sword-swallowing, chainsaw-juggling
Other body modifications	Piercings, stretched earlobes and silver tooth veneers

For **Lucky Diamond Rich, performing came naturally. Not content with juggling chainsaws and swallowing swords, he used his skin as a canvas and turned himself into a living artwork.**

Born Gregory McLaren in New Zealand, Lucky joined a travelling circus as a teenager and received his first tattoo aged 16 – a small juggling club, which he had placed on his hip because he was worried his mother wouldn't approve! Lucky was instantly attracted to what was then a subversive art form, and he described his early tattoos as "postcards", representing all the different areas he had visited.

As his performing career took off, Lucky decided to experiment with layering, and had his designs overlaid with a 100% coating of black ink – including the eyelids, ears and gums. This was then overlaid in parts with white, and more coloured designs added on top! Lucky's devotion to ink was finally recognized in 2006, when GWR named him the ◎ **most tattooed man**. Today, his coverage exceeds 200%.

Lucky estimates that he has spent more than 1,000 hours having his body modified by hundreds of artists. These days, though, he prefers tattooing others, and has stepped back from performing. He's proud to share his family's Aboriginal heritage with the Quandamooka people of North Stradbroke Island in Queensland, Australia, and is now a support worker at an alcohol and drug recovery centre in Victoria, where he assists Aboriginal men with their rehabilitation.

1

Lucky has multiple layers of tattoo, with full-colour designs inked on top of his all-over black body suit.

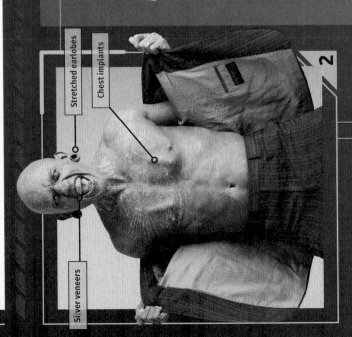

2

Stretched earlobes

Chest implants

Silver veneers

4. Posing on a 10-ft-tall (3-m) unicycle for a GWR photo-shoot with Editor-in-Chief, Craig Glenday, looking on. Lucky says that being a GWR title holder is an "honour and a privilege", and that he enjoys being recognized from his book appearances.

5. Lucky surpassed the record held by the UK's Tom Leppard, the "Leopard Man of Skye", who had 99.5% ink coverage. Lucky states that he has had it easier than earlier tattoo record holders, as many of the stigmas historically attached to the tattoo art form have since been dispelled.

1. Lucky pictured with his proud mother before embarking on his record-breaking tattooing odyssey... and before he acquired his current name: "I'm lucky by nature, rough diamonds are the most precious and my spirit has become rich from learning about how to be a good human!"

2. "Everyone's different with how they react to me," says Lucky. "But it's like the weather: I can't change it so I just have to accept it." He adds: "Under this skin, I'm no different to anyone else, I'm just heavily tattooed... What other people think of me is none of my business! I'm comfortable in my own skin today."

3. Lucky is proud of his native heritage, and is seen here bearing the Australian Aboriginal flag. It was designed by Harold Thomas of the Luritja people, and has protected legal and political status.

Find out more about Lucky in the Hall of Fame section at www. guinnessworldrecords.com/2023

Itinerary

Despite its repeated use on book covers, one form of transport that Phileas Fogg doesn't use in the novel is a hot-air balloon!!

Novel inspiration
Our globetrotting survey of superlatives is inspired by Jules Verne's 1873 book Around the World in Eighty Days, which will celebrate its 150th anniversary in 2023. Can amateur adventurer Phileas Fogg and his valet Passepartout win a bet by circling the globe within the slim time frame?

AROUND THE WORLD
IN EIGHTY DAYS
JULES VERNE

ILLUSTRATED FIRST EDITION

Around the World in 300 Records

Welcome aboard GWR's Global Grand Tour!
Since the COVID-19 pandemic, we've all had
to get used to travelling less frequently. So to
keep your spirit of adventure alive and well, GWR
is bringing the world to you! At each stop on our virtual
circumnavigation of record-breaking locations, you'll
find an "At a glance" box of stats and facts, followed
by our selection of must-see superlatives. Think of it
as an appetite-whetter... Who knows, once lockdowns
and face coverings are finally a thing of the past,
this imaginary tour could become your springboard
to new adventures in the real world! Bon voyage!

USA

1: Gateway Arch

Wherever you are in St Louis, Missouri, you'll likely spot the city's majestic Gateway Arch. The **tallest commemorative monument**, it rises to 192 m (630 ft) – the equivalent of 63 storeys – with a span of the same width. The stainless-steel edifice was completed on 28 Oct 1965 to memorialize the westward expansion across the continent after the Louisiana Purchase of 1803, when the state was bought from Napoleon's France – a transaction that doubled the size of the USA at the time. For a commanding view extending nearly 50 km (30 mi), take a tram ride to the top of the arch.

2: Cedar Point Amusement Park

Adrenaline junkies will be spoiled for choice at this entertainment extravaganza in Sandusky, Ohio. Expect non-stop thrills with the **most rides in an amusement park** – 72 at the last count. Among the 17 rollercoasters there is the 420-ft-tall (128-m) Top Thrill Dragster, the world's **first strata rollercoaster**. This is defined as a coaster with a full-circuit track and a drop of 400–499 ft (121.9–152 m). Hold on tight!

3: The Narrows

Zion National Park in Utah is a haven for campers and hikers. Its host of natural wonders includes Crawford Arch, a curved rock formation whose apex is c. 300 m (1,000 ft) above the ground. But for one of its most beguiling sights, visit The Narrows – the world's **deepest slot canyon**. Forged as the waters of the Virgin River cut through the Navajo Sandstone, it's some 600 m (2,000 ft) deep, yet its walls are just 10 m (32 ft) apart at most. It snakes for 25 km (16 mi) through the park, and takes around 13 hours to walk.

4: Dollywood

Dolly Parton is a country-music icon, rising from "dirt-poor" roots (her words) to achieve stellar success. She has notched up the **most decades with a Top 20 hit on Billboard's Hot Country Songs chart** – six. Her Dollywood theme park in Pigeon Forge, Tennessee, pairs rollercoasters and thrill rides with gentler experiences, such as the Dollywood Express heritage narrow-gauge railway. And, of course, plenty of live music.

5: Graceland

Another Tennessee must-see is this Colonial Revival-style mansion in Memphis. It was bought in 1957 by Elvis Presley, who – 45 years after his death – remains the **bestselling solo artist**, with 1 billion sales worldwide. Join the hundreds of thousands of fans who trek here annually to marvel at the kitsch delights of the Jungle Room and chart the course of The King's remarkable life in the Trophy Building.

6: State Theatre

Film buffs touring the Midwest will want to stop off in Washington, Iowa, for screen time at the **oldest continuously operating cinema**. This venerable movie house opened its doors on 14 May 1897, and as of 5 Jan 2022 had been in continuous operation for 124 years 236 days. The first moving picture to appear here was shown using a cinématographe made in Paris, with tickets as cheap as 15¢ each (about $5 or £3.60 today).

7: Mauna Loa

Hawaii may be an idyllic holiday destination, but it's also home to Mauna Loa, the **largest active volcano**. Its broad, gentle dome is 120 km (75 mi) long and 50 km (31 mi) wide, with hardened lava flows that occupy more than 5,125 km² (1,980 sq mi) of the island. It has blown its top 33 times since 1843, the year of its first confirmed eruption.

8: Dodger Stadium

The Brooklyn Dodgers quit their native New York in 1957 to head for sunny California and rename themselves the Los Angeles Dodgers. Since Dodger Stadium opened in 1962, nearly 150 million fans have trooped into it. It's the **largest Major League Baseball stadium** by seating capacity, accommodating 56,000 fans in its standard configuration. (True, the Oakland Coliseum has the potential to seat more, but only when additional sections are opened up.) The park has also seen concerts by acclaimed artists such as The Beatles, Michael Jackson and Beyoncé (see pp.164–65), so why not book yourself in for a game or a gig?

9: San Antonio

Anyone hooked on tales of the Wild West should high-tail it to this Texan city to see the Alamo Mission. In 1836, around 200 besieged fighters including Davy Crockett and James Bowie held out here for 13 days against some 2,500 Mexican troops before being overcome. A fitting location, then, for the ◐ **tallest cowboy-boot sculpture**. Standing 10.74 m (35 ft 3 in) tall, it's the work of Bob "Daddy-O" Wade, and proof positive that everything's bigger in Texas. Find it outside the North Star Mall at 7400 San Pedro Avenue.

10: Hyperion

Somewhere within California's Redwood National Park stands a superlative <u>Sequoia sempervirens</u>, or coast redwood. Nicknamed Hyperion, it's the **tallest tree**, having reached 116.07 m (380 ft 9.7 in) by 2019 – comfortably surpassing the height of London's Elizabeth Tower (better known as "Big Ben"). This titan of the forest also has the **deepest crown** (measured from its top to the start of the foliage), at 90.9 m (298 ft 2.7 in). Hyperion was discovered on 25 Aug 2006, but its location has remained a closely guarded secret in an effort to protect it.

11: Devils Tower

This photo-op-friendly mound in Wyoming was created more than 50 million years ago after lava pushed through the sedimentary rock, then gradually cooled and shrank. As the enclosing softer rock eroded away over time, the freestanding monolithic landmark emerged. It's composed of the **tallest volcanic columns** – some soaring to 867 ft (264 m) above the plains. Fans of classic sci-fi movies will know it as the mysterious mountain in Steven Spielberg's <u>Close Encounters of the Third Kind</u> (USA, 1977).

12: The Best Man

Forget Las Vegas: anyone seeking a truly "quick" wedding should head for Shelbyville, Illinois. It's home to the **fastest wedding chapel** – the <u>Best Man</u>, which can hit speeds of 99 km/h (62 mph). The Reverend Darrell Best fitted out this former fire truck with stained-glass windows, pews, a pulpit and even a pipe organ. Couples can get hitched on the road, or parked up at a site of their choice... then hitch a ride on the chapel to their reception!

At a glance

- **Area:** 9,833,517 km²
- **Population:** 334.9 million
- **Key Facts:** The USA boasts some major superlatives, including the world's **largest economy**, with an estimated GDP of $22.94 trillion as of Oct 2021, according to the International Monetary Fund. Given its vast expanse, it's little wonder that the country also has the **most airports** – 19,919, according to the most recent figures. Trivia note: did you know there have been 27 versions of the "Stars and Stripes" flag since its adoption as the USA's standard in 1775?

ROUTE 66

USA 20¢
UNITED STATES AIR MAIL

Canada

At a glance

- **Area:** 9,984,670 km²
- **Population:** 37.9 million
- **Key Facts:** Canada is the second-largest country by area, and shares the world's **longest boundary** with the USA, at 8,963 km. It also has the **longest coastline**, at 243,798 km – including tens of thousands of islands – and is home to the **largest island created as a direct result of human action**: Quebec's 2,020-km² Île René-Levasseur, formed when the Manicouagan Reservoir was deliberately flooded, is large enough to fit New York City 2.5 times over.

1: Peak 2 Peak Gondola
Got a head for heights? Then make for Whistler in British Columbia, where you'll find the **highest cable-car above ground** – 436 m (1,430 ft) at its loftiest. It's not one for acrophobics, as this is about 55 m (180 ft) higher than the roof of the Empire State Building. For an added thrill, you can even choose a special glass-bottomed gondola! The cable-way runs for around 4.4 km (2.7 mi) and connects the peaks of the Whistler and Blackcomb mountains. The ride also includes the **longest unsupported span between two cable-car towers** – a gap of 3.02 km (1.87 mi).

2: Festival de la Galette de Sarrasin
There's a smorgasbord of incentives to visit this Quebecois buckwheat-crêpe-themed event, from the mouth-watering dishes to eye-catching traditional crafts. And had you been there on 3 Aug 2019, you could have witnessed the **largest demolition derby**. This superlative wrecking extravaganza saw 125 daredevil drivers tear around a dirt track for 50 min in Saint-Lazare-de-Bellechasse, courtesy of organizers Nicolas Tremblay, Julien Fournier and Paul Morin. Driving a 2001 Toyota Corolla, Mathieu Langlois was the eventual winner, walking away with a prize of CAN$10,000 ($7,563; £6,233).

3: Saint-Louis-du-Ha! Ha!
Only in Canada can you send home a postcard from a town that boasts the **most exclamation marks in a place name**! This Quebecois municipality (population: 1,318) was christened with its uniquely double-barrelled appellation in 1874. "Ha! Ha!" refers to the archaic French word "hâ-hâ", a landscape feature that creates or acts as an invisible boundary line, in this case most probably the nearby Lake Témiscouata.

4: Rogers Centre
Home to the Toronto Blue Jays baseball team, and formerly known as the SkyDome, this stadium can accommodate 67,000 concert-goers, 55,000 Canadian football fans and 50,600 baseball aficionados (although not all at the same time!) It's perhaps best known, however, for housing the **largest retractable roof**. Completed in Jun 1989, it spans 209 m (685 ft) at its widest and covers an area of 3.2 ha (8 acres). It takes 20 min to open, and once the roof is fully retracted the entire field and 91% of the seats are uncovered.

5: CN Tower
Chances are that if you stop off in Toronto you'll see the CN Tower – whether you're planning to or not – for this communications and observation tower rises 553.34 m (1,815 ft 5 in)

Pitch-perfect view
With the roof of the Rogers Centre open, the nearby CN Tower can look down on Toronto Blue Jays' home games. <u>GWR</u>'s founding editor Ross McWhirter was at hand when the tower's antenna was fitted, to confirm it as the **tallest tower**, a title it held for more than 30 years. In 1999, Ashrita Furman spent nearly an hour climbing its steps the hard way – by pogo stick! (See opposite.)

Saint-Louis-du-Ha! Ha! 6
Rivière-du-Loup 54

into the city sky. Topped out on 2 Apr 1975, it was once the **tallest structure** and **tower** (until the completion of the Burj Khalifa and Canton Tower, respectively).

Running around the top of its 360 Restaurant, a giddy 356 m (1,167 ft 11 in) above ground level, is the **highest external walk on a building**. If you're brave enough to give it a go, you'll experience a "hands-free", harness-secured "edgewalk" along a ledge just 1.5 m (5 ft) wide. (See how relaxed <u>GWR</u> Editor-in-Chief Craig Glenday is in the photo below!)

You can reach the LookOut Level observation platform at 346 m (1,135 ft) in less than a minute, via one of six glass-fronted elevators outside. But if you're serial GWR title holder Ashrita Furman (USA), that's insultingly easy. On 23 Jul 1999, he achieved the **fastest time to pogo-stick up the CN Tower**, bouncing its 1,899 steps in 57 min 51 sec.

6: Windsor Pumpkin Regatta
This annual competition sees contestants paddle 800 m (2,624 ft) across Nova Scotia's Lake Pesaquid in "personal vegetable craft" – that's hollowed-out pumpkin gourds to the rest of us! And yes, motorized pumpkins are allowed. The event marked its 21st year in 2019, making it the **longest-running pumpkin boat race**. And though COVID-19 restrictions put things on hold for the following two years, hopes are high for 2022.

7: Montréal Olympic Stadium Tower
There are many reasons why once-upright edifices begin to lean over, but some are built that way in the first place. This architectural marvel measures 165 m (541 ft 4 in) tall and has a curved angle of 45°, making it the **tallest leaning tower**. Fancy a trip to the top? A funicular built on two levels will whisk you up the outer wall of the tower to the

observatory in a couple of minutes. There, a panoramic view awaits you, stretching 80 km (50 mi) into the distance on clear days.

8: Rideau Canal Skateway
As temperatures plummet, Canada becomes a skating winter wonderland. When this waterway running through Ottawa in Ontario temporarily freezes over each year, it creates the **largest naturally frozen ice rink**, extending for 7.8 km (4.8 mi) with an overall maintained surface area of 165,621 m² (1.782 million sq ft), equivalent to 90 Olympic-size skating rinks. Join the 20,000 visitors who hit the ice daily, warm up en route at the many fire pits, and re-energize with one or two "beaver tails" – deep-fried cinnamon-and-sugar treats.

9: Festival International de Jazz de Montréal
With around 3,000 artists and some 650 concerts per year (most of them free), Quebec's jumbo jazz jamboree is well worth making time for. In Jul 2004, for its 25th anniversary year, more than 1.9 million people did just that, making it the **largest jazz festival**.

10: Niagara Falls
Located on the border with the USA, this cascade receives 22.5 million visitors a year, making it the **most visited waterfall**. About 6 million cu ft (169,900 m³) of water pours over the waterfall every minute. To visualize that, imagine nearly 70 Olympic-size swimming pools! Don't miss the chance to get up close to the Falls on a sightseeing boat tour – just don't forget your waterproofs!

On 30 Jun 1859, Charles Blondin, aka Jean-François Gravelet (FRA), made the **first tightrope crossing of the Niagara Gorge**. He made his traverse along a 1,100-ft-long (335-m) rope strung 160 ft (48 m) above the thunderous cataracts.

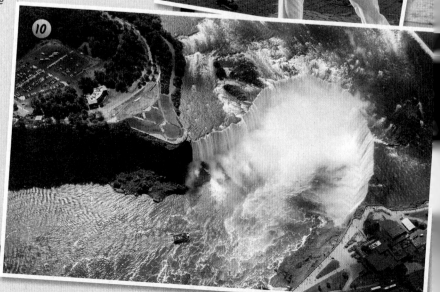

Mexico

1: Yucatán cave systems
Intrepid explorers of the Yucatán Peninsula can take the plunge into the **longest underwater cave system**, the Sistema Sac Actun ("White Cave System") and Dos Ojos ("Two Eyes"). These connected caverns have a combined total length of 371.95 km (231.12 mi) – four times that of the Panama Canal. The caves are accessed through sinkholes known as <u>cenotes</u>, which the Maya people believed to be portals to the underworld and where they deposited sacred objects and even, it is believed, human sacrifices!

2: Día de los Muertos
Every November, Mexico comes alive for a colourful and joyous celebration of the dead. Giant skeletons parade through the streets, and private altars known as <u>ofrendas</u> are decorated with photographs and belongings of the deceased. The **largest Day of the Dead altar** was organized by the local government of Hidalgo on 1 Nov 2019 and covered 1,044.3 m² (11,240 sq ft) – about twice the size of a basketball court! It was festooned with a multitude of offerings, including 600 candy skulls, 1,000 bouquets of flowers and 1,000 candles.

3: La Quebrada
The death-defying cliff-divers of La Quebrada ("The Ravine") in Acapulco plunge 35 m (115 ft) into a mere 3.6 m (12 ft) of water – the **highest head-first dives** performed regularly. A tradition that began with local fishermen in the 1930s has grown into one of the city's main tourist attractions, with divers aged 15–70 staging spectacular shows several times a day. The fearless freefallers made a notable appearance in the 1963 Elvis Presley movie <u>Fun in Acapulco</u>.

4: El Macro Mural Barrio de Palmitas
In 2014–15, an art collective known as the German Crew spent 14 months painting the city of Pachuca red... and yellow and blue and pink! With help from local residents, they decorated 209 walls with a single vibrant artwork – the **most walls covered by a mural**. The 20,000-m² (215,200-sq-ft) painting was part of a government project designed to unite the community and rehabilitate the local neighbourhood.

5: Great Pyramid of Cholula
Also known as Tlachihualtepetl ("man-made mountain"), this vast adobe monolith in the state of Puebla is the **largest pyramid by volume**. Although shorter than the Pyramid of Khufu in Egypt (see p.154), its volume is greater by almost 2 million m³ (7 million cu ft). The present incarnation was built by the Olmeca-Xicalanca people in 650–800 CE. It receives c. 220,000 visitors a year.

Sea's a crowd
The National Marine Park off Mexico's Yucatán Peninsula is home to the **largest group of underwater life-size statues**. <u>The Silent Evolution</u>, a group of 480 figures based on local people, is the work of Jason deCaires Taylor (UK). The sculptures help to promote the recovery of natural reefs.

At a glance
- **Area:** 1,964,375 km²
- **Population:** 130.2 million
- **Key Facts:** Mexico is the 10th most populous country in the world, with around 25% of its people living in or around the capital, Mexico City. Among its many natural treasures are the **tallest underwater stalactite** – the 12.8-m Tunich Ha of the Sistema Chac Mool cave system – and the Árbol del Tule in Oaxaca: a Montezuma cypress (<u>Taxodium mucronatum</u>) with a trunk circumference of c. 36.2 m – the **greatest tree girth**.

Volume: 4.45 million m³

Caribbean

1: Harewood Rum 1780
No trip to the Caribbean would be complete without sampling a glass or two of rum, the liquor distilled from sugar that has become synonymous with the region. The **oldest rum** dates to 1780 and was distilled in Barbados. In 2011, a cache of forgotten bottles was discovered in the basement of a country house in West Yorkshire, UK. The last 16 bottles were auctioned off in Dec 2014, fetching £100,000 ($155,320) for charity.

2: Bee hummingbirds
Twitchers will have to keep their eyes peeled if they want to spy the **smallest bird**. Native to Cuba, male bee hummingbirds (<u>Mellisuga helenae</u>) reach a length of just 57 mm (2.24 in) and weigh 1.6 g (0.05 oz) – lighter than a playing card. Bee hummingbirds can beat their wings more than 80 times per second and eat half their body weight in nectar every day.

3: St Thomas Aquinas University
Caribbean culture vultures will find the **first university in the New World** in present-day Santo Domingo in the Dominican Republic. Founded as a seminary for Roman Catholic monks in 1518, the Universidad Santo Tomás de Aquino was made a university by a papal bill on 28 Oct 1538 and officially recognized by the Spanish Court in 1558.

4: Toro Bike
If you want to combine daredevilry with your sightseeing, head to the Toroverde adventure park in Puerto Rico and take a ride on the **longest bicycle zipwire**. You'll pedal over the jungle canopy, along 322.25 m (1,057 ft) of highwires.

5: The Merengue
Despite its African and Spanish influences, merengue music is unique to the island of the Dominican Republic. The **largest merengue dance** featured 844 participants in the capital city of Santo Domingo on 3 Nov 2019.

6: Sint Maarten & Saint-Martin
At just 87 km² (33.6 sq mi), Saint Martin is the world's **smallest inhabited shared island**, divided between the French Saint-Martin and the Dutch Sint Maarten. No trip here is complete without a visit to Maho Beach for a terrifying view of the aircraft that make a low-altitude approach to the Princess Juliana International Airport. Whoosh!!

7: Hercules beetles
Visitors to the islands of Guadeloupe and Dominica would be advised to watch out for these mighty flying insects, the **longest beetle species**! One specimen of the subspecies <u>Dynastes hercules hercules</u> was measured at 172 mm (6.77 in).

At a glance
- **Area:** 223,768 km²
- **Population:** 38.7 million
- **Key Facts:** The Caribbean (also archaically described as the West Indies) is a region comprising 13 independent countries but also many territories and dependencies. There are more than 700 islands – the largest of which is Cuba (as big as the next five largest islands combined). The name "Caribbean" derives from the Spanish word "Carib", used to describe the indigenous Kalingo (or Karina or Karino) people who originally inhabited the region.

100%

EN SANTO DOMINGO, Imprenta de Andres Josef Blocquerst

Año 1801.

Elevation: 6,310 m

Central & South America

1: Belize Barrier Reef Reserve
Australia might claim the most famous (and **longest**) barrier reef (see p.146), but if you're in Central America don't miss the **largest reef system in the northern hemisphere**. At 963 km² (371.8 sq mi), the Belize Barrier Reef Reserve is almost 2.5 times larger than the Caribbean island of Barbados and second in size only to the Great Barrier Reef. The submarine shelf and reef stretch from Mexico in the north all the way to Guatemala in the south, and is a go-to destination for snorkelling, sailing and diving. It's also a precious habitat for countless threatened species such as sea turtles, manatees and crocodiles.

2: Mount Chimborazo
If Mount Everest is the **highest mountain**, then its peak must sit farther from Earth's core than any other point on the planet, right? Well... no. The Himalayan giant soars to the greatest height above sea level, but the **farthest mountaintop from Earth's centre** is that of Chimborazo in Ecuador. A distance of 6,384.4 km (3,967.1 mi) separates the summit of this Andean peak from our world's core – that's more than 2 km (1.2 mi) farther than the top of Everest. This is possible because Earth is an "oblate spheroid" – i.e., it bulges at the Equator.

3: Galápagos Islands
Located off the Ecuadorian coast, the Galápagos archipelago played a key role in the theory of evolution. In 1835, naturalist Charles Darwin spent 19 days here,

researching for his groundbreaking work On the Origin of Species (1859). It's also home to the **most northerly penguin** – the Galápagos penguin (Spheniscus mendiculus), mainly found on the isles of Fernandina and Isabela, up to 0.16°N.

4: Kerepakupai Merú
Set on an upper tributary of the Caroní River is Venezuela's prime tourist destination: the **tallest waterfall**. It plunges 979 m (3,212 ft) – about 18 times the drop of Niagara Falls (see p.117) – from the cliffs of Auyán-tepui mountain. You might know it as Angel Falls, named after US pilot Jimmie Angel, who spotted it from the air in 1933. Its local name, in the indigenous Pemón language, translates roughly as "waterfall of the deepest place".

5: San Bartolo
Archaeologist William Saturno was trekking through the ancient Guatemalan city of San Bartolo in 2001 when he made a once-in-a-lifetime find: the **oldest Mayan mural**, dating to 100 BCE. The vibrant artwork tells the story of creation and offers insights into the civilization, such as how their kings ruled by divine right. The jungle site is also home to the **oldest Mayan writing**, dating to 300-200 BCE.

6: Amazon rainforest
Imagine yourself in a place with tree canopies so dense that you can't see the sky. That's the

Amphibious Amazon
Despite facing increasing threats, this vast rainforest continues to support a rich array of wildlife. Out of the 8,000-plus known amphibians such as frogs, more than 1,150 live in Brazil, where 60% of the Amazon lies; it's the **country with the most amphibians**.

8

1,115 steps

9

10

view within the **largest tropical rainforest**, which spans nine countries and around 6.5 million km² (2.5 million sq mi). The verdant forest is sustained by the Amazon river, which discharges water at a peak rate of 340,000 m³ (12 million cu ft) every second! Although not the world's **longest river** (see p.141), it's the **largest river by flow**.

7: Rio de Janeiro Carnival
Brazil's famous fiesta has come a long way since its origins in the early 18th century as a water fight with optional lemon juice or mud... Boasting extravagant costumes and street parades soundtracked by thunderous samba drums, Rio's annual gala is the world's **largest carnival**. It is usually staged during the first week of March and attracts some 2 million people each day.

8: Monserrate Cerro Abajo
Red Bull's bone-rattling event sees daring cyclists negotiate the Cerro de Monserrate, a hill in the centre of the Colombian capital, Bogotá, for the **longest downhill bicycle stair race**. Some 80% of the 2.4-km (1.49-mi) course comprises steps – more than a thousand of them, in fact! France's Adrien Loron won the 2021 edition in 4 min 31 sec. We'd recommend you stick to walking...

9: Salar de Uyuni
In south-west Bolivia lies the **largest salt flat**, covering some 10,000 km² (3,860 sq mi) - almost the same size as Jamaica. It contains c. 10 billion tonnes (11 billion tons) of salt. In the rainy season (Dec-Apr), a shallow layer of water forms over the arid lake bed, giving rise to stunning reflections. Got a taste for more saline adventures? Then why not stop at the **largest salt hotel** here? There are 16 bedrooms in the Palacio de Sal, a 4,500-m² (48,440-sq-ft) facility with floors, walls, ceilings, beds and even a nine-hole golf course all made from sodium chloride! The present hotel was rebuilt in 2007 with a million salt blocks.

10: Isla Escudos de Veraguas
This tiny island off the coast of Panama has an aptly diminutive endemic resident: the pygmy three-toed sloth (*Bradypus pygmaeus*). The critically endangered critter - both the **rarest** and **smallest sloth** - is no bigger than 53 cm (1 ft 8 in), only slightly longer than a new-born human baby. A three-hour boat ride away, this isle is not easy to reach, but fans of the **slowest mammals** will surely be rushing to see this mini marvel.

11: Machu Picchu
Only a handful of outsiders had seen this Inca citadel since the original inhabitants abandoned it in the late 16th century, but it caught global attention in 1911 when publicized by US academic Hiram Bingham. Built in the Andes mountains of the Cusco region in southern Peru, it has gone on to become the **most visited Inca site**. In 2018, a record 1,578,030 people made a pilgrimage here to clamber among the unmistakable cloud-shrouded ruins and hang out with the local llamas.

12: Monumental Cabo de Hornos Lighthouse
The Atlantic and Pacific oceans clash at Cape Horn, South America's southern tip, where high winds and rough seas have claimed many a ship. In a bid to prevent further tragedy, a lighthouse was built on Isla Hornos in Chile's Tierra del Fuego in 1991. Simpler navigation beacons are found farther south, but located at 55.96°S it's the **most southerly lighthouse**.

At a glance

- **Area:** 18,504,123 km²
- **Population:** 521.1 million
- **Key Facts:** Latin America is renowned for its natural beauty and rich tapestry of indigenous cultures, both past and present. The region boasts records in every corner, from its tropical jungles and reefs to superlative rivers and lakes. One of its most iconic wonders must be the Andes – the **longest continental mountain range** on Earth. They include some of the planet's tallest peaks, more than 50 of them exceeding 6,000 m above sea level.

11

12

Flashes every 5 sec

11-m (36-ft) tower

UK & Ireland

At a glance

- **Area:** 313,883 km²
- **Population:** 72.3 million
- **Key Facts:** The United Kingdom is made up of four countries: England, Scotland, Wales and Northern Ireland. Buckingham Palace in London is home to Her Royal Majesty Elizabeth II, who celebrated her 70th year on the throne on 6 Feb 2022 and is the **longest-reigning queen**. The island of Ireland is home to the famous Guinness stout that, back in the 1950s, inspired a certain book of records...

1: Alton Towers
Thrill-seekers will be in seventh heaven at this theme park and resort in Staffordshire, England. Among its 10 rollercoasters is The Smiler, which transports passengers at 85 km/h (52.82 mph) through the ○ **most track inversions in a rollercoaster** – 14. There's also a waterpark, high-ropes adventure and a crazy golf course.

2: Crown Jewels
For more than 600 years, the royal regalia of the kings and queens of England has been stored in the Tower of London (see #4). This collection of crowns, robes and sceptres comes to around 140 objects and is on public display. It includes St Edward's crown, which has 444 precious and semi-precious stones and is the **most valuable crown**, at an estimated £3.5 m ($4.5 m).

3: St Patrick's Tower
In the Liberties neighbourhood of the Irish capital, Dublin, you'll find a decommissioned windmill that stands 45.7 m (150 ft) tall. St Patrick's Tower was built in 1757 as part of the Thomas Street Distillery, which at its peak produced more than 2 million gallons of whiskey a year. In 1860, with the advent of the steam age, the sails were removed, and by the 1920s, the distillery had closed. Today, the **tallest windmill** stands unoccupied.

4: Tower of London
This historic fortress on the north bank of the River Thames was founded in the 11th century, during the Norman Conquest. A UNESCO World Heritage Site, it is home to the world's **oldest museum**.

The Royal Armouries Museum opened its doors to the public in 1660, although the collection could be viewed by appointment for up to eight years before that. Objects on display include the **tallest suit of armour**, which stands 2.05 m (6 ft 8 in). It was said to have been worn by John of Gaunt, 1st Duke of Lancaster, in the 14th century. In fact, the suit is German in origin, and dates to around 1540.

5: Stratford-upon-Avon
This West Midlands market town has become famous around the world as the birthplace of the Bard, William Shakespeare (1564–1616). The **best-selling playwright** – who penned Hamlet, Macbeth and Romeo and Juliet – is estimated to have sold in excess of 4 billion copies of his works. There are a total of five houses in Stratford with historical links to Shakespeare, including Hall's Croft (below), where his daughter Susanna lived. The Royal Shakespeare Company also stages its world-renowned performances in the town. To see, or not to see, that is the question...

6: Croke Park
Ireland's national stadium in Dublin is the headquarters of the Gaelic Athletic Association and stages the All-Ireland finals in sports such as Gaelic football, hurling and camogie. The 1961 Senior Football Championship final between Down and Offaly (inset) drew 90,556 spectators

King Henry VIII

Mr. WILLIAM SHAKESPEARES COMEDIES, HISTORIES, & TRAGEDIES.

– the **largest crowd for a Gaelic football game**. The **hurling** record of 84,856 – for the 1954 final between Cork and Wexford – was also achieved at Croke Park.

7: The Beatles
Take a magical mystery tour around the northern English city of Liverpool in homage to the **best-selling group**, who racked up estimated sales of more than 1 billion singles and albums. Book a ticket to ride on a tour bus and see where the band grew up. At Pier Head, you'll find John, Paul, George and Ringo captured in bronze by sculptor Andy Edwards. Come together at Penny Lane for a selfie and visit the city's Fab Four museums before heading to Mathew Street to twist and shout at The Cavern Club, the legendary venue where The Beatles played 292 times in 1961–63.

8: Giant's Causeway
Northern Ireland's only UNESCO World Heritage Site is a group of 40,000 interlocking basalt columns on the Atlantic coast. The columns are the result of ancient volcanic activity, although popular legend attributes them to the Irish giant Finn MacCool. At Port Noffer, you can find Finn's "Giant's Boot" – a weathered stone in the shape of a shoe (UK size 93.5!). Basalt is the **most common volcanic rock**, accounting for more than 90% of all such material at the Earth's surface.

9: World Gravy Wrestling Championships
The Rose 'N' Bowl pub in the English village of Stacksteads is home to a saucy sporting competition in which combatants grapple in a pool of cold Lancashire gravy. Points are earned for costumes and all-round entertainment. Six-time champion Joel Hicks has racked up the **most wins** of the event, while the **women's** record of two is shared by Emma Slater and The Oxo Fox, aka Roxy Afzal.

10: Loch Ness
These tranquil waters in the Scottish Highlands have become a Mecca for cryptozoologists, who believe that a sea monster lurks somewhere beneath the surface of the 56-km² (22-sq-mi) lake. Although no concrete evidence of Nessie has been found, reports of strange "water beasts" in the area date back to the 6th century. No one has searched more fervently than Steve Feltham, who moved to the area in 1991 and has spent 30 years conducting the **longest continuous vigil seeking the Loch Ness Monster**. He lives in a converted mobile library on the shore, and scans the loch in search of the monster every day.

11: Ffestiniog Railway
Founded on 23 May 1832, Ffestiniog Railway in Wales is the **oldest independent railway company**. It winds 13.5 mi (21.7 km) through the picturesque scenery of Snowdonia National Park, climbing 700 ft (213 m) from the harbour in Porthmadog to the town of Blaenau Ffestiniog. If you'd prefer to see Wales by narrowboat, then hop on the Llangollen Canal and travel across the River Dee on the world's **tallest navigable aqueduct**: the 38.4-m-tall (126-ft) Pontcysyllte Aqueduct.

12: Stonehenge
One of the world's most iconic prehistoric landmarks, the stone circle on Salisbury Plain in Wiltshire, England, was constructed in the Late Neolithic period around 2,500 BCE. The site comprises the **largest trilithons** – structures built from two upright stones with a third laid on top. The heaviest blocks each weigh more than 45 tonnes (99,200 lb)!

6 x champ Joel Hicks

2 x champ Roxy Afzal

viewing platform at 276 m

1,665 steps!

France

1: Eiffel Tower
Dominating the Parisian skyline is the iconic Eiffel Tower, which stands 300 m (984 ft) tall – or 324 m (1,063 ft) if you include the antennas on top. It was built for the Paris <u>Exposition Universelle</u> and named after the engineer Gustave Eiffel, whose company designed and constructed the tower. At the time of its inauguration on 31 Mar 1889, the wrought-iron lattice tower was the **tallest structure** in the world, and it remains the **tallest iron structure**. It is also the **most visited paid-for monument**, attracting 6–7 million paying customers every year.

2: Versailles
No trip to Paris is complete without a stroll around the **largest garden**. The grounds at the Palace of Versailles – about 20 km (12 mi) west of the city centre – were created by André Le Nôtre in the late 17th century for King Louis XIV. Today, they cover more than 800 ha (1,976 acres) – the equivalent of over 30,500 tennis courts! – of which 100 ha (247 acres) encompass the magnificent formal garden, famed for its fountains, orangeries, paths and "bosquets" (groves of perfectly aligned trees). Dotted around the grounds are also 221 sculptures made from bronze, marble or lead.

3: Millau Viaduct
If you leave Paris and head towards the Mediterranean, you can enjoy the breathtaking views from the world's **tallest bridge**. The Millau Viaduct – which spans the Tarn Valley in the Occitanie region – is supported by seven concrete piers, the tallest of which (#2) measures 244.9 m (804 ft) from the ground to the road deck. If the 87-m-tall (285-ft) pylons are included, the structural height reaches a maximum of 336.4 m (1,103 ft). For the <u>highest</u> **bridge**, turn to p.152.

4: Tour de France
The world's most famous bicycle race has been snaking its way through France – and sometimes into neighbouring countries – since 1903. It attracts the **largest audience for a sporting event**, with upwards of 12 million spectators lining the course every year across the 23-day competition.

5: The Louvre
Art lovers should stop off at this iconic museum in Paris, where the walls are lined with 35,000 works of art. It's the **most visited gallery**; its busiest year, in 2018, saw a record 10.2 million tourists pass through its doors. The star attraction, of course, is the priceless painting <u>Mona Lisa</u> by Leonardo da Vinci, which in 1911 infamously became the **most valuable object stolen** (don't worry, it was recovered in 1913!)

For the highest bridge, turn to p.152.

At a glance
- **Area:** 551,500 km², including Corsica in the Mediterranean; 643,801 km² including the five largest of its 13 overseas territories (French Guiana, Guadeloupe, Martinique, Mayotte and Réunion)
- **Population:** 62.8 million; 68 million including all 11 populated overseas territories
- **Key Facts:** France is the **most visited country**, drawing 89.4 million tourists (2018 figure). Owing to its territories, it has the **most time zones** (13 at certain points in the year).

Pier 2   336.4 m

324 m

244.9 m

Height of Eiffel Tower

Holy matri-money!
Back in 2004, when Vanisha Mittal (IND) and Amit Bhatia (UK) were planning their wedding, their venue of choice was the Palace of Versailles! The bride's father – billionaire steel magnate Lakshmi Mittal – picked up the bill... a mere $55 m (then over £28 m), making it the **most expensive wedding!**

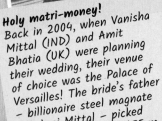

Italy

At a glance

- **Area:** 301,340 km², including the islands of Sardinia and Sicily
- **Population:** 62.3 million
- **Key Facts:** The Roman Empire dates back to the founding of Rome in 753 BCE but the modern Italian Republic was only established in 1861. Italy can boast the **most World Heritage Sites** (58 as of Jul 2021), including Pompeii (destroyed and preserved by the eruption of Mount Vesuvius in 79 CE), the city of Venice and Mount Etna.

1: Venice
Often named the most beautiful and most romantic place on Earth, Venice is also the **most water-logged city**. Built on a series of 118 small islands in the Venetian Lagoon, the municipality is frequently flooded, although with increasing – and worrying – regularity outside the high-water season. An unexpected high tide in Nov 2019, for example, saw 80% of the city submerged. The Venetians, though, have adapted well, using the 3.8-km-long (2.3-mi) Grand Canal as its major thoroughfare, taking <u>vaporetto</u> water-buses, and linking the streets with some 400 bridges.

2: Mount Etna
Rising 3,329 m (10,921 ft), Etna, on the island of Sicily, is the largest active volcano in Europe. It's also one of the world's most active, and provides volcanologists with the **longest record of volcanic eruptions** – it has flared up around 200 times since it was first documented in 1500 BCE. Etna also emits the **largest steam rings**: 200-m-wide (650-ft) vortices that can last up to 10 min.

3: Colosseum
Completed in 80 CE, the Flavian amphitheatre or Colosseum in Rome covers 2 ha (5 acres) – equivalent to three soccer pitches. It's not only the **largest amphitheatre** ever built but also the largest still standing. At the height of Imperial Rome, up to 87,000 people would flock to the four-storey arena to see gladiators and wild beasts locked in mortal combat.

4: Holy See (Vatican)
The world's **smallest country** is the Vatican, or Holy See, which exists as an enclave within Rome. The home of the Pope – and a population of 825 (as of 2019) – it covers just 0.44 km² (0.17 sq mi), meaning that you could fit 18 Vaticans into the gardens of Versailles (see opposite). Nevertheless, the papal residence is the **largest religious palace**, with its 1,000+ rooms – including the famous Sistine Chapel – covering more than 16 ha (40 acres).

The Pontifical Swiss Guard in the Vatican City is the **oldest military unit**, dating back to Jan 1506 (and with roots predating 1400)

An earthquake in 1349 destroyed about three-fifths of the outer wall

Buon appetito!

Italians have a BIG appetite for their national dishes:

Largest...	Metric	Holder
Cappuccino	4,250 litres	Altoga/Fiera Milano Fairground
Cazöla	931.4 kg	Piazza Litta, Ossana
Mortadella	920.8 kg	Gino Venturi
Pancetta	150.5 kg	Ponte dell'Olio/Piacenza
Panettone	332.2 kg	Davide Comaschi
Pizza	1,261.6 m²	NIPfood/Fiera Roma
Tiramisu	3,015 kg	Associazione Cons.erva
Longest...		
Breadstick	116.5 m	Terminal Nord
Focaccia	169.2 m	PIAZZAGRANDE
Mozzarella	106.1 m	Ente Provinciale Turismo di Avellino
Porchetta	44.9 m	Butchers of Monte San Savino
Salami (cooked)	16 m	Fratelli Daturi
Tiramisu	273.5 m	Galbani Santa Lucia

IL GRISSINO
PIÙ LUNGO DEL MONDO
110METRI
TERMINAL NORD

Spain

1: Gran Telescopio Canarias (GTC)
Located on La Palma in the Canary Islands is the **largest single optical telescope**. The GTC – which achieved "first light" on 13 Jul 2007 – has a mirror comprising 36 hexagonal segments, giving it a total diameter of 10.4 m (34 ft). For a 90-min daytime tour, book in advance with one of the GTC's "Starlight Guides".

2: Sobrino de Botín
Famed for its roast suckling pig – as celebrated by Ernest Hemingway in his novel <u>The Sun Also Rises</u> – Sobrino de Botín in Madrid is the world's **oldest restaurant**. It has been operating continuously since it was opened in 1725 by French cook Jean Botín. Today, it's owned by Antonio González and his family, who have been serving Madrileños for three generations.

3: La Tomatina
On the last Wednesday in August, the town of Buñol near Valencia holds its annual tomato festival. In 2012, at the peak of the event's popularity, c. 40,000 people indulged in the **largest food fight**, throwing at least 40 tonnes (88,180 lb) of tomatoes at each other!

4: The Cross of the Fallen
Standing 152.4 m (500 ft) tall above an underground church in the Valley of the Fallen, Madrid, is the **largest free-standing cross**. This monumental burial complex originally housed the remains of Francisco Franco, who ruled Spain from 1939 until his death in 1975, although in 2019 he was exhumed and moved to a more modest cemetery elsewhere in the city.

5: Spanish Christmas Lottery
It's been tradition since 1812 for Spaniards to enter the annual Christmas lottery, which offers the world's **largest lottery prize fund**. In 2021, a total of €2.4 bn (£2.19 bn; $2.93 bn) was up for grabs, with the top prize, known as "El Gordo" ("The Fat One"), paying out €4 m (£3.6 m; $4.8 m).

6: Basílica de la Sagrada Família
Dominating the skyline of Barcelona is Antoni Gaudí's still-unfinished Sagrada Família, the **tallest Art Nouveau church**. On 8 Dec 2021, the inauguration of the Marian Tower took the height of the basilica to 138 m (452 ft). This is one of 18 monumental spires, only nine of which are finished; the taller Jesus Tower, which has no completion date as yet, is set to reach 172.5 m (566 ft), which would make this the **tallest church** (see p.154).

7: Aqueduct of Segovia
The **largest Roman aqueduct still in use** – after an amazing 19 centuries! – is the 28-m-high (92-ft) waterway in modern-day Segovia. It transports water over 32 km (20 mi) from the Fuenta Fría river to the city, where the famous 683-m-long (2,240-ft) bridge section is supported by two rows of 166 single and double semi-circular arches.

At a glance

- **Area:** 505,370 km², including the Balearic and Canary Islands.
- **Population:** 47.2 million
- **Key Facts:** A key driver in Spain's economy is tourism, and as of 2021, the country boasts the **most Blue Flag beaches**, with 614. A constitutional monarchy was re-established in 1978, and the current "living embodiment of Spain", King Felipe VI, stands 1.97 m tall, making him the **tallest king**. Spain also has the **oldest wordless national anthem**, "Marcha Real" ("Royal March"), which was written in 1761.

152.4 m

93.1 m

Height of the Statue of Liberty (including pedestal)

Portugal

At a glance

- **Area:** 92,090 km², including the islands of Madeira and the Azores.
- **Population:** 10.2 million
- **Key Facts:** Portugal occupies c. 20% of the Iberian Peninsula and is home to the **largest area of cork forest** (736,000 ha) – 34% of the worldwide total. Its long history as an empire (nearly 600 years) – extending to Africa, the Americas, Oceania, and South and Southeast Asia - means that today, there are c. 250 million Portuguese speakers globally.

1: Morgadinha dress
In 2020, the Cultural, Recreational and Social Association of Teivas – a town 235 km (146 mi) north of the capital, Lisbon – commissioned the **largest traditional dance costume**. The 8-m-tall (26-ft) Morgadinha dress is based on the attire worn when performing a dance of the same name during the midsummer St John festival.

2: Stilted runway
Madeira International Airport has the **longest bridge-supported runway**, which stretches 1,020 m (3,346 ft) over the ocean and extends the landing strip to a total of 2,781 m (9,124 ft).

3: Parque Eduardo VII
This beautifully verdant park in Lisbon is home to the world's largest Portuguese flag – it's 20 m (65 ft) wide! – and was also the site chosen by the hypermarket Modelo for an ambitious PR stunt. To show support for Portugal's efforts in the 2010 FIFA World Cup, Modelo set the record on 5 Jun for the **most balls released**, which saw picnickers showered in 10,000 red balls.

4: Arroz de Sardinha
The **largest serving of Portuguese rice and sardines** was dished up by the Confraria dos Sabores Poveiros in the fishing community of Póvoa de Varzim on 6 Jul 2019. A 2-m-wide (6-ft 6-in) pan was filled with 1,027 kg (2,264 lb) of filleted fish, onion, garlic, red peppers, tomatoes, sweet paprika and rice, and served to the community to remind them of the joys of fresh regional produce and the importance of local cuisine.

5: Livraria Bertrand
The world's **oldest bookseller** can be found at Rua Garrett, in the trendy Chiado neighbourhood of Lisbon. Pedro Faure opened the shop in 1732 before passing it to his son-in-law, Pierre Bertrand, after whom the business is named. The original premises were destroyed in an earthquake in 1755 but rebuilt; the current store dates to 1773.

6: Giant waves of Nazaré
Feel the full force of the Atlantic Ocean as it pummels the Portuguese coast at Praia do Norte in Nazaré. The waves aren't the only thing breaking here: records are too! Brazil's Rodrigo Koxa achieved the **largest wave surfed (unlimited)** on 8 Nov 2017, catching a 24.38-m (80-ft) swell; the **female** record is 22.4 m (73 ft 6 in) by Maya Gabeira (BRA) on 11 Feb 2020.

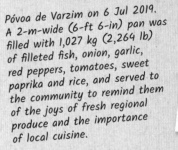

Maya Gabeira in action, riding a wave taller than the White House!

Nordic countries

At a glance

- **Area:** 3,487,860 km²
- **Population:** 27.7 million
- **Key Facts:** The Nordic countries comprise five sovereign states (Denmark, Finland, Iceland, Norway and Sweden) and the autonomous territories of the Faroe Islands and Greenland – the **largest island**, with an area of 2,175,600 km². Norway is the **most democratic country**, according to the Economist Intelligence Unit's 2020 Democracy Index, while Iceland is the **most peaceful country** – topping the 2021 Global Peace Index, ahead of Denmark.

1: Polar Park Arctic Wildlife Centre

An hour's drive from Narvik, at a latitude of 68.69°N, lies the **most northerly zoo**. Here in the snowy surrounds of the Norwegian countryside, wolves prowl and musk ox bulls go head to head in the mating season. And make sure you drop in on the brown bears, whose numbers in the park were swelled in the spring of 2020 by the delivery of three cubs.

2: Tromsø Arctic-Alpine Botanic Garden

Operated by the Norwegian Arctic University Museum, the **most northerly botanical garden** lies within the Arctic Circle in Norway at 69.40°N. Warmed by the Gulf Stream, the garden's 28 themed collections house plants from every continent, including a selection from Africa capable of surviving an Arctic winter. Flowering season usually runs from May to Oct; there are no gates, and visitors can enter for free whenever they wish.

3: Vikersundbakken

Sports fans with a head for heights should make for the **tallest ski-flying hill** in Vikersund, Norway. Inaugurated in 1936, it was rebuilt for the 2012 Ski Flying World Championships and now stands 225 m (738 ft) tall. Vikersundbakken has witnessed multiple world records, including the **longest competitive ski jump**: 253.5 m (831 ft 8 in), by Austria's Stefan Kraft on 18 Mar 2017.

4: Kajaani Castle

History buffs should trek to 64.22°N in Finland, where the ruins of the **most northerly castle** await. Constructed on a small river island between 1604 and 1619, Kajaani Castle once served as a prison and held the outspoken Swedish historian Johannes Messenius. It was blown up by the Russians in 1716 after a five-week siege.

5: Samsø Labyrinten

Lose yourself among the twists and turns of the **largest permanent tree maze**, which covers 60,000 m² (645,835 sq ft) – the same as 12 soccer fields. The Labyrinten is located on the small Danish island of Samsø.

6: ICEHOTEL

If you're looking for somewhere cool to stay, you'd be hard pushed to find somewhere more chilled than the ICEHOTEL in Jukkasjärvi, Sweden. Rebuilt every winter using blocks of frozen water harvested from the River Torne, it's the **largest ice structure**, with a total floor area in 2021 of around 2,870 m² (30,892 sq ft). There are 15-20 standard rooms besides 12 "art suites" designed and sculpted by international artists.

7: Vestmannaeyjar puffin colony

The Icelandic islands of Vestmannaeyjar (aka the Westman Islands, population: 4,300) are home to the **largest super-colony of puffins** (Fratercula arctica) – with an estimated 830,000 breeding pairs during the Apr–Aug nesting season. This is roughly 20% of the world puffin population, and around 386 birds for every islander!

Amazing space

The Samsø Labyrinten was constructed using Norway spruce and 10,000 newly planted deciduous trees. The maze is carbon-neutral and has encouraged biological diversity in the area. Its pathways total 5.5 km (3.4 mi) in length.

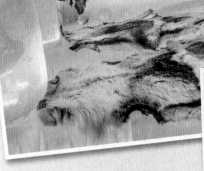

8: Globen
The Avicii Arena leaves an unmistakable mark on the skyline of the Swedish capital, Stockholm. The **largest hemispherical building**, it stands 85 m (288 ft) tall and has a total volume of 600,000 m³ (21 million cu ft). Commonly known as Globen, it opened on 19 Feb 1989 and stages ice hockey and futsal games, as well as musical performances.

9: Skiing
For centuries, skis have played a key role in the Nordic concept of _friluftsliv_ – "open-air living", as popularized in modern times by the Norwegian playwright Henrik Ibsen. In Sep 2021, archaeologists in Norway's Digervarden Ice Patch recovered the second of the **oldest pair of skis** – seven years after finding the first! The wooden skis with birch bindings date back 1,300 years. The one found in 2014 is now on display at the Norwegian Mountain Centre in Lom; the other is currently being studied at the Museum of Cultural History in Oslo.

10: Blokhus sandcastle
On 2 Jul 2021, the small Danish seaside town of Blokhus unveiled the ▶ **tallest sandcastle**, an elaborate construction rising 21.16 m (69 ft 5 in) into the air. A team of 30 sculptors commissioned by Kulturhuset & Skulpturparken Blokhus used more than 5,805 tonnes (6,400 tons) of sand to construct the seaside-themed stronghold.

11: Olde the gentoo penguin
Odense Zoo in Denmark is home to a herring-loving geriatic who never fails to pull in the crowds. Olde ("Great-granny" in Danish) is a female gentoo penguin (_Pygoscelis papua_) who celebrated her 42nd birthday on 16 May 2021. She is the **oldest living penguin in captivity**. Gentoos typically live for around 15-20 years, but this OAP (old-age penguin) shows no sign of slowing down!

12: Bakken amusement park
Thrill-seekers should make a beeline for Bakken, the 439-year-old amusement park located in the Danish capital of Copenhagen. Bakken opened in 1583 and is the **oldest operating amusement park** in the world. It boasts quirky stalls, independent shops and 31 rides, including Rutschebanen, a wooden rollercoaster that was built in 1932.

Top of the world?
In Aug 2021, researchers in Greenland found an uncharted island that they called Qeqertaq Avannarleq. They claimed it was 800 m (2,600 ft) farther north than Oodaaq – an islet located at 83.67°N that's considered to be the **northernmost land**. Fancy a trip to find out?!

COVID-19 virus (wearing a crown!)

Minions!

Doctor carrying a syringe of vaccine

Cyclists

Blokhus seamark

Beach huts

Dragon

Germany

1: Munich Oktoberfest

Inaugurated some 200 years ago to mark a royal wedding, Oktoberfest – the **largest beer festival** – is now part beverage celebration, part fun fair, with rides and sideshows alongside a head-spinning array of alcohol. The 2018 iteration, held from 22 Sep to 7 Oct, saw 7.5 million litres (2 million gal) of beer downed. The 6.3 million visitors supped from steins across a 31-ha (76.6-acre) site – about three-quarters the size of the **smallest country**, the Vatican (see p.127).

2. Weihenstephan Abbey

Beer lovers should also make a pilgrimage to the **oldest working brewery**. This former Benedictine monastery in Bavaria was granted a licence in 1040 CE. If you're in the area, why not also call in for a tipple at the world's second-oldest working brewery? Weltenburg Abbey, near Kelheim, lies about 60 km (37 mi) to the north; beer was first produced here in 1050 CE.

3: Burghausen Castle

Germany is hardly short of castles. In fact, it's home to more than 2,000 of them! But topping a ridge above the town of Burghausen, between the Salzach river and Wöhrsee lake, this medieval marvel stands out as the world's **longest castle**, at 1,051 m (3,448 ft). Formerly a second home to the dukes of Bavaria, it houses a main inner courtyard, where the family once lived, and five large outer courtyards. Stroll along the battlements, take in the stunning views from the tower, and try to keep your lunch down in the torture museum - eek!

4: Bridges of Hamburg

"Pontists" will appreciate the chance to travel over the nearly 2,500 road-, rail- and foot-bridges that crisscross Hamburg: the **city with the most bridges**. Despite being known as the "Venice of the North", Hamburg boasts more bridges over its rivers, lakes and canals than the actual Venice – in fact, more than <u>six times</u> as many!

5: Spreuerhofstrasse

Just 31 cm (1 ft 0.2 in) at its most slender, this passageway in the city of Reutlingen, south of Stuttgart, is the **narrowest street**, dating to the early 18th century. Claustrophobes beware: it's barely wide enough for a child to fit through. And, as one wall is moving gradually inwards, you'd best squeeze in a visit soon!

6: Ludwigsburg piggy bank

Germany's passion for <u>wurst</u> (sausages) is no secret, but that's not its only porcine claim to fame... In Ludwigsburg, you can bank on a selfie with the **largest piggy bank**. The money-box mascot of Kreissparkasse stands 5.58 m (18 ft 3 in) tall and is almost twice the length of a classic VW camper-van.

At a glance

- **Area:** 357,022 km²
- **Population:** 79.9 million
- **Key Facts:** Germany boasts Europe's largest economy and its second-highest population, behind Russia. It has produced some of the finest minds from physicist Einstein to philosophers such as Hegel. Nowadays, it hosts many annual highlights in the cultural calendar, from the Berlin Film Festival and Frankfurt Book Fair to Gamescom in Cologne, the **largest gaming festival** (2019 attendance: 373,000).

This (not so) little piggy...

Money boxes, or "still banks" as they're known by collectors, have a surprisingly long history, dating back to at least the 2nd century BCE. The earliest-known pig-shaped ones hail from Java in Indonesia: terracotta wild boars dating to the 1100s.

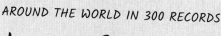

Low Countries

At a glance

- **Area:** 74,657 km²
- **Population:** 29.7 million
- **Key Facts:** Much of Belgium, the Netherlands and Luxembourg lie under, or at, sea level – hence why they came to be called the "Low Countries". Approximately 27% of the Netherlands is below sea level, making it the **lowest country** on the planet. Not surprisingly, it's also home to the **largest tidal barrier**, the 9-km-long Oosterscheldedam, which helps repel incoming storm surges from the North Sea.

1: Kusttram
All aboard for the **longest tram route**! The 68-km (42-mi) "Coast Tram" service skirts the Belgian coastline from Knokke to De Panne. Coincidentally, it makes 68 stops along the way.

2: Canal jumping
To navigate the Netherlands' waterways, locals learned to vault across them, a skill that became a sport: fierljeppen ("far leaping"). Marrit van der Wal (NLD) holds the **female leap** record, clearing a distance of 18.19 m (59 ft 8 in) in Burgum in 2019. Countryman Jaco de Groot took the **male** record – 22.21 m (72 ft 10 in) – in Zegveld in 2017.

3: Ghent Altarpiece
For all its fame, the Mona Lisa has only been purloined once (see p.126). The **most stolen painting**, meanwhile, is the Ghent Altarpiece – also known as the Adoration of the Mystic Lamb – a large Flemish artwork comprising 12 panels, begun by Hubert van Eyck and completed by his brother, Jan, in 1432. It's been the victim of 13 crimes and seven thefts. In 1934, two of the panels were stolen, of which only one has been recovered. Catch it while you can!

4: Waffles
They've been around in some form for millennia, but waffles are now closely tied to this region – Belgium in particular.

Even an ardent aficionado would struggle to eat the **tallest stack of waffles**, though: it towered 91.5 cm (3 ft) tall, and was served up on 28 Jun 2020 by Belgian brothers Francis and Michel De Buck in their café, De Buck Au Pingouin, in Blankenberge.

5: Pinkpop Festival
Every year, some 50,000 music-lovers flock to the Dutch province of Limburg for Pinkpop. The **longest-running annual pop-music festival**, it was held for 50 consecutive years (1970–2019) before COVID lockdowns forced it to pause. But don't panic (at the disco): the party was due to return in 2022.

6: Diary of Anne Frank
This moving journal has sold more than 30 million copies and has been translated into 55 languages, making it the **best-selling diary**. Frank's memoir describes life as she, her family and friends hid from Nazi persecution in Amsterdam, Netherlands, during WWII. Visit the Anne Frank House museum to walk in the footsteps of the diary's author.

East, South & Central Europe

At a glance

- **Area:** 6,040,692 km²
- **Population:** 605 million
- **Key Facts:** Europe is the second smallest of the seven continents, yet its heartland, from the brisk Baltic Sea to the balmy Mediterranean, is bursting with the history of many cultures and empires. Marvel at the **oldest Viking ships** (700–750 CE) on the Estonian isle of Saaremaa; spend 10-centimes in Switzerland to say you've used the **oldest coin in circulation** (minted since 1879); or head to Çatalhöyük in Turkey to see its neolithic cave-homes, the world's **oldest houses** at c. 7,500–5,700 BCE.

1: Large Hadron Collider
Some 100 m (328 ft) below the ground at the European Organization for Nuclear Research (CERN), near the Swiss city of Geneva, physicists are striving to replicate conditions in the aftermath of the Big Bang. To do so, they use accelerators such as the Large Hadron Collider (LHC) to hurl protons together at near the speed of light. With a circumference of 27 km (16.7 mi), this gigantic ring is the **largest scientific instrument**. CERN is also home to the Compact Muon Solenoid (shown), used in studies into dark matter and the search for extra dimensions. The LHC itself is off limits, but science aficionados can sign up for a free guided tour around CERN's laboratory.

2: Theatre of Dionysus
The Acropolis at the heart of Athens, Greece, isn't all about its crowning Parthenon temple (see pp.102–03). On its southern slope, you'll find the **first permanent theatre**, built c. 500 BCE to honour Dionysus, the god of wine and revelry. Originally seating some 17,000 people, the venue was "in the round", with stone rows built on an incline overlooking the stage. As well as tragedies and comedies, the theatre also hosted drama competitions in which the audience could vote for their favourite play.

3: Dentaprime HQ
Calling all Davids, Davinas, Donnas, Danutas and Devendras: if you're ever in Bulgaria, don't skip its third-largest city, Varna, or you'll miss a unique selfie opportunity. Opened in 2020, this delightfully designed dental clinic is the **largest building shaped as an alphabet letter**; its total floor area is 3,647 m² (39,256 sq ft). It's particularly striking at night when fully illuminated. Regardless of your name, if you're visiting this Black Sea port city, it definitely makes for a diverting D-tour!

4: Predjama Castle
In south-west Slovenia, near the town of Postojna, you can explore a unique semi-subterranean stronghold. Standing 35 m (115 ft) tall, this is the **largest cave castle** in the world. Game of Thrones fans will adore it – especially in July, when it plays host to costumed medieval games. In the nearby Postojna Cave Park, you can take an underground ride through a spellbinding "karst" landscape – limestone that has dissolved into dream-like Daliésque formations.

5: Meet a Mangalitza!
Travel through rural Hungary and you might think you're seeing things when you first spot a Mangalitza pig, as it has a rather unusual feature. Clad in a long, thick coat similar to sheep's fleece, the Mangalitza is the world's **hairiest domestic pig**. It originated here in the 19th century.

6: Spit cake
No visit to Lithuania is complete without sampling a šakotis, or spit cake. Sweet batter is slowly ladled on to a rod (spit) while it's baked in a special oven or over an open fire. This eventually

gives the dessert a branch-like appearance – hence its other name "tree cake". The **largest spit cake** weighed 85.8 kg (189 lb 2 oz) and was baked by a team of five from UAB Romnesa in Druskininkai in 2015. The sweet treat is traditionally served at weddings or at Christmas.

7: Hofburg Palace
In addition to schnitzel, classical music and Red Bull, Austria's also famous for some highly trained Lipizzaner stallions (actually bred in Slovenia). If you enjoy dressage routines, you'll want to trot on over to the Spanish Riding School at the Hofburg in Vienna, the **largest palace riding school**. Dating to the 18th century, the 55 x 18-m (180 x 59-ft) baroque hall – replete with chandeliers! – is the scene for elaborate performances by the talented equines and their equally skilled riders.

8: Kırkpınar Oil Wrestling Festival
Turkish wrestling has evolved its own unique rules and customs. Participants cover themselves in olive oil before a bout, making it harder for opponents to gain a secure hold. If you're gripped by the idea of seeing it in the flesh (so to speak), make for the Sarayiçi Peninsula, where the **oldest wrestling competition** is usually held towards the end of June. This week-long festival has been staged since the mid-14th century. The winner receives a prized golden belt, which is paraded through the nearby city of Edirne.

9: Keret House
Poland's capital city, Warsaw, is a tourist's delight, from the Copernicus Science Centre to the picturesque Old Town, which was rebuilt after WWII based largely on paintings by the 18th-century artist Canaletto. You'll also find the **narrowest home** here. Keret House is a tiny raised residence measuring just 92 cm (3 ft) at its slimmest and 152 cm (4 ft 11 in) at its widest, yet it squeezes in a bedroom with

separate kitchen and bathroom, connected by a ladder. As it doesn't conform to local building regulations, technically the house is classed as an art installation.

10: Na zdraví!
Raise a glass in the Czech Republic, where beer has been brewed for more than a thousand years. The country is home to such well-known breweries as Staropramen and Pilsner Urquell. You'll be in good company: the Czechs have the **largest beer consumption per capita** – 188.6 litres (49.8 gal) were purchased per citizen in 2019.

11: National Day of Folk Costume
Folk art is a great way to keep cultural heritage alive. Romania's annual National Day of Folk Costume turns the spotlight on historical attire, music and performance. The May 2017 event included the **most people in traditional Romanian clothing** – 9,643 – and the **largest Romanian folk dance**, featuring 9,506 participants, both organized by Transylvania's Bistriţa-Năsăud community. Traditional dress here is not only colourful but laden with hidden symbology. Look out for grape vines (eternal life), snails (evolution) and flowers (fleeting beauty).

North Asia

1: Banpo Grand Bridge
Spanning the Han River in the South Korean capital, Seoul, is a bridge with added aquatic appeal. The **longest bridge fountain** at 1,140 m (3,740 ft), it features 380 movable nozzles, which shoot water out to more than twice the length of a bowling lane. In the evenings, LED lights imbue the dancing sprays with a kaleidoscope of colours.

2: Lake Baikal
Travel to south-east Siberia to gaze into the **deepest lake**. At 1,642 m (5,387 ft), Baikal could fit a stack of five Eiffel Towers (see p.126)! It's also the **largest freshwater lake by volume** – 23,615 km³ (5,666 cu mi) – and the **oldest lake** at 20–25 million years. In winter, its frozen surface is ideal for skating, sledging and snowmobile rides; summer offers kayaking, swimming and hiking.

3: Laika
Pay your respects at a rocket-themed memorial in Moscow, which salutes a stray pooch that made history. On 3 Nov 1957, as the sole passenger in the Sputnik 2 spacecraft, Laika lifted off from the Baikonur Cosmodrome in Kazakhstan to become the **first animal to orbit Earth**. Tragically, she survived only a few hours into the flight – something that was only revealed in 2002 – but her legacy nevertheless represents a giant leap in the story of space exploration.

4: Intellectual Intelligence Museum
Lovers of riddles and mental conundrums will enjoy a testing time at this museum in the Mongolian capital, Ulaanbaatar. There are in excess of 5,000 puzzles for visitors to pit themselves against, while among the exhibits is the **largest collection of chess sets** – 438, as of 2019 – owned by Tumen-Ulzii Zandraa (MNG). As well as buying sets, he also makes his own, using materials such as ebony, stone and cow horn.

5: Sky Deck
If vertiginous heights make you queasy, perhaps look away now... Travel 478 m (1,568 ft) up Seoul's Lotte World Tower and you'll discover a viewing platform with a see-through base – the **highest glass observation deck**. Just a 45-mm-thick (1.7-in) panel separates visitors from thin air, but it can bear more than 500 kg (1,100 lb) per m² – equivalent to a grand piano. Reach the Sky Deck in style via the Sky Shuttle – the **tallest double-decker elevator**, rising to 496 m (1,627 ft).

6: Beringia dog-sled race
The dramatic Kamchatka Peninsula in the far east of mainland Asia is home to hot springs, snow-capped peaks and volcanoes. In 1992, the region also hosted the **longest dog-sled race ever** – the Beringia-92, which covered 2,044 km (1,270 mi) from Esso to Markovo. Although around half that length today, the annual race continues for anyone harbouring "bark-and-ride" ambitions.

7: T Express
At Yongin-si's Everland theme park – the largest in South Korea - one ride immediately stands out. The 56-m-high (183-ft 9-in) T Express is the **tallest wooden rollercoaster** (a title it has shared

Deepest surface lakes by continent

Continent	Depth
Asia: Baikal	1,642 m
Africa: Tanganyika	1,470 m
South America: O'Higgins (aka San Martín)	836 m
North America: Great Slave (aka Tu Nedhé/Tucho/Tıdeè)	614 m
Europe: Hornindalsvatnet	514 m
Oceania: Hauroko	462 m
Antarctica: Radok	362 m

with Sweden's <u>Wildfire</u> since 2016).
The ride, which opened in 2008, hurtles
riders along its creaky tracks at up to
104 km/h (64.6 mph)!

8: Mongolian wrestling
Wrestling has been part of Mongolian tradition
for millennia; 13th-century emperor Genghis Khan
encouraged it among his troops to keep them
fighting fit. It remains the country's favourite
sport and interested tourists have a host of
nationwide contests to choose from each year.
Competitors win bouts by forcing their opponents
to touch the ground with a body part other
than the feet. The **largest Mongolian wrestling
tournament** involved 6,002 participants and was
organized by the Mongolian National Wrestling
Federation in Ulaanbaatar from 17 to 25 Sep 2011.

9: Cold Pole Festival
With average January temperatures of -10°C (14°F),
be sure to pack plenty of layers if you're heading
to Siberia. Russia's far-eastern republic of Sakha
is home to the **coldest permanently inhabited
places**, a record jointly held by the towns of
Oymyakon (shown) and Verkhoyansk. Both have
registered temperatures of -67.7°C (-90°F) – so
cold that many cars have to be kept running, to
prevent their engines from freezing! Winter's end
is warmly welcomed at the Cold Pole Festival
every March, hosted by Chyskhaan, a figure
from pagan folklore dubbed
the "Lord of Frost".

10: Mongolian steppes
If you're touring this expansive, rugged region,
avoiding crowds won't be an issue... Mongolia is the
most sparsely populated sovereign country, with
some 3,198,913 citizens occupying 1,553,556 km²
(599,831 sq mi) of land. That works out at a mere
2.05 people per km² (5.3 people per sq mi).

11: Thousand Camel Festival
You might associate camels with warmer climes,
but north/central Asia boasts its own humped
ruminant. Populations of Bactrian camels (<u>Camelus
bactrianus</u>) have dwindled worryingly, though,
prompting efforts to boost their profile. Get a sense
of just how important these animals are to this
region at the world's **largest camel race**, staged
in the Gobi Desert city of Dalanzadgad, Mongolia.
In 2016, a record 1,108 jockeys took part.

12: Incheon
This South Korean industrial port city has been
finding innovative ways to redevelop its docks in
recent years – not least than with a 23,688.7-m²
(254,983-sq-ft) artwork of book spines depicting
the four seasons, painted on 16 silos. The **largest
outdoor mural** was produced by 22 artists in 2018
using approximately 865,400 litres
(228,600 gal) of paint.

At a glance
- **Area:** 18,882,616 km²
- **Population:** 223 million
- **Key Facts:** Spanning
Eurasia, Russia is the
largest country, almost
twice the size of the USA.
It includes Europe's longest
river – the 3,645-km
Volga – and largest lake –
Ladoga, at 18,130 km². Under
Genghis Khan and his heirs,
Mongolia once embodied the
largest contiguous empire
(24 million km² in the late
13th century). The Korean
Peninsula, which split in
1945, remains divided along
communist and democratic
lines. South Korea is now
a high-tech dynamo thanks
to brands such as Samsung.

One hump or two?
Mongolia's annual
"camelot" is part of a local
festival dating back to
1997. Now a two-day event,
it incorporates two races,
camel polo and various
team sports, all centred on
double-humped Bactrians.
Their one-humped cousins
are known as dromedaries.

Middle East

1: Jericho cable car

In the Bible, Jesus fasted for 40 days and 40 nights on the Mount of Temptation and was tested by the Devil there. Many identify the site as Mount Quarantana, which overlooks Jericho in Palestine and now hosts a Greek Orthodox monastery. In the past, it took visitors an hour to climb it, but today a 12-cabin cable car whisks you there in five minutes. It's the **lowest aerial cable-car route**, linking a station at Elisha's Spring, at 219.9 m (721 ft) below sea level (bsl), with another on the Mount that's still about 50 m (164 ft) bsl. The 1,328-m-long (4,356-ft) ride offers a breathtaking panorama over Jericho – thought to be the **oldest continually inhabited city**, with roots back to at least 9000 BCE.

2: Shibam

This Yemeni city represents an early example of vertical urban planning. Many of its population of around 7,000 live in densely clustered residential mud-brick high-rise buildings, some more than 30 m (98 ft) tall and consisting of 12 storeys. The lofty dwellings first started to arise after Shibam was flooded in 1532–33, with most of its 500-odd towers built over the next few decades, making it the **oldest skyscraper city**.

3: EpiQ Coaster

Thrill-seekers are guaranteed an adrenaline rush at the Quest amusement park within the Doha Oasis project

in Qatar. The resort has more than 30 rides and attractions, including the **tallest indoor rollercoaster** – the *EpiQ* – which more than lives up to its name, topping out at 56.7 m (186 ft).

4: Enot Tsukim Nature Reserve

Find some respite from white-knuckle rides at this haven for nature on the shore of the Dead Sea in Israel. At around 430 m (1,410 ft) below sea level, this protected area is the **lowest nature reserve** on Earth and the **lowest wetland**. Although the Dead Sea is too salty to support plants, this 5.8-km-long (3.6-mi) oasis has lower salinity because of fresh groundwater from the Judaean Mountains. Its roll call of local wildlife includes the striped hyena (*Hyaena hyaena*, Israel's largest carnivore) and the Middle Eastern jewel beetle (*Steraspis squamosa*) – one of 210 species of insect documented here. Get even closer to nature with the guided tours and hiking expeditions on offer.

5: Cemetery at Ur

The city-state Ur, now in Iraq, was the site of the **first royal cemetery**, with around 1,800 graves dating back to 2600 BCE. Of these, 16 were elaborate tombs containing spectacular artefacts, such as ornate jewellery (inset), and the remains of servants and courtiers. While there, make time to visit the nearby ziggurat – the dominant style of religious building in ancient Mesopotamia – that was constructed during the reign of Ur-Nammu (c. 2113–2095 BCE). Located in Muqayyar, it was

At a glance

- **Area:** 6,472,375 km²
- **Population:** 362.2 million
- **Key Facts:** Stretching from Israel to Iran, including the entire Arabian Peninsula, the Middle East incorporates the 560,000-km² Rub' al Khali, the **largest continuous sand desert** covering an area greater than Metropolitan France! The region combines ancient historical sites such as Damascus in Syria – the **oldest capital city**, inhabited since c. 2500 BCE – with the ultra-modernity of Dubai, typified by the Burj Khalifa, the ◑ **tallest building** (see p.155).

Larger-than-life Levantine fare

Outsized helpings of traditional Middle Eastern dishes for devotees of gargantuan gastronomy.

Largest...	Weight	Prepared by
Falafel	101.5 kg	Hilton Dead Sea Resort & Spa (JOR)
Kibbeh	233 kg	Al-Midan (LBN)
Fatteh (serving)	3,438.2 kg	Chef Ramzi Choueiri & Al-Kafaàt University students (both LBN)
Fattoush	4,432.5 kg	Municipality of Kab Elias (LBN)
Hummus (serving)	10,452 kg	Chef Ramzi Choueiri & Al-Kafaàt University students

originally three storeys, of which only the first and part of the second levels survive today. Its exterior was rebuilt in the 1980s.

6: Maraya Concert Hall

Aficionados of ancient history will marvel at the tombs and monuments at Al-Hijr – the first Saudi Arabian UNESCO World Heritage Site. If you're in the area, find some time for reflection at the Maraya Concert Hall, the **largest mirrored building**. Created by the Royal Commission for AlUla (SAU), Maraya – which means "mirrored" in Arabic – is encased in a 9,740-m² (104,840-sq-ft) glass façade that reflects the dramatic volcanic landscape. The 500-seat hall hosts concerts and other events year-round.

7: Dokaae clock

The holy city of Mecca in Saudi Arabia is the destination for millions of the faithful who join in the annual Hajj pilgrimage. Whether you're there to worship at the nearby Great Mosque of Mecca – Islam's most sacred site – or simply as a tourist, be sure to check the time on the 120-storey Makkah Clock Royal Tower (see p.155). It features the world's **largest clock face** – at 43 m (141 ft), its diameter is around twice the length of a bowling lane. It's well worth making the trip up, and not just for the viewing deck: the tower's top four floors are given over to an astronomy museum.

8: Jebel Jais Flight

Indulge your need for speed on this thrilling ride in the emirate of Ras Al Khaimah. The **longest zip wire** spans an unbroken distance of 2,831 m (9,288 ft) – greater than that of 26 soccer pitches! Daredevils travel at up to 150 km/h (93 mph), from a height of 1,680 m (5,511 ft) above sea level, zooming over the Jebel Jais mountain. Created by Toro Verde and Ras al Khaimah Tourism Development Authority (both UAE), it offers three minutes of exhilaration – or sheer terror! – but memories for a lifetime.

9: Almas caviar

Caviar is synonymous with fine living and deep pockets, and the **most expensive caviar** of all is almas, produced from the pale-golden eggs of the beluga sturgeon (_Huso huso_) that live in the southern Caspian Sea, off Iran. In 2006, just 1 kg (2 lb 3 oz) of this "black gold" regularly fetched in the region of £20,000 (then $34,500). Top tip: connoisseurs traditionally place caviar between the index finger and the thumb before consuming it.

10: Pearl Diving Pool

The Middle East may be better known for its arid terrain, but Deep Dive Dubai in the UAE is making a splash with the world's ◔ **deepest swimming pool**, opened in 2021. The main flooded shaft plunges down 60 m (196 ft 10 in) – three times the height of the White House. What's more, this indoor SCUBA-diving facility for both training and recreation boasts a sunken-city theme straight out of a sci-fi movie. Artful props enhance the experience, from a submerged library to a luxury car in a garage. You can also drop in for a game of underwater table football!

Africa

Mourning dress
Its prominent double-barred wooden cross makes the <u>kanaga</u> one of the most instantly recognizable masks of the Dogon people. It's worn by members of the Awa society at funeral rituals known as <u>dama</u>.

1: Sigui festival
The Dogon people of Mali are famous for their spectacular mask dances. They're performed by the Awa society, a group of male-only initiates who carve their own masks and learn how to speak <u>sigi so</u> ("language of the bush"). Among the Awa's responsibilities is the festival of the Sigui, which can play out over more than five years, with each Dogon village taking turns to host a series of feasts and rituals. Celebrating the passage of knowledge to new inductees, the **longest religious ceremony** only takes place once every 60 years; the next Sigui is due to begin in 2032.

2: University of Al-Karaouine
Founded in 859 CE in the Moroccan city of Fez, the **oldest seat of higher learning** has been educating students for more than 1,000 years and counts Pope Sylvester II and the geographer/diplomat Leo Africanus among its alumni. It was established as a mosque, with an adjoining school and library, and wasn't officially designated a university until 1963. Today, it draws scholars from around the globe, particularly those with an interest in Islamic studies and Arabic linguistics.

3: East Africa soda lakes
The Rift Valley in Kenya and Tanzania is home to the **most alkaline lakes**, which reach 50°C (122°F) and pH levels of 10 to 12 – caustic enough to burn skin! That doesn't deter the lesser flamingo (<u>Phoeniconaias minor</u>), though, which gathers in vast flocks to feed off the algae, turning its plumage that familiar shade of red-pink. The soda lakes owe their corrosiveness to high concentrations of sodium carbonate, chlorine and phosphorus produced by local volcanoes.
East Africa is also home to the **saltiest lake** – the Gaet'ale Pond, located in Ethiopia's Afar Region. It has 43.3% salt by weight, making it even saltier than the Dead Sea.

4: Marble berry
<u>Pollia condensata</u> is a perennial herbaceous plant found in African forests that produces vivid metallic-blue fruits. These brilliant baubles are the **shiniest organic objects**, approximately 30% as reflective as a silver mirror. Because marble berries have no nutritional value, scientists believe that this shininess is an evolutionary ploy to tempt birds into picking the fruit for use as nest decorations – in this way, encouraging seed dispersal.

5: Biete Medhane Alem
The Ethiopian town of Lalibela is famous for its rock-hewn churches. They're thought to have been carved from the stony landscape around the 12th century CE, as part of a plan to create a "New Jerusalem". Grandest of them all is the 33.5-m-long (110-ft) Biete Medhane Alem ("House of the Saviour of the World"), the **largest monolithic church**. Join worshippers as they seek the blessing of the Lalibela Cross, a 7-kg (15-lb) processional artefact housed within.

Safari spotters' guide
Take an African supersized safari with these big beasts!

Largest...	Species	Weight / height
Land animal	African bush elephant	4–7 tonnes / 3–3.7 m
Rhinoceros	Southern white rhinoceros	3.6 tonnes / 1.7 m
Freshwater mammal	Hippopotamus	3.6 tonnes / 1.45 m
Primate	Eastern lowland gorilla	163 kg / 1.75 m
Bird	North African ostrich	156 kg / 2.7 m
Lemur	Indri	7.5 kg / 72 cm
Tallest...		**Height**
Land animal	Giraffe	5.5 m

6: Sudwala Caves
Formed from Precambrian dolomite rock in Mpumalanga, South Africa, the **oldest caves** on Earth are believed to have emerged around 240 million years ago. The Sudwala Caves opened to the public in the 1960s and can now be visited year round. Underground, you'll find 150-million-year-old speleothems (mineral formations) like the "Lowveld Rocket" and the "Screaming Monster". If you're feeling particularly adventurous, try the Crystal Tour – but only if you're up to wading through water and crawling along tunnels!

7: Tsingy de Bemaraha National Park
The Grand Tsingy in Madagascar is a 600-km² (6,450-sq-ft) Jurassic-era limestone massif, which over millions of years has been eroded to form a "stone forest" of sharp pinnacles. Plan a guided trek through the **largest stone forest** to take in the otherworldly landscape with its up to 90-m-tall (295-ft) natural spires. There are also 11 species of lemur inside the park.

Situated some 400 km (250 mi) off the east coast of Africa, Madagascar is the **oldest island**, and the fourth largest in the world. It split off from the Indian subcontinent around 80-100 million years ago.

8: Sahara
Covering 10 countries and an area roughly 5,800 times the size of Greater London, the Sahara is the **largest hot desert** in the world. Its blistering heat, wind-swept dune fields (ergs) and towering sand ridges (draa) can make for inhospitable conditions for travellers, but it remains a place of natural wonder. One creature who has made the desert home is the smallest fox, the 40-cm-long (1-ft 3-in) fennec, whose giant ears help to keep it cool.

9: Couscous
Steamed semolina is a delicious staple of North African cuisine, and can be served as a side dish, dessert or the main event. You'd have needed a hearty appetite to polish off the **largest bowl of couscous**, which was prepared at the 2004 International Fair of Algiers in Algeria and weighed 6.04 tonnes (13,315 lb) – the same as an adult elephant (see opposite)!

10: Great Sphinx of Giza
One of Egypt's best-known landmarks, the Sphinx is a limestone statue of a mythological creature with a lion's body and a human's head. It's believed that the face is that of King Khafre (c. 2575–2465 BCE), although the nose has been missing for centuries. Carved from a single block, the Sphinx is the **largest monolithic sculpture** at 73.5 m (241 ft) long. It stands near to the Pyramid of Khufu, a record setter in its own right (see p.154 and p.160).

At a glance

- **Area:** 30,293,969 km²
- **Population:** 1.37 billion
- **Key Facts:** Humans have inhabited Africa longer than any other continent – the **oldest Homo sapiens bones**, dating back c. 300,000 years, were unearthed in western Morocco. Today, Africa is the continent with the **most countries** – 54, the newest of which is South Sudan – and the **most boundaries** – 108; or 110, if including the Sahrawi Arab Democratic Republic. It also boasts two superlative waterways: the 6,695-km Nile, the world's **longest river**; and the Congo, the **deepest river**, with a maximum depth of 220 m.

69 m (226 ft)

Central & South Asia

Average weight:
1 x jackfruit =
10–15 x pineapple

1: Nanga Parbat
Also known as Diamir, this Himalayan peak in the Pakistani-administered region of Kashmir is the ninth-highest in the world at 8,125 m (26,656 ft). It has a fearsome reputation among climbers, who must contend with its unstable glaciers and propensity for storms. With roughly one in five attempts to summit Nanga Parbat ending in tragedy, no wonder it's nicknamed "Killer Mountain"! It's also the **fastest-rising mountain**, growing 7 mm (0.27 in) each year.

2: Darvaza Crater
In a natural gas field in Turkmenistan's Karakum Desert lies the "Door to Hell": a blazing crater that has been burning since 1971. It is thought to have formed after the ground collapsed when drilling equipment breached a subterranean void, and geologists set the resulting crater alight to prevent a large leak of methane gas. The result is the **longest-burning methane crater**.
 In Nov 2013, Canadian adventurer George Kourounis descended to the bottom of the 30-m-deep (98-ft) pit wearing a heat-resistant aluminium suit, becoming the **first person to explore the Darvaza Crater**.
 The end may be in sight for this fiery landmark, though; in Jan 2022, the Turkmen government announced plans to extinguish it.

3: Jackfruit
No trip to Bangladesh would be complete without sampling its national fruit, the jackfruit. Specimens grow up to 0.9 m (2 ft 11 in) long and can weigh five times as much as a bowling ball – making them the **largest tree-borne fruit**. A single mature jackfruit tree (Artocarpus heterophyllus) can produce as many as 200 fruit a year. Its low cost and high nutritional value makes the jackfruit a staple ingredient of Bangladeshi cuisine, featuring in everything from soups to salads and curries.

4: Thaipusam
Every year in Jan/Feb, Tamil Hindus come together to celebrate the occasion when Murugan, the Hindu god of war, was gifted a divine spear to defeat the demon Surapadman and his brothers. Followers engage in kavadi, acts of devotion that range from carrying pots of rice milk to impaling skewers through their cheeks. The **largest Thaipusam festival** takes place in Malaysia. As many as 1 million devotees embark on an 8-hr trek from the Sri Mahamariamman Temple in the capital, Kuala Lumpur, to the holy Batu Caves some 15 km (9 mi) away.

5: Sri Ranganathaswamy Temple
This 1,000-year-old sacred site, situated on the island of Srirangam in Tamil Nadu, India, is dedicated to Ranganatha, a form of the Hindu deity Vishnu. The complex features an ornamental 13-tiered gopuram (entrance tower), completed in 1987, which soars to 72 m (236 ft). This stunning example of Dravidian architecture – both the **tallest** and the **largest Hindu temple complex** on the planet – has been nominated as a UNESCO World Heritage Site and is currently pending evaluation.

6: Sepilok Orangutan Rehabilitation Centre

Living in the canopy of tropical rainforests in Indonesia, orangutans (Pongo) are the **largest tree-dwelling mammals**. Since 1964, the **longest-running orangutan sanctuary** has helped more than 300 rescued orphans back into the wild. The home for ailing apes is based in the 43-km² (16.6-sq-mi) Kabili-Sepilok Forest Reserve in the Malaysian state of Sabah, on Borneo. It is actively involved in conservation education, as well as assisting other endangered species such as sun bears (the **smallest bears**), gibbons and elephants. It's open all year to visitors and for volunteers looking to go the extra mile.

7: Angkor Wat

First constructed by the Khmer King Suryavarman II during his reign in 1113–1150 CE, the temple of Angkor Wat in Cambodia is the **largest religious structure** ever built. Take a stroll around its 162.6-ha (401-acre) grounds to admire the ornate galleries and central temple-mountain. Angkor Wat was originally dedicated to the Hindu god Vishnu before gradually transforming into a Buddhist centre of worship. It once hosted a population of around 80,000 people, but it was abandoned during the mid 15th century.

8: Lake Toba

Around 75,000 years ago, a supervolcanic eruption on the modern-day island of Sumatra nearly wiped out humanity... On a cheerier note, it also created the now-idyllic Lake Toba, which at c. 100 x 30 km (62 x 18 mi) is the **largest crater lake**. Toba also contains the isle of Samosir, the original home of the Toba Batak people. With an area of 630 km² (243 sq mi), Samosir is the **largest island in a lake on an island**.

9: Statue of Unity

On an island near the Sarovar Dam, in the Indian state of Gujarat, stands a 182-m-tall (597-ft) likeness of Sardar Vallabhbhai Patel, one of India's founding fathers. The world's **tallest statue** is so prominent in the landscape that it is visible from 7 km (4.3 mi) away. Take a ride up the elevator inside the statue to the viewing gallery, located 153 m (501 ft) off the ground, which offers sweeping views of the surrounding reservoirs and mountains, or visit at night to see a laser show projected on to the sculpture.

10: Mountain River Cave

Deep within Vietnam's Phong Nha-Ke Bàng National Park lies Hang Son Đoòng, the **largest cave**. Its entrance was discovered by a local farmer in 1991, although another 18 years would elapse before a formal survey was made; we now know it extends for at least 6.5 km (4 mi). Those explorers willing to make the 6-hr journey through the jungle, and the 200-m (656-ft) descent inside the hollow, will be rewarded with one of Earth's most spectacular hidden wonders.

11: Istana Nurul Iman

For a dazzling display of royal opulence, take a trip to Brunei, a sovereign state located on the north coast of Borneo. A few kilometres south-west of the capital, Bandar Seri Begawan, is the Palace of the Light and Faith, official home of the 29th Sultan of Brunei and also the seat of the country's government. The world's **largest occupied palace**, it contains 1,788 rooms – more than double that in Buckingham Palace – including a 5,000-seat banqueting hall, a mosque and a garage for 110 cars. It also has an air-conditioned stable for 200 polo ponies and five swimming pools. It's worth noting that the royal residence is open to visitors for only three days each lunar year, during the festival of Hari Raya, marking the end of Ramadan.

Height: 4 x Statue of Liberty (minus pedestal)

182 m

At a glance

- **Area:** 10,551,875 km²
- **Population:** 2.5 billion
- **Key Facts:** This region is famed for its geological extremes, from the 8,848.8-m Mount Everest (aka Sagarmāthā or Chomolungma), the **highest mountain**, to the **deepest point in the sea**, the 10,935-m Challenger Deep in the Pacific Ocean. Its architectural wonders, often with a spiritual link, are no less awe-inspiring than those formed by nature; Thailand alone is home to some 35,000 temples!

THAILAND

China

1: Great Wall of China
The world's **longest wall** is, in fact, a network of walls, trenches, towers and gates, rebuilt and added to by several dynasties over 2,000 years. A 2012 survey estimated its total historical extent at more than 20,000 km (12,400 mi), though now only a few hundred kilometres remain intact. Some of the most popular stretches today are found in Jiankou, Mutianyu and Jinshanling.

2: Yuan-Dao Guanyin Temple
Visitors to Taiwan can find peace at the Yuan-Dao Guanyin Temple. Standing watch over the complex is a seated statue of the Buddhist goddess of mercy, Guanyin, who in some guises possesses as many as a thousand arms and eyes. Twenty years in the making, this is the **largest steel sculpture**, at 30.3 m (99 ft) tall and 35.9 m (117 ft) wide.

3: Sakyamuni Pagoda
Yingxian County in Shanxi is home to a 1,000-year-old tiered tower known as the Muta. From a stone base, the building rises five levels to 67.3 m (220 ft) – making it the **tallest wooden pagoda**. Built in 1056 CE during the Liao Dynasty, the structure has withstood earthquakes and wartime artillery fire.

4: The Forbidden City
Occupying a 72-ha (178-acre) site in the heart of Beijing, the Forbidden City is a sprawling complex of imposing courts, halls and gardens. Home to Emperors of the Ming and Qing dynasties between 1420 and 1924, it earned its name owing to the fact that most citizens were barred from entering. Today, however, the Forbidden City's gates are firmly open to tourists. In fact, this UNESCO World Heritage Site is the **most visited palace**, receiving more than 17 million guests in 2018.

5: Giant pandas
These monochromatic mammals are a national treasure. As few as 1,864 giant pandas (Ailuropoda melanoleuca) live in their native habitat, the temperate forests in the mountains of south-west China. They feed almost entirely on bamboo, with males growing up to 300 lb (136 kg). The **largest giant-panda habitat** is the 9,245-km² (3,569-sq-mi) Sichuan Giant Panda Sanctuaries, which claims 30% of the global population.

6: Terracotta Army
In 1974, farmers near Xi'an in Shaanxi Province stumbled across pits containing around 8,000 clay soldiers, officials and other figures. This "Terracotta Army" – the **largest group of life-size statues** – was created to stand vigil over the tomb of Qin Shi Huangdi, the first Emperor of China, who died in 210 BCE. A museum now exists on the site.

At a glance

- **Area:** 9,596,960 km²
- **Population:** 1.39 billion
- **Key Facts:** China has the world's **largest population**. Its territory crosses five geographical time zones, but since 1949 it has observed only one, so it's the **largest country in one time zone**. A blend of tradition and modernity, it boasts both the Rongbuk Monastery – the **highest temple**, at 5,100 m above sea level – and the Guangdong Science Center – the **largest science museum**, with an area of 126,514 m².

Japan

At a glance

- **Area:** 377,915 km²
- **Population:** 124.6 million
- **Key Facts:** Japan comprises five islands: Honshū, Hokkaido, Kyūshū, Shikoku and Okinawa. The former is home to Tokyo, the **largest capital city**, with a population of 37,468,302. The country boasts the **oldest ruling house**, with the Yamato Dynasty providing a succession line of 126 emperors. Those with a sweet tooth should head to Kyoto and seek out the **oldest candy shop** – Ichimonjiya Wasuke, selling sweets since c. 1000 CE.

1: Japanese macaques
Inhabiting the mountainous Jigokudani area of Honshū, Japanese macaques (<u>Macaca fuscata</u>) are the **most northerly primates**, barring humans. The snow monkeys keep warm in the -15°C (5°F) winters by bathing in hot volcanic springs.

2: Ghibli Museum
Get "spirited away" to Mitaka City to revel in the wistful world of Studio Ghibli. The museum was designed by Hayao Miyazaki, the director behind classic movies such as <u>My Neighbour Totoro</u> (1988) and <u>Howl's Moving Castle</u> (2004). As the **most successful non-English animation studio**, it has grossed $1.39 bn (£1.04 bn) from 19 feature films.

3: Gundam Factory
Mecha fans need to include Yokohama on their itinerary. To mark the 40th anniversary of anime TV series <u>Mobile Suit Gundam</u> in 2020, the Gundam Factory revealed an 18-m-tall (59-ft) version of the RX-78-2 Gundam, which comes to life every hour. It is the **largest humanoid robot**.

4: Ryōgoku Sumo Hall
Take a trip to the Yokoami neighbourhood of Tokyo to experience Japan's national sport: sumo. This ancient form of wrestling is steeped in ritual, with super-sized combatants purifying the <u>dohjō</u> (ring) with salt before waging battle. With a capacity of 11,908, Ryōgoku is the **largest sumo stadium** and holds three of the six official tournaments (<u>honbasho</u>) – in January, May and September. Ringside seats are highly prized, but beware of flying wrestlers!

5: Sapporo Snow Festival
Every February, Hokkaido's largest city hosts a seven-day celebration of snow. It began in 1950, when a collection of sculptures by students in Odori Park drew 50,000 people. Since 1974, the festival has included an International Snow Sculpture Contest. Teams spend weeks creating spectacular arctic artworks such as the **largest <u>Star Wars</u> snow sculpture** in 2015, which featured a lightsaber-wielding Darth Vader and was crafted from 3,175 tonnes (3,499 tons) of the white stuff.

6: Cherry blossom
Spring comes to Japan in a colourful blizzard of pink and white petals produced by <u>sakura</u> trees. LEGOLAND in Nagoya celebrated the national flower by creating their own year-round version with toy bricks. At 4.38 m (14 ft 4 in) tall and 4.93 m (16 ft 2 in) wide, it is the ▶ **largest LEGO-brick cherry-blossom tree**.

23 m (75 ft)

Spring has sprung
If you're hoping to catch Kyoto's <u>sakura</u> trees in full bloom, don't leave it too late! Studies of the city's cherry-blossom seasons show that 2021's peak arrived on 26 Mar – the earliest since records began in 812 CE.

Australia

1: Lone Pine Koala Sanctuary

Wildlife aficionados will surely want to stop by in Brisbane to see this venerable institution. Set up in 1927 by Claude Reid, it's the world's **oldest koala sanctuary** and home to more than 130 of these cuddly Aussie icons. You'll have plenty of chances to perfect your snapshots of them, as koalas spend up to 19 hr a day asleep - they're not lazy, just conserving energy, as the eucalyptus leaves that they feed on are very low on nutrients.

2: National Penny-farthing Championships

Its origins may lie in France, but this distinctive early bicycle is celebrated in style every year in the Tasmanian town of Evandale at the **largest penny-farthing competition**. As well as several different races, the event runs a Victorian-themed fair. Novice high-wheelers are welcome... though good luck packing one in your suitcase!

3: Wave Rock

Should you find yourself in Hyden, east of Perth, make time for a selfie-stop at the aptly named Wave Rock. Around 2.7 billion years old, and reaching 12 m (39 ft) tall, its graceful curve formed over the millennia as its granite was eroded away by the acidic soil that once covered it. With an exposed area of 1,320 m² (14,200 sq ft), it's the **largest flared slope**. Find it on Hyden Rock's north face.

4: Great Barrier Reef

If there's one must-see on your trip to Australia, it's this majestic coral structure off Queensland's coast. At 2,027 km (1,260 mi), it's the **longest reef** (made up of thousands of mini reefs).

Dive in to mingle with some 1,500 fish species (10% of the world's total, no less!), including many a _Finding Nemo_ star, from clownfish and blue tangs to sea turtles and starfish. Top tip: avoid jellyfish by visiting in winter (Jun-Aug).

5: Stadium Australia

Given Australians' passion for sport, it's little wonder that they'd build a superlative venue in Sydney for the Summer Olympics in 2000. It was designed to hold 110,000 spectators – the **highest capacity for an Olympic stadium** - though some 114,000 crammed in for the event's closing ceremony. Today, it welcomes fans of rugby league and soccer alongside concert-goers.

6: Daintree rainforest

Time-travel back to the age of the dinosaurs in this lush tropical wonderland on the coast of Queensland. Daintree is the world's **oldest rainforest** – dating back around 180 million years; compare that to a "mere" 55 million years for the Amazon (see p.122). At around 1,200 km² (460 sq mi), it's also the country's largest contiguous block of rainforest.

At a glance

- **Area:** 7,741,220 km²
- **Population:** 25.8 million
- **Key Facts:** Australia is the **smallest continent** but the **largest continental island**. It's also the **flattest continent**, with no major mountain ranges and a mean elevation of just 330 m. That said, perhaps its most famous geological feature defies the desert relief: Uluru – the **largest sandstone monolith**. Home to many unique animals, one of Australia's most iconic is the red kangaroo (_Osphranter rufus_), the **largest marsupial**.

New Zealand

1: Birding bonanza

New Zealand boasts a bounty of feathered record breakers. These include the ground-dwelling kākāpo (Strigops habroptila), or owl parrot, the **heaviest parrot**. Males weigh up to 4 kg (8 lb 13 oz). They are critically endangered, so keen "twitchers" must submit to a quarantine process before travelling to one of their island homes.

The national bird, from which New Zealanders derive their nickname, is the kiwi; for a chance to see one in the wild, head to a conservation park or nature reserve, or sign up for a wildlife tour. The brown kiwi (Apteryx australis) lays the **largest eggs relative to body size**. One female weighing 1.7 kg (3 lb 12 oz) produced a 406-g (14-oz) egg – almost one-quarter of her body mass!

The very rare yellow-eyed penguin (Megadyptes antipodes) is the **least social penguin**. Endemic to New Zealand and a few subantarctic islands, it nests alone, out of sight from other birds.

2: Baldwin Street

South Island's second-largest city, Dunedin, contains this short road, unremarkable save for a 34.8% gradient (19°), making it the **steepest street**. What a great way to test your calf muscles! If you're there in July, stay for the annual Cadbury Jaffa Race, when thousands of candies are sent rolling down the hill.

3: Frying Pan Lake

Outdoorsy types will love the rugged beauty of the Waimangu Volcanic Rift Valley. Here, you'll find steamy Frying Pan Lake (aka Waimangu Cauldron) – the **largest hot spring**, at c. 3.8 ha (9.3 acres). Its average temperature hits 60°C (140°F) and it's acidic too, so you'd best leave it to the thermophilic (heat-loving) life-forms – mainly micro-organisms such as bacteria and algae – that can take the heat.

4: Ranfurly tree

Legend has it that in 1901, Lord Ranfurly, then-Governor of New Zealand, planted a Sitka spruce (Picea sitchensis) on Campbell Island – one of the country's most southerly isles. Its nearest companion is some 222 km (138 mi) away, making it the **remotest tree**. Expedition cruises occasionally pay visits, but in case you can't book, here's a snap of the solitary spruce.

5: Matainaka Cave

For one of the country's most distinctive sights, you'll have to go underground. Visit South Island's Otago coast for the **longest sea cave** at 1.54 km (0.95 mi). With its sandstone walls worn away by the constant action of the waves, it's growing longer by the year. Why not hire a kayak and paddle through this shadowy subterranean world?

6: Wellington

Immerse yourself in the history of Aotearoa (the Māori name for New Zealand), with an emphasis on indigenous culture, at the Museum of New Zealand Te Papa Tongarewa. A five-minute ride on the locality's iconic red funicular brings you to the hills, a panoramic vantage point for snapshots of the planet's **most southerly capital city** (among sovereign countries), at 41.28°S.

At a glance

- **Area:** 268,838 km²
- **Population:** 4.9 million
- **Key Facts:** A third of New Zealand is officially protected as a nature reserve. Volcanic activity over millennia has shaped its distinctive landscape - immortalized in the Lord of the Rings movies. It's one of only two countries to have two national anthems (the other is Denmark). And it produced Edmund Hillary who, along with Tenzing Norgay, claimed the **first ascent of Everest** in 1953.

LEGO ENGINEER

David Aguilar

At the age of five, David Aguilar from Andorra was introduced to LEGO®. Who could have foreseen the groundbreaking inventions this encounter would lead to?

Born without a right forearm, David (who also goes by the nickname Hand Solo) built his first LEGO prosthetic arm when he was just nine years old. Although the pieces available to him then weren't really suitable for practical use, the fire had been sparked and he persevered with honing the LEGO limb.

Aged 18, he made a crucial breakthrough, redeploying parts from a LEGO Technic Rescue Helicopter (set #9396) to create his Mark-I (MK-I) model, a nod to superhero Iron Man's first suit of armour. With a grabber hand and moveable elbow, the **first functional LEGO prosthetic arm** was strong enough for press-ups!

Fast-forward to 2021 and David is already working on MK-VI, with which he hopes to make the elbow and hand sections independently manoeuvrable. He's excited too about the possibilities of 3D-printing artificial limbs from scratch. This inspirational inventor is now a sought-after speaker, appearing at a NASA innovation summit in 2019, among others. David's rising profile enables him to encourage all of us to think outside the (LEGO) box and to realize our full potential.

David's MK-II arm (above) incorporates parts from the LEGO Technic Air Race Jet kit (#42066).

VITAL STATISTICS

Name	David Aguilar Amphoux
Birthplace	Andorra la Vella, Andorra
Nickname	Hand Solo
Academic status	Bioengineering student
Current GWR titles	• First functional LEGO prosthetic arm • First foot-controlled LEGO prosthetic arm • First LEGO prosthetic arm with a stylus

1

2

3

MK-I

MK-II

MK-III

MK-IV

1. A nine-year-old David shows off his very first attempt at a LEGO prosthetic. "LEGO was my first toy as a kid: it felt that you could build an infinite amount of things. Imagination was the only limit!"

2. The MK-II prosthetic featured a pincer to pick objects up and could also bend. By equipping it with a LEGO motor, David was able to lift heavier objects.

3. With each new iteration, David's designs advanced the functionality of his prostheses. Crucially, these plastic-brick designs are much more affordable than conventional prosthetics, which are also costly to maintain.

4. When news of David's innovative work reached Zaure Bektemissova in France, she swiftly got in touch with the inventor. Her eight-year-old son Beknur was born with only partially developed limbs, and she was struggling to find him suitable prosthetics. In response, David created two brand-new LEGO limbs: the MK-Beknur to pick up objects – the
⊙ **first foot-controlled LEGO prosthetic arm** – and the eMK-Beknur, which is the
⊙ **first LEGO prosthetic arm with a stylus.**

5. In 2020, David teamed up with the editor of *Briques Mag*, Sébastien Mauvais, on the TV show *LEGO MASTERS France*. They went on to lift the LEGO-brick champions trophy.

6. David riding his INOKIM OX Super electric scooter, which has a specially modified braking system and artificial limb. This was developed by David's dad, Ferran Aguilar (inset), who has built bespoke vehicles for his son since he was a boy. Recently, the pair collaborated on the book *Pieza a Pieza* ("Piece by Piece"), which recounts David's life story to date. It was published in 2021, and the subtitle neatly sums up his extraordinary engineering abilities: "The Story of the Boy Who Built Himself".

Find out more about David in the Hall of Fame section at www.
guinnessworldrecords.com/2023

LONGEST CAR

On 1 Mar 2022, a classic GWR title holder officially regained its crown. *American Dream* is a 30.51-m-long (100-ft 1.5-in) super-stretch limo that can accommodate 75 passengers. It was originally designed by legendary custom-car builder Jay Ohrberg, and – in a slightly shorter incarnation – made headlines as the world's lengthiest automobile back in 1986: But upkeep costs and other challenges (where can you *park* it?!) saw it become a neglected, rusted wreck. In 2019, property tycoon and car collector Michael Dezer spotted its sad remains on eBay and snapped it up from then-owner Michael Manning (pictured; all USA). With the help of a team of auto-repair experts – and at a cost of some $250,000 (£190,725) – the duo brought *American Dream* back to life. Why not seek it out? It's on display at Dezerland Park in Orlando, Florida, USA. You can't miss it!

MISSIONS

Epic Engineering

EXPLORATION

DISCOVERY

RESEARCH

2023

American Dream houses a large waterbed, swimming pool, Jacuzzi, bathtub, mini-golf course and even a helipad!

HIGHEST BRIDGE

Beipanjiang First Bridge stands 565.4 m (1,854 ft 11 in) above China's Beipan River, between Yunnan and Guizhou. This cable-stayed road bridge opened on 29 Dec 2016. One World Trade Center, the tallest building in North America, would fit under the bridge's deck. For the **tallest bridge**, see p.126.

FIRST DOUBLE-HELIX BRIDGE

Singapore's 280-m (918-ft) Helix Bridge is the only one of its kind built to date. Designed by Cox Architecture and Architects 61, with engineers Arup, it uses two intertwining steel helices to create a complex tubular truss. It opened fully on 18 Jul 2010 at an overall cost of SGD$82.9 m ($60.2 m; £39.3 m).

LONGEST BRIDGE-TUNNEL

The Hong Kong–Zhuhai–Macau crossing in China's Pearl River Estuary is 29.6 km (18.4 mi) long. It consists of three cable-stayed bridges totalling 22.9 km (14.2 mi), a 6.7-km (4.2-mi) undersea tunnel and four artificial islands. Including approach highways, it stretches for 55 km (34.2 mi).

TYPES OF BRIDGE

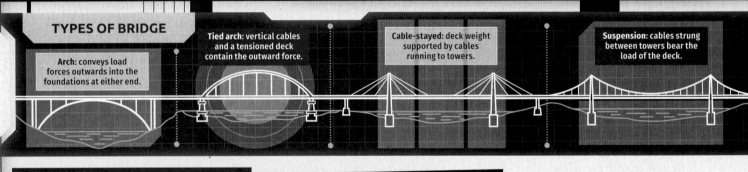

Arch: conveys load forces outwards into the foundations at either end.

Tied arch: vertical cables and a tensioned deck contain the outward force.

Cable-stayed: deck weight supported by cables running to towers.

Suspension: cables strung between towers bear the load of the deck.

LONGEST 3D-PRINTED STEEL BRIDGE

The 8.7-m (28-ft 7-in) MX3D Bridge spans the Oudezijds Achterburgwal, a canal in the De Wallen district of Amsterdam, Netherlands. Dutch engineering firm MX3D used robotic 3D-printing technology for its construction; as a result, it is a continuous piece of metal, with no joints or separate sections.

The bridge was formally opened by Queen Máxima of the Netherlands (left) on 15 Jul 2021.

Oldest vehicular suspension bridge

As of 2021, the Union Chain Bridge had been in place for 201 years. It straddles the River Tweed between the British towns of Horncliffe in Northumberland and Fishwick in Berwickshire. The bridge originally used wrought-iron chains to support the deck. It has a 2-tonne (4,400-lb) weight limit and only one car can cross at a time.

First tilting bridge

The Gateshead Millennium or "Winking" Bridge opened on 17 Sep 2001 and stretches 126 m (413 ft) across the River Tyne in Newcastle upon Tyne, UK. Rather than lifting vertically, the bridge rotates lengthwise on pivots on either bank. When it opens to allow boats to pass below, its motion mimics a very slow blink of an eye – hence its nickname.

First curling bridge

To date, the only curling bridge in the world is the "Rolling Bridge" at Paddington Basin in London, UK. Designed by Heatherwick Studio and completed in

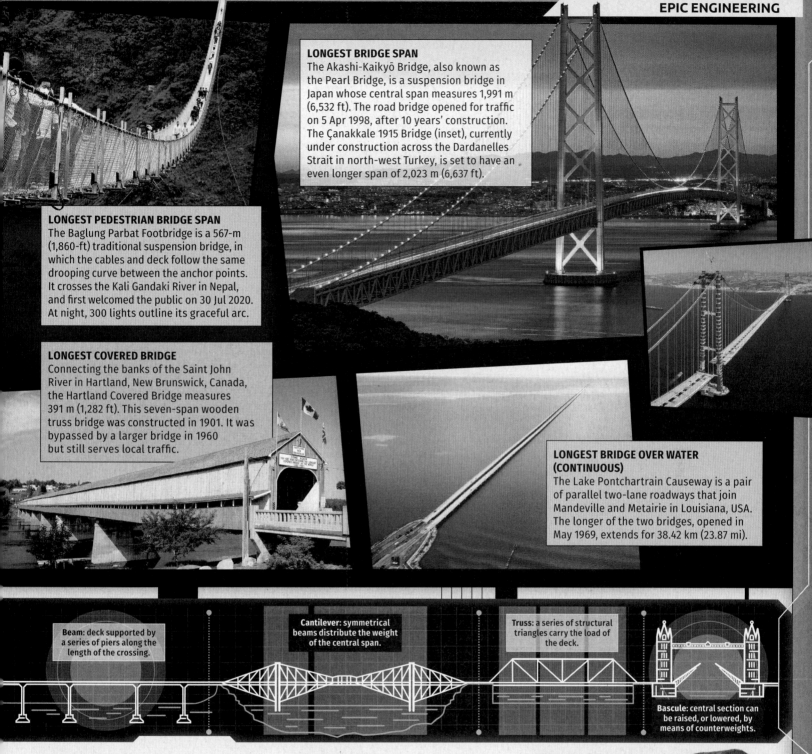

LONGEST BRIDGE SPAN

The Akashi-Kaikyō Bridge, also known as the Pearl Bridge, is a suspension bridge in Japan whose central span measures 1,991 m (6,532 ft). The road bridge opened for traffic on 5 Apr 1998, after 10 years' construction. The Çanakkale 1915 Bridge (inset), currently under construction across the Dardanelles Strait in north-west Turkey, is set to have an even longer span of 2,023 m (6,637 ft).

LONGEST PEDESTRIAN BRIDGE SPAN

The Baglung Parbat Footbridge is a 567-m (1,860-ft) traditional suspension bridge, in which the cables and deck follow the same drooping curve between the anchor points. It crosses the Kali Gandaki River in Nepal, and first welcomed the public on 30 Jul 2020. At night, 300 lights outline its graceful arc.

LONGEST COVERED BRIDGE

Connecting the banks of the Saint John River in Hartland, New Brunswick, Canada, the Hartland Covered Bridge measures 391 m (1,282 ft). This seven-span wooden truss bridge was constructed in 1901. It was bypassed by a larger bridge in 1960 but still serves local traffic.

LONGEST BRIDGE OVER WATER (CONTINUOUS)

The Lake Pontchartrain Causeway is a pair of parallel two-lane roadways that join Mandeville and Metairie in Louisiana, USA. The longer of the two bridges, opened in May 1969, extends for 38.42 km (23.87 mi).

Beam: deck supported by a series of piers along the length of the crossing.

Cantilever: symmetrical beams distribute the weight of the central span.

Truss: a series of structural triangles carry the load of the deck.

Bascule: central section can be raised, or lowered, by means of counterweights.

2004, the wood-and-steel pedestrian bridge uses hydraulic rams to curl its eight segments like a scorpion's tail. When closed it forms an octagon, and when extended it reaches 12.9 m (42 ft 4 in) across a canal inlet.

Widest bridge

The San Francisco-Oakland Bay Bridge in California, USA, is a complex of bridges that traverse San Francisco Bay. The East Span (opened 2013) has an overall deck width of 78.74 m (258 ft 4 in). It incorporates 10 lanes of roadway, a 4.7-m-wide (15-ft 5-in) bike path, and a gap where the central pylon supports the two bridge deck sections. The bridge is designed to withstand a magnitude-8.5 earthquake.

Longest...
Plastic bridge

The Aberfeldy Golf Club in Perth and Kinross, UK, incorporates a reinforced-plastic bridge over the River Tay that measures 113 m (370 ft 9 in) in length and has a main span of 63 m (206 ft 8 in).

Bascule bridge span

Serving both road and rail traffic, the Rethe Bascule Bridge has a bascule (drawbridge) section measuring 104.2 m (341 ft 10 in) between its pinion bearings. It crosses a shipping channel in Hamburg, Germany.

Germany is also home to the **longest canal bridge**. The 918-m (3,011-ft) Magdeburg Water Bridge connects the Mittellandkanal with the Elbe-Havel Canal and can be used by ships of up to 1,350 tonnes (2.9 million lb).

Combined road and rail bridge span

The Tsing Ma Bridge in Hong Kong, China, which opened to the public in May 1997, has a main span of 1,377 m (4,518 ft). This record will eventually pass to the Yavuz Sultan Selim Bridge in Turkey, but as of 2021 no rail infrastructure had been installed there.

Floating bridge

The pontoon-supported section of the USA's Evergreen Point Floating Bridge measures 2,349.5 m (7,708 ft). It connects Seattle to the suburb of Bellevue, Washington, across Lake Washington.

LONGEST ARCH BRIDGE SPAN

The Pingnan Third Bridge has a main span of 575 m (1,886 ft). It crosses the Xunjiang River near Pingnan in Guangxi, China, and opened for traffic on 28 Dec 2020. The structure is known as a "through-arch bridge", a design in which the deck passes through the load-bearing arch and is supported by cables.

Tallest Buildings

1. Wooden building

Located on the banks of Lake Mjøsa in the Norwegian town of Brumunddal, Mjøstårnet is an 18-storey mixed-use tower standing 85.4 m (280 ft) tall. It was designed by Voll Arkitekter and built by HENT and Moelven Limtre (all NOR), with construction finishing in Mar 2019. Mjøstårnet contains offices and apartments, a hotel, a restaurant and a swimming pool. Its load-bearing structures are made from glued laminated timber, or "glulam" – layers of lumber bonded together with durable adhesive.

2. Wooden structure

A truss tower in Gliwice, Poland, rises 118 m (387 ft) into the air – two metres taller than the **tallest tree**, Hyperion (see p.117). Constructed in 1935, it was originally used for radio transmissions and currently serves as a mobile phone tower. Although the Gliwice tower is the tallest wooden structure currently standing, it remains some way short of the **tallest ever** – the 190-m (623-ft) Mühlacker transmission tower in Germany, which was demolished in 1945.

3. Lighthouse

Although not primarily built to aid navigation, the 133-m-tall (436-ft) Jeddah Port Control Tower in Saudi Arabia is included in The National Geospatial Intelligence Agency's "List of Lights". The concrete-and-steel observation tower was built in 1990 on a pier by the entrance to Jeddah Seaport. It has a focal height (i.e., the height of its lamp as measured from sea level) of 137 m (449 ft) and produces three white flashes every 20 sec.

4. Pyramid

The Pyramid of Khufu at Giza, Egypt, was originally 146.7 m (481 ft) tall, although erosion and vandalism have reduced its height to 137.5 m (451 ft). Designed as a tomb for the pharaoh Khufu, it was finished in c. 2560 BCE following an estimated 27 years of building work and is the oldest of the Seven Wonders of the Ancient World. The Great Pyramid was the **tallest structure built by humans** for almost 4,000 years, until the short-lived 160-m (524-ft) spire of the UK's Lincoln Cathedral was completed in 1311 CE.

5. Pagoda

Completed in 2007, Tianning Pagoda in Changzhou, China, is 153.7 m (504 ft) tall. Construction took five years and cost around 300 million yuan ($38.5 m; £19.2 m). The 13-storey temple is topped by a golden spire with a 30-tonne (66,140-lb) bronze bell that can be heard from as far away as 5 km (3 mi). The Tianning Pagoda is the fifth such temple to have been built on the site since the Tang Dynasty (618–907 CE).

6. Church

Ulm Minster, a Lutheran church situated in the German state of Baden-Württemberg, has a spire that tops out at 161.53 m (530 ft). The minster was built in phases over the course of several centuries, between 1377 and 1890. It was declared complete at just 100 m (328 ft) in 1543; work was not resumed until the 19th century, when the lower parts of the building were renovated and reinforced, and a towering spire was added on to the 14th-century foundation.

In Spain, work continues on the unfinished Basilica de la Sagrada Família in Barcelona (see p.128). Designed by Antoni Gaudí, the church has been under construction since 1882 and will eventually measure 172.5 m (566 ft) to the top of its central tower.

7. Wind turbine

The Gaildorf Pilot Project near Stuttgart in Germany has four enormous hybridturm (hybrid tower) turbines with a hub height of 178 m (584 ft) and rotors that extend to 246.5 m (808 ft). The turbines were built by engineering firm Max Bögl Wind AG (DEU) and connected to the power grid on 19 Dec 2017. They each have reservoirs at their bases that feed a pumped-storage power station in the valley, generating 42 gigawatt-hours per year.

8. Ferris wheel

Opened on 21 Oct 2021, the Ain Dubai observation wheel on Bluewaters Island in the UAE measures 250 m (820 ft) from the ground to the top of its rim. See pp.148–49 for more.

The **tallest centreless observation wheel**, a futuristic take on the traditional amusement ride, stands 142.5 m (467 ft) over the Bailang River in Weifang, Shandong, China.

9. Minaret

The tallest building in Africa is a 264.3-m (867-ft) minaret housed inside Djamaa el Djazaïr, a massive modern religious complex in the Algerian capital of Algiers. As it sits in a seismically active area, the minaret is designed to withstand a magnitude-9 earthquake. Djamaa el Djazaïr covers an area of around 400,000 m² (4.3 million sq ft), including a 20,000-m² (215,000-sq-ft) prayer hall designed to accommodate 37,000 worshippers. It was constructed between 2012 and 2019 at a reported cost of around $1 bn (£773.8 m) and completed on 29 Apr 2019.

10. Iron structure

Originally standing 300 m (984 ft) high – now 330 m (1,082 ft) thanks to a TV antenna completed in Mar 2022 – the Eiffel Tower is an iconic element of the Parisian skyline (see p.126). Yet its proposed construction caused outcry among the city's artists, who argued that the "Iron Lady" would be a blot on the landscape. The Eiffel Tower was constructed from 18,038 metallic parts and took two years to build. It was inaugurated on 31 Mar 1889, in time for the Exposition Universelle. The tower would remain the **tallest structure** in the world until 27 May 1930, and the completion of the 319-m (1,046-ft) Chrysler Building in New York City, USA.

11. Hotel

The Gevora Hotel in Dubai, UAE, measures 356.33 m (1,169 ft) from ground level to the top. The building, instantly recognizable by its golden façade, consists of 75 floors and 528 rooms. Facilities include four restaurants, an open-air pool deck, a luxury spa and a health club. The high-end hotel took four years to construct and was inaugurated on 9 Feb 2018.

12. Steel building

Situated in the heart of downtown Chicago, Willis (formerly Sears) Tower is the third-tallest building in North America. The 108-storey steel skyscraper tops out at 442 m (1,450 ft), weighs 201,848 tonnes (222,500 tons) and has 416,000 m² (4.47 million sq ft) of floor space. It took 2,000 construction workers three years to build the tower, finishing in May 1973. Subsequent supertall buildings (i.e., skyscrapers more than 300 m, or 984 ft, tall) have been constructed around a core of reinforced concrete.

13. Residential building

Central Park Tower in New York City, USA, is a 472.4-m-high (1,550-ft) skyscraper containing 179 luxury apartments and amenities including a rooftop pool, gym and private members club. The tower is owned by the Extell Development Company (USA) and was topped out on 17 Sep 2019. The "cheapest" units in the building reportedly sold for more than $6 m (£4.8 m), and the larger penthouse apartments were listed at $63 m (£50.6 m).

The three tallest hotels in the world are all in Dubai: the Gevora (see 11 above), the J W Marriott Marquis Dubai (355 m; 1,165 ft) and Rose Rayhaan by Rotana (333 m; 1,093 ft).

14. Unoccupied building

Goldin Finance 117 is a 128-storey skyscraper in the Chinese city of Tianjin that topped out in Sep 2015 at a height of 596.6 m (1,957 ft). At the time, this made it the world's fifth-tallest building. However, the tower's owner ran into financial difficulties and was forced to suspend work on the skyscraper in December of that year, leaving it unfinished and unoccupied. In response to this and other public failures, in Apr 2020 the Chinese government promulgated new urban planning regulations effectively banning the construction of new buildings greater than 500 m (1,640 ft) in height.

15. Clock tower

The Makkah Clock Royal Tower in Mecca, Saudi Arabia, is 601 m (1,972 ft) tall. It is part of a complex of seven hotels called the Abraj Al Bait, which lies close to Islam's sacred Great Mosque of Mecca and cost an estimated $16 bn (£9.8 bn) to construct. The tower boasts the **largest clock face**, with a diameter of 43 m (141 ft) – six times larger than the one on the Elizabeth Tower of the UK's Houses of Parliament, commonly called "Big Ben".

16. Twisting tower

The Council on Tall Buildings and Urban Habitat defines a "twisting" building as one that progressively rotates its floor plates or its façade as it gains height. The Shanghai Tower in China is a 632-m-tall (2,073-ft) mixed-use building whose 128 floors twist a total of 120° between the ground and the roof. This deflects wind loads, allowing the tower to be built with less steel bracing and a less pronounced taper than comparable structures. The Shanghai Tower was officially completed on 2 Sep 2014.

17. Tower

The Tokyo Skytree rises 634 m (2,080 ft) above the Sumida district of the Japanese capital. Completed in Feb 2012, one of the Skytree's main functions is broadcasting TV and radio signals; its predecessor, the Tokyo Tower (333 m; 1,092 ft), had become surrounded by too many high-rise buildings to give complete digital terrestrial television coverage.

18. ◗ Building

Tallest of them all is the Burj Khalifa, which soars into the skies above Dubai to a height of 828 m (2,716 ft) – twice that of the Empire State Building. The tower's three-winged design was inspired by the spider lily, *Hymenocallis*, a regional desert flower. Burj Khalifa was developed by Emaar Properties (UAE) and officially opened on 4 Jan 2010. Features include the **most floors in a building** (163) and the **highest outdoor observation deck** (555.7 m; 1,823 ft) – the appropriately named At the Top, Burj Khalifa SKY, which can be found on the building's 148th floor.

Goldin Finance 117's "walking stick" design was to be crowned with an atrium shaped like a cut diamond.

Each of the four clock faces of the Makkah Clock Royal Tower are covered by 98 million pieces of glass mosaic and illuminated by 2 million LED lights.

Mitsubishi Electric's NexWay elevator in unit OB-3 of the Shanghai Tower travels 121 floors at a speed of 73.8 km/h (45.8 mph), making it the **fastest elevator**.

Bionics

First powered exoskeleton

In development from 1965 to 1971, the Hardiman was an experimental 1,500-lb (680-kg) hydraulic lifting suit created by General Electric (USA) for the US Army. It was designed to enable users to carry objects as heavy as 750 lb (340 kg). Hardiman was abandoned at the prototype stage, however, due to its alarming tendency towards "violent and uncontrolled motion".

Fastest letter selection using a brain-computer interface

By monitoring electrical activity in the brain, it is possible to pick out specific signals that can be used to control external devices. This technique shows promise for those who have difficulty writing or speaking. In May 2021, a team from Stanford University (USA) tested a brain-computer interface that allowed paralysed users to compose sentences at speeds of 90 characters per minute. It works by having users visualize writing letters by hand.

An early attempt at a more direct approach, the **first thought-to-speech system** was described in Apr 2019 by a team from the University of California, San Francisco (USA). This device monitored the neural activity of people while they imagined speaking, and used this to generate mostly understandable synthesized speech.

Most mind-controlled prosthetics

In Dec 2014, Leslie Baugh of Colorado, USA, who lost both his arms in an accident, became the first person able to use two nerve-controlled prosthetic arms at once. He first needed surgery to connect the nerves that formerly controlled his limbs

FIRST POWERED EXOSKELETON APPROVED FOR GENERAL USE

A powered exoskeleton is an external body suit equipped with technologies that aid, or improve, limb capability. On 26 Jun 2014, the ReWalk Personal became the first such device cleared for home and public use by the United States Food and Drug Administration.

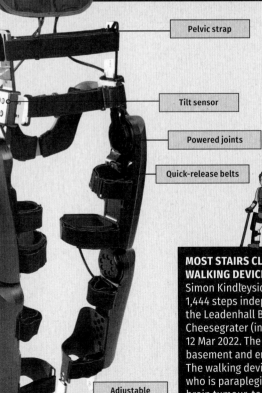

Control unit and battery

Pelvic strap

Tilt sensor

Powered joints

Quick-release belts

Adjustable ankle joints

FARTHEST DISTANCE WALKED BY A PERSON WITH PARAPLEGIA

Michael Roccati (ITA), who was paralyzed in a motorcycle accident, is now able to walk thanks to a spinal-cord implant developed by French neuroscientist Grégoire Courtine and Swiss neurosurgeon Jocelyne Bloch. As part of physical therapy, he walked 500 m (1,640 ft) in early 2022.

to the bionic arms. He also had to train his mind to work with the prostheses before finally being able to move both arms with his brain. The prosthetics were developed by researchers at Johns Hopkins Applied Physics Laboratory in Laurel, Maryland, USA.

Fastest artificially assisted reaction times

Another area of research in bionics is in the use of electrical stimulation – either of the nerves or muscles – to control body parts whose connecting nerves have been damaged (see above). In May 2019, researchers from the University of Chicago (the same team that developed DextrEMS, see opposite) generated an artificially assisted reaction time of 50 milliseconds using electro-muscular stimulation. That's five times faster than usual.

Most common neuroprosthesis

Cochlear implants have been fitted to more than 736,900 people worldwide, according to figures released by the United States National Institutes of Health in Dec 2019. These devices pair an external microphone with an implant inside the skull that directly stimulates the auditory nerve, restoring some degree of hearing to individuals who are otherwise completely deaf.

MOST STAIRS CLIMBED IN A ROBOTIC WALKING DEVICE IN EIGHT HOURS

Simon Kindleysides (UK) ascended 1,444 steps independently within the Leadenhall Building, aka the Cheesegrater (inset), in London, UK, on 12 Mar 2022. The ascent started in the basement and ended at the 50th floor. The walking device allows Kindleysides, who is paraplegic after suffering a brain tumour, to climb by detecting subtle shifts in the balance of his body and then initiating forward steps.

BIONIC TECHNOLOGY

The term "bionic" describes artificial devices used to overcome impairments or enhance abilities. Bionic technologies mimic or assist the functions of human body parts and systems, rather than simply acting as physical placeholders. Below, we set out the four basic types.

Monitoring
Implants and external devices that sense body functions. Examples include blood-sugar monitors, electrocardiograms and fitness trackers.

Orthotics
Devices that support weak or impaired body functions. Examples include exoskeletons, hearing aids and cardiac pacemakers.

Prosthetics
Devices that replace lost body functions. Examples include artificial limbs, cochlear implants and artificial hearts.

Cyborg augmentation
Devices that enhance existing abilities or senses, or add new ones. Examples include high-power industrial exoskeletons and implants to enable the detection of magnetic fields.

MOST PRECISE BIONIC HAND CONTROLLER

The "independence index" is a scale used to describe the extent to which each finger is able to move independently, rated on a scale of 0 to 1. In Oct 2021, a team at the University of Chicago, led by Dr Pedro Lopes (PRT), tested a system called DextrEMS, which combined electrical stimulators with mechanical brakes, achieving an independence index of 0.6 (not far off the 0.8 of a typical human).

DextrEMS actuators used to position fingers for playing guitar chords

LARGEST COMPETITION FOR USERS AND DEVELOPERS OF ASSISTIVE DEVICES

Cybathlon is a championship designed to drive improvements to assistive technologies. The 2016 edition, held on 8 Oct, attracted 66 teams from as far afield as China and Brazil. The event, organized in partnership with Swiss university ETH Zurich, is held every four years. It challenges teams to complete mundane tasks, such as walking down stairs while carrying multiple objects.

MOST DRUMBEATS IN ONE MINUTE USING A DRUMSTICK PROSTHETIC

Jason Barnes performed 2,400 beats in 60 sec in Atlanta, Georgia, USA, on 25 Jul 2018. Barnes used a prosthetic arm created by Gil Weinberg (both USA). He wore an electromyographic band that senses muscle activity from his forearm and triggers the motorized artificial arm into drumming.

Most of the mass of the suit, and any object being carried, is transferred via the legs to the ground.

BEST-SELLING EXOSKELETON

According to figures released by robotics firm Innophys (JPN) on 7 Jul 2021, a total of 20,000 Muscle Suits have been sold since the product was introduced in Feb 2016. The Muscle Suit is a hip-and-back exoskeleton, designed to give wearers an additional 25.5 kg-force (56.2 lb-force) of lifting power.

STRONGEST HUMAN EXOSKELETON

The Guardian XO is a robotic full-body suit manufactured by Sarcos Robotics (USA) that enables its operator to lift objects weighing up to 90 kg (198 lb). That's about the same as a full-grown adult kangaroo! The operator bears only around 5% of that load. Sarcos unveiled its prototype in Apr 2019. The suit is designed to handle objects that are too heavy for a human to comfortably lift on a regular basis, but typically too small for the practical deployment of mechanical hoists and forklifts.

Trainspotting

LARGEST DISPLAY OF STEAM LOCOMOTIVES
Da'an Locomotive Expo Park (CHN) presented a fleet of 79 steam engines in Jilin, China, on 30 Jun 2021. Remarkably, China Railway didn't retire the last of these QJ-series locomotives from main-line service until 2002.

FIRST SOLAR-POWERED TRAIN IN SCHEDULED SERVICE
The Byron Bay Solar Train carried its first paying customers on 16 Dec 2017. Its roof incorporates a thin-film solar-panel array that can generate 6.5 kW of power. The train runs along a 3-km (1.8-mi) stretch of the previously disused Murwillumbah line between North Beach and Byron Beach in New South Wales, Australia.

MOST POWERFUL STEAM LOCOMOTIVE IN OPERATION
The Union Pacific "Big Boy" 4014 is capable of a tractive effort – i.e., pulling force – of 135,375 lbf (602 kN) at 10 mph (16 km/h). It was built in Nov 1941 by the American Locomotive Company, and retired in 1959. Exhumed from a museum in 2012, it re-entered service on 4 May 2019 to pull excursion trains.

LONGEST RAIL NETWORKS

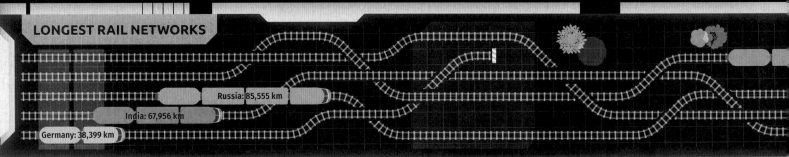

Russia: 85,555 km

India: 67,956 km

Germany: 38,399 km

BUSIEST RAILWAY COMPANY
Over the course of 2019, Indian Railways carried 8,439,000,000 passengers according to statistics compiled by the International Union of Railways. The overall passenger load transported by the company changed only a little during 2020 – dropping to 8,086,000,000 – despite the ongoing COVID-19 pandemic.

Busiest railway network (country)
An estimated 8,989,900,000 journeys were made on Japan's railways in 2019, according to the International Union of Railways. The largest single operator is the East Japan Railway Company, which is second only to Indian Railways in terms of passenger numbers.

Busiest metro system
In 2019, the Beijing Subway in China had an average daily ridership of 10,869,000 people, and carried 3,962,351,000 passengers during the year. The following year, pandemic restrictions brought these numbers down to 6,269,000 and 2,293,984,000 respectively.

First trainspotter
The earliest confirmed trainspotter was Fanny Johnson (UK), who in 1861 – at the age of 14 – began keeping a journal entitled "Names of the engines on the Great Western that I have seen". She noted the numbers of various locomotives that passed near her home in Westbourne Park, London, UK. The pastime is still popular today, as shown by the **most followed trainspotter on TikTok** (see pp.210–11).

First regular passenger railway service
The Oystermouth Railway, later to become the Swansea and Mumbles Railway, began serving customers in Swansea, UK, on 25 Mar 1807.

First underground rail system
The inaugural section of the London Underground opened on 10 Jan 1863, with the first passenger journeys on the following day. The initial stretch of what was then named the Metropolitan Railway ran 6 km (3.7 mi), between Paddington and Farringdon Street. To build the line, engineers employed the "cut and cover" system, with its brick-lined tunnels constructed in trenches and later reburied.

The **most extensive underground rail system** is that of China's Shanghai Métro. Its overall track length extended to 831 km (516 mi) with the opening of two driverless metro lines on 30 Dec 2021.

All passenger numbers are based on 2019 figures, to avoid distortion from the effects of COVID-19 lockdowns.

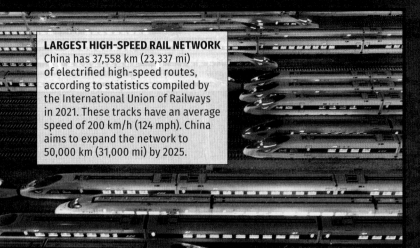

LARGEST HIGH-SPEED RAIL NETWORK
China has 37,558 km (23,337 mi) of electrified high-speed routes, according to statistics compiled by the International Union of Railways in 2021. These tracks have an average speed of 200 km/h (124 mph). China aims to expand the network to 50,000 km (31,000 mi) by 2025.

FASTEST MAGLEV TRAIN
Operated by the Central Japan Railway Company, the L0 (A07) series is a magnetically levitated (maglev) train. It achieved a speed of 603 km/h (374.68 mph) on a test track in Yamanashi, Japan, on 21 Apr 2015. The L0 could travel from Paris to Berlin in less than three hours.

FASTEST STEAM LOCOMOTIVE
On 3 Jul 1938, the London North Eastern Railway's Class A4 No.4468 *Mallard* reached a speed of 125 mph (201.16 km/h) during tests of a new brake system in Rutland, UK. The streamlined Class A4 locomotives were designed for high-speed services on the relatively level and straight East Coast Main Line, and routinely exceeded 100 mph (160 km/h) in passenger service. Today, *Mallard* is displayed at the National Railway Museum in York, UK.

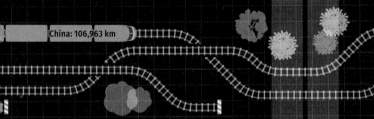

China: 106,963 km   USA: 148,433 km

The **most stations in an underground rail system** is 468, in New York City, USA, although only 277 are actually underground. It was reported in Jan 2022 that traveller numbers had dropped to 2.2 million people - about 40% of the pre-pandemic level.

Largest railway station (platforms)
Built in 1903–13, Grand Central Terminal at Park Avenue and 42nd Street in New York City contains 44 platforms. They are located on two underground levels, with 41 tracks on the upper level and 26 on the lower. The creation of a commuter terminal for the Long Island Rail Road, currently scheduled for late 2022, will add an extra four platforms and eight tracks.

The **longest railway platform** is at Gorakhpur Junction, a station in Uttar Pradesh, India. The No.1 platform measures 1,366 m (4,481 ft), including ramps, and 1,355 m (4,445 ft) without them.

Greatest distance by a runaway train
On 27 Mar 1884, an uncrewed set of eight boxcars loaded with coal travelled 97 mi (156 km) in the USA.

At about 5 p.m., a storm tore the roof off a roundhouse in Akron, Colorado, sending the boxcars rolling east. As the line descended on to the Great Plains, they accelerated to speeds of up to 40 mph (64 km/h). At Benkelman, Nebraska, two railroad engineers gave chase in a locomotive, successfully coupling with the train and bringing it to a stop at 7.30 p.m.

Longest urban streetcar/tram route
Public Transport Victoria Route 75 runs 22.8 km (14.1 mi) from Vermont South, in the eastern suburbs of Melbourne, Australia, to the city's central business district. The route was expanded to its current extent on 26 Jan 2014.

Australia also boasts the **longest straight railroad**. For 478 km (297 mi) on the Nullarbor Plain, the Trans-Australian Railway runs dead straight, although not level, from Mile 496 between Nurina and Loongana, Western Australia, to Mile 793 between Ooldea and Watson, South Australia.

LONGEST CHILDREN'S RAILWAY LINE
The Gyermekvasút (Children's Railway) in Hungary is an 11.7-km-long (7.2-mi) narrow-gauge railway line staffed by children aged 10-14 under supervision. Also known as Line 7, it has a one-way journey time of c. 50 min and stops at seven stations between Hűvösvölgy and Széchenyihegy, on the Buda side of Budapest. The railway has been in continuous operation since 31 Jul 1948.

Tallest Ferris Wheel

Towering 250 m (820 ft) above an artificial island in the UAE, Ain Dubai is a hi-tech, supersized reimagining of the traditional amusement ride. To give you an idea of its scale, we've presented it alongside one of the great engineering feats of the ancient world – the Great Pyramid of Giza in Egypt.

Ain Dubai uses a total of 2,400 km (1,491 mi) of cables – 12 times longer than the nearby Suez Canal.

GUINNESS WORLD RECORDS

Opened on 21 Oct 2021, Ain Dubai takes its passengers on a revolutionary 38-min journey through the skies, providing a waterfront view of Dubai's unmistakable skyline from Bluewaters Island.

The **tallest Ferris wheel** measures 250 m (820 ft) from the ground to the top of its rim and is fitted with 48 cabins, giving it a total capacity of 1,750 people. Ain Dubai is 82.5 m (270 ft) taller than the previous record holder, the Las Vegas High Roller, and more than three times the height of the **first Ferris wheel**. The inset picture also visualizes that 1893 engineering marvel on the Giza Plateau, far from its actual home in Chicago, Illinois, USA. Though it was smaller, George Ferris' original wheel could accommodate 2,160 passengers into its 36 cabins.

The Chicago Ferris wheel was built in just six months, but scaling up Ain Dubai to the height of a 60-storey building introduced a number of unprecedented challenges. In total, it took the

project's lead contractor, Hyundai Engineering & Construction, six years to get Ain Dubai turning. The 192 tensioned cables that provide the wheel's structure and strength could only be attached once the rim was complete and in position. This meant that the wheel had to be constructed from eight pizza-slice-shaped segments, attached to the hub by steel trusses and reinforced with a temporary steelwork around the rim. To see how it compares to other colossal constructions, turn to pp.154–55.

Round-Up

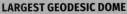

LARGEST GEODESIC DOME
The Jeddah Superdome's self-supporting roof has a diameter of 210.1 m (689 ft 3 in), enclosing a space that is 46 m (150 ft 11 in) high and wide enough to contain an Olympic-size running track. This multipurpose event space, located in Saudi Arabia's second city, was built between Feb 2020 and Jun 2021 (construction process pictured).

First AI inventor
In Jul 2021, DABUS – a neural network created by Stephen Thaler (USA) – became the first artificial intelligence to be named in a successful patent application. DABUS and Thaler were co-listed as inventors on South African patent ZA2021/03242 "Food Container and Devices and Methods for Attracting Enhanced Attention". The innovations described in the patent – a plastic container that used fractal geometry to make it easier to heat and an attention-grabbing pulsed light – resulted from DABUS processing solutions until it arrived at a potentially useful one.

Most powerful laser
The ELI-Nuclear Physics facility in Măgurele, Romania, has two 10-petawatt (PW) lasers that can be used jointly to focus 20 petawatts of laser energy on to a target. A petawatt is a quadrillion (10^{15}) watts. Built as part of the European Union's Extreme Light Infrastructure research project, they were first tested at 10 petawatts in Mar 2019.

The **highest-intensity laser beam** is 110 zettawatts per cm², achieved by the Center for Relativistic Laser Science (CoReLS) in Gwangju, South Korea. A zettawatt is a sextillion (10^{21}) watts. The test results were published on 6 May 2021.

Most complete human genome sequence
The term "genome" describes an organism's full DNA set, made up of billions of base pairs. On 27 May 2021, international research group the Telomere-to-Telomere (T2T) Consortium published a draft research paper of a sequence called T2T-CHM13, which encompasses all 3.055 billion base pairs of a sample human genome. Previous genome sequences were unable to decipher several long stretches of confusing repeating patterns.

Deepest undersea core sample
On 14 May 2021, a core was taken from the seabed in the Japan Trench, 8,023 m (26,322 ft) below sea level. The sample was collected using the Giant Piston Corer, a 40-m-long (131-ft) coring drill deployed from the Japanese Research Vessel *Kaimei*. Deep-sea cores can be used to gather data on historic climate shifts.

Longest wastewater tunnel
The Túnel Emisor Oriente (Eastern Discharge Tunnel) in Mexico City is 62.1 km (38.58 mi) long, with a diameter of 7 m (22 ft 11 in). This massive storm drain carries wastewater from Mexico City's endorheic basin (a lake with no outflow) under the mountains to the north, to a point where it can drain into the Pánuco River. It is longer than both the **longest road tunnel** – Norway's Lærdal Tunnel, at 24.5 km (15.2 mi) – and the **longest rail tunnel** – the Gotthard BaseTunnel, at 57 km (35.42 mi), between Göschenen and Airolo in Switzerland.

MOST UAVs AIRBORNE SIMULTANEOUSLY
Shenzhen High Great Innovation Technology Development (CHN) launched 5,164 unmanned aerial vehicles skywards in Shenzhen, Guangdong, China, on 18 May 2021. The drones were carefully arranged in lines for a dramatic light display. Each one weighed 0.54 kg (1 lb 3 oz) – about as heavy as a tin of beans.

LARGEST SHEET OF CHAINMAIL
Hill House in Helensburgh, UK, is encased in a 2,700-m² (29,062-sq-ft) chainmail sheet supported by a steel frame. Known as the "Hill House Box", it was designed by Carmody Groarke Architects for the National Trust for Scotland in order to protect this Art Nouveau showpiece – designed by Charles and Margaret Mackintosh – during restoration. The metal covering was completed on 31 May 2019.

The chainmail keeps off the rain, allowing the water-damaged landmark to dry out.

LONGEST PUBLIC-TRANSIT CABLE-CAR ROUTE
Mexico City's Line 2 measures 10,555.3 m (34,630 ft) – about four times the length of Washington, DC's National Mall – from Constitución de 1917 station to Santa Marta station. Created by Sistema de Transporte Público Cablebús (MEX), it was inaugurated on 8 Aug 2021. The system has the capacity to transport 200,000 people per day and has 308 cabins.

Largest tunnel-boring machine

Built by Herrenknecht (DEU), the Mixshield S880 *Qin Liangyu* has a maximum shield diameter of 17.63 m (57 ft 10 in), a length of 120 m (393 ft 8 in) and weighs 4,850 tonnes (5,346 tons). It was used by Bouygues Construction (FRA) to excavate the Chek Lap Kok to Tuen Mun subsea road tunnel in Hong Kong, China. The 5-km-long (3.1-mi) tunnel section was created between 25 Mar and 3 Nov 2015, when *Qin Liangyu*'s shield diameter was reduced to 14 m (45 ft 11 in) to complete the project alongside another Herrenknecht machine.

The **fastest tunnel-boring machine** is the 3.4-m-diameter (11-ft) Robbins Mk 12C, built to excavate the Katoomba Carrier sewage redirection tunnel in Australia's Blue Mountains. In Aug 1994, it achieved a single-day distance record of 172.4 m (565 ft), removing 1,565.3 m³ (55,278 cu ft) of rock en route.

Longest journey in a fuel-cell vehicle without refuelling

From 23 to 24 Aug 2021, a hydrogen-powered Toyota Mirai was driven 1,360.37 km (845.29 mi) without refuelling in Gardena, California, USA. The event was organized by Toyota Motor North America and the drivers were Wayne Gerdes and Bob Winger (all USA).

Largest Rube Goldberg

The cartoonist Reuben Garrett Lucius Goldberg became famous for his detailed depictions of inordinately complex inventions, and inspired inventors to create real-life equivalents. Chevrolet Menlo, Wang Xiqi and Guan Jian (all CHN) created a 427-step Rube Goldberg to turn on a neon light, as verified in Langfang, Hebei, on 24 Sep 2021.

TALLEST RIDEABLE BICYCLE

Adam Zdanowicz (POL) rode a 7.41-m-tall (24-ft 3.7-in) bike in Białystok, Poland, on 21 Dec 2020. It took him about a month to plan and design the bicycle, with another three weeks or so devoted to building it. The Christmas-tree-shaped bike is constructed entirely from recycled materials.

FASTEST ELECTRIC AIRCRAFT

On 16 Nov 2021, the Rolls-Royce *Spirit of Innovation*, flown by test pilot Steve Jones (UK), averaged 555.9 km/h (345.4 mph) over a 3-km (1.8-mi) course in Wiltshire, UK. This experimental aircraft is based on the Nemesis NXT racing plane, but is fitted with a custom-made 400-kW (536-hp) electric motor (inset).

LONGEST TUNNEL FLOWN THROUGH IN AN AEROPLANE

On 4 Sep 2021, stunt pilot and Red Bull Air Racer Dario Costa (ITA) flew his racing plane 1.73 km (1.07 mi) through the Çatalca Tunnels, on Turkey's Northern Marmara Motorway. With only 4 m (13 ft) between the wingtips and the walls, Costa navigated the tunnels at an average speed of 245 km/h (152 mph).

Upon emerging from the tunnels after his 44-sec flight, Costa celebrated with a mid-air loop.

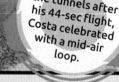

FIRST UNDERWATER ROUNDABOUT

On 19 Dec 2020, the Eysturoy Tunnel in the Faroe Islands opened to traffic. It includes a submarine roundabout located beneath the Skálafjørður, a fjord that splits the island of Eysturoy. The tunnel joins the towns of Runavík and Strendur, both located on the island, with the Faroese capital of Tórshavn on the isle of Streymoy.

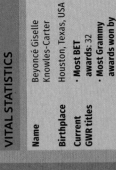

Name Beyoncé Giselle Knowles-Carter

Birthplace Houston, Texas, USA

Current GWR titles

- **Most BET awards:** 32
- **Most Grammy awards won by a vocalist:** 28
- **Most Grammy nominations (female):** 79
- **Most MTV Video Music Awards:** 30

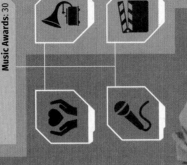

MUSIC MEGASTAR

Beyoncé

She has sold more than 200 million records worldwide, starred in Hollywood films and is obliterated music-industry records. She is a fashion icon, activist and philanthropist. Little wonder they call her "Queen Bey".

From an early age, Beyoncé demonstrated a huge talent for singing and dancing. Aged eight, she joined Girl's Tyme, which would evolve into one of the most successful girl groups in history: Destiny's Child.

The trio parted ways in 2006, but as a solo artist Beyoncé went from strength to strength. Hits such as "Crazy in Love" and "Single Ladies (Put a Ring On It)" became dancefloor staples, while "Halo" has been streamed more than 1 billion times on Spotify. With 2016's *Lemonade*, she became the **first act to debut at No.1 in the USA with their first six studio albums.**

Beyoncé continues to push boundaries both on and off the stage – so much so that in 2021 she was among the inaugural 12 celebrities inducted into the Black Music & Entertainment Walk of Fame in Atlanta, Georgia.

The records don't stop with Beyoncé. Her husband, Jay-Z, boasts his own GWR titles (see pp.180–81), and now even their children are getting in on the act; breaking records has become a Knowles family tradition.

A FILM BY BEYONCÉ

HOMΣCOMING

NOW STREAMING | NETFLIX

Beyoncé wrote and directed the award-winning 2019 Netflix concert film *HOMECOMING.*

Find out more about Beyoncé in the Hall of Fame section at www. guinnessworldrecords.com/2023

1. In 2015, Beyoncé visited Haiti to see how the island had recovered in the wake of the 2010 earthquake. Her BeyGOOD foundation has also given grants to Black business owners and families affected by the COVID crisis.

2. Presenting fellow pop legend Michael Jackson with an award in 2003. Beyoncé credits Jackson as one of her greatest musical inspirations, who "helped me to become the artist I am".

3. Together with Destiny's Child bandmates Kelly Rowland and Michelle Williams, Beyoncé achieved unprecedented chart success. Their single "Independent Women Pt 1", released in Aug 2000, spent the **most weeks at No.1 on the US singles chart by a girl group** – 11.

4. Beyoncé voiced lioness Nala and curated the soundtrack for the 2019 remake of *The Lion King*. She was joined on the track "BROWN SKIN GIRL" by daughter Blue Ivy (b. 7 Jan 2012), who is the **youngest individually credited Grammy winner**, aged 9 years 66 days.

5. As The Carters, Beyoncé and husband Jay-Z released the studio album *Everything is Love* and embarked on two world tours. They have won the **most Grammy awards by a married couple** – 51.

6. At the 63rd Grammy Awards on 14 Mar 2021, Beyoncé added four more trophies to her collection to take her career tally to 28. This is the **most Grammys won by a woman**, and also **by a vocalist**, since the awards began in 1959.

4

5

6

MOST VIEWERS FOR A NETFLIX ORIGINAL DEBUT
Released on 17 Sep 2021, the Netflix Original series *Squid Game* (Siren Pictures) was watched by 142 million subscriber households in its first month – two-thirds of the streaming service's subscription base. The nine-part survival thriller was created by South Korean filmmaker Hwang Dong-hyuk and reached the No.1 position in 97 territories. Its plot sees 456 contestants risk their lives in a series of challenges for 45.6 bn won ($38.8 m; £28.1 m) in prize money.

A month after the show's debut, Bloomberg revealed that *Squid Game* had boosted the stock-market value of Netflix by $19 bn (£13.8 bn).

MISSIONS

Entertainment

The challenges in *Squid Game* are all inspired by traditional South Korean playground activities.

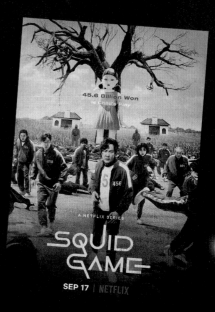

Visual & Special Effects

LARGEST ANIMATRONIC

A spinosaurus built by Stan Winston Studio (USA) for *Jurassic Park III* (USA, 2001) weighed 25,000 lb (11,340 kg) and was nearly 45 ft (13.7 m) long. The 1,000-hp (735-kW) hydraulic puppet was mounted on a motorized cart.

MOST 3D-PRINTED FACES IN A STOP-MOTION MOVIE

For its cryptozoological comedy *Missing Link* (CAN/USA, 2019), animation studio LAIKA (USA) used 106,000 colour 3D-printed faces. Each bore a different expression approved by the director that could be switched between animation frames.

3,260 LED panels, covering 720 m² (7,750 sq ft)

MOST PHOTO-REAL ANIMALS CREATED FOR A MOVIE

The Lion King (USA/UK, 2019) featured 86 different computer-generated (CG) species, as created by the UK's Moving Picture Company. More than 1,280 artists, including 130 animators, built their virtual menagerie using 237,000 reference images.

LARGEST LED VOLUME SHOOTING STAGE

The near-circular (310°) Pixomondo and William F White International LED stage in Vancouver, Canada, is 27.4 m deep, 24.3 m wide and 8.3 m tall (90 ft x 80 ft x 27 ft 3 in). Wall and ceiling LED panels create VFX without needing greenscreens.

VISUAL EFFECTS SOCIETY'S TOP 10 MOST INFLUENTIAL VFX MOVIES

10. *The Abyss* (USA, 1989)

9. *Alien* (UK/USA, 1979)

8. *Close Encounters of the Third Kind* (USA/UK, 1977)

7. *King Kong* (USA, 1933)

6. *Tron* (USA, 1982)

First Oscar for Special Effects

The inaugural Academy Award for Best Special Effects (now Visual Effects) was won on 29 Feb 1940 by *The Rains Came* (USA, 1939), ahead of *The Wizard of Oz*. The movie used a split-screen combination of live action and miniatures to depict a devastating earthquake and flood.

The **most Oscars for Visual Effects** is eight (including two Special Achievement awards), won by Dennis Muren (USA) for his work on titles such as *Jurassic Park* and *The Abyss*.

MOST VISUAL-EFFECTS SHOTS IN A MOVIE

The number of VFX shots in blockbusters continues to grow, with India's film industry now racing ahead of Hollywood. S S Rajamouli's medieval fantasy epic *Baahubali: The Beginning* (IND, 2015) contained around 4,500 separate VFX shots created by more than 600 staff working for 16 different studios.

First cloud tank used in a movie

The appearance of atmospheric skies can be created by injecting liquids into a tank filled with layers of salt and fresh water. The first cloud-tank shot in a feature film was made by Scott Squires, under the supervision of Douglas Trumbull (both USA), for Steven Spielberg's *Close Encounters of the Third Kind*.

First digital face replacement in a movie

In *Jurassic Park*, stuntwoman Nathalie B Bollinger performed the scene where Lex Murphy (Ariana Richards) falls through a ceiling panel while being chased by a velociraptor. Richards' face was subsequently added into the shot via digital face replacement by ILM (see right).

Most indoor rain for a movie

A stormy scene from *Bad Times at the El Royale* (USA, 2018) was shot on a set beneath 42 "rain heads" capable of dropping 2,000 gal (9,092 litres) of water – the equivalent of 50 bath-tubs' worth – every minute, which then needed to be drained and recirculated.

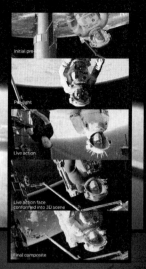

LONGEST SINGLE VISUAL-EFFECTS SHOT

The opening shot of Alfonso Cuarón's *Gravity* (USA/UK, 2013) lasts for 12 min 46 sec without any apparent cuts. The scene depicts astronauts – including characters played by Sandra Bullock and George Clooney – servicing the Hubble Space Telescope until a debris field hits them. The effects were provided by Framestore (UK).

Initial pre...

Pre-light

Live action

Live action face conformed into 3D scene

Final composite

LARGEST VISUAL EFFECT

The interior of Planet Ego in *Guardians of the Galaxy Vol. 2* (USA, 2017) was created as a highly detailed "hero" shot by Wētā FX (NZ). The studio drew upon Mandelbulb (3D-fractal) research to produce the effect, which required the rendering of a record 361 billion polygons.

MOST COMPLICATED CG MODEL IN A MOVIE

The malevolent robot Devastator in *Transformers: Revenge of the Fallen* (USA, 2009) was constructed from 52,632 individual pieces made from 11.7 million polygons overlaid with 6,467 textures. It was the work of ILM (see below).

5. *Jurassic Park* (USA, 1993)

3. *2001: A Space Odyssey* (UK/USA, 1968) & *The Matrix* (USA/AUS, 1999)

2. *Blade Runner* (USA, 1982)

1. *Star Wars: Episode IV – A New Hope* (USA, 1977)

Largest cinematic battle sequences

Peter Jackson's *Lord of the Rings* trilogy (NZ/USA, 2001–03) contained combat scenes with more than 200,000 characters. They were created by Wētā FX's crowd-simulation software "Massive", which used AI to determine how characters interacted.

Largest movie production budget

Avatar (USA, 2009) had a production budget of $425 m (£246 m), according to The Numbers. The sci-fi odyssey became the **first movie to gross $2 bn** on the weekend of 29–30 Jan 2010, and as of 21 Mar 2022 was the **highest-grossing movie** outright, having earned $2,845,899,541 (£2.1 bn) at the global box office.

Most high explosives detonated in a movie take

A trio of explosions using 300 lb (136.4 kg) of TNT equivalent was filmed on 8 Mar 2019 for the James Bond movie *No Time to Die* (UK/USA, 2021). The single shot took place on the UK's Salisbury Plain and was the work of EON Productions, MGM Studios, Universal Pictures, Chris Corbould and Event Horizon (all UK).

LONGEST-RUNNING VISUAL-EFFECTS STUDIO

Industrial Light & Magic (ILM) was founded on 26 May 1975 by director George Lucas during the making of *Star Wars: Episode IV – A New Hope* (1977, top right). It went on to create VFX for more than 350 movies, including such landmarks as *The Abyss* and *Jurassic Park*, winning multiple Oscars. ILM continues to work on the *Star Wars* franchise, providing effects for Disney's *The Mandalorian* (2019, bottom right).

100 Years of Disney

9. *Inside Out* (2015)
Metascore: 94
Gross: $853.6 m

7. *Snow White and the Seven Dwarfs* (1937)
Metascore: 95
Gross: $184.9 m

Top 10 Disney animations
Metacritic ranks movies out of 100 based on reviews by professional critics, and the most acclaimed Disney animated films are a magical mix of old and new.

10. *Toy Story 3* (2010)
Metascore: 92
Gross: $1.07 bn

8. *WALL·E* (2008)
Metascore: 95
Gross: $532.5 m

MOST OSCARS WON
He may have died in 1966, but Walter Elias Disney (USA) still holds this lifetime record, attaining 26 Academy Awards (four honorary). The first was in 1932 (above; see **1**) and the last was given posthumously in 1968 for *Winnie the Pooh and the Blustery Day*.

Once upon a time, on 16 Oct 1923, Walt Disney and his brother Roy founded the Disney Brothers Cartoon Studio (later renamed The Walt Disney Company). In 2023, this pioneering studio celebrates its centenary – 100 years of record-breaking movies, TV, videogames and theme parks. And with exciting acquisitions such as Marvel and Star Wars continuing to expand its empire, Disney's "happy ever after" is far from over.

1. First full-colour cartoon
Hitting the big screen in 1932, the original Technicolor animation was Disney's *Flowers and Trees*, a "Silly Symphonies" 8-min short that also became the **first cartoon to win an Oscar** that same year (see left).

2. Highest-grossing animation (inflation adjusted; domestic market)
Inspired by a 19th-century Brothers Grimm story, Disney's first full-length feature – *Snow White and the Seven Dwarfs* (1937) – showed the true potential for animation at the cinema. While another fairytale adaptation wears the box-office crown today (see **10**), if inflation is taken into account then *Snow White* still reigns supreme – just. Its lifetime sales of $184.9 m (£124.3 m) in the US market alone equates to approximately $1.55 bn (£1.13 bn) in today's money.

3. First Disney platform videogame
Starring its much-loved mascot, the **first Disney videogame** was simply titled *Mickey Mouse* (Nintendo) and involved the character intercepting falling eggs; it was released on the Game & Watch on 9 Oct 1981. Several other titles followed, but it was not until six years later that its first platformer arrived, with *Mickey Mousecapade* (Hudson Soft) debuting on the Nintendo Entertainment System on 6 Mar 1987.

4. Highest-grossing single entertainment title
The 1994 animated movie *The Lion King* was adapted for the stage by theatre director Julie Taymor. It opened on Broadway in 1997 and was a roaring success, spawning productions the world over. The show had grossed over $9.1 bn (£7 bn) as of 2020, making it the single most lucrative entertainment title, surpassing any individual movie, book, play, musical or videogame (not adjusted for inflation).

5. Most successful Disney videogame
Released for the PlayStation 2 in 2002, *Kingdom Hearts* (Square) had shipped 6.3 million units as of 26 Jan 2019, according to VGChartz. This was the debut of a groundbreaking gaming franchise that brought together characters from across the Disney universe.

6. Toy Story (1995)
Metascore: 95
Gross: $365.3 m

4. Fantasia (1940)
Metascore: 96
Gross: $83.3 m

2. Dumbo (1941)
Metascore: 96
Gross: $6 m

5. Beauty and the Beast (1991)
Metascore: 95
Gross: $438.7 m

3. Ratatouille (2007)
Metascore: 96
Gross: $626.5 m

1. Pinocchio (1940)
Metascore: 99
Gross: $84.3 m

TALLEST THEME-PARK CASTLE
Inspired by real-life palaces and forts in Europe, the unmistakable Cinderella Castle at Disney's Magic Kingdom soars to 57.3 m (188 ft) at its tip. It has been the centrepiece of Walt Disney World in Florida since the theme park threw open its doors in 1971. The iconic structure was further enshrined in Disney lore when added to its logo in 1985.

6. Most songs from a soundtrack album on the US Hot 100 simultaneously
On 11 Feb 2006, nine tracks from the movie *High School Musical* featured in the Hot 100 chart. Its highest-placed song, "Breaking Free", leaped 82 places from No.86 to No.4 in its second week on the countdown, a record climb at the time.

7. Highest-grossing pirate movie
No other screen swashbuckler has accrued more "pieces of eight" than the second instalment in the *Pirates of the Caribbean* franchise: *Dead Man's Chest* (2006). Its box-office booty stands at a timber-shivering $1.06 bn (£774 m).

8. Most expensive animated film
A modern retelling of Rapunzel, *Tangled* (2010) had a reported production budget of $260 m (£168 m), much of which went into animating those lengthy locks.

9. First film with a female co-director to gross $1 bn
Frozen, co-written and co-directed by Jennifer Lee and Chris Buck (both USA), has earned $1.27 bn (£927.6 m) since its 2013 release. Lee and Buck reprised their

roles for 2019's *Frozen II* (**10**), which is now the all-time **highest-grossing animation**, earning $1.45 bn (£1.06 bn), putting it in 10th place among all movies.

11. Highest-grossing original animation
Pixar joined the Disney family in 2006. The $1.24 bn (£905.7 m) taken by *Incredibles 2* (2018) makes it the top non-spin-off cartoon. Among all animations, it's beaten only by the *Frozen* films (**9, 10**), which draw on Hans Christian Andersen's 1844 tale *The Snow Queen*.

12. Highest-grossing Disney movie
Disney has acquired some of Hollywood's live-action heavyweights in recent years, including Marvel (in 2009) and Lucasfilm (in 2012). Factoring in these additions to its portfolio, its top-earning release to date is *Avengers: Endgame* (2019), on $2.8 bn (£2 bn).

13. Most in-demand digital original TV show
Disney got in on the streaming game in Nov 2019 with Disney+. Flagship title *The Mandalorian* was the most popular online original series in 2020–21, according to Parrot Analytics. Its global demand was 57.6 times greater than the average TV show (see more overleaf).

Box-office figures from The Numbers, as of Oct 2021; Metascore methodology at metacritic.com

Demand expressions between
6 Mar 2021 and 5 Mar 2022

PARROT ANALYTICS

To assess cross-platform interest in a TV series – from streaming to likes and hashtags on social media – GWR works with Parrot Analytics. Their "Demand Expressions per capita" (DEx/c) value compares global engagement with a series against the average. A value of 10 means that a series is 10 times in greater demand than average.

Variety: *The Tonight Show Starring Jimmy Fallon* (NBC), 26.2

Horror: *American Horror Story* (FX), 31.6

Documentary: *Cosmos: Possible Worlds* (National Geographic), 14.6

Comedy: *The Big Bang Theory* (CBS), 43.0

Medical drama: *The Good Doctor* (ABC), 41.8

TV show (overall): *Attack on Titan* (MBS), 75.4

*millions of hours watched within first 28 days, as of 1 Mar 2022

TOP 10 NETFLIX SHOWS*

10 *The Witcher* (season 2; 2021). Fantasy drama; 484

9 *13 Reasons Why* (season 2; 2018). Teen drama; 496

8 *Inventing Anna* (limited series; 2022). Crime drama; 511

7 *The Witcher* (season 1; 2019). 541

6 *All of Us Are Dead* (season 1; 2022). Survival drama/horror; 560

HIGHEST-EARNING TV ACTOR

Dwayne "The Rock" Johnson (USA) earned an estimated $270 m (£200.1 m) for the year ending 31 Dec 2021, according to *Forbes*. He's the star – and subject – of the biographical sitcom *Young Rock* (NBC, 2021–).

Reese Witherspoon (USA) holds the **female** record, with earnings of around $115 m (£85.2 m) for the same period. She's the star and producer of *The Morning Show* (Apple TV+, 2019–).

Highest-rated TV series (current)

The Underground Railroad (Amazon Prime Video, 2021) has a Metascore of 92 on the review aggregator Metacritic, making it the highest review-rated show of the latest full calendar year. Based on Colson Whitehead's eponymous novel, the limited series is a fantasy set in the 19th century. It follows plantation slaves Cora and Caesar as they make a bid for freedom using a mysterious subterranean railway line, pursued by bounty hunter Ridgeway. The show won the Golden Globe Award for Best Miniseries or Television Film.

Most Emmy wins for Outstanding Host for a Reality or Competition Program

RuPaul Charles (USA) has picked up six Emmys for *RuPaul's Drag Race* (Logo TV/VH-1, 2016–21). As a producer, he is also a four-time winner of Outstanding Competition Program for the show in 2018–21, and won Outstanding Unstructured Reality Program for *Drag Race: Untucked!* in 2021. This takes his total count to 11, making him the most awarded Black winner in Emmy history.

First openly transgender Emmy nominee (lead role)

On 13 Jul 2021, Michaela Jaé Rodriguez (USA) was nominated for Outstanding Lead Actress in a Drama Series ahead of the 73rd Primetime Emmy Awards. She was shortlisted for her performance as Blanca Rodriguez in *Pose* (FX); see also p.182. The **first openly transgender nominee** was Laverne Cox (USA) in 2014, for playing Sophia Burset in *Orange is the New Black* (Outstanding Guest Actress in a Comedy Series).

In 2021, Netflix secured 44 Emmy wins, taking home more awards than any other broadcaster for the first time. It also tied CBS's record from 1974 for the **most wins by a network in a year**.

The Handmaid's Tale (Hulu) was nominated 21 times in 2021 but failed to convert any of them to wins, breaking the record of 17 achieved by *Mad Men* (AMC) in 2012 for the **largest Emmy Award "shutout"**.

Most Nickelodeon Kids' Choice Awards blimps won for Favorite TV Show

A revival of the US teen sitcom *iCarly* (Nickelodeon, 2021; original series 2007–12) claimed its fourth

Film adaptation: *Cobra Kai* (Netflix), 34.8

Comic adaptation: *WandaVision* (Disney+), 61.3

Book adaptation: *Game of Thrones* (HBO), 73.1

Reality TV: *Shark Tank India* (Sony), 27.0

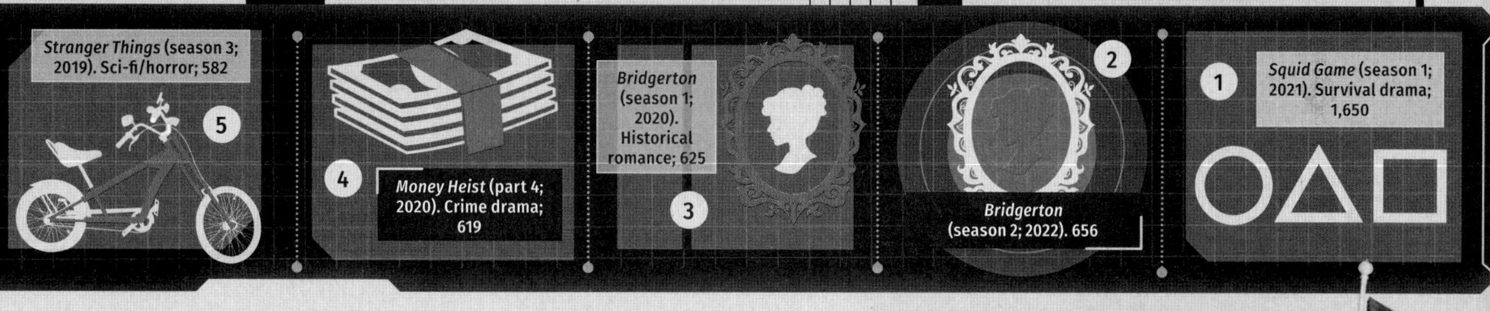

Legal drama: *Billions* (Showtime), 39.1

Stranger Things (season 3; 2019). Sci-fi/horror; 582

5

4 *Money Heist* (part 4; 2020). Crime drama; 619

Bridgerton (season 1; 2020). Historical romance; 625

3

Bridgerton (season 2; 2022). 656

2

1 *Squid Game* (season 1; 2021). Survival drama; 1,650

Favorite TV Show award at the Nickelodeon Kids' Choice Awards on 9 Apr 2022 – a ceremony co-hosted by Miranda Cosgrove, who reprised her role as Carly Shay in the latest series. The sitcom ties with *Home Improvement* (ABC, 1991–99; syndicated to Nickelodeon) for the most wins in the category.

The **most public votes received for a kids' awards show** is 513,183,993, by Nickelodeon Brazil Kids' Choice Awards, as verified on 15 Sep 2021.

Most submissions to an online casting call in 24 hours
On 10 Aug 2021, Netflix (USA) received 4,139 responses from hopefuls to an online casting call in Los Angeles, California, USA. The event, which was staged to promote the launch of Netflix Reality, sought to recruit contestants for various TV shows.

Oldest host of a TV music talent show
Song Hae (KOR, b. 27 Apr 1927) was 94 years 350 days old on 12 Apr 2022, as verified in Seoul, South Korea. A legend in the Korean entertainment industry, he has hosted the talent show *National Singing Contest*

since 1988 – a role that has earned him the affectionate nickname of "Korea's Favourite Grandpa".

Longest-running live TV music show hosted by the same presenter
As of 17 Sep 2021, Tamori (aka Kazuyoshi Morita) had fronted *Music Station* for 34 years 167 days. He made his debut on 3 Apr 1987. The show has been broadcast weekly by TV Asahi (both JPN) since 24 Oct 1986.

Longest screen kiss in a TV show (unscripted)
Brooke Blurton and Jamie-Lee Dayz (both AUS) smooched for 5 min 11 sec during season 7 of *The Bachelorette Australia* (Network 10) in Sydney, New South Wales, on 2 Nov 2021. The previous record was set on *The Bachelor Australia*, six years earlier.

MOST EMMY NOMINATIONS FOR A COMEDY DEBUT
In 2021, the first season of *Ted Lasso* (USA, Apple TV+/Doozer Productions, 2020-) received 20 Emmy nominations. It stars Jason Sudeikis as an American college football coach hired to revive the fortunes of an English soccer team owned by Rebecca Welton (Hannah Waddingham). It converted seven nominations to wins, included Outstanding Comedy Series.

Books & Publishing

BEST-SELLING BOOK
Though exact figures are impossible to come by, research conducted by the British and Foreign Bible Society in 2021 suggested that 5–7 billion copies of the Christian Bible had been produced in the 1,500 years since its contents were standardized.

Oldest written archive
An organized collection of 2,500 inscribed clay tablets dating to around 2350 BCE was discovered in 1974 in the ruins of the ancient city of Ebla, located in what is now western Syria. The tablets contain the official records of the Eblaite state, with information on land ownership and trade deals, as well as dictionaries for translating the languages of other ancient civilizations.

Oldest continuously operating library
Situated at the foot of Mount Sinai in Egypt, the library of St Catherine's Monastery was established between 527 and 565 CE on the orders of Byzantine Emperor Justinian I. It is home to one of the most important collections of early Christian manuscripts in the world: the 3,300 items known as the "Old Collection".

Largest chained library
Before the adoption of the printing press in Europe, books were both hugely valuable and very difficult to replace. Some medieval libraries protected their collections by anchoring books to the shelf using a chain that passed through the binding. Established in the 12th century, the chained library at Hereford Cathedral in the UK holds 227 medieval manuscripts and around 1,200 early printed books.

First audiobook
Joseph Conrad's novella *Typhoon* (1902) was packaged as a set of four LP records by the British Royal National Institute of Blind People in 1935.

First ebook
A copy of the United States Declaration of Independence was typed up on a Xerox Sigma V mainframe by University of Illinois student Michael Hart on 4 Jul 1971. This simple plain-text file, accessible to anyone connected to the ARPAnet (an early version of the internet), became the nucleus of the Project Gutenberg public-domain ebook service (see right).

Most expensive printed book
On 26 Nov 2013, US billionaire businessman David Rubenstein purchased a copy of the *Bay Psalm Book* for $14.16 m (£8.74 m) at Sotheby's in New York City, USA. The hymn book was produced by the residents of the Massachusetts Bay Colony in 1640 and is the first book ever printed in British North America. Only 11 copies survive of the original 1,700 made.

Largest trade publisher
Penguin Random House publishes 70,000 digital and 15,000 print titles every year. The publisher posted revenues of €3.37 bn ($3.78 bn; £2.87 bn) for the 2019 financial year, according to the 2020 edition of the Global 50 Ranking of the Publishing Industry.

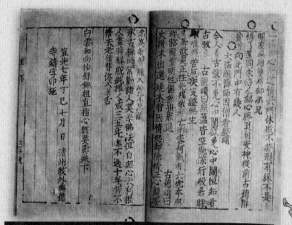

OLDEST BOOK PRINTED USING MOVABLE METAL TYPE
The *Buljo jikji simche yojeol* (generally known simply as the *Jikji*) is a Korean collection of Zen Buddhist teachings printed in Jul 1377 – a whole 73 years before the Gutenberg Bible. The *Jikji*'s colophon states that it was "printed using metal type", a claim backed up by the appearance of pairs of identical type throughout its 39 leaves, suggesting resetting and reuse.

LARGEST COLLECTION OF COMIC BOOKS
At the last official count, Bob Bretall of Mission Viejo, California, USA, had amassed a haul of 101,822 unique comics. The *Spider-Man* fan keeps the majority of the collection in his three-car garage, but he also has a "comic room" (pictured) with special editions and other associated comic-book memorabilia.

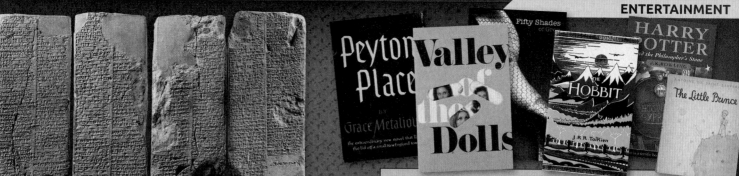

FIRST LIBRARY

The Assyrian king Ashurbanipal assembled a library in his palace in Nineveh (in present-day northern Iraq) between 668 and 631 BCE. It contained 30,000 clay tablets inscribed with cuneiform writing. While earlier royal archives are known (see opposite), this was the first effort to organize literary texts with no administrative purpose.

BEST-SELLING FICTION BOOK

It is impossible to state with certainty which novel has sold the most copies ever, as reliable and independently verified sales data only began to be collected on a significant scale in the early 2000s. Popular sensations such as *Peyton Place* (1956) by Grace Metalious and *Valley of the Dolls* (1966) by Jacqueline Susann received much contemporary media attention and sold up to 30 million copies, but their popularity did not endure. Titles said to have sold more than 100 million copies include *The Hobbit* (1937) by J R R Tolkien, *The Little Prince* (1943) by Antoine de Saint-Exupéry and *Harry Potter and the Philosopher's Stone* (1997) by J. K. Rowling. The **best-selling fiction book (independently verified figures)** is E L James's *Fifty Shades of Grey* (2011), which had global sales of 16,994,323 copies as of Nov 2021.

MOST PROLIFIC BOOK THIEF

Stephen Blumberg (USA) stole at least 23,600 rare books from 268 different libraries across North America between the 1970s and 1990. Blumberg was turned in by a former accomplice in 1990 and convicted in Jul 1991 on four counts of possessing and transporting stolen property.

BEST-SELLING FICTION BOOK (CURRENT)

Stephenie Meyer's *Midnight Sun* had recorded combined worldwide sales of 1,847,843 over the course of 2020, according to The NPD Group and Nielsen Book Research. The novel was a retelling of Meyer's young adult classic *Twilight* (2005), with events seen from the perspective of vampire Edward Cullen rather than series narrator Bella Swan.

LARGEST ADVANCE FOR A NON-FICTION BOOK

A total of $65 m (£50 m) was offered to former US president Barack Obama and First Lady Michelle Obama for their memoirs (published respectively as *A Promised Land* in 2020 and *Becoming* in 2018). Trade-publishing giant Penguin Random House (see opposite) won the bidding war for the two books.

LARGEST LIBRARY

The US Library of Congress in Washington, DC, is currently home to more than 173 million items. Its collection is spread across *c.* 838 mi (1,348 km) of shelves and includes more than 41 million books and other print materials, 4.1 million recordings and 15 million photographs. Its nearest rival, the British Library in London, is not far behind with 170 million items.

MOST POISONOUS BOOK

Dr Robert Kedzie's *Shadows from the Walls of Death* (1874) includes 86 leaves of wallpaper containing up to 36 g (1.2 oz) of arsenic. The book warned the public of the arsenic-based dyes used by contemporary wallpaper manufacturers. Only four copies remain, with the poisonous leaves sealed in plastic (inset) or an air-tight container.

MOST EXPENSIVE BOOK (PRIVATE SALE)

The *Sherborne Missal*, a richly illustrated medieval manuscript, was acquired by the British Library in Aug 1998 as part of a deal worth £15 m ($24.88 m). The 694-page book was made at Sherborne Abbey in Dorset, UK, between 1399 and 1407 by a team led by artist John Siferwas and scribe John Whas.

Puzzles

The World Puzzle Federation governs the annual World Puzzle Championship (WPC) and the World Sudoku Championship (WSC). The WPC was first held in 1992 – making it the **longest-running puzzle championship** – and it challenges competitors to solve logic-based brain-teasers. Fancy taking part? Then get a taster with this selection of puzzles, all drawn from past competitions. Good luck!

Solutions on p.251

Most wins of the World Puzzle Championship					
Category	Name	Medals	Gold	Silver	Bronze
Individual	Ulrich Voigt (DEU)	19	11	6	2
Under 18s	Qiu Yanzhe (CHN)	4	4	0	0
Over 50s	Taro Arimatsu (JPN)	4	4	0	0
Team	USA	28	15	8	5

Correct as of 11 Jan 2022

WORD SEARCH
Find the three occurrences of the word SENEC in the grid shown here. You may use any of the given eight directions (below right).

Senec in Slovakia was the location of the 25th World Puzzle Championship in Oct 2016

C	E	S	N	C
E	E	E	E	E
N	S	N	C	N
E	E	E	S	E
S	N	C	S	E

CLASSIC SUDOKU
Place a digit from 1 to 9 into each of the empty cells so that each digit appears exactly once in each row, column and 3x3 outlined box.

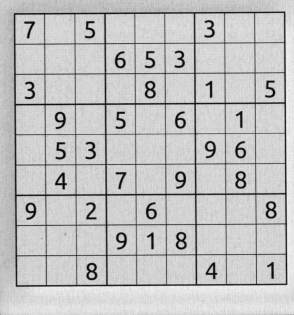

SNAKE
Place a one-cell-wide snake into the grid so it does not touch itself, not even diagonally. The head and tail of the snake are marked with circles. Numbers outside the grid indicate how many cells in that row or column are occupied by the snake.

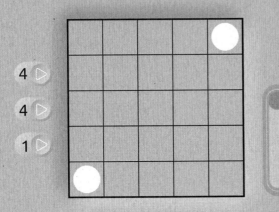

DIAGONAL SUDOKU
Place a digit from 1 to 9 into each of the empty cells so that each digit appears exactly once in each row, column and 3x3 outlined box. Each main diagonal contains each digit from 1 to 9.

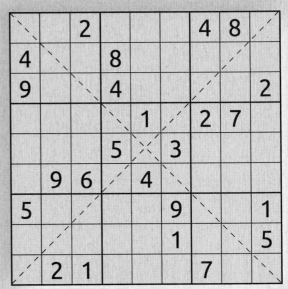

CROSSWORD

Enter the given words – all chess Grandmasters – into the grid, so that they can be read horizontally from left to right or vertically from top to bottom. All words must be interconnected, and each word must be used exactly once. No other words of two or more letters may arise. Some letters are already given; each such letter must be used by exactly one word, and each word must contain exactly one of these letters.

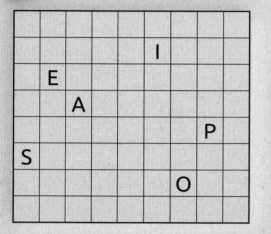

TAL

PETROSIAN

SPASSKY

FISCHER

KARPOV

KASPAROV

DISSECTION

Divide the grid into three congruent pieces, using horizontal, vertical and diagonal lines. Cells can be cut in half by a diagonal line. Other ways to cut a cell into smaller parts are not allowed. The pieces must have identical shape and size, but they can be rotated and reflected.

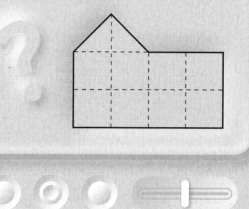

HEXA WORDS

Fill in the whole grid with letters. Six hexagonal cells around each blue cell must contain one of the words from the given list (in any order). Each word should be used exactly once.

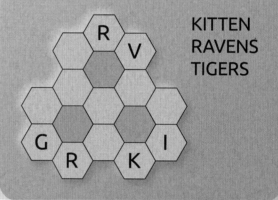

KITTEN
RAVENS
TIGERS

SPOT THE DIFFERENCE

Circle 10 differences between the image of the Taj Mahal and its reflection. The differences are clearly intentional, such as things that have disappeared, moved or changed size, shape or orientation.

MOVING MATCHES

The figure below shows nine decimal digits assembled from matchsticks. You are given a configuration of matchsticks. Move at most two matchsticks to produce the largest possible positive integer. (The integer must be written in base 10, using only the digits as shown below and nothing else. Rotating the whole configuration/ changing the point of view is not allowed.)

Jigsaw Puzzles

MOST FOLLOWED JIGSAW PUZZLER ON YOUTUBE
As of 1 Jan 2022, Karen Puzzles (aka Karen Kavett, USA) had 143,000 subscribers on her YouTube channel. While other YouTubers may feature jigsaws occasionally, Karen's channel is entirely devoted to them.

First "dissected" puzzle
The popularizing of interlocking picture puzzles is credited to the British map engraver John Spilsbury. In 1766, he published a map of Europe mounted on wood and cut along national boundaries using a marquetry saw. The aim was to help children to learn geography. It was known as a "dissection"; the first recorded use of the term "jigsaw puzzle" was in 1906, after the invention of the tool of the same name.

Largest jigsaw puzzle by area
No jigsaw ever covered a larger area than the one-off 6,122.68-m² (65,904-sq-ft) puzzle created by DMCC (UAE), as confirmed in Dubai, UAE, on 7 Jul 2018. The 12,320-piece wooden puzzle, depicting the late Sheikh Zayed bin Sultan Al Nahyan, covered the equivalent of 23 tennis courts.

The **largest jigsaw puzzle by piece count** was another one-off, this time made by a team of 1,600 students from Vietnam's University of Economics

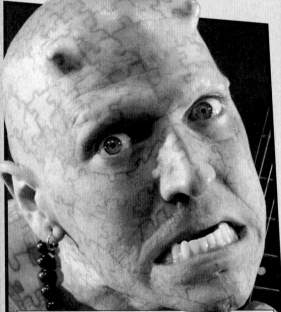

MOST JIGSAW-PUZZLE TATTOOS
Artist, actor and sideshow performer The Enigma (aka Paul Lawrence, USA) has a body suit of 2,123 tattooed puzzle pieces, as ratified for *Lo Show dei Record* in Milan, Italy, on 13 Apr 2011. The body-mod devotee has been inked by more than 200 artists, and also has horn implants and a variety of piercings. He has also reshaped his ears.

Ho Chi Minh City. On 24 Sep 2011, they joined together their 551,232-piece image of a lotus flower and a mind map – a diagram for visualizing and memorizing information – at the Phu Tho Stadium. It covered an area of 344.52 m² (3,708.38 sq ft) – about a third again larger than a tennis court.

Pintoo of Taiwan, China, manufactures the **largest plastic jigsaw by piece count**, with 4,800 elements. The finished puzzle measures 86.3 x 115 cm (2 ft 9 in x 3 ft 9 in) – about the size of a bath towel – and depicts a stylized map of the island. Plastic is the third most common material used in jigsaw puzzles, behind cardboard and wood.

The **largest online jigsaw puzzle by piece count** is the *Million Piece Mission*, created by the US Air Force. It is a 1.03-gigapixel image of the National Museum of the US Air Force, broken into 1.2 million pieces. The puzzle was launched on 15 Jun 2020 in reaction to the USAF's halting of its outreach programme owing to the COVID-19 pandemic.

For the **largest commercially available puzzles**, see right.

Longest jigsaw puzzle marathon
Held on 30–31 Oct 2010, the Hannut Marathon jigsaw contest in Belgium gave 112 teams a total of 25 hr to solve as many puzzles (ranging from 500 to 2,000 pieces) as possible.

SMALLEST COMMERCIALLY AVAILABLE JIGSAW PUZZLE BY AREA
Based on the completed size of a 1,000-piece jigsaw, the (now out of print) miniature Tomax Puzzles by Standard Project (CHN) measured just 182 x 257 mm (7.17 x 10.12 in), as confirmed in Hong Kong, China, on 12 Dec 2009. Each piece averaged 0.467 cm² (0.072 sq in).

The **smallest jigsaws by piece size** are those produced by Selegiochi (ITA). Their 99-piece nano-puzzles have shapes with an average surface area of just 0.361 cm² (0.05 sq in). The finished size is 6.5 x 5.5 cm (2.5 x 2.1 in) – smaller than a playing card.

100%

100%

Most people solving a jigsaw puzzle at one location
Chello Multicanal (ESP) assembled 9,569 participants for a mass puzzle session during the Fira de Barcelona in Spain between 27 Dec 2011 and 4 Jan 2012.

Largest collection of jigsaw puzzles
Luiza Figueiredo (BRA) owned 1,047 unique jigsaw sets, as of the most recent count on 9 Jul 2017 in São Paulo, Brazil. She has been collecting since 1967. Her puzzle passion began after she solved her first jigsaw when she was seven years old.

Konrad and Renata Wachulec (both POL) have spent 20 years amassing the **largest collection of windmill jigsaws**. You can see their 505 puzzles on Instagram @windmills_puzzles_and_we.

Most expensive jigsaw puzzle sold at auction
A hand-crafted wooden jigsaw realized $27,000 (£15,279) at a charity auction in Gettysburg, Pennsylvania, USA, on 28 Sep 2005. Custom-made by the award-winning American jigsaw enthusiast Rachel Page Elliott, *The Outing* was cut into 467 interlocking pieces, many of which were shaped as birds, cats, horses and dogs. It pictured a golden retriever and her five puppies playing in the grass and was sold to benefit the Golden Retriever Foundation.

PIECING IT ALL TOGETHER
Regular jigsaw pieces do not have universally agreed names, so you will hear dissectologists (jigsaw solvers) use a wide variety of terms. Here, with the help of the World Jigsaw Puzzle Federation (WJPF), we humbly suggest a basic classification to help with standardization in the dissectology community:

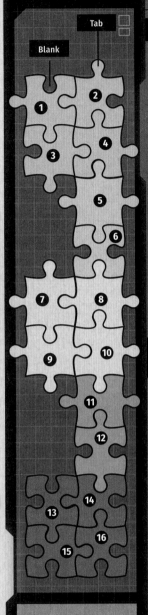

Tab

Blank

KEY
1: Quarter to
2: 9 [o'clock]
3: Quarter past
4: 3 [o'clock]
5: Square
6: Noner
7: Left crown
8: Up crown
9: Down crown
10: Right crown
11: Level/quarter past 9
12: Plumb/6 [o'clock]
13. Downie
14. Leftie
15. Rightie
16. Uppie

LARGEST COMMERCIALLY AVAILABLE JIGSAW PUZZLE BY PIECE COUNT

Travel Around Art by Grafika (FRA) contains 54,000 pieces. First sold in 2020 for *c.* £450 ($610), it depicts a gallery wall hung with more than 50 famous paintings. At 8.64 x 2.04 m (28 ft 4 in x 6 ft 8 in), it is also the **largest commercially available jigsaw puzzle by area**.

The World Jigsaw Puzzle Federation considers the above to be a composite of smaller puzzles, so the **largest single-image puzzle** is the 42,000-piece *Around the World*, aka *World Landmarks,* by Educa Borrás (ESP, left), designed by Adrian Chesterman. On 27 Apr 2018, a 100-strong team (right) in Mutilva, Spain, completed it in a record 22 hr 29 min 20 sec.

FASTEST TIME TO COMPLETE A 1,000-PIECE JIGSAW PUZZLE IN COMPETITION

At the 2018 British Jigsaw Championship, held in Newmarket, Suffolk, on 24 Jun, Sarah Mills (UK) solved a 1,000-piece artwork in 1 hr 55 min – averaging one piece every 6.9 sec. Mills is now a seven-time national champion.

LARGEST HAND-CUT WOODEN JIGSAW PUZZLE (PIECES)

In 2021, Jill Walterbach (USA) unveiled her 101,010-piece jigsaw in the game-and-puzzle magazine *AGPI Quarterly*. Measuring 22 m long by 0.3 m tall (72 x 1 ft), the "wrap-around" puzzle is a single abstract artwork painted in acrylics on 0.25-in-thick (0.6-cm) maple-veneered MDF. It comprises 37 pieces vertically and 2,730 horizontally, each one cut using a Seyco scroll saw.

WORLD JIGSAW PUZZLE CHAMPIONSHIP (WJPC)

Invigilated by the WJPF (see opposite), the **first WJPC** took place in Valladolid, Spain, on 28–29 Sep 2019. Jana Hanzelková (CZE) topped the individual rankings with the **fastest time to complete a 500-piece jigsaw** – 46 min 35 sec. Subsequent WJPC events were cancelled owing to COVID-19, but 2022 was expected to mark their return.

FIRST PLAYABLE JIGSAW PUZZLE VINYL RECORD

On 23 Sep 2016, UK trio Sugar Coat released a 7-inch vinyl version of their debut single "Me Instead" as a playable jigsaw puzzle. One of 35 different pressings of the record, it was designed by Cameron Allen of Royal Mint Records and based on the artwork of a jigsaw puzzle found in a charity shop.

World Jigsaw Puzzle Championship

1	Fastest 500 pieces (pairs)	34 min 34 sec	Demelza Becerra Robledillo & Ángel Heras Salcedo (both ESP)
2	Fastest 500 pieces (individual)	46 min 35 sec	Jana Hanzelková (CZE)
3	Oldest competitor at the WJPC	76 years 68 days	Dora Maria Polle Karczauninkat (DEU, b. 23 Jul 1943)

GET A PIECE OF THE ACTION

If you think you've got what it takes to compete against the world's best dissectologists, visit **worldjigsawpuzzle.org** to register for the next world championship!

LARGEST SPHERICAL JIGSAW PUZZLE

Unima Industrial (HK) Ltd of China produced a jigsaw with a 4.77-m (15-ft 7.8-in) circumference depicting Winnie-the-Pooh and friends. Hollow, and comprising curved plastic pieces, it was made in Hong Kong, China, and displayed and ratified at the city's Convention and Exhibition Centre on 10 Jan 2005.

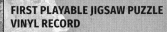

Pop Music

SLOWEST CLIMB TO No.1 ON THE US SINGLES CHART
Glass Animals' (UK) alt-pop slow-burner "Heat Waves" took 59 weeks to summit the *Billboard* Hot 100. The track finally hit No.1 on 12 Mar 2022, beating Mariah Carey's 35-week trek to the top with "All I Want for Christmas Is You" in 2019.

MOST CONSECUTIVE UK CHRISTMAS No.1s
LadBaby, aka Mark and Roxanne Hoyle (both UK), secured their fourth festive chart-topper in a row in 2021, with "Sausage Rolls for Everyone" – aided by pop stars Ed Sheeran and Elton John. All the proceeds went to The Trussell Trust, a food-poverty charity.

MOST GOLDEN MELODY AWARDS FOR SONG OF THE YEAR
"Queen of C-pop" Jolin Tsai (CHN) has won Song of the Year three times at the Chinese-speaking world's equivalent of the Grammys: for "Marry Me Today" (2007, with David Tao), "The Great Artist" (2013) and "Womxnly" (2019).

MOST *DAESANG* AWARDS WON AT THE MNET ASIAN MUSIC AWARDS
BTS (KOR) triumphed in all four *daesang* ("grand prize") categories at the 2021 Mnet Asian Music Awards to take their total to 17. The K-pop kings are members of the GWR Hall of Fame and hold multiple music and social-media records; in 2021, they posed with just a selection of their certificates for a special photoshoot.

MUSIC CONSUMPTION IN 2021

According to the International Federation of the Phonographic Industry, people listened to 18.4 hr of music per week on average in 2021 – the highest engagement in music ever. Here's how the world tuned in to get its music fix...

Live (including livestreaming) 2%

Social-media platforms (e.g., Facebook, Instagram, VK) 3%

Other (e.g., TV, on-demand premium video services, music swapped with family and friends) 5%

Purchased music (e.g., CDs, vinyl, DVDs, downloads) 9%

MEAT LOAF (1947–2022)
Rock star Meat Loaf (USA, b. Marvin Lee Aday) passed away on 20 Jan 2022. His three *Bat Out of Hell* albums (released in 1977, 1993 and 2006) are the **best-selling album trilogy**, with reported sales of 65 million. The classic first instalment sold 44 million alone, making it the **best-selling rock album by a solo artist**.

Most streamed track on Spotify in 24 hours
"Easy on Me" by Adele (UK, see right) was streamed 19,749,704 times on 15 Oct 2021. The heartfelt piano number racked up 84,952,932 streams in the seven days up to and including 21 Oct 2021, making it also the platform's **most streamed track in one week**.

The **male** record in 24 hours is 16,103,849 streams, for "As It Was" by Harry Styles (UK) on 1 Apr 2022. The lead single from the ex-One Direction star's third studio album (*Harry's House*), "As It Was" topped Spotify charts in 34 different countries.

Most followers on Spotify
Ed Sheeran (UK, see right) had 95,345,034 followers on the music streaming platform as of 12 Apr 2022. This was 17 million more than his nearest challenger, **female** record holder Ariana Grande (USA), who had 78.2 million. The **group** with the most followers were BTS (KOR, see above), with 47.9 million.

Most simultaneous Top 10 entries on the US singles chart
On the *Billboard* Hot 100 dated 18 Sep 2021, Drake (CAN) occupied an incredible nine of the Top 10 chart positions – including the entire Top 5. All nine tracks were new entries and were taken from the rapper's sixth studio album, *Certified Lover Boy*.

Most simultaneous new entries on the US singles chart
Twenty-six tracks from Taylor Swift's (USA) re-recorded studio album *Red (Taylor's Version)* debuted on the *Billboard* Hot 100 on 27 Nov 2021. They were headed by "All Too Well (10 Minute Version) (Taylor's Version)", which became the **longest song to reach No.1 on the *Billboard* Hot 100**, with a running time of 10 min 13 sec.

Most Grammy nominations
Jay-Z (USA, b. Shawn Carter) earned three nominations for the 64th Annual Grammy Awards on 3 Apr 2022, taking his career total to 83 (see also pp.164–65).

YOUNGEST PERSON TO WIN THE FILM MUSIC AWARDS "TRIPLE CROWN"

The *James Bond* theme "No Time to Die" (2020) earned Billie Eilish (USA, b. 18 Dec 2001) a Grammy, a Golden Globe and an Oscar. She was just 20 years 99 days old when she claimed the latter, on 27 Mar 2022.

BIGGEST-SELLING DIGITAL SINGLE

"Save Your Tears" by The Weeknd (CAN, b. Abel Tesfaye) registered 2.15 billion "subscription streams equivalent" worldwide, making it the most-purchased song of 2021 according to the International Federation of the Phonographic Industry. The Weeknd also won this accolade in 2020, with 2.72 billion streams for "Blinding Lights".

FIRST LATIN SOLO ARTIST TO REACH No.1 ON SPOTIFY

On 24 Mar 2022, singer and TV personality Anitta (BRA, b. Larissa de Macedo Machado) climbed to No.1 on Spotify's Global Top 200 daily chart with "Envolver" ("Wrap"). The raunchy reggaeton tune had racked up 6.39 million streams.

MOST STREAMED TRACK ON SPOTIFY

"Shape of You" by Ed Sheeran (UK) had been streamed 3,026,657,640 times by 23 Jan 2022 – the first track to reach the 3-billion milestone. It had been the platform's most popular song since 22 Sep 2017, taking the crown from Drake's "One Dance". In Apr 2022, Sheeran won a High Court battle over the track, after claims he had plagiarized another song were rejected by the judge.

Ad-supported audio streaming (e.g., free tier of Spotify or Deezer)	Short-form video apps (e.g., TikTok, Triller)	Radio (e.g., broadcast live, catchup, internet radio stations)	Video streaming (e.g., YouTube, DailyMotion, Niconico)	Paid-for subscription audio streaming (e.g., Spotify Premium, Apple Music, Melon)
9% ADs	11%	16%	22%	23%

Most consecutive years with a Japanese No.1 single

KinKi Kids (JPN), comprising Koichi and Tsuyoshi Domoto, extended their chart-topping streak to 26 years with "Kojundo Romance" on 28 Mar 2022.

First winner of the Best Global Music Performance Grammy

At the 2022 Grammys, Arooj Aftab (PAK/USA, b. SAU) became the inaugural recipient of this new award category for her 7-min 42-sec song "Mohabbat", taken from the 2021 album *Vulture Prince*.

At the same ceremony, Bad Bunny (PRI, b. Benito Ocasio) became the **first winner of the Best Música Urbana Album Grammy**, for his 2020 album *EL ÚLTIMO TOUR DEL MUNDO* ("The Last Tour of the World").

Longest officially released song

On 19 May 2021, Mark Lee and The Pocket Gods (both UK) released "Song for First Contact", which lasts 48 hr 17 min. This was surpassed on 1 Oct 2021 by Earthena (CAN), whose epic number "Symphony of the Crown" plays out over 48 hr 39 min 35 sec.

Highest annual earnings for a musician (current year)

Bruce Springsteen (USA) netted $590 m (£437.3 m) in the calendar year 2021, according to *Rolling Stone*. This was due in large part to the sale of Springsteen's publishing copyrights and master recordings from his 50-year career to Sony Music for an estimated $500 m (£378.1 m) – the **largest publishing sale by a musician**. The Boss's back catalogue includes 20 studio albums.

30 was also 2021's biggest-selling album, shifting 5 million copies between 19 Nov and 31 Dec!

MOST ALBUM OF THE YEAR BRIT AWARDS WON BY A SOLO ARTIST

Adele (UK) won Best British Album of the Year for the third time in 2022, for her fourth studio album *30* (inset). She also claimed the Best British Artist of the Year award, introduced in 2022 to replace the previous Male and Female categories at the **first gender-neutral BRIT Awards**.

I'd Like to Thank...

BAFTAs

Most wins by a film

On 4 Mar 1971, the Western *Butch Cassidy and the Sundance Kid* (1969) picked up nine British Academy of Film and Television Arts (BAFTA) awards. They included both Best Actor and Best Actress in a Leading Role (Robert Redford and Katharine Ross, respectively), and Best Screenplay (William Goldman).

Most wins by an actor

Peter Finch (AUS, b. UK) won five BAFTAs for Best Actor in a Leading Role. His last, for *Network* (1976), was awarded posthumously on 28 Mar 1977.

MOST WINS BY AN ACTRESS

Dame Judi Dench (UK) won six BAFTAs between 1966 and 2002, the latest coming for *Iris* (2001). She's shown above with Sir Kenneth Branagh, her director in *Belfast* (2021; see Oscars).

Most wins for Best Costume Design

Milena Canonero (ITA; 1982, 1986, 2007 and 2015) and Jenny Beavan (UK; 1987, 2002, 2016 and 2022) have each won four BAFTAs. Beavan's latest award was for the crime comedy *Cruella* (2021).

Most nominations for Best Original Music before winning

On 13 Mar 2022, at the 10th attempt, legendary film composer Hans Zimmer (DEU) claimed his first-ever BAFTA, for soundtracking the sci-fi movie *Dune*.

MOST NOMINATIONS FOR A SCI-FI FILM

On 3 Feb 2022, Denis Villeneuve's epic *Dune* (2021) received 11 nominations, from which it won five awards on 13 Mar 2022. It ties with Alfonso Cuarón's *Gravity* (2013) as the most-nominated sci-fi movie.

GOLDEN GLOBES

Most wins by an actress

On 15 Jan 2012, Meryl Streep (USA) extended her own record with an eighth competitive Golden Globe. Her first win was for Best Actress in a Supporting Role in *Kramer vs. Kramer* (1979), and her most recent was for Best Performance by an Actress in a Motion Picture – Drama in *The Iron Lady* (2011), as British prime minister Margaret Thatcher.

Jack Nicholson and Alan Alda (both USA) tie for the **most wins by an actor**, with six each. Nicholson's awards include Best Motion Picture Actor – Drama for the acclaimed *Chinatown* (1974), *One Flew Over the Cuckoo's Nest* (1975) and *Terms of Endearment* (1983). Alda's wins all came for his portrayal of Hawkeye Pierce in the legendary CBS TV show *M*A*S*H*, between 1975 and 1983.

FIRST TRANSGENDER WINNER

On 9 Jan 2022, Michaela Jaé Rodriguez (USA) was awarded Best Actress in a TV Drama. She was recognized for her portrayal of Blanca Rodriguez-Evangelista in *Pose* (FX, 2018–21). (See also p.172.)

OLDEST WINNER

O Yeong-su (KOR, b. 19 Oct 1944) was aged 77 years 82 days when he was awarded Best Supporting Actor – Television on 9 Jan 2022. He portrayed Oh Il-nam (#001) in Netflix's global survival smash *Squid Game* (2021–).

Most wins by a film

Musical comedy drama *La La Land* (2016) was nominated for seven Golden Globes and won all of them. The roll call included Best Motion Picture – Musical or Comedy, alongside nods for both lead players, Ryan Gosling and Emma Stone.

Most nominations

• **Actor**: 22, by Jack Lemmon (USA) between 1960 and 2000. He won four times, the last in 2000 for the TV movie *Inherit the Wind* (1999).
• **Actress**: 32, by Meryl Streep from 1979 to 2020.
• **Film**: 11, for *Nashville* (1975) in 1976. It secured only one win: Best Original Song – Motion Picture, for the song "I'm Easy".

FIRST WIN BY A DEAF ACTOR

At the 94th Academy Awards on 27 Mar 2022, Troy Kotsur (USA) won Best Supporting Actor for playing Frank Rossi in *CODA* (2021). His co-star Marlee Matlin (USA) had previously secured the **first win by a deaf actress** for her role in *Children of a Lesser God* (1986). She was aged just 21 years 218 days at the 1987 ceremony, making her also the **youngest Best Actress winner**.

OSCARS

Most nominations for a Black actor

Denzel Washington (USA) picked up his 10th Academy Awards nomination in Feb 2022, for *The Tragedy of Macbeth* (2021).

FIRST ANIMATED FILM TO BE NOMINATED FOR BEST DOCUMENTARY

Jonas Poher Rasmussen's *Flee* (2021) – about a gay Afghan refugee – was shortlisted on 8 Feb 2022. In a first for the Oscars, it was put up for Best Animation, Documentary and International Feature Film.

First person to receive nominations in seven different categories

On 8 Feb 2022, Sir Kenneth Branagh (UK) was shortlisted for Best Director (for the second time), Best Picture and Best Original Screenplay for his drama *Belfast*. He'd previously been nominated for Best Actor, Best Supporting Actor, Best Adapted Screenplay and Best Live Action Short Film.

OLDEST FEMALE WINNER OF BEST DIRECTOR

Dame Jane Campion (NZ, b. 30 Apr 1954) was 67 years 331 days old on 27 Mar 2022, when she was awarded Best Director for *The Power of the Dog* (2021). The honour also made Campion the **first woman to receive two nominations for Best Director**, while the movie itself attracted the **most nominations for a film with a female director** – 12.

MOST WINS BY AN ACTRESS
Audra McDonald (USA) has won six acting awards at the Antoinette Perry Awards, aka the Tonys. Her latest was for the title role in *Lady Day at Emerson's Bar & Grill* (2014). She is also the only person to win in four different acting categories.

TONY AWARDS
Most…
• **Wins by a musical**: *The Producers* won 12 out of 15 nominations on 3 Jun 2001, including Best Musical. Directed by Susan Stroman, with a cast including Matthew Broderick and Nathan Lane, it broke the previous record of 10, held by *Hello Dolly!* since 1964.
• **Acting category wins by a production**: at the 4th Tony Awards on 9 Apr 1950, the cast of the original Broadway production of Rodgers & Hammerstein's musical *South Pacific* walked away with wins in four acting categories. This represents every category for which the cast was eligible.
• **Nominations for a musical**: on 3 May 2016, *Hamilton* earned 16 nominations. Its music, lyrics and books are by Lin-Manuel Miranda.
• **Nominations for a play**: Jeremy O Harris's *Slave Play* received nods in 12 categories on 15 Oct 2020. Unfortunately, Harris's work also holds the record for the **most nominations for a play without a win**.
• **Nominations for an actress**: Julie Harris and Chita Rivera (both USA) have each been nominated 10 times over the course of their careers.
• **Awards won by different productions of the same play**: Arthur Miller's *Death of a Salesman* (1949) was voted Best Play at the 1949 awards and Best Revival for productions in 1984, 1999 and 2012.

MOST WINS BY A COMPOSER
Stephen Sondheim (USA) received seven Tonys, including Best Score for *A Little Night Music* (1973) and *Sweeney Todd* (1979). The greatly admired songsmith passed away on 26 Nov 2021.

NICKELODEON KIDS' CHOICE AWARDS

Most wins
Nickelodeon started its annual Kids' Choice Awards (KCAs) in 1988, handing out trophies called blimps for pop-culture categories that are voted on by the public. No **female** celebrity has been awarded more blimps at the KCAs than Selena Gomez (USA), who won 11 times from 2009 to 2019. Will Smith (USA) holds the **male** record, with 11 wins between 1991 and 2009.
Taylor Swift (USA) has the **most nominations**, with 35 between 2010 and 2022. Will Smith leads the **male** category, with 27 between 1989 and 2020.

Most wins by a male singer
Justin Bieber (CAN) took home his ninth blimp at the 35th Nickelodeon KCAs in Santa Monica, California, USA, on 9 Apr 2022. He picked up the Favorite Music Collaboration award for "Stay", his chart-topping single with The Kid LAROI.
The **female** record in this category is held by Ariana Grande (USA), who has won eight times for her music. (Selena Gomez has more awards, but her total includes six for acting.)

Most wins by a music group
BTS (KOR) have won six blimps: Favorite Global Music Star (2018 and 2021), Favorite Music Group (2020–22) and Favorite Song for "Dynamite" (2021). Their victory in 2022 was the K-pop septet's third consecutive award in the category.

MOST WINS BY A CARTOON
SpongeBob SquarePants (USA) has been voted Favorite Cartoon on 19 occasions, in 2003–07 and 2009–22. The late Stephen Hillenburg's animated comedy series won its 14th consecutive blimp on 9 Apr 2022.

Most wins by an author
A KCA blimp for Favorite Book was awarded from 1995 to 2016. *Harry Potter* writer J. K. Rowling (UK) racked up seven wins, in 2000–02, 2004, 2006–08.
The **male** record is held by *Diary of a Wimpy Kid* creator Jeff Kinney (USA), who took home the coveted blimp six times, in 2010–12, 2014–16.

Most wins by a movie franchise
Only two film franchises have won three Favorite Movie gongs. TV cartoon spin-off *Alvin and the Chipmunks* was the first, in 2008, 2010 and 2012. The feat was later equalled by three *Hunger Games* book adaptations in 2013–15.

GRAMMYS
Most wins by a group
U2 (IRL/UK) have collected 22 Grammy statues since 1988. Their most successful year was 2006, when they picked up five awards. The **most wins by a group in a single year** is eight, by Santana (USA) in 2000.

Most wins by a rapper
Rappers Jay-Z (b. Shawn Carter, USA) and Ye, aka Kanye West, USA, have each pocketed 24 awards, a total both men reached at the 64th Annual Grammys on 3 Apr 2022.

MOST WINS FOR BEST ROCK ALBUM
Foo Fighters (USA) have won five Best Rock Album Grammy awards, from *There Is Nothing Left to Lose* in 2001 to *Medicine at Midnight* in 2022. Tragically, drummer Taylor Hawkins (far left) died on 25 Mar 2022.

Most consecutive nominations for Record of the Year
Six artists have received three back-to-back nominations for Record of the Year, the latest being singer Billie Eilish and her co-writer/producer brother Finneas O'Connell on 23 Nov 2021. Eilish's sole female precedent, Roberta Flack, secured three in 1973–75.

First songwriter to win consecutive Song of the Year awards
In 2021, Dernst "D'Mile" Emile II (USA) won Song of the Year as a co-writer on H.E.R.'s "I Can't Breathe". He followed it up on 3 Apr 2022 with his co-writing credit on Silk Sonic's "Leave the Door Open".

MOST CONSECUTIVE NOMINATIONS FOR SONG OF THE YEAR
H.E.R. (Having Everything Revealed, aka Gabriella Wilson, USA) is the sixth act to have three consecutive Song of the Year Grammy nominations. The R&B singer was shortlisted for "Hard Place" at the 2020 ceremony, "I Can't Breathe" in 2021 and "Fight for You" at the 64th Grammys on 3 Apr 2022. She won in 2021 (pictured).

Top 25 Gaming Records

Settle back and switch on as we present our favourite videogame records, from the earliest programmes to today's billion-dollar industry, compiled by a panel of GWR's gaming gurus. In these 25 entries, you'll find iconic characters, best-selling smash hits and critical darlings. Whether you're mad for Mario, potty for Pokémon or fanatical for Fortnite, it's time to discover the records that took gaming to the next level.

25 LARGEST MULTIPLAYER PVP BATTLE

EVE Online (CCP Games, 2003) is a space-based massively multiplayer online role-playing game (MMORPG) famed for its epic player-versus-player (PVP) battles where in-game damage can cost thousands of real-world dollars. On 6 Oct 2020, the 14-hr skirmish known as "Fury at FWST-8" drew 8,825 players and saw 1,308 battleships destroyed.

24 MOST CRITICALLY ACCLAIMED MMORPG

It has been almost 18 years since *World of Warcraft* was released to rave reviews in Nov 2004. Since then, Blizzard Entertainment's influential MMORPG has maintained a Metacritic score of 93 out of 100, helped by various updates and expansions. Millions of gamers still log in every day to do battle against a cast of evil warlocks, dragons and supernatural beings – as well as each other.

23 MOST CRITICALLY ACCLAIMED SUPERHERO SERIES

Not every superhero story works as a videogame, but the Dark Knight's blend of sneaking, investigating and pummelling always goes down well. The four main instalments of Rocksteady's *Batman: Arkham* series have an average rating of 86.87% on Metacritic. More than 30 million units have been shipped since 2009's *Arkham Asylum*, and the "Arkhamverse" was set to expand in 2022 with *Suicide Squad: Kill the Justice League*.

22 LARGEST CAST FOR A VIDEOGAME

With their million-dollar budgets and huge development teams, modern videogames can rival movie productions. Rockstar Games' epic Western *Red Dead Redemption 2* (2018) was eight years in the making and called on 1,200 actors to provide dialogue or motion-capture performances. The game was released to instant critical acclaim and rustled up a reported $725 m (£564 m) in its first three days.

21 LONGEST-RUNNING FIGHTER SERIES

With the release of 2020's *Street Fighter V: Champion Edition*, Capcom's one-on-one brawler franchise had been active for 32 years. The original game, *Street Fighter*, was released in the arcades on 30 Aug 1987. The series blew up with the sequel, with characters such as Ryu, Ken and Chun-Li – and their signature moves – becoming famous around the world. *Street Fighter* titles have amassed total sales of almost 50 million units.

BEST-SELLING COIN-OPERATED FIGHTING VIDEOGAME

Street Fighter II: The World Warrior (1991) was a knockout blow to other beat-'em-ups, selling 200,000 cabinets. Players had a choice of fighters and could put together strings of attacks that we now know as "combos".

20 LARGEST COLLECTION

Antonio Romero Monteiro (USA) has amassed 20,139 videogames in Richmond, Texas, USA, as verified on 2 Feb 2019. Rarities include every game for the Japan-only Nintendo 64DD, and the seldom-seen Game Gear title *CJ Elephant Fugitive* (Codemasters, 1994). Antonio's favourite? Konami's *Super Castlevania IV* (1991) for the Super NES.

19 LARGEST VIDEOGAME CONVENTION

Since the first Game Developers Conference in 1988 (attendance: 25), videogame conventions have grown into global events where industry bigwigs rub shoulders with cosplayers. The 2019 edition of gamescom, an annual trade fair in Cologne, Germany, attracted 373,000 visitors in five days. Fans and pros alike will hope to return in even greater numbers as COVID-19 restrictions ease.

18 FASTEST COMPLETION OF *SUPER MARIO BROS.*

Speedrunning – completing the playthrough of a game in the quickest possible time – has become a thriving subculture, with dedicated livestreams, forums and even conventions. One of the most popular challenges is Nintendo's 1985 classic, *Super Mario Bros.* On 2 Dec 2021, "Niftski" (USA) completed the game in 4 min 54.881 sec, with the aid of a PC emulator, glitches and some pixel-perfect timing. This is just 0.083 sec off the fastest theoretically possible time.

17 BEST-SELLING FIRST-PERSON SHOOTER SERIES

On 21 Apr 2021, Activision-Blizzard announced that its *Call of Duty* franchise had sold more than 400 million units since the release of the original game on 29 Oct 2003. There have been 18 main-series titles, plus another 15 spin-off games and console exclusives. Over the course of its annual releases, *Call of Duty* has expanded beyond its World War II setting to include Cold-War spycraft and drone-filled sci-fi battlefields.

16 LONGEST VIDEOGAME MARATHON

Dancing queen Carrie Swidecki (USA) strutted her stuff for 138 hr 34 sec playing *Just Dance 2015* (Ubisoft, 2014) on 11–17 Jul 2015 in Bakersfield, California, USA. Carrie first caught the exergamer bug playing the arcade game *Dance Dance Revolution* (Konami, 1998) and hasn't stopped dancing since. She was inducted into the International Video Game Hall of Fame in 2018.

CARRIE ON DANCING
Carrie also holds GWR titles for **most high scores achieved on a dance videogame series in 24 hours** – 276, on 23 Jul 2016 – and the **longest videogame marathon on a mobile game** – 55 hr 1 min 51 sec, on *Pokémon GO* on 4–7 Jun 2019.

15 LONGEST-RUNNING SOCCER SERIES

With the release of *FIFA 22* on 1 Oct 2021, EA Sports' *FIFA* franchise had been active for 27 years 290 days. The series kicked off on 15 Dec 1993 with *FIFA International Soccer*, and has sold more than 325 million units. French World Cup-winner Kylian Mbappé (right) was the face of its latest release; the player with the **most FIFA cover appearances**, though, is Brazilian forward Ronaldinho, with nine.

14 MOST POPULAR SOCIAL SIMULATION

Not every gamer seeks the high-octane carnage of a *Gears of War* or *GTA*. Since its original release in 2000, the *Sims* series has captivated fans with the daily interactions of its virtual denizens and has reportedly sold 200 million units across all formats. It was created by Will Wright, who was inspired to build a "virtual dollhouse" after his home was destroyed in a fire. The series' most popular iteration is *The Sims* 4 (Maxis, 2014), which had 10 million monthly active users during spring 2020 and 36 million registered players as of 31 Mar 2021.

13 FIRST MULTIPLATFORM VIDEOGAME

Originally coded for a PDP-1 computer at the Massachusetts Institute of Technology in 1961–62 by Steve Russell (USA), *Spacewar* was implemented on a variety of different machines at universities across the USA. Players fought while flying starships around a star with simulated gravity. *Spacewar* also gave rise to the **first videogame tournament**: the Intergalactic *Spacewar* Olympics, held on 19 Oct 1972 at Stanford University.

FIRST VIDEOGAME
A draughts (checkers) program designed by Christopher Strachey (UK) for the Ferranti Mark I computer was first played in Jul 1952. The human operator was pitted against the computer, with the board shown on a Williams tube display.

12 HIGHEST-GROSSING MOBILE GAME

MOST CONSECUTIVE WINS IN *HONOR OF KINGS*
On 26 Jan 2019, "Saobai" (CHN) claimed his 333rd *Honor of Kings* victory in a row. The 18-year-old esports player was watched by an official GWR adjudicator and a streaming audience of 15 million people.

Honor of Kings (Tencent Games, 2015) had earned an estimated $12.8 bn (£9.3 bn) as of 6 Oct 2021, according to industry analysts. Although not particularly well known internationally (where it is marketed as *Arena of Valor*), this mobile MOBA is a cultural phenomenon in its native China. In 2020, developer Tencent claimed *Honor of Kings* had reached 100 million daily users, around half of which are female.

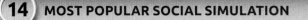

Sony's PlayStation 2 (PS2) shipped 155 million systems over its 13-year lifespan between 2000 and 2012. The PS2 led a revolution in home entertainment, as it and other sixth-generation consoles enabled users to play games, go online and watch DVD movies through one device. Although superseded by the PS3 in 2006, Sony continued PS2 production for another six years, during which time many third-party developers continued to release new games for the aging, but still popular, platform (see below).

MOST GAMES RELEASED FOR A SINGLE CONSOLE
One of the key reasons for the PlayStation 2's success was its huge and diverse library of games. Between the console's launch on 4 Mar 2000 and the release of the **last PS2 game** (*Pro Evolution Soccer 2014*) on 13 Nov 2013, approximately 4,380 unique titles were given a physical release for the platform.

The adventures of Lara Croft have been enthralling gamers for more than 25 years, with sales of her *Tomb Raider* series totalling 85 million copies as of 28 Oct 2021, according to publisher Square Enix. Lara has shown startling longevity, evolving from the cartoon pin-up of 1996's *Tomb Raider* (below, left) to the grittier heroine of the 2013 reboot. Developer Crystal Dynamics used performance-capture techniques to create a more realistic character.

MOST MAGAZINE COVERS FOR A VIDEOGAME CHARACTER
Lara Croft's impact on popular culture is shown by her appearance on at least 1,230 magazine covers. This includes not only gaming titles but those covering culture, lifestyle and film. The fearless artefact-hunter has starred in three Hollywood movies, portrayed by Angelina Jolie (twice) and Alicia Vikander. A sequel starring Vikander is slated for release in 2022.

Developed by computer scientist Alexey Pajitnov for the Soviet Electronika 60 micro-computer in 1984, *Tetris* has spawned more than 200 official variants developed for at least 70 unique systems. These include titles for in-flight entertainment systems, word processors and LCD keychain games. Top players have developed strategies and techniques such as "hypertapping" to outwit the classic puzzler. For more on the latest *Tetris* world champion, see p.105.

FIRST VIDEOGAME IN SPACE
On 1 Jul 1993, the Soyuz TM-17 rocket blasted off for the *Mir* space station with a Nintendo Game Boy and *Tetris* among its payload. It belonged to cosmonaut Aleksandr Serebrov, who went on to spend 196 days in orbit. The cartridge was auctioned off in 2011 for $1,220 (£789).

HIGHEST-EARNING eSPORTS TEAM

Team Liquid are the dominant force in competitive gaming, having earned $38,476,764 (£28.3 m) from 2,148 tournaments as of 11 Feb 2022. The Dutch-based organization fields multiple teams across a range of gaming disciplines. The majority of its prize money ($23 m, or £16.8 m) comes from its *Dota 2* team, which won The International in 2017 and was runner-up in 2019. However, Team Liquid has also earned seven-figure prize pots with teams that compete in *Fortnite*, *StarCraft* and *Counter-Strike: Global Offensive* (pictured).

7 LARGEST USER-GENERATED CONTENT PLATFORM

Launched without much fanfare in 2004, *Roblox* has grown into a global phenomenon. It is not a conventional videogame, but rather a platform that allows users to create and share their own games (or "experiences"). Thousands of these games are published every week. COVID-19 lockdowns saw a surge in activity on the platform, with 43.2 million daily users as of 16 Aug 2021.

MOST VISITED GAME IN *ROBLOX*
"Adopt Me!" had been visited more than 27.2 billion times as of 11 Feb 2022. Created by *Roblox*-ers "Bethink" and "NewFissy", the game initially revolved around raising virtual children. A 2019 update focusing on adopting pets led to a massive spike in popularity.

6 FASTEST ENTERTAINMENT PROPERTY TO GROSS $1 BILLION

BEST-SELLING ACTION-ADVENTURE GAME
GTA V's success continues thanks to *GTA Online*, which has kept players engaged long after they had completed the story of Trevor, Michael and Franklin. As of 7 Feb 2022, *GTA V* had sold 160 million units, earning around $6.4 bn (£4.6 bn).

Upon its release on 17 Sep 2013, the criminal classic *Grand Theft Auto V* heralded a new era of Hollywood-style blockbuster videogames. It was developed over five years with a budget of $265 m (£166.2 m), but earned back its development costs in a matter of hours. Soon after, it was announced that *GTA V* had achieved sales of $1 bn (£621.3 m) in just three days, a mark that is yet to be equalled by any videogame or movie.

BEST-SELLING RPG SERIES

The first pair of *Pokémon* games, *Red* and *Green* (inset below), were an immediate smash hit for Nintendo when they came out in Feb 1996. Since then, seven further generations of *Pokémon* RPGs (role-playing games) have been made, comprising 37 individual titles. As of Mar 2021, *Pokémon* had sold 380 million games and spawned 25 feature films – the **most movie spin-offs from a videogame series**.

MOST DOWNLOADED MOBILE GAME ON DEBUT
Released on 6 Jul 2016, *Pokémon Go* is an augmented-reality game that spawns virtual Poké-monsters in the real world around us. By the end of its first month, 130 million people had put the game on their phones.

4 MOST CRITICALLY ACCLAIMED

Beginning with 1986's ground-breaking *The Legend of Zelda*, new entries in Nintendo's *Zelda* series have always been a big deal. However, it was the first 3D instalment of the series, *Ocarina of Time* – released on 21 Nov 1998 – that earned Link's adventures the top spot among the all-time greats. As of 22 Oct 2021, *Ocarina of Time* had a score of 99 out of 100 on review-aggregator Metacritic, making it the all-time **most critically acclaimed videogame**; four games currently sit behind it, each with a Metascore of 98.

LARGEST COLLECTION OF *ZELDA* MEMORABILIA
Like every entry on this list, the *Zelda* series has its share of superfans. Anne Martha Harnes (NOR) has been hooked since 1994, when she first played *A Link to the Past* on the SNES. In 2008, she started gathering Zelda merchandise and, at the last count, had collected 1,816 unique items.

3 MOST CONCURRENTLY PLAYED

Despite being the youngest game on this list, *Fortnite Battle Royale* (2017) has achieved a level of popularity rivalled only by the game at the number one spot. About 80 million players check in for a round or two every month, and there are typically *c.* 4 million players active on any given day. For special live events, these figures rise even higher. On 1 Dec 2020, the Galactus Event – the climax of a three-month collaboration with Marvel – saw 15.3 million players wage war against The Devourer of Worlds.

MOST FOLLOWED TWITCH STREAMER (FEMALE)
Fortnite's popularity with streamers is a key factor in its global success. One of the biggest of these online personalities is Pokimane, aka Imane Anys (CAN, b. MAR), who had 7,230,762 followers on Twitch as of 8 Feb 2021.

2 MOST UBIQUITOUS CHARACTER

Since Mario's first appearance – as "Jumpman" – in 1981's *Donkey Kong* arcade cabinet, Nintendo's plucky plumber has appeared in an amazing 240 unique games, as well as numerous ports and remakes. In addition to his usual platforming adventures, these games have seen Mario try his hand at everything from karting and golf to painting and even teaching how to type. In 2022, Mario is due to make a return to the big screen for the first time since 1993, with Chris Pratt donning the blue overalls and red cap.

MOST EXPENSIVE GAME
On 11 Jul 2021, a mint-condition copy of *Super Mario 64* – sealed in its box since 1996 – was sold by Heritage Auctions for $1.56 m (£1.12 m). This beat a record set by a copy of *The Legend of Zelda* that sold for $870,000 (£631,000) just two days earlier.

BEST-SELLING LUIGI VIDEOGAME
Mario's nervous little brother Luigi has long lived in his sibling's shadow, and didn't get a game of his own until 2001. However, his latest adventure, *Luigi's Mansion 3* (2019), is proof that he has a dedicated fan base, selling 9.59 million copies as of 31 Mar 2021.

1 BEST-SELLING GAME

With its blocky graphics and completely open-ended gameplay, *Minecraft* was no one's idea of a smash hit back when it was first released in 2011. It quickly gained a huge following, however, and is now a perennial fixture of the gaming world. As of Apr 2021, *Minecraft* had sold 238 million copies worldwide. Recent updates have given it state-of-the-art graphical overhauls (right) and spin-off adventure games such as *Story Mode* (below).

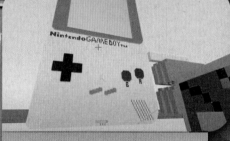

FIRST GAME BOY VIDEOGAME RECREATED IN *MINECRAFT*
There are many GWR titles inspired by the creativity of *Minecraft* players, but few are more impressive than the functioning Game Boy that YouTuber MrSquishy (USA) showed off in 2017. The virtual handheld could play *Pokémon Red* (see opposite) using a clone of the Game Boy's processor made from 375,000 command blocks!

Giant's Orchestra

We love supersized musical instruments here at GWR, though sadly we've never been able to bring them together in a true "big band". With international travel still a tricky prospect, we've opted to imagine what such a troupe might look like when their tour hit the Sydney Opera House in Australia. Long strings and big bores make for really deep notes, so they would probably sound like a tuneful earthquake. Even the smallest of these instruments can play a G# below the lowest note on a grand piano, while others approach the limits of human hearing.

This violin is based on a late 18th-century model by master luthier Johann Georg Schönfelder II.

Incredibly, every instrument here is fully playable – although it might take more than one person to do it!

Take the **largest violin** (**1**), for example. Made by a group of master luthiers from Vogtland, Germany, it is seven times larger than standard and is 4.27 m (14 ft) from top to bottom. It requires three musicians to play it: one to press the strings and two to handle the 5.2-m (17-ft) bow.

Our string section also features the **largest ukulele** (**2**), a 3.9-m-long (12-ft 9-in) behemoth 7.5 times larger than a soprano model. Lawrence Stump (USA) made this über-uke, after helping his son build a ukulele for a school project.

You'd need strong lungs to play the **largest saxophone** (**3**) playable by one person. It stands 2.7 m (8 ft 10 in) tall and boasts a bell diameter of 39.1 cm (1 ft 3 in). Created by J'Elle Stainer (BRA), this subcontrabass sax has a lowest note of 25.95 Hz – only just audible to the human ear.

Definitely not playable by one person, the **largest accordion** (**4**) is 2.53 m (8 ft 3 in) tall, 1.9 m (6 ft 2 in) wide and weighs approximately 200 kg (440 lb) – about as heavy as the three people you'll probably need to play it. Dubbed Castelfidardo, after the town in Italy where it was constructed, it's built to a 5:1 scale and was more than 1,000 hours in the making.

Relative to a standard-sized instrument, the **largest drum kit** (**5**) is this 5.2:1-scale replica created by Drumartic (AUT). It includes a bass drum with a 2.9-m (9-ft 6-in) diameter – wider than that of a discus thrower's circle. And it's not called "The Big Boom" for nothing.

Rounding off this outsized orchestra is the **largest piano** (**6**), a 1.8-tonne (4,000-lb) jumbo grand built by Daniel Czapiewski (POL). It's 2.49 m (8 ft 2 in) wide, 1.92 m (6 ft 3 in) high and has 156 keys (68 more than normal) spanning 12 octaves – which you'll need to keep up with this band!

Round-Up

LARGEST eSPORTS TEAM FOR PEOPLE WITH DISABILITIES

Permastunned Gaming is a multinational eSports collective exclusively for gamers with disabilities that had 33 members by Apr 2022. The brainchild of Belgium-based Alexander Nathan (b. NLD, above), the group specializes in games such as *Dota 2*, *Call of Duty* and *Tekken*, among others.

Fastest theatrical production

On 20 Feb 2022, Rubber Chicken Theatre (UK) staged a rendition of *Return to the Forbidden Planet* in 9 hr 59 min 3 sec in Stirling, UK. The clock started when the production team were handed the scripts, with no one involved aware of the title beforehand. The performance had to last a minimum of 90 min and have an audience of at least 50 paying customers.

Longest radio interview

Himal FM's Bhanu Bhakta Niraula chatted with activist and tourism expert Ang Phinjo Sherpa (both NPL) for 25 hr 26 min in Kathmandu, Nepal, on 8–9 Nov 2021.

The **longest video livestream marathon** is 45 hr 45 min, by influencer and business entrepreneur-turned-hip-hop artist Mahmoud "TheRealMood" Shehada (CAN) in Dubai, UAE, on 16–18 Dec 2021.

▶ Smallest mobile nightclub

The "Doof Shed" measures 1.097 m² (11.808 sq ft) and comes complete with dancefloor, sound system and dynamic lighting. Created by twins Harry and Evangelos "Boonie" Labrakis (both AUS), the dinky disco was verified on 15 May 2021 in Sydney, New South Wales, Australia.

Most money pledged for a Kickstarter project

Fantasy writer Brandon Sanderson (USA) crowdfunded a fantastical $41,754,153 (£31.7 m) between 1 Mar and 1 Apr 2022. His project – to cover the self-publication of four new novels – reached its initial goal of $1 m (£746,800) in less than 35 minutes.

Highest-earning dead celebrity

Children's author Roald Dahl (UK, 1916–90) earned $513 m (£380 m) in the 12 months leading up to 30 Oct 2021, according to *Forbes*. This was due largely to the purchase by Netflix of The Roald Dahl Story Company – in which the writer's heirs still held a 75% stake.

Longest-running videogame series

With the launch of *Space Invaders Gigamax* (Square Enix) on 26 Mar 2020, the retro shooter game had been firing for 41 years 284 days. The original Taito title was released on 16 Jun 1978.

Fastest Any% completion of *Elden Ring* (PC)

"RockCandy" (USA) battled through the Lands Between in 25 min 48 sec on 19 Apr 2022, as verified by Speedrun.com. This was equalled by "Hyp3rsomniac" (USA) five days later. Bandai Namco's action-RPG was co-created by videogame director Hidetaka Miyazaki and *Game of Thrones* writer George R R Martin.

SMALLEST PURPOSE-BUILT CINEMA IN OPERATION

The Little Prince Micro-Cinema in Stratford, Ontario, Canada, has an area of just 16.29 m² (175.34 sq ft), as verified on 27 Nov 2021. The 13-seat venue, built in 2019, plays short films in the day with free admission, while feature-length movies are screened in the evening.

YOUNGEST *RUPAUL'S DRAG RACE* WINNER

Krystal Versace, aka Luke Fenn (UK, b. 10 Oct 2001), was 20 years 46 days old when her victory in the Series 3 finale of *RuPaul's Drag Race UK* aired on 25 Nov 2021. The franchise's youngest-ever finalist started doing drag at 13. She lip-synced her way to glory to Dusty Springfield's cover of "You Don't Own Me".

BETTY WHITE (1922–2021)

Actress and comedian Betty White (USA, b. 17 Jan 1922) made her screen debut in 1939 and was still performing in 2019, more than 80 years on – the **longest TV career by an entertainer (female)**. The "Golden Girl" died on 31 Dec 2021.

FIRST DEAF ACTOR TO PLAY A LIVE-ACTION MARVEL SUPERHERO

The Eternals (USA, 2021) featured Lauren Ridloff (USA) in the role of Makkari. Ridloff, a Tony-nominated actor who has appeared in zombie series *The Walking Dead*, blazed a trail as the super-fast superhero; she communicates with the other characters using American Sign Language.

FIRST VIDEOGAME TO WIN A HUGO AWARD

On 18 Dec 2021, *Hades* (Supergiant Games, 2020) won the inaugural Best Video Game category at the prestigious sci-fi and fantasy literary awards. The critically acclaimed dungeon crawler challenges players to help Zagreus – the son of Hades – escape from the Underworld.

HADES

MOST EPISODES OF A LIVE CHILDREN'S TV SHOW

On 19 Jan 2022, TV Tokyo's weekday kids' show *Oha Suta* aired its 5,500th episode in its 25th year of being on Japanese television. GWR's Fumika Fujibuchi stopped by to present an official certificate to host Subaru Kimura (centre) and presenter Ike Nwala (right).

Largest Soul Train dance

To mark 50 years since the debut of the *Soul Train* variety show, on 21 Nov 2021 US cable network BET asked 536 people to shake their stuff in New York's Marcus Garvey Park. As per tradition, dancers formed two rows then took it in turns to boogie in between.

Most times to watch a movie at the cinema

Between 16 Dec 2021 and 15 Mar 2022, Ramiro Alanis (USA) watched 292 screenings of *Spider-Man: No Way Home* (see below) in Riverview, Florida, USA. Ramiro became a two-time holder of this record, having seen his 191 viewings of *Avengers: Endgame* (USA, 2019) topped by Arnaud Klein (FRA), who watched *Kaamelott: First Instalment* (FRA/BEL, 2021) 204 times in 2021.

YOUNGEST OPERA SINGER

Victory Brinker (USA, b. 4 Feb 2012) was only 7 years 314 days old at the start of a run of concerts at the Pittsburgh Public Theater in 2019. The *America's Got Talent* classical vocalist can reach over three octaves and sing in eight languages.

First female winner of the Filmfare Lifetime Achievement Award

Iconic playback singer Lata Mangeshkar (IND) passed away on 6 Feb 2022. Known as the "nightingale of Bollywood", in 1994 she became the first woman – and only the third-ever person – to be presented with a Lifetime Achievement Award at the Filmfare Awards, which honour artistic and technical excellence in the Hindi movie industry.

Most southerly game of musical chairs

On 28 Dec 2021, a group of 15 competitors and 17 helpers – representing eight different countries – led by Cindy Y Chang (USA/JPN) played musical chairs at 89.999848°S, near the South Pole in Antarctica. The song list included "Ice Ice Baby" by Vanilla Ice and Run DMC's "Walk This Way". The last man sitting was Joshua Leyba of the USA.

YOUNGEST MARIACHI SINGER

Mateo Adalberto López (USA, b. 28 Aug 2014) has been performing with mariachi bands since 21 Apr 2019, at the age of just 4 years 236 days. After his Mexican folk-music songs went viral on social media, he has featured on *Mexico's Got Talent* and NBC's *Little Big Shots*.

LARGEST ORCHESTRA

On 13 Nov 2021, a total of 8,573 musicians – including school children and professionals from the Simón Bolívar Orchestra – gathered en masse to play Tchaikovsky's *Slavic March* in Caracas, Venezuela. The players, who were aged between 12 and 77, were all part of the El Sistema (VEN) music-education programme.

MOST EXPENSIVE COMIC

A copy of Marvel's *Amazing Fantasy #15* (1962, far left) realized $3.6 m (£2.6 m) at Heritage Auctions on 9 Sep 2021. The comic features the first appearance of Spider-Man and originally sold for 12 cents.

On 13 Jan 2022, page 25 of *Marvel Super-Heroes Secret Wars #8* (left) fetched $3.36 m (£2.45 m) – the **most expensive comic-book page sold at auction**.

Spidey is the highest-grossing movie superhero, with total box-office takings of $8 bn (£5.9 bn) as of Jan 2022.

MOST VIEWED MOVIE TRAILER IN 24 HOURS

A teaser for *Spider-Man: No Way Home* (USA, 2021) accrued 355.5 million global views on 23–24 Aug 2021. The clip showed star Tom Holland cast into the Marvel multiverse, pitting him against villains from previous incarnations of the *Spider-Man* franchise, along with other actors to have formerly played the lead role.

To mark the movie's release, 601 diehard Spidey fans assembled at Jio World Drive in Mumbai, India, on 15 Dec 2021. The **largest gathering of Spider-Men** was organized by Sony Pictures Entertainment (IND).

Cristiano Ronaldo

Cristiano Ronaldo has spent his footballing career rewriting the record books. In 2021, he cemented his legacy as one of the greatest players in the game's history by becoming the top scorer in men's internationals.

Born in the Portuguese archipelago of Madeira, Ronaldo's skills took him on a sporting journey around the biggest clubs in European football – from Sporting Lisbon to Manchester United, Real Madrid and Juventus. He evolved from a dazzling winger into a complete centre-forward, notching up an incredible 450 goals in 438 games for Real to become their all-time leading scorer. In the UEFA Champions League he reigned supreme, setting records for **most appearances** (183) and **most goals** (140).

But Ronaldo is arguably proudest when he pulls on his national shirt. He made his debut for Portugal in 2003 and became a talisman for his teammates, captaining them to glory at Euro 2016. At the delayed EURO 2020 tournament, Ronaldo struck five times in four games to equal the **most men's international soccer goals** – a record long held by Iran's Ali Daei, who scored 109 goals between 1993 and 2006. Ronaldo overtook Daei during a World Cup qualifier on 1 Sep 2021 (see **6**), and by 29 Mar 2022 he had reached 115 goals. He had also played 186 internationals, putting him joint-third on the men's all-time list (see p.222). Will Ronaldo be able to add this record to his collection before he calls time on his career?

VITAL STATISTICS

Name Cristiano Ronaldo dos Santos Aveiro

Birthplace Madeira, Portugal

Current world records
Most goals in...
- **Internationals (male):** 115
- **UEFA European Championships:** 14
- **Champions League games:** 140

Trophies & awards
7 x domestic league titles
5 x Champions League titles
5 x FIFA Ballon d'Or
1 x UEFA European Championship

1

2

3

"Always good to be recognized as a world record breaker. Let's set the numbers even higher!"

1. As a youth player on Madeira, Ronaldo was nicknamed Abelhinha ("Little Bee"). He spent two years playing for Nacional before signing for Sporting Lisbon at the age of 12, and moving to mainland Portugal.

2. Ronaldo joined Manchester United in 2003 and became an instant hero with the Old Trafford faithful, going on to score 118 goals in 292 games. Ronaldo returned to United in 2021 and played his first English league match for 12 years 118 days – the **longest gap between English Premier League appearances.**

3. In 2009, Ronaldo joined Real Madrid for a then-world-record fee of £80 m ($130 m). He helped the Spanish giants dominate the UEFA Champions League, winning four titles in nine seasons. In 2013/14, he broke the record for **most goals in a UEFA Champions League season,** scoring 17 times in 11 matches.

4. On-field success has helped to make Ronaldo arguably the world's most famous sportsperson. As of 16 Feb 2022, he had the **most followers on Instagram** (402 million) and was the **most liked person on Facebook** (150.8 million).

5. Ronaldo led Portugal to victory at EURO 2016, where they overcame host nation France 1–0 in the final. He struck his first international goals at EURO 2004, and now holds the tournament record for both **appearances** (25) and **goals** (14).

6. On 1 Sep 2021, Ronaldo achieved the **most men's international soccer goals** with two headers against the Republic of Ireland. Of his current tally of 115, he has scored 28 with his head.

6

Find out more about Ronaldo in the Hall of Fame section at www. guinnessworldrecords.com/2023

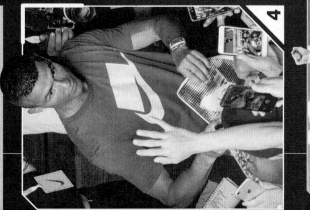

4

5

NEWEST REPUBLIC
On 30 Nov 2021, the island nation of Barbados officially removed the UK's Queen Elizabeth II as head of state and became a republic – i.e., a nation ruled by an elected president, as opposed to a monarch. At the stroke of midnight, a 21-gun salute in the capital, Bridgetown, signalled the handover to the country's first president and new head of state, Dame Sandra Mason, although Prime Minister Mia Mottley retained power as head of the government. Mason and Mottley are pictured opposite (centre and far left, respectively) in a group that also includes Bajan cricketing legend Sir Garfield Sobers, singer Rihanna and the UK's Prince Charles.

At the same ceremony, Rihanna was declared a National Hero of Barbados. She and Sobers are the sole living incumbents of this honour.

Modern World

EXPLORATION

DISCOVERY

RESEARCH

B

2023

DOWN WITH THIS SORT OF THING

WHAT ARE WE PROTESTING AGAINST AGAIN

IT'S A SIGN

BLACK LIVES MATTER

Among other musical achievements, Rihanna has scored the most US No.1 singles in a year by a female – four (2010).

Taking Action

YOUNGEST *TIME* PERSON OF THE YEAR
Climate activist Greta Thunberg (SWE, b. 3 Jan 2003) was named Person of the Year by *TIME* magazine aged 16 years 354 days on 23 Dec 2019. She's pictured here in Nov 2021 in Glasgow, UK, speaking to fellow protesters who had flocked to the Scottish city during the UN's COP26 climate-change conference (see also p.215).

LONGEST JOURNEY BY A FULL-BODY PUPPET
A giant puppet dubbed Little Amal travelled *c.* 8,000 km (4,970 mi) from Gaziantep, Turkey, to Manchester, UK, between 27 Jul and 3 Nov 2021. Representing a nine-year-old Syrian refugee, Amal ("Hope" in Arabic) visited 65 European cities – London is pictured – to spotlight Syria's refugee crisis.

LARGEST ANTI-WAR RALLY
On 15 Feb 2003, a crowd of approximately 3 million gathered in Rome, Italy, to oppose the USA's threat to invade Iraq. Police and media statistics indicate that millions more demonstrated in nearly 600 cities worldwide, with 10–15 million pacifists taking to the streets to protest globally.

LARGEST LGBTQ+ MARCH
A reported 5 million people attended WorldPride NYC 2019 in New York City, USA, on 28–30 Jun. The march marked the 50th anniversary of the infamous police raid on Manhattan's Stonewall Inn on 28 Jun 1969 – a catalyst for the gay-rights movement.

LARGEST DONATION OF...

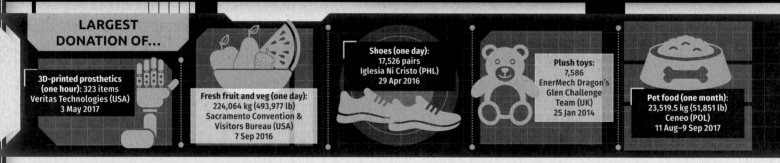

3D-printed prosthetics (one hour): 323 items
Veritas Technologies (USA)
3 May 2017

Fresh fruit and veg (one day): 224,064 kg (493,977 lb)
Sacramento Convention & Visitors Bureau (USA)
7 Sep 2016

Shoes (one day): 17,526 pairs
Iglesia Ni Cristo (PHL)
29 Apr 2016

Plush toys: 7,586
EnerMech Dragon's Glen Challenge Team (UK)
25 Jan 2014

Pet food (one month): 23,519.5 kg (51,851 lb)
Ceneo (POL)
11 Aug–9 Sep 2017

LONGEST HUMAN CHAIN (MULTIPLE COUNTRIES)
On 23 Aug 1989, in an act of solidarity calling for independence from the USSR, around 2 million people joined hands in three Baltic states. In total, it stretched some 675 km (419 mi) across Estonia, Latvia and Lithuania.

The longest human chain spanned 1,050 km (652 mi) on 11 Dec 2004, from Teknaf to Tentulia in Bangladesh.

Assessing the size of crowds inevitably involves some conjecture and estimation. With expert guidance, GWR uses data from many sources, such as the news and social media, organizers, local law enforcement and retrospective studies/reports.

First recorded labour strike
In the 29th year of Pharaoh Ramses III's reign (*c.* 1157 BCE), the artisans of the Royal Necropolis at Deir el-Medina, Egypt, downed tools in response to late rations. The event is documented on the "Turin Strike Papyrus".

First country to pass women's suffrage
New Zealand's governor, Lord Glasgow, signed the Electoral Bill on 19 Sep 1893, making his country the earliest self-governing nation in the contemporary Western world to permanently grant women the right to vote. Many pre-colonial societies had women's suffrage (or an equivalent), though. For

example, women voted, and vetoed, on war councils in North America's indigenous Iroquois confederation, which may date as far back as the mid-12th century.

Largest environmental mobilization
On 22 Apr 1970, the very first Earth Day saw some 20 million people across the USA engage with environmental issues via a range of activities. These included protest marches, rallies, teach-in lectures and community clean-ups. The one-day mobilization was spearheaded by peace activist John McConnell – who, in 1969, had proposed a day to honour our planet, Senator Gaylord Nelson from Wisconsin and environmentalist Denis Hayes (all USA).

Longest hotel-workers' strike
On 15 Jun 2003, all 130 employees at the Congress Plaza Hotel in Chicago, Illinois, USA, went on strike owing to grievances over wages and contracts. The action ended 9 years 349 days later, on 30 May 2013.
The **longest pub-workers' strike** began on 3 Mar 1939, prompted by the appointment of a

MOST VALUABLE ENVIRONMENTAL AWARD

On 17 Oct 2021, five winners each received the inaugural Earthshot Prize of £1 m ($1.4 m) for their cutting-edge ideas to tackle climate change. The award was launched in 2020 by the UK's Prince William and Sir David Attenborough. Among the recipients were Bahamian conservationists Coral Vita, who have devised a revolutionary system of growing coral on land and reseeding it in the ocean (pictured). A network of such farms could help to regenerate reef ecosystems.

LARGEST ANTI-RACISM MOVEMENT

Black Lives Matter (BLM) was co-founded in 2013 by Patrisse Cullors, Alicia Garza and Opal Tometi (all USA). Engagement with BLM has sky-rocketed, notably after George Floyd's murder on 25 May 2020. In the following month, c. 15–26 million people in the USA alone joined a BLM demonstration.

LARGEST ANIMAL-RIGHTS MARCH

On 9 Sep 2017, an estimated 20,000–30,000 people took part in the "Animal Parade" held in Tel Aviv, Israel. They were calling for improved animal welfare in agriculture, a ban on fur products and a wider take-up of veganism. The event was organized by around 25 animal charities, including Vegan Friendly (ISR).

LONGEST PEACE VIGIL BY AN INDIVIDUAL

Concepción "Connie" Picciotto (b. María de la Inmaculada Concepción Martín, ESP) maintained a sit-in against nuclear weapons for 34 years 177 days. The vigil lasted from 1 Aug 1981 until her death, aged 80, on 25 Jan 2016. Her camp was in Lafayette Square, opposite the White House in Washington, DC, USA.

Connie started the vigil with fellow anti-nuclear protester William Thomas, who died in 2009.

School supplies:
18,012 kg
(39,709 lb)
Xiaomi
Technology India
8 Nov 2019

Underwear (one hour):
10,289 pairs
Ryan Avery and The
Action Center (both USA)
10 Oct 2021

Bicycles (one hour):
979
DaVita Villagewide (USA)
26 Apr 2017

Baked goods:
24,480 kg (53,969 lb)
Grupo Bimbo (MEX)
22 Oct 2020

Books (one week):
657,061
Rotary Clubs of Jamaica
1–8 May 2010

non-unionized worker at Downey's bar in Dublin, Ireland. A picket remained outside the tavern until 27 Nov 1953 – a duration of 14 years 269 days – making this one of the longest strikes on record.

Most non-violent revolutionary movements in one decade

Worldwide, the 2010s (2010–19) saw the emergence of 96 primarily peaceful civil-resistance campaigns. Among them were anti-corruption protests in North Africa and the Middle East – what came to be known as the "Arab Spring" – and the Catalan independence movement in Spain. That decade also saw the rise of Black Lives Matter in 2013 (see above), the Global Climate Strike in 2019 and the **largest women's-rights protest**: c. 4.47 million people took part in 2017's "Women's March on Washington" in the US capital, as well as in sister marches nationally and internationally.

Most money raised by a...			
Event	Fundraiser	Amount	Cause (year)
Remote music festival	"One World: Together at Home", by Global Citizen and WHO	$127.9 m (£102.4 m)	COVID relief efforts (2020)
Walk/run (individual)	Captain Sir Tom Moore (UK)	£32.8 m ($44.5 m)	NHS (2020)
Walk/run by an amputee (individual)	Terry Fox (CAN)	CAN$14.7 m ($12.7 m; £5.2 m)	Cancer research (1980)
Livestream fundraiser	Z Event 2021 (FRA)	€10.06 m ($11.64 m; £8.50 m)	Various (2021)
Swim	BT Swimathon (UK)	£1.97 m ($3.3 m)	Various (1998)
Broadway show	Hugh Jackman (AUS)	$1.78 m (£1.14 m)	AIDS relief (2012)

Correct as of 1 Apr 2022

LARGEST GENERAL STRIKE

Some 250 million workers took part in a widespread national strike in India on 26 Nov 2020. Triggered by discontent over employment and welfare laws, it was backed by 10 trade unions and several left-wing political parties. The action affected all services and industries nationwide, including transport, agriculture, banking and shipping.

Cryptomania

First decentralized cryptocurrency

In summer 2008, a user known as Satoshi Nakamoto joined an online community called "Cypherpunks". He passed around a paper titled *Bitcoin: A Peer-to-Peer Electronic Cash System*, which promised to solve a problem the community had been wrestling with for years: how to make a secure, trustworthy digital currency without a centralized controlling authority.

Over the following months, Nakamoto developed his idea, which used a publicly visible, cryptographically secure ledger (an innovation he called a "blockchain") to log all transactions. It also used community resources to validate their authenticity (through a process called "mining"). By the beginning of 2009, he had Bitcoin, the **first blockchain**, up and running and mined the "genesis block" on 3 Jan, earning 50 bitcoin as a reward.

First bitcoin transaction

On 9 Jan 2009, Nakamoto sent bitcoin early adopter Hal Finney (USA) 10 bitcoin. However, this was only a test – Finney had helped debug the original Bitcoin software, and wanted to check the blockchain was updating correctly.

The **first commercial bitcoin transaction** – in which the cryptocurrency was used to purchase something – took place on 22 May 2010. American programmer Laszlo Hanyecz offered 10,000 bitcoin online to anyone who ordered him two pizzas. Someone accepted the bitcoin (then worth $41; £28) and ordered Hanyecz pizza costing $25 (£17) in return. Hanyecz considered the deal to be "free pizza", as bitcoin mining was then easy, and doesn't regret his purchase, even though those bitcoin would have been worth *c.* $350 m (£268 m) as of 24 Feb 2022.

First cryptocurrency exchange

As the community surrounding Bitcoin grew, new financial institutions appeared to serve its needs. Alongside various peer-to-peer services, American developer Dustin Dollar's BitcoinMarket (which began operations on 17 Mar 2010) quickly established itself as an important player. It allowed users to trade bitcoin as well as exchange it for fiat currencies such as the US dollar. BitcoinMarket was the premier cryptocurrency exchange for about one year, before being eclipsed by a more user-friendly exchange called Mt. Gox.

Largest cryptocurrency hack

The meteoric rise of Mt. Gox would come to serve as a cautionary tale. As it grew, it began to operate more like a conventional bank; customers would keep bitcoin in accounts hosted on the site, meaning that while Mt. Gox's servers recorded their ownership, on the Bitcoin blockchain it was all still registered to Mt. Gox's wallets.

In 2013, hackers managed to obtain log-in credentials for these online "hot" wallets, and transferred out more than 850,000 bitcoin, bankrupting the exchange. At the time that the hack was announced, in Feb 2014, the stolen currency – drawn from both Mt. Gox's own assets and customer accounts – was worth $450 m (£270 m).

First seizure of cryptocurrency

Many early adopters of Bitcoin were attracted by the prospect of a currency that was beyond the reach of the state – one that could not be seized or its value manipulated by a central authority. In practice, however, human error and investigative zeal mean that the promise of a fully anonymous currency is hard to maintain. The first person to have cryptocurrency seized by law-enforcement authorities was an alleged drug dealer in South Carolina, USA, whose 11.02 bitcoin (which then had a value of $968; £629) were confiscated as part of a bust on 12 Apr 2013.

The **largest cryptocurrency seizure** was carried out on 8 Feb 2022 by the US Department of Justice. They took $3.6 bn (£2.6 bn) from Ilya Lichtenstein and Heather Morgan (both USA), who stand accused of attempting to launder the 119,754 bitcoin that were stolen in the 2016 hack of the Bitfinex exchange.

Most valuable cryptocurrency

Although it has inspired many other coins, Bitcoin – as the **oldest cryptocurrency** – remains the gold standard of digital assets. As of 24 Mar 2022, one bitcoin had a value of $42,989 (£32,486) and the currency as a whole had a market capitalization of $816.69 bn (£617.17 bn). One of the biggest winners from this astonishing growth is its mysterious creator, Satoshi Nakamoto. No one has heard from him since 2011, and the extent of his holdings is not clear, but just that 50-bitcoin reward is now worth $2.1 m (£1.59 m).

FIRST COUNTRY TO ADOPT BITCOIN AS LEGAL TENDER

On 9 Jun 2021, El Salvador passed a law that made bitcoin legal tender – meaning that organizations and individuals would be required to accept bitcoin as payment of a debt. It was hoped that this move, which was condemned by the World Bank, would reduce the cost of international transfers – an important consideration for a country that is reliant on money sent home by workers overseas.

MOST VALUABLE FAN TOKEN

Fan tokens are NFTs that grant their owners access to exclusive clubs associated with sports teams. The most valuable fan tokens are those of English Premier League side Manchester City, which had a combined value of $47.1 m (£35.6 m) as of 24 Mar 2022.

NOTABLE NFTs

Developed in 2014 (see below right), non-fungible tokens, or NFTs, use the same blockchain technology as cryptocurrencies to create unique, tradeable assets that can be used to authenticate the ownership of more or less anything. And we mean *anything*! Here are some of the wilder things that have been offered for sale...

"Non-Fungible Twig"
by BetweenTwoNaps
Owning the NFT confers ownership of the actual twig

"Just setting up my twttr"
by Jack Dorsey
The founder of Twitter's first tweet

"A Year of Farts"
by Alex Ramírez-Mallis
52 min of fart recordings

"Morons" by Burnt Banksy
A Banksy print mocking the art market, burned to mock the NFT market

"Right Arm" by Oleksandra Oliynykova
Tattoo placement rights for the right arm of a Croatian tennis player

"Fyre Festival Sandwich" by Trevor DeHaas
A limp cheese sandwich from a failed music festival

"Random Number" by The N Project
Just that: the buyer gets a random number

MOST EXPENSIVE NFT ARTWORK (LIMITED EDITION)

A piece called *Everydays: The First 5000 Days*, by digital artist Beeple (aka Mike Winkelmann, USA), was auctioned by Christie's for $69,346,250 (£53,339,818) on 11 Mar 2021. The piece is a composite of Beeple's 13 years of daily artworks. The winning bid came from blockchain entrepreneur MetaKovan (aka Vignesh Sundaresan, IND/SGP).

MOST EXPENSIVE NFT COLLECTIBLE

NFT collectibles are limited-edition sets of artwork built around pre-rendered templates. NFTs from one of the earliest sets – "CryptoPunks" by Larva Labs (CAN) – now command sky-high prices. The most expensive is CryptoPunk #5822, which was purchased for $23.7 m (£17.4 m) by crypto entrepreneur Deepak Thapliyal on 12 Feb 2022.

HIGHEST FLOOR PRICE FOR AN NFT COLLECTION

Although it is the rarest CryptoPunks (see above) that command the highest prices, the smaller and more exclusive NFT collection known as the "Bored Ape Yacht Club" – made by Yuga Labs (USA) – is the most expensive to buy into. As of 21 Mar 2022, the value of the cheapest NFT in the set (the "floor price") is $295,225 (£224,006).

FIRST TRADEABLE NFT

Quantum (see below left) established the NFT concept, but it was only a technology demonstration. The first NFTs designed to be traded on the open market were the CryptoKitties, developed by Dapper Labs (CAN) as part of a videogame of the same name and released on 28 Nov 2017.

FIRST NFT

During a hackathon called "Seven on Seven", which took place in New York City, USA, on 5 May 2014, artist Kevin McCoy was paired with developer Anil Dash (both USA). Together, they designed a blockchain-based system (which they called a "monegraph", but we now know as an NFT) to authenticate digital artwork. At the end of the event, McCoy minted an NFT – *Quantum* – which he then sold to Dash for just $4 (£2.36).

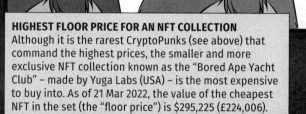

HIGHEST NFT TRANSACTION VOLUME

Players of Axie Infinity, made by Vietnamese videogame developer Sky Mavis, collect and mint NFTs representing digital pets called Axies, which are traded in the game's NFT marketplace. Between its release in Mar 2018 and 24 Mar 2022, players spent $4bn (£3 bn) in the game.

Most NFTs are hosted on the Ethereum blockchain and the transactions take place in ETH. They have been converted to fiat currency here for clarity.

Dressed to Impress

For thousands of years, humans have used clothes not only for survival, but as a means of self-expression, with trending styles and notions of beauty perpetually evolving. Cast an eye over our history of fashionable superlatives, from Stone Age jewellery to 21st-century pop couture.

OLDEST MANNEQUIN
A life-size torso and head was discovered in the tomb of the Egyptian pharaoh Tutankhamun (c. 1341–1323 BCE). It was stored by a chest of clothing and is thought to have been used to display outfits for the young ruler. Dowel holes in the shoulders suggest that the mannequin originally had arms.

MOST EXPENSIVE HAT SOLD AT AUCTION
A bicorn hat reputedly worn by Napoleon Bonaparte at the Battle of Marengo in 1800 sold at auction for €1.8 m ($2.2 m; £1.4 m) in 2014. It was one of around 120 such hats worn by Napoleon, each made by Parisian firm Poupard et Cie.

MOST VALUABLE GRILL JEWELLERY
A gem-laden grill worn by Katy Perry in her "Dark Horse" music video was valued at $1 m (€758,282) on 11 Oct 2017. The dental decoration was the creation of cosmetic dentist Dr William Dorfman (USA).

OLDEST WOVEN CLOTHING
A V-necked linen shirt found in the Tarkhan cemetery, south of the Egyptian capital of Cairo, has been carbon-dated to 3482–3102 BCE. The Tarkhan dress, as it is known, features knife-pleated sleeves and bodice, and is made from three pieces of hand-woven linen.

MOST EXPENSIVE SWEATER SOLD AT AUCTION
A grey mohair five-button cardigan sported by Nirvana frontman Kurt Cobain during the band's appearance on MTV Unplugged in 1993 sold for $334,000 (£260,230) on 26 Oct 2019. The thrift-store cardigan is worn and damaged, with a missing button, cigarette burns and a mysterious crunchy brown stain around the right front pocket.

FIRST SUNGLASSES
Inuit "snow goggles" dating to the 3rd century CE have been found at Alaskan and Siberian archaeological sites. They consist of a wood or bone eye mask perforated by thin slits that protects the wearer's eyes from dazzling sunlight reflecting off the snow.

MOST VALUABLE NECKLACE
"The Incomparable" was valued in 2013 at $55 m (£34 m). Made by Switzerland-based jewellers Mouawad, the necklace contains a 407.48-carat flawless diamond along with 102 "satellite" diamonds cut into various shapes.

MOST TOXIC MAKE-UP
Venetian ceruse (aka "spirits of Saturn") was used as a skin whitener in Europe in the 16th and 17th centuries. A mixture of highly toxic powdered white lead (lead carbonate) and vinegar, its application could cause hair and teeth loss, pitting of the skin and even early cognitive decline.

OLDEST JEWELLERY
A group of 33 perforated shell beads from the sea snail Tritia gibbosula were created and worn at least 142,000 years ago during the Early Middle Stone Age. The shells were excavated between 2014 and 2018 from the Bizmoune Cave near Essaouira in Morocco.

100%

A grand habit was the required "court dress" for women in the royal court of King Louis XIV of France.

WIDEST SKIRT

If our fashion-conscious Pharoah wanted to step out in a skirt, he would definitely be noticed in a *grand habit*... He would also have to go through doors sideways! The most extravagant examples of this 18th-century ensemble measured up to 7 ft (2.1 m) in width, with skirts supported by cane-and-fabric undergarments known as panniers.

LONGEST SHOES

The poulaine (aka the "piked shoe" or "Crakow") was worn by both men and women between the 1340s and 1460s. Contemporary accounts suggest that these slender-pointed shoes could extend to a maximum length of 2 ft (60 cm).

MOST EXPENSIVE GLOVE SOLD AT AUCTION

A white rhinestone-studded glove that once belonged to Michael Jackson (USA) was bought for $420,000 (£253,360) on 21 Nov 2009. Jackson wore the glove on Motown's 25th-anniversary TV special in 1983 – when he famously moonwalked for the first time while performing "Billie Jean".

OLDEST SOCKS

A pair of red woollen socks discovered in the ancient Egyptian city of Oxyrhynchus date to the 4th century CE. They are divided into two toes, to enable them to be worn with sandals.

MOST EXPENSIVE JEANS

This 129-year-old pair of Levi Strauss & Co. "XX" blue jeans were bought by an anonymous collector for $100,000 (£75,300) in May 2018. Despite looking almost new, they actually date from 1893, just 20 years after Levi Strauss patented his metal-riveted denim design. One caveat: the jeans were a special order for Arizona storekeeper Solomon Warner, who wore a 44-in (111-cm) waist and 36-in (91-cm) leg.

MOST DIAMONDS SET IN ONE RING

This elaborate marigold flower ring was set with 12,638 individual cut diamonds by Renani Jewels of Meerut, Uttar Pradesh, India, on 30 Nov 2020. India has always been a global centre of diamond production and trade, and it is estimated that around 90% of the natural diamonds on the market today were cut in the coastal city of Surat.

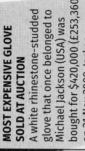

100%

OLDEST SHOES

Ancient sagebrush sandals associated with several indigenous groups in North America have been carbon-dated to 9,300–10,500 years old. Examples of this style of footwear are known as "Fort Rock" sandals, after the cave in Oregon, USA, where the first pairs were found.

MOST EXPENSIVE SHOES FROM A FILM SOLD AT AUCTION

A pair of ruby slippers worn by Judy Garland in *The Wizard of Oz* (USA, 1939) sold for $666,000 (£450,621) on 24 May 2000. It is one of five pairs known to have survived from production. Dorothy's slippers were silver in L Frank Baum's original novel, and were likely changed to better stand out against the movie's Technicolor Yellow Brick Road.

Going, Going, Gone!

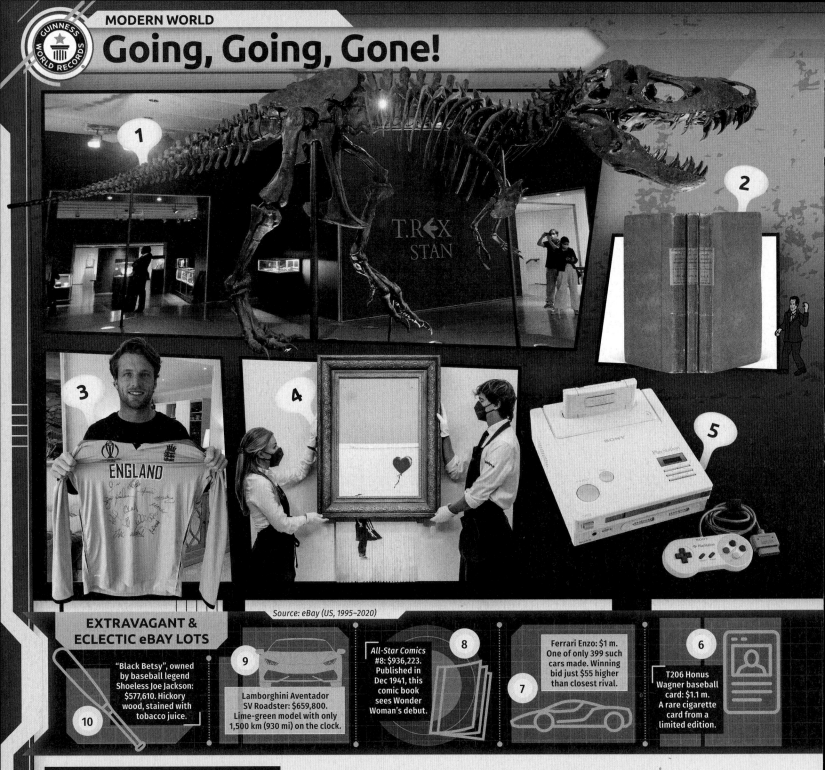

T.REX STAN

Source: eBay (US, 1995–2020)

EXTRAVAGANT & ECLECTIC eBAY LOTS

10 "Black Betsy", owned by baseball legend Shoeless Joe Jackson: $577,610. Hickory wood, stained with tobacco juice.

9 Lamborghini Aventador SV Roadster: $659,800. Lime-green model with only 1,500 km (930 mi) on the clock.

8 *All-Star Comics* #8: $936,223. Published in Dec 1941, this comic book sees Wonder Woman's debut.

7 Ferrari Enzo: $1 m. One of only 399 such cars made. Winning bid just $55 higher than closest rival.

6 T206 Honus Wagner baseball card: $1.1 m. A rare cigarette card from a limited edition.

LARGEST GAVEL

Jim Bolin (USA) created a wooden gavel – used by auctioneers and judges – measuring 5.09 m x 1.54 m (16 ft 8 in x 5 ft), as ratified on 20 Aug 2019 in Marshall, Illinois, USA. It sits outside the city's county courthouse, here shown with local judge Tracy W Resch. In an auction house, gavels are used to signify the end of bidding, hence the expression "hammer price".

MOST EXPENSIVE SOLD AT AUCTION

1. Dinosaur bones

A *Tyrannosaurus rex* skeleton dubbed "Stan" realized $31,847,500 (£24.6 m) at Christie's in New York City, USA, on 6 Oct 2020. Named after amateur palaeontologist Stan Sacrison, who found the remains in 1987, it is one of the most complete *T. rex* specimens ever unearthed. "Stan" will be one of the star exhibits at a new natural-history museum in Abu Dhabi, UAE.

2. Printed work by a female author

A three-volume first edition of Mary Shelley's 1818 Gothic horror story *Frankenstein* (see also p.174) sold for $1,170,000 (£845,865) at Christie's in New York on 14 Sep 2021. It's thought to beat a copy of *Emma*, by Jane Austen, that took £180,000 ($354,240) in 2008.

3. Cricket shirt (online)

The No.63 shirt worn by England's Jos Buttler in the ICC World Cup final sold on eBay for £65,100 ($80,157) on 8 Apr 2020. The wicketkeeper auctioned the top to raise money for hospitals in the wake of COVID-19. Buttler wore it during the super over that saw England defeat New Zealand to win the competition.

4. Banksy artwork

The half-shredded *Love is in the Bin* (2018) by anonymous British street artist Banksy realized £18,582,000 ($25.3 m) when sold at Sotheby's in London, UK, on 14 Oct 2021. This infamous piece started life as 2006's *Girl with Balloon*, achieving a then-record sale price for Banksy of £1.04 m ($1.35 m) in 2018. After the hammer had fallen, however, the work self-destructed via a shredder built into its frame – after which, it was renamed.

5. Videogame console (online)

A Nintendo PlayStation Super NES CD-ROM Prototype created by both Sony and Nintendo in 1992 sold for $360,000 (£275,807) at Heritage Auctions on 8 Mar 2020. It is reportedly the last of 200 prototypes made via a failed joint venture by the two companies. For the **most expensive videogame**, see p.191.

All sales figures include auction fees unless otherwise stated

ILLUSTRATOR
ポケモンイラストレーター

ポケモンカードゲームイラストコン
テストにおいて、あなたのイラストは、
優秀であることが認められました。
そこで、あなたをポケモンカード公
式認定イラストレーターと認め、そ
の栄誉をたたえます。

100%

7

8

9

6

10

11

5
House with a war-proof bunker:
$2.1 m. An ex-missile silo in
New York State with a secret
subterranean
chamber.

4
**The town of Albert in Texas,
USA: $2.5 m.** Five citizens
live on the 13-acre (5.2-ha)
site. Seller's additions
include a tavern.

**Lunch with Warren Buffett:
$2.6 m.** An annual charity
event, held by one of the
world's richest people.

3

2
Gulfstream II: $4.9 m.
Private jet with a range
of high-end facilities.
Accommodates up to
12 passengers.

Gigayacht: $168 m. Luxury
405-ft (123-m) yacht with
helipad, spa, cinema, gym,
10 VIP suites and more.

1

6. Fancy-dress crown
A plastic crown once worn by the late US hip-hop
artist The Notorious B.I.G. (b. Christopher Wallace)
sold for $594,750 (£461,856) at Sotheby's in New York
City on 16 Sep 2020. The rapper donned the headwear
during a photoshoot with photographer Barron
Claiborne just three days before he was killed.

7. Watch
On 9 Nov 2019, a one-off stainless-steel edition of
the Patek Philippe Grandmaster Chime achieved
31 m Swiss francs (£24.3 m; $31.1 m) at the eighth Only
Watch charity auction held at Christie's in Geneva,
Switzerland. Its unique features include two dials (one
golden opaline, one ebony-black) in a reversible case,
and an inscription that reads "The Only One".

8. *Pokémon* trading card (online)
A near-mint Pikachu Illustrator Trainer Promo
Hologram card sold for $900,000 (£662,730) at Goldin
Auctions on 24 Feb 2022. Designed by Pikachu creator
Atsuko Nishida, it is one of only 41 known copies.

9. Coin
On 9 Jun 2021, a 1933 Double Eagle sold for $18,872,250
(£13.3 m) at Sotheby's in New York City. It has a face
value of $20 and is the only coin of its kind that the US
government has authorized for private ownership.

10. Worn trainers/sneakers
An autographed pair of Michael Jordan's Nike Air
Ships fetched $1,472,000 (£1.1 m) at a Sotheby's sale
in Las Vegas, USA, on 24 Oct 2021. They were worn by
the legendary player in 1984 in his fifth game for the
Chicago Bulls, during his NBA rookie season.

11. Cow
Poshspice (pictured) may not be the world's costliest
cow, but she *is* the most expensive of the Limousin
breed. She rustled up 250,000 guineas (£262,000;
$358,610) at Harrison & Hetherington auctioneers in
Carlisle, UK, on 29 Jan 2021. However, a young Friesian
heifer named Mist realized $1.3 m (£914,000) at auction
in Vermont, USA, on 13 Jul 1985. She was bought by a
syndicate led by Boston lawyer Jerome Rappaport.

**MOST EXPENSIVE *STAR WARS*
ACTION FIGURE SOLD AT
AN ONLINE AUCTION**
A rocket-firing Boba Fett toy
sold for $185,850 (£144,354)
via Hake's Auctions on
7 Nov 2019. Made by toy
company Kenner in 1979,
this prototype was never
released for public sale.
Most were destroyed in
the factory at the time,
and only a handful
have ever come
to market.

Fast Food

FIRST FAST-FOOD RESTAURANTS
A retail revolution took place in the Roman Empire of the 1st and 2nd century CE, inspired by the explosion of city sizes. It saw the rise of outlets with masonry sales counters open to the street. These eateries – often ornately decorated (inset) – typically featured a rear kitchen area and worktops from which hot dishes and drinks were served.

Largest fast-food chain (by outlets)
As of 31 Dec 2020, McDonald's (USA) owned 39,198 locations globally, ahead of Subway's 37,540 and Starbucks' 32,660. Founded in 1940 by Richard and Maurice McDonald, the burger chain is now also the largest by **revenue**, with an income of $19.2 bn (£14.1 bn) in 2020. Factoring in their franchisees, however, results in a total system-wide revenue of $93.3 bn (£68.7 bn) for the same period.

Most northerly fast-food restaurant
There is a Subway sandwich outlet located at 71.2883°N, 156.7835°W in Utqiaġvik, Alaska, USA, approximately 530 km (330 mi) above the Arctic Circle. No branch within a chain of fast-food restaurants is closer to the North Pole.

The **most southerly** is the Domino's Pizza in Punta Arenas, Chile, located at 53.1381°S, 70.8895°W. This branch of the 18,300-strong global fast-food franchise is situated 1,496 km (930 mi) north of the Antarctic Circle. There are more southerly eateries, though these are not part of a fast-food chain; The Galley Takeaways, for example, is a fish-and-chip shop located at 46.6001°S, 168.3459°E in Bluff, on New Zealand's South Island.

Largest burger restaurant
I'M HUNGRY in Jeddah, Saudi Arabia, had an area of 2,860 m² (30,784 sq ft) – approximately 1.3 times the size of an ice hockey rink – when measured on 12 Dec 2019.

Fastest time to assemble a hamburger
On 21 Aug 2021, Tom Sinden (UK) built a burger in 7.81 sec in Warlingham, Surrey, UK. As per GWR guidelines, the cheese, tomato, onion and lettuce were pre-sliced, and the patty was pre-cooked.

Largest...
- **Onion bhaji**: 175.48 kg (386 lb 13 oz), made by Oli Khan and Surma Takeaway Stevenage (both UK) in London, UK, on 4 Feb 2020.
- **Fish and chips (serving)**: 54.99 kg (121 lb 3 oz), created by Resorts World Birmingham (UK) on 9 Feb 2018.
- **Fried chicken (serving)**: 1,667.3 kg (3,675 lb 12 oz), made by Karafesu Project Council in Nakatsu, Japan, on 15 Sep 2019.

Longest chimichanga
Macayo's (USA) made a 7.8-m-long (25-ft 7-in) version of this spicy Mexican snack in Phoenix, Arizona, USA, on 25 Sep 2021.

Highest-altitude pizza delivery on land
Between 5 and 8 May 2016, Pizza Hut Africa (ZAF) and Yum! Brands (USA) transported a pepperoni pizza 5,897 m (19,347 ft) up to the summit of Mount Kilimanjaro in Tanzania.

On 4 Jul 2012, Pizzas 4 Patriots (USA) sent 30,000 pizzas to US Armed Forces stationed in Afghanistan via DHL Express. The **largest pizza delivery** was shared between troops at Kandahar Airfield, Bagram Airbase and Camp Bastion (now Camp Shorabak).

The **farthest distance to deliver a pizza** is 19,870 km (12,346 mi), by Paul Fenech (AUS) in association with youth cancer charity Canteen and STA Travel. He hand-delivered the (cold) Margherita pizza to Niko Apostolakis in Wellington, New Zealand, on 1 Jul 2006, after a three-day trip from Opera Pizza in Madrid, Spain.

MOST EXPENSIVE CHICKEN NUGGET SOLD AT AUCTION
On 4 Jun 2021, eBay user "polizna" sold a single McDonald's chicken nugget for $99,997 (£70,709). It's unknown if the nugget realized its high price because it was part of an exclusive meal launched in collaboration with K-pop icons BTS, or because it resembled a crewmate from the popular videogame *Among Us* (Innersloth, 2018).

MOST EXPENSIVE FRENCH FRIES
The Crème de la Crème Pommes Frites went on sale for $200 (£143.79) at Serendipity 3 in New York City, USA, on 12 Jul 2021. The wallet-busting dish is complemented with a Mornay dipping sauce made with cream from 100%-grass-fed Jersey cows and Swiss raclette-style truffled-gruyère cheese that has been aged for three months. It's finished with a dusting of 23-karat edible gold.

Guérande truffle salt

Baccarat crystal Arabesque serving plate

Mornay sauce

Crete Senesi Pecorino Tartufello cheese

Upstate Chipperbec potatoes blanched in Dom Pérignon Champagne and thrice-fried in French goose fat

Shaved black summer truffles

MOST VALUABLE FAST-FOOD BRANDS

1. Starbucks $38.44 bn
2. McDonald's $33.83 bn
3. KFC $15.07 bn
4. Subway $8.18 bn
5. Domino's Pizza $6.08 bn
6. Taco Bell $5.80 bn
7. Dunkin' $5.74 bn
8. Pizza Hut $5.13 bn
9. Haidilao $4.52 bn
10. Tim Hortons $4.05 bn

"Brand value" is a measure of a company's overall worth, factoring in its income as well as its reputation, brand identity and other intangible assets.

Source: Brand Finance, 2021

LARGEST SKEWER OF KEBAB MEAT

On 31 Dec 2008, a rotisserie spit loaded with 4,022 kg (8,866 lb) of chicken meat was presented in Paphos, Cyprus, by Zith Catering Equipment (CYP). The mountainous mass of meat weighed more than the average hippopotamus.

MOST BIG MACS CONSUMED

Donald Gorske (USA) ate his 32,672nd Big Mac® in Fond du Lac, Wisconsin, USA, on 1 Jan 2022. He usually eats 14 of the twin-patty treats each week, purchasing them in bulk and microwaving them at home. In the course of nearly 50 years, he's only gone without one on eight days.

LARGEST PIZZA COMMERCIALLY AVAILABLE

Moontower Pizza Bar in Burleson, Texas, USA, can prepare you a 1.98-m² (21.31-sq-ft) pizza. Dubbed *The Bus* for its rectangular shape, it costs $299.95 (£224.86) plus tax, includes one topping, and is deliverable within a limited area. It takes a while to make, though, so orders must be submitted 48 hr in advance.

LARGEST COLLECTION OF FAST-FOOD RESTAURANT TOYS

When he's picking up a snack, Percival R Lugue (PHL) makes sure to hang on to any freebies. By 4 Nov 2014, he'd stockpiled 10,000 fast-food toys, as verified in Apalit, Pampanga, Philippines. He's had to build a house for them, which his friends refer to as the "Giant Happy Meal Box".

LARGEST COLLECTION OF HAMBURGER-RELATED ITEMS

At the last official count, Hamburger Harry, aka Harry Sperl (DEU) of Daytona Beach, Florida, USA, had amassed 3,724 burger-related items. They include the burgermobile from the movie *Good Burger* (USA, 1997) and a burger waterbed. Harry's prize possession is a Harley-Davidson motorcycle named the *Hamburger Harley*.

TikTok

FASTEST TIME TO REACH 1 MILLION FOLLOWERS
K-pop sensations BTS (KOR; @bts_official_bighit) raced to a million TikTok followers in just 3 hr 31 min on 25 Sep 2019. The septet are also the **most followed music group**, with 49 million fans on the network. (For more on BTS, see p.180.)

MOST FOLLOWED CHEF
Burak Özdemir (TUR; @cznburak) has rustled up a tasty 57.2 million fans with videos of himself preparing classic Turkish dishes. His nickname "CZN" derives from a textiles company called Cinzano that was owned by his father.

MOST FOLLOWED FAMILY
The "First Family of TikTok" are the D'Amelios (all USA), left to right: Heidi (@heididamelio), Charli (@charlidamelio), Marc (@marcdamelio) and Dixie (@dixiedamelio). Combined, their fan count stands at 216.9 million people – about the same as the entire population of Brazil! Of the total, 64% are Charli's.

MOST LIKED VIDEO
A clip of US-based Bella Poarch (b. PHL; @bellapoarch) lip-syncing and pulling faces to the track "Soph Aspin Send (M to the B)" by Millie B has 56.4 million likes. In May 2021, Poarch released her own debut single, meaning the US Navy veteran-turned-influencer is now also the **most followed musician**, with 89 million fans.

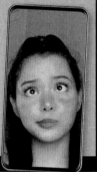

TOP 10 MOST FOLLOWED PEOPLE ON TIKTOK

Source: Social Blade, as of 14 Apr 2022

10 Spencer Polanco Knight: 55 million

9 Burak Özdemir: 57.2 million

8 Dixie D'Amelio: 57.3 million

7 Kimberly Loaiza: 61.6 million

6 Zach King: 68.1 million

TikTok

Fastest time for a social-media platform to reach 1 billion monthly active users*
On 27 Sep 2021, TikTok announced that it had hit 1 billion monthly active users, just five years after it launched. The short-form video-sharing network was first released on 26 Sep 2016 (initially as A.me) by the Chinese web-tech company ByteDance. It was rebranded globally as TikTok in Sep 2017. This means it far outpaced Facebook (which took 8.7 years), YouTube (8.1 years) and Instagram (7.7 years).

Most downloaded app (current year)*
TikTok was downloaded 656 million times worldwide in 2021 – over 100 million more than its nearest competitor, Instagram. Of that total, 94 million downloads were in the USA alone. The results were published in a report produced by Apptopia.

Highest-earning contributor
Queen of TikTok Charli D'Amelio – the **most followed TikToker** (see above) – earned around $17.5 m (£12.9 m) in 2021, according to *Forbes* on 7 Jan 2022. Alongside endorsement deals, her wealth was boosted by the launch of a clothing line for Hollister, and shows on Hulu and Snapchat's Snap Originals, all in tandem with her sister and fellow TikTok star, Dixie.

D'Amelio was the **first person to reach 100 million followers** on 22 Nov 2020. She's also the **most liked user**, with 10.8 billion likes. The **most liked male** is shared between @vietdoosan and @anurupakofficial, each with 8.6 billion, according to Social Blade.

Most viewed live music performance
More than 5.5 million unique viewers tuned in to Ed Sheeran's (UK) live set for TikTok on 25 Jun 2021 (including two replays on the following day). The hour-long gig featured 12 songs. Staged during the UEFA European Football Championship, the TikTok Euro 2020 show took place at Portman Road – home to the musician's beloved soccer team, Ipswich Town FC.

Most comments on a video
On 24 Sep 2021, anonymous *Minecraft* aficionado @meqs posted "Comment for a cookie". To date, 10.7 million TikTokers had obliged the request.

Most followed...
• **Musician (male)**: American beatboxer Spencer X (b. Spencer Polanco Knight; @spencerx) has racked up 55 million fans. As well as solo videos of his own compositions and cover versions, the self-described "mouth music man" has collaborated with artists such as Alicia Keys and DJ Marshmello.
• **Twins**: With videos embracing dance, gymnastics, comedy skits, pranks and challenges, brothers Lucas and Marcus Dobre-Mofid (both USA; @dobretwins) have 35.3 million fans on their shared profile.
• **Trainspotter**: College student Francis Bourgeois (UK; @francis.bourgeois) has (t)racked up 2.2 million followers. He rekindled his childhood love of trains during lockdown in 2020 and his unbridled enthusiasm has made him a runaway success, popular far beyond just the railfan community. (See also pp.158–59.)

*All figures as of 14 Apr 2022 unless otherwise stated; all records are exclusive to the TikTok platform unless marked with ***

MOST VIEWED VIDEO

Posted on 9 Dec 2019, "Zach Kings Magic Broomstick" had been seen 2.2 billion times by 15 Mar 2022. In the video, Zach King (USA; @zachking) dons Hogwarts regalia and appears to levitate on a broomstick, before it's revealed to be another of his signature illusions. The magic-loving social-media star – formerly TikTok's most followed man – first rose to fame on Vine.

MOST FOLLOWED MALE

Italy-based comedian Khabane "Khaby" Lame (b. SEN; @khaby.lame) has accrued 136.3 million fans for his parodies of "life hack" videos. "It's my face and my facial expressions that make people laugh," he told *The New York Times*.

HIGHEST-EARNING CONTRIBUTOR (MALE)

Josh Richards (USA; @joshrichards) earned an estimated $5 m (£3.7 m) in 2021, as reported by *Forbes* on 7 Jan 2022. This places the multi-talented TikToker joint-fourth overall on the list of the platform's highest earners for the year.

MOST FOLLOWED ACTRESS

American dancer and all-round entertainer JoJo Siwa (b. Joelle Joanie Siwa; @itsjojosiwa) has 41.1 million fans. As well as voicing Jay and Kira in *The Angry Birds Movie 2* (FIN/USA, 2019), she has starred in many TV dramas and is also a judge on the US reality show *So You Think You Can Dance*.

5 Will Smith: 71.3 million (most followed actor)

4 Addison Rae: 87.3 million

3 Bella Poarch: 89 million

2 Khabane Lame: 136.3 million

1 Charli D'Amelio: 139.3 million

Guinness World Records itself has grown a loyal following of 19.5 million fans. TikTok is the perfect bite-sized format to show off amazing record holders. Below are our top 10 most watched TikTok posts in the year 2021 – a snapshot of GWR's diverse talent in a (coco)nut shell!

Record (*since broken)	Views (millions)	Holder
Largest mouth gape (male)	95.2	Isaac Johnson (USA)
Most coconuts smashed with one hand in one minute* (1)	50	Abheesh P Dominic (IND)
Shortest woman	38	Jyoti Amge (IND)
Fastest time to jump-pot 15 pool balls (2)	33.4	Florian "Venom" Kohler (FRA)
Longest fingernails on a pair of hands (female)*	30	Ayanna Williams (USA)
Most Big Macs eaten in a lifetime	27.8	Donald Gorske (USA)
Longest nose on a living person	23	Mehmet Özyürek (TUR)
Longest time to mouth-spray water	22.6	Kirubel Yilma (ETH)
Largest mouth gape (female) (3)	17.6	Samantha Ramsdell (USA)
Tallest Mohican	15	Joe Grisamore (USA)

LEARN ON TIKTOK WITH GUINNESS WORLD RECORDS

TikTok isn't just a showcase for some of GWR's incredible record holders (see table right). The platform has also been a springboard for a few homegrown GWR stars, who hosted a series of "Learn on TikTok" content in 2021. Among them are (left to right): mad scientists Orbax & Pepper, Editor-in-Chief Craig Glenday and sports fanatic Will Munford.

Largest Producer of Beef

The USA produced 12.35 million tonnes (13.61 million tons) of bovine meat in 2020, according to the 2021 edition of the Food and Agriculture Organization of the United Nations' *Food Outlook* report. That's 2.5 million tonnes (2.75 million tons) more than its nearest rival, Brazil. But what would all this beef look like if it was dished up in a single serving?

The US president would be able to see (and smell!) the behemoth burger from the White House lawn.

White House

Millions of tonnes of beef can be hard to visualize, so we've pictured it as an XXXXXL-size double cheeseburger. For scale, we've served up this multi-storey meatfest in the centre of the US National Mall, with the Washington Monument as its skewer. The diameter of the two patties would be approximately 420 m (1,377 ft).

Even if we ignore the grease stains on the National Mall, this burger comes with a heavy environmental cost. Global beef production accounts for around 2.83 billion tonnes (3.12 billion tons) of greenhouse gas every year, or around 6% of all global emissions. Although more efficient than the global average, US beef production still creates an estimated 243 million tonnes (268 million tons) of CO_2 annually – that's about the same as the carbon footprint of Belgium and the Netherlands combined!

As massive as this burger is, the USA has an appetite to match. The nation is the **largest consumer of beef**, eating 12.39 million tonnes (13.65 million tons) annually, which equates to an average of 37.6 kg (83 lb) per person – or 415 Big Macs-worth of beef. This still doesn't come close to beating the two-a-day, 730-a-year regimen of Donald Gorske, the man who has achieved the ◗ **most Big Macs eaten in a lifetime** (see p.209).

Round-Up

Safest city

The Danish capital Copenhagen achieved a score of 82.4 on *The Economist's Safe Cities Index 2021*. Toronto, Canada, came a close second, with 82.2. The report assesses 60 cities worldwide. Scores are out of 100, and based on performance in 76 different categories, including personal and digital safety, robustness of infrastructure and – as of 2021 – environmental security.

Highest temperature recorded in Antarctica

On 6 Feb 2020, a temperature of 18.3°C (64.9°F) was registered at Argentina's Esperanza research station, at the tip of the Antarctic Peninsula, and later ratified by the World Meteorological Organization.

The **highest temperature in the Arctic Circle** was 38°C (100.4°F), logged four months later on 20 Jun at Verkhoyansk (67.55°N, 133.38°E) in the region of the Sakha Republic (aka Yakutia) in Russia.

Largest Ugandan rolex

Comprising a fried egg and vegetables wrapped in a chapati, the "rolex" is one of Uganda's staple street foods. Raymond Kahuma (UGA) made a 204.6-kg (451-lb) version – some 700 times heavier than usual – in the village of Kasokoso, Wakiso District, on 4 Nov 2021. "It felt so surreal to win a GWR title," he said. "Surreal wouldn't even be the word – *crazy!*"

Longest megillah

Avner Moriah (ISR) created a 28.03-m (91-ft 11-in) megillah – a scroll referring to the biblical narrative of the Book of Esther – as verified in Har Adar, Israel, on 18 Dec 2020. Fifteen years in the making, it comprises 29 sheets of cowskin parchment painted with watercolour and gouache, with details added in gold, silver and copper leaf.

Largest chalk street artwork (individual)

On 24 Jul 2021, Giovanni Bassil (LBN) used chalk to recreate a 200-m² (2,152.7-sq-ft) version of his country's flag in Beirut, Lebanon. The size of a typical cinema screen, his artwork was all the more impressive given the high temperatures, which rendered the asphalt hot, making his chalk break repeatedly.

Most pledges received for a campaign

Thanks to the "Save Your Food" project, a total of 880,749 people vowed to reduce food loss and waste, as verified on 26 Jan 2022. The scheme was initiated by the Ministry of Agriculture and Forestry of Turkey, in conjunction with the UN Food and Agriculture Organization. On 21 Mar, the same ministry also created the **largest online album of people planting trees**, collecting 383,783 unique photographs.

MOST EXPENSIVE HAMBURGER

"The Golden Boy", added to the menu at De Daltons restaurant in Voorthuizen, Netherlands, in Apr 2022, will set you back a whopping €5,000 (£4,231; $5,557). The epic epicurean delight is crafted by chef Robbert Jan De Veen using Wagyu beef, king crab, thinly sliced vintage Joselito Bellota Ibérico jamón, Wyke Farms cheddar and Dom Pérignon champagne-battered onion rings. It's topped off with beluga caviar, smoked duck-egg mayonnaise, white truffle, a barbecue sauce flavoured with Kopi Luwak coffee and Macallan single-malt whisky, and pickled tiger tomato steeped in Japanese matcha tea. The buns are infused with Dom Pérignon and coated in gold. Customers must give two weeks' notice.

LONGEST ACTIVE CAREER IN THE AIR FORCE

Robert Taylor (UK) served in the RAF from 10 Jan 1969 to his retirement on 11 Feb 2020 – a total of 51 years 32 days. A radar specialist, he says he chose to remain in the Service for so long "mainly through respect for and genuine commitment to the RAF".

HIGHEST VOLTAGE FROM A FRUIT BATTERY

Professor Saiful Islam and the Royal Society of Chemistry (both UK) generated 2,307.8 V from a battery of 2,923 lemons in Manchester, UK, on 15 Oct 2021. It delivered a current of 0.84 milliAmps and 1.94 W of power. With the UN's COP26 summit just days away, the event was staged to highlight the importance of innovative strategies to bring about a zero-carbon world.

LONGEST MARRIAGE FOR A LIVING COUPLE

GWR was sad to hear of the passing of Eugene Gladu on 3 Jan 2022. He and his wife Dolores (née Nault; both USA) had been married for 81 years 223 days. Their wedding took place in Woonsocket, Rhode Island, USA, on 25 May 1940 (inset). We offer condolences to their family and welcome new applications for this category.

MOST EXPENSIVE *POKÉMON* TRADING CARD

An ultra-rare PSA Grade 10 Pikachu Illustrator card was purchased privately by YouTuber Logan Paul (USA) for $5,275,000 (£3.86 m) on 22 Jul 2021. Paul received his GWR certificate on 2 Apr 2022, after making his WWE debut at WrestleMania 38. He entered the ring wearing his prized trading card around his neck.

doo doo doo doo doo doo.

FIRST YOUTUBE VIDEO WITH 10 BILLION VIEWS

On 13 Jan 2022, "Baby Shark Dance" by PINKFONG (KOR) received its 10-billionth view on YouTube. The catchy children's dance-and-music-singalong was first uploaded in 2016, going on to surpass Luis Fonsi's "Despacito" in 2020 as the platform's **most viewed music video** and **most viewed video** outright.

MOST YOUTUBE CHANNELS WITH OVER 100,000 SUBSCRIBERS BY AN INDIVIDUAL

As of 31 Jul 2021, the UK's Jack Massey Welsh owned 10 YouTube channels, each of which had more than 100,000 subscribers. He made his name with the *JackSucksAtLife* channel, for which he videos himself playing *Minecraft* while adding a comic commentary.

Most viewed YouTube music video in 24 hours by a solo artist

BLACKPINK singer/rapper Lisa, aka Pranpriya Manobel (THA), released her debut solo single "LALISA" on 10 Sep 2021, and the accompanying video was watched 73.6 million times over its first 24 hours online. This eclipsed the 55.4 million views clocked up by Ariana Grande's "thank u, next" on 30 Nov 2018.

Fastest time to reach 1 million likes on Instagram

Juliette Freire's (BRA) Instagram post announcing that she had won *Big Brother Brasil* generated 1 million likes in only 3 min on 4 May 2021. This was twice as fast as the previous record, set by US singer Billie Eilish only the day before.

Instagram's **most liked image** is a photo of an egg posted by the Egg Gang on the "world_record_egg" account. As of 1 Feb 2022, it had 55,746,040 likes.

Longest-running hacker convention

DEF CON was first held in Las Vegas, Nevada, USA, in 1993, and has been staged annually for 28 years. In 2020, it took the form of a virtual event titled DEF CON SAFE MODE. The convention attracts a wide range of people involved in computer security, including hackers, lawyers and cryptographers; plain-clothes officials from law enforcement, the military and national security agencies also attend.

DEF CON 27 (held from 8–11 Aug 2019) attracted some 30,000 attendees, making it the **largest hacker convention**.

Largest programming competition

CodeVita attracted 136,054 participants on 10 Apr 2021. It was organized by Tata Consultancy Services of Mumbai, India. Aimed at students, CodeVita emphasizes the importance of coding in an increasingly technology-focused world by promoting the idea of programming as a sport.

FASTEST TIME TO REACH 1 MILLION FOLLOWERS ON INSTAGRAM

It took Kim "V" Tae-hyung (KOR) just 43 min to secure a million Instagram fans on 6 Dec 2021. His fellow members of K-pop sensation BTS all launched their own Instagram pages on the same day at the same time.

> Leah clearly has a taste for nuggets. In 2020, she also set the three-minute record of 775.1 g (1 lb 11 oz).

▶ MOST CHICKEN NUGGETS EATEN IN ONE MINUTE

Leah Shutkever (UK) downed 352 g (12.42 oz) of crispy-coated chicken bites in Milan, Italy, on 10 Feb 2022. Discover more of this speed-eating legend's GWR titles on p.82.

MOST DELEGATES REGISTERED FOR A CLIMATE CONFERENCE

In all, 39,509 delegates applied to attend the 26th UN Climate Change Conference of the Parties (aka COP26). It was hosted by the UK, in partnership with Italy, at the SEC Centre in Glasgow from 31 Oct to 13 Nov 2021. Attendees included indigenous representatives from the Amazon rainforest (above), while climate activists such as Ocean Rebellion (right) and Greta Thunberg (see p.200) staged protests outside.

Ellie Simmonds

HALL OF FAME

Para swimmer Ellie Simmonds hung up her goggles in 2021, ending a glittering career in the pool that saw her break multiple world records, win 19 Paralympic and World Championship gold medals, and become an iconic figure of disability sport.

Ellie started swimming at five years old and was entered into the British Swimming talent programme aged 10, after she was spotted at an event. Born with achondroplasia – a form of dwarfism – she competed in the women's S6 and SM6 classifications of para swimming. Ellie exploded on to the international scene at the age of just 13, winning two gold medals at the 2008 Beijing Paralympics. She was voted the BBC Young Sports Personality of the Year and became a household name in the UK.

As the home favourite at the 2012 Paralympics in London, the pressure was on Ellie. She rose to the challenge in style, smashing the S6 400 m world record by five seconds in the final and winning a second gold, in the SM6 200 m individual medley, also in world-record time. After winning another Paralympic title at Rio 2016, Ellie competed for the final time at the delayed Tokyo Paralympics in 2021 – fittingly, racing against the next generation of para athletes that she herself had done so much to inspire.

VITAL STATISTICS

Name Eleanor May Simmonds, OBE

Birthplace Walsall, West Midlands, UK

Current world records (S6 freestyle unless indicated; LC = long course, SC = short course)
- **LC 800 m:** 11:03.41
- **SC 200 m:** 2:44.21
- **SC 400 m:** 5:27.58
- **SC 4 x 100 m** (34 pts): 4:26.20
- **SC 200 m individual medley (SM6):** 3:05.13
- **SC 4 x 100 m medley:** 4:56.23

Ellie is a patron of the Dwarf Sports Association UK. "It's about recognizing abilities not disabilities."

1. Ellie was named in the 2013 New Year Honours list, and visited Buckingham Palace in London to be awarded an OBE (Officer of the Order of the British Empire) for her services to Paralympic sport. Four years prior to this, at the age of 14, she'd become the **youngest recipient of an MBE** (Member of the Order of the British Empire).

2. At Beijing 2008, 13-year-old Ellie collected her first Paralympic gold medal in the S6 100 m freestyle and added the S6 400 m freestyle title.

3. Roared on by a home crowd at the London 2012 Games, Ellie secured two golds, a silver and a bronze, setting world records in both the S6 400 m freestyle and the SM6 200 m individual medley.

4. Ellie has become a familiar face in the UK media, appearing on primetime TV shows such as *The Jonathan Ross Show* in May 2021.

5. At the 2019 World Para Swimming Championships, Ellie medalled alongside her compatriot Maisie Summers-Newton – one of a number of swimmers to have acknowledged Ellie as an idol and inspiration.

6. Ellie has also worked with the World Against Single Use Plastic (WASUP) charity to clean up her home town of Walsall – part of a volunteering drive in advance of the 2022 Commonwealth Games, due to be held in the nearby city of Birmingham.

Ellie with one of her GWR certificates. "If you really want something, only you can stop yourself from achieving it."

Find out more about Ellie in the Hall of Fame section at www.
guinnessworldrecords.com/2023

FIRST QUALIFIER TO WIN A TENNIS SINGLES GRAND SLAM (OPEN ERA)
At the 2021 US Open, Emma Raducanu (UK, b. CAN) served up a sporting triumph against the odds that became known as the "Fairytale of New York". Playing in only her fourth WTA event, and ranked 150 in the world, Raducanu came through three qualifying and seven main-draw matches to clinch the title – without even dropping a set. The 18-year-old beat Leylah Fernandez (CAN, opposite, left) 6–4, 6–3 in the **first open-era Grand Slam singles final contested by unseeded players**. Their combined age was just 37 years 307 days.

Sports

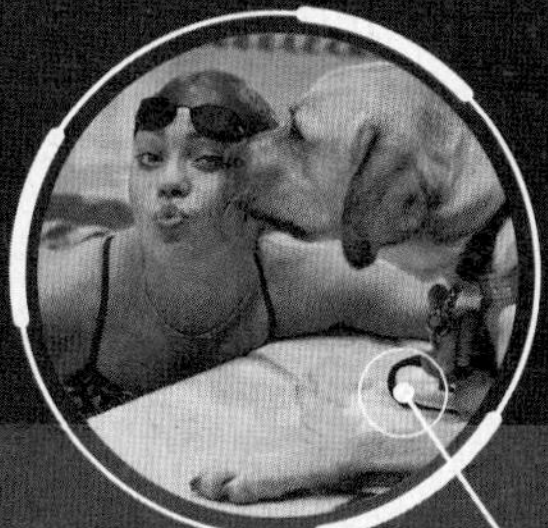

EXPLORATION

DISCOVERY

RESEARCH

2023

Raducanu's triumph at the 2021 US Open netted her a cool $2.5 m (£1.8 m) in prize money.

US OPEN 2021

Winter Games

HIGHEST FIGURE SKATING SHORT PROGRAMME SCORE (MALE)

Nathan Chen (USA) was awarded 113.97 for his short programme on 8 Feb at the Capital Indoor Stadium in Beijing. Chen performed to "La Bohème", landing a quad flip among his jumps. He won gold in the men's singles with an overall score of 332.60 – 22 points ahead of his nearest rival.

MOST GOLD MEDALS WON AT A WINTER OLYMPICS (COUNTRY)

Norway claimed 16 gold medals at Beijing 2022 – two more than the previous best for a single Winter Games. The Scandinavian country topped the podium in six different sports, with medal leader Johannes Thingnes Bø (inset) winning four events in the biathlon alone.

The 2022 Winter Olympics and Paralympics took place in Beijing, China, on 4–20 Feb and 4–13 Mar respectively. We've selected some of the finest record-breaking performances on snow and ice.

Most Winter Olympic appearances by an athlete

Speed skater Claudia Pechstein (DEU, b. 22 Feb 1972) participated in her eighth Winter Games in Beijing, equalling the record set by ski-jumper Noriaki Kasai (JPN) between 1992 and 2018. Pechstein took to the ice for the final of the women's mass start aged 49 years 362 days on 19 Feb – making her the **oldest Winter Olympic competitor (female)**. Cheryl Bernard was listed as an alternate for the Canadian curling team in 2018 at the age of 51, but she did not compete.

The **oldest Winter Olympic competitor (male)** is Carl August Kronlund (SWE, b. 25 Aug 1865), who took part in the inaugural men's curling event aged 58 years 156 days on 28 Jan 1924 in Chamonix, France.

MOST INDIVIDUAL GOLD MEDALS WON AT DIFFERENT OLYMPIC GAMES

On 7 Feb 2022, speed skater Ireen Wüst (NLD) won the women's 1,500 m to complete her fifth consecutive Olympics with an individual title. Wüst increased her overall medal tally to 13 in Beijing (six golds, five silvers and two bronze) – the **most speed skating Olympic medals**.

Highest total score in ice dance figure skating

Gabriella Papadakis and Guillaume Cizeron (both FRA) claimed gold in Beijing with a total score of 226.98. The 2018 Olympic silver medallists opened with the **highest rhythm dance score in ice dance** – 90.83 – on 12 Feb and scored 136.15 in the free dance two days later. See Stop Press (pp.246–47) for more.

In the pairs competition on 18–19 Feb, Sui Wenjing and Han Cong (both CHN) delighted home fans by recording the **highest total score in pairs figure skating**: 239.88. This included the **highest pairs short programme score**: 84.41.

Fastest 10,000 m speed skating (male)

Nils van der Poel (SWE) won gold in 12 min 30.74 sec on 11 Feb 2022 – the only current speed skating world record not set at altitude. Van der Poel is also the **5,000 m** world record holder, having set a time of 6 min 1.56 sec in Salt Lake City, Utah, USA, on 3 Dec 2021.

MOST SHORT TRACK SPEED SKATING MEDALS

Arianna Fontana (ITA) earned a gold and two silvers in Beijing to take her Olympic medal total to 11. Fontana – nicknamed *L'Angelo Biondo* ("The Blonde Angel") – won her first medal at Turin 2006 at the age of 15. Over the next 16 years, she amassed two golds, four silvers and five bronze, winning Olympic medals at every contestable distance.

Winter Olympic winners

	Record	Name	Sport	Date
First gold medallist		Charles Jewtraw (USA)	Speed skating	26 Jan 1924
First gold medallist (female)		Herma Szabo-Plank (AUT)	Figure skating	29 Jan 1924
Most medals won	15	Marit Bjørgen (NOR)	Cross-country skiing	2002–18
Most medals won (male)	13	Ole Einar Bjørndalen (NOR)	Biathlon	1998–2014
Most golds at a single Games	5	Eric Heiden (USA)	Speed skating	1980
Most golds at a single Games (female)	4	Lidiya Skoblikova (USSR)	Speed skating	1964
Youngest individual medallist	14 years 363 days	Scott Allen (USA, b. 8 Feb 1949)	Figure skating	6 Feb 1964
Youngest individual medallist (female)	15 years 69 days	Andrea Mitscherlich (GDR, b. 1 Dec 1960)	Speed skating	8 Feb 1976
Youngest gold medallist	13 years 85 days	Kim Yun-mi (KOR, b. 1 Dec 1980)	Short track speed skating	24 Feb 1994
Youngest gold medallist (male)	16 years 259 days	Billy Fiske (USA, b. 4 Jun 1911)	Bobsleigh	18 Feb 1928
		Toni Nieminen (FIN, b. 31 May 1975)	Ski jumping	14 Feb 1992
Oldest gold medallist	54 years 102 days	Robin Welsh (UK, b. 20 Oct 1869)	Curling	30 Jan 1924
Oldest gold medallist (female)	43 years 106 days	Anette Norberg (SWE, b. 12 Nov 1966)	Curling	26 Feb 2010

MOST LUGE OLYMPIC MEDALS

Natalie Geisenberger (DEU) won seven Olympic medals in the luge between 2010 and 2022. She topped the podium in the women's singles and the team relay at three consecutive Olympics – Sochi 2014, Pyeongchang 2018 and Beijing 2022 – and claimed a bronze in the singles at Vancouver 2010. Geisenberger is also a nine-time world champion.

MOST ALPINE SKIING GOLD MEDALS AT A SINGLE WINTER OLYMPICS (COUNTRY)

Switzerland dominated the Alpine skiing programme in Beijing, winning five of the 11 events: the men's downhill (Beat Feuz, pictured) and giant slalom (Marco Odermatt), and the women's downhill (Corinne Suter), Super-G (Lara Gut-Behrami) and combined (Michelle Gisin).

Fastest 1,000 m short track speed skating (female)
Suzanne Schulting (NLD) won her Olympic women's 1,000 m quarter-final in 1 min 26.514 sec on 11 Feb, breaking a world record that had stood for almost a decade. She claimed the gold medal later that day.

On 23 Oct 2021, Schulting teamed up with Selma Poutsma, Yara van Kerkhof and Xandra Velzeboer (all NLD) to clock the **fastest women's 3,000 m relay** – 4 min 2.809 sec – also in Beijing.

MOST WINTER OLYMPIC...
Curling medals

Oskar Eriksson (SWE) won four Olympic medals across three Games between 2014 and 2022. He was a member of Sweden's victorious men's curling team in Beijing, and also earned a bronze in the mixed doubles alongside Almida de Val.

Luge gold medals (male)
Tobias Arlt and Tobias Wendl (both DEU) triumphed in the doubles and the team relay events at three consecutive Olympics – Sochi 2014, Pyeongchang 2018 and Beijing 2022 – for a total of six gold medals. "The Tobys" were part of a powerhouse German luge squad who won every event at Beijing, alongside Johannes Ludwig and **female** and **overall luge medal** record holder Natalie Geisenberger (see above).

Women's ice hockey gold medals (country)
Canada secured their fifth Olympic women's ice hockey title since 2002 in Beijing, defeating the USA 3–2 in the final on 17 Feb. They dominated the tournament, scoring 57 goals in seven matches on their way to gold. The team was led by forward Sarah Nurse, who recorded the **most points in an Olympic women's ice hockey tournament** – 18. Nurse contributed an Olympic-record 13 assists and five goals, finding the net in the final.

MOST WINTER PARALYMPIC...
Biathlon gold medals

Vitaliy Lukyanenko (UKR) won eight Paralympic golds in the biathlon between 2006 and 2022. He triumphed in the men's visually impaired 6 km and 10 km events in Beijing – part of a dominant Ukrainian biathlon team who claimed 22 medals in 18 events. Lukyanenko has participated in six Games, winning a total of 11 biathlon medals and a further four in cross-country skiing.

Snowboarding gold medals

Brenna Huckaby (USA) won her third Paralympic title on 11 Mar, competing in the banked slalom. She also earned a further bronze in the snowboard cross. Huckaby matched the golden career tally of para snowboard pioneer Bibian Mentel-Spee (NLD), who passed away in 2021.

Wheelchair curling medals

Ina Forrest (CAN) claimed her fourth Paralympic medal – a bronze – when Canada won the third-place match against Slovakia on 11 Mar. Paralympic wheelchair curling teams are mixed: two of Forrest's teammates in Beijing, Dennis Thiessen and skip Mark Ideson, claimed the **male** record with their third medals.

YOUNGEST FREESTYLE SKIING OLYMPIC GOLD MEDALLIST

Eileen Gu (CHN, b. USA, 3 Sep 2003) carved her name into Olympic history when she won the big air event aged 18 years 158 days in Beijing on 8 Feb 2022. The home favourite claimed a dramatic victory with her final run, landing a double cork 1620 safety grab – a trick she had never attempted before – to pip France's Tess Ledeux by 0.75 points. Gu went on to win another gold in the halfpipe (above) and a silver in slopestyle.

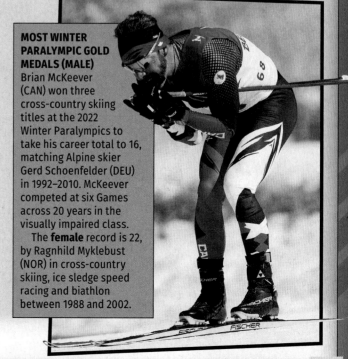

MOST WINTER PARALYMPIC GOLD MEDALS (MALE)

Brian McKeever (CAN) won three cross-country skiing titles at the 2022 Winter Paralympics to take his career total to 16, matching Alpine skier Gerd Schoenfelder (DEU) in 1992–2010. McKeever competed at six Games across 20 years in the visually impaired class.

The **female** record is 22, by Ragnhild Myklebust (NOR) in cross-country skiing, ice sledge speed racing and biathlon between 1988 and 2002.

Soccer

MOST EPL GOALS SCORED FOR ONE CLUB

Sergio Agüero (ARG) netted 184 English Premier League (EPL) goals for Manchester City between 15 Aug 2011 and 23 May 2021. He scored a brace against Everton on his final league appearance to surpass Wayne Rooney's 183 goals for Manchester United. Agüero's total includes the **most EPL hat-tricks**: 12.

Most men's international caps

In Sep 2021, FIFA released an update of their "Century Club" for men's international appearances. Top of the list was Soh Chin Ann, recognized for 195 of his 219 matches for Malaysia between 19 Nov 1969 and 18 Oct 1984 (minus 24 games at the Olympics). Soh, a centre-back, made his international debut aged 19 and played for his country for nearly 15 years, helping them qualify for the 1972 and 1980 Olympic football tournaments.

Another Malaysian player whose feats were retrospectively acknowledged by FIFA was Mokhtar Dahari, who was ratified as the third-highest scorer in men's internationals with 89 goals. Dahari (b. 13 Nov 1953) also became the **youngest player to score 50 international goals**, reaching his half-century aged 22 years 273 days against India on 12 Aug 1976.

Most consecutive Bundesliga titles

Bayern Munich sealed their 10th German top-flight league title in a row with a 3–1 win over Borussia Dortmund on 23 Apr 2022. This is the longest title streak by any club in Europe's so-called "Top 5" leagues – Spain, Germany, Italy, England and France. Bayern's latest triumph saw midfielder/forward Thomas Müller become a league champion for the 11th time – the **most Bundesliga titles won by a player**.

Bayern also hold the overall record for **most German top-flight league titles**: 32, with 31 coming in the Bundesliga era (1963–) and one earlier triumph in 1931/32.

Most French top-flight league titles

Paris Saint-Germain claimed their 10th Ligue 1 crown on 23 Apr 2022, matching the feat of AS Saint-Étienne between 1956/57 and 1980/81. Olympique de Marseille have won the division nine times, with one additional table-topping season in 1928/29 during the amateur era.

PSG's Marco Verratti (ITA) had further cause to celebrate, as he lifted the Hexagoal trophy for the eighth time: the **most Ligue 1 titles won by a player**.

Most consecutive La Liga appearances

Iñaki Williams (ESP) featured in 224 successive Spanish top-flight matches across six years between 20 Apr 2016 and 17 Apr 2022. Williams, a forward for Athletic Bilbao, surpassed Juan Antonio Larrañaga's record of 202 consecutive games on 1 Oct 2021.

Longest EPL unbeaten away run

On 19 Sep 2021, Manchester United (UK) defeated West Ham United 2–1 at the London Stadium to record their 29th consecutive away league game without defeat. The Red Devils won 19 and drew 10 during their streak, which began on 17 Feb 2020 and finally came to an end on 16 Oct 2021, with a 4–2 loss at Leicester City.

MOST GOALS SCORED IN A BUNDESLIGA SEASON

Bayern Munich's Robert Lewandowski (POL) struck 41 times in the German top division during the 2020/21 season. He scored in the final minute of Bayern's final league match, against Augsburg, to outdo the legendary Gerd Müller, who hit 40 goals for Bayern in 1971/72.

Most generations of one family to score for the same Serie A club

Daniel Maldini (ITA) enjoyed a dream debut for AC Milan on 25 Sep 2021, finding the net away against Spezia. Daniel's father, defender Paolo, scored his final Serie A goal on 30 Mar 2008; his grandfather, Cesare, last found the net for Milan in the league on 3 Sep 1961.

Most consecutive UEFA Champions League seasons to score

On 28 Sep 2021, both Karim Benzema (FRA) and Lionel Messi (ARG) found the net to register their 17th successive Champions League campaign with a goal. Messi (see opposite) scored his first goal for new club Paris Saint-Germain against Manchester City, while Benzema struck during Real's shock 2–1 defeat to Sheriff Tiraspol.

Italy scored 93 goals during their 37-game unbeaten streak and conceded just 12 – a goal difference of +81.

LONGEST UNBEATEN RUN IN MEN'S COMPETITIVE INTERNATIONAL MATCHES

Italy went unbeaten for 37 games between 10 Oct 2018 and 8 Sep 2021, recording 30 wins and seven draws under coach Roberto Mancini. Their streak included victory over England in the UEFA EURO 2020 final on 11 Jul 2021 (pictured). The Azzurri's run was finally ended by Spain, who beat them 2–1 in the UEFA Nations League.

MOST OLYMPIC WOMEN'S FOOTBALL APPEARANCES
Formiga (b. Miraildes Maciel Mota, BRA) played in 33 matches at the Olympics between 1996 and 2021. The Tokyo Games was the midfielder's seventh Olympic tournament – every edition of women's football staged to date.

Most appearances in the UEFA Women's Champions League
On 24 Apr 2022, Wendie Renard (FRA) became the first player to feature in 100 games in the Women's Champions League. The Olympique Lyon centre-back scored a penalty – her 31st European goal – as her side beat rivals PSG 3–2 in their semi-final first-leg tie.

As of the same date, the **most UEFA Women's Champions League goals** was 57 – by Renard's Lyon teammate Ada Hegerberg (NOR).

Most goals scored in an Olympic women's tournament
Vivianne Miedema (NLD) struck 10 times at the Tokyo Games on 21–30 Jul 2021 in Japan. The Dutch ace scored eight goals in three Group F matches and added a brace in the quarter-final.

The **men**'s record is 12, by Ferenc Bene (HUN) at the 1964 Olympics – also staged in Tokyo. This included all six goals in Hungary's 6–0 demolition of Morocco on 11 Oct.

Most wins of the Copa América
On 10 Jul 2021, Argentina overcame hosts Brazil 1–0 at the Maracanã Stadium in Rio de Janeiro to win their 15th South American national team championship. This equalled the mark set by Uruguay from 1916 to 2011.

LARGEST ATTENDANCE AT A WOMEN'S MATCH
A total of 91,648 spectators watched the UEFA Women's Champions League semi-final first-leg clash between FC Barcelona and VfL Wolfsburg at the Camp Nou in Spain on 22 Apr 2022. The hosts ran out 5–1 winners, beating their own attendance record from the previous round.

AVUI SOM #91.648

MOST WINS OF THE AFC WOMEN'S ASIAN CUP
China claimed a record ninth Asian Cup with a 3–2 win over South Korea on 6 Feb 2022 in Navi Mumbai, India. The Steel Roses overturned a 2–0 half-time deficit thanks to an injury-time winner by Xiao Yuyi. First staged in 1975, the AFC Women's Asian Cup has been won by seven different countries to date.

Most wins of the CAF Champions League
Egyptian side Al Ahly won their 10th Confederation of African Football Champions League title on 17 Jul 2021. The 42-time domestic champions defeated South Africa's Kaizer Chiefs 3–0 at Stade Mohammed V in Casablanca, Morocco.

Most wins of futsal's Best Men's Player in the World award
Futsal is a form of indoor football played by teams of five, where technique and skill are at a premium. Ricardinho (PRT, b. Ricardo Filipe da Silva Braga) was named best male player by the Futsal Planet website six times, in 2010 and 2014–18. He retired in 2021 after guiding his country to their first-ever Futsal World Cup, lifting the trophy on 3 Oct in Kaunas, Lithuania.

The **women**'s record is eight, by Amandinha (BRA, b. Amanda Lyssa de Oliveira Crisóstomo) consecutively between 2014 and 2021.

MOST GOALS SCORED IN LA LIGA
Lionel Messi (ARG) left FC Barcelona in 2021 having hit 474 Spanish top-flight league goals in 520 games. This total included the **most La Liga hat-tricks** (36). Over the course of 17 seasons with the Catalan giants, Messi won the league's top-scorer award eight times, in 2010, 2012–13 and 2017–21 – the **most wins of the Pichichi Trophy**. The Argentinian maestro led Barcelona to 10 La Liga titles during his time at the club.

YOUNGEST PLAYER AT THE UEFA EUROPEAN CHAMPIONSHIPS
Kacper Kozłowski (b. 16 Oct 2003) was 17 years 246 days old when he played for Poland during their 1–1 draw against Spain at the delayed UEFA EURO 2020 tournament on 19 Jun 2021. The midfielder came off the bench to break the record set by Jude Bellingham just six days earlier, during England's 1–0 win over Croatia. See below for more age-related EURO records.

UEFA EUROs: Oldest & Youngest

Record	Age	Name	Date
Youngest player (knock-out stages)	18 years 4 days	Jude Bellingham (UK, b. 29 Jun 2003)	3 Jul 2021
Youngest goalscorer	18 years 141 days	Johan Vonlanthen (CHE, b. COL, 1 Feb 1986)	21 Jun 2004
Youngest goalscorer (final)	20 years 64 days	Pietro Anastasi (ITA, b. 7 Apr 1948)	10 Jun 1968
Oldest goalscorer (final)	34 years 71 days	Leonardo Bonucci (ITA, b. 1 May 1987)	11 Jul 2021
Oldest goalscorer	38 years 257 days	Ivica Vastić (AUT, b. 29 Sep 1969)	12 Jun 2008
Oldest outfield player	39 years 91 days	Lothar Matthäus (DEU, b. 21 Mar 1961)	20 Jun 2000
Oldest player	40 years 86 days	Gábor Király (HUN, b. 1 Apr 1976)	26 Jun 2016

Super Bowl

MOST TOUCHDOWNS (TDs)

Jerry Rice crossed into the end zone eight times in four Super Bowls: for the 1988–89 and 1994 San Francisco 49ers, and the 2002 Oakland Raiders. The Hall of Fame wide receiver amassed a series of offensive records, including the **most points** (48), **most yards receiving** (589) and **most receptions** (33).

Every year, the champions of the National Football League are decided in a playoff match between the winners of the National Football Conference and the American Football Conference. The Super Bowl has become one of sport's showpiece events, filled with pageantry, drama and explosive action.

TEAM

Most wins

Two franchises have won six Super Bowls apiece: the Pittsburgh Steelers (1974–75, 1978–79, 2005 and 2008) and the New England Patriots (2001, 2003–04, 2014, 2016 and 2018). The Patriots have also made the **most Super Bowl appearances** (11).

Highest score

The 1989 San Francisco 49ers beat the Denver Broncos 55–10 at Super Bowl XXIV. Jerry Rice (see left) set the record for **most receiving TDs in a game** – three – which he would go on to equal at Super Bowl XXIX. There, the 1994 49ers beat the San Diego Chargers 49–26 to record the **highest aggregate score**, with QB Steve Young throwing the **most TD passes in a game** – six.

Most interceptions in a game

The 2002 Tampa Bay Buccaneers put on a defensive masterclass at Super Bowl XXXVII, making five interceptions against the Oakland Raiders. Three were returned for touchdowns.

The **most sacks in a game** is seven, by the 1975 Pittsburgh Steelers, the 1985 Chicago Bears, the 2015 Denver Broncos and the 2021 LA Rams.

INDIVIDUAL

Youngest player

Jamal Lewis (b. 26 Aug 1979) took to the field at Super Bowl XXXV aged 21 years 155 days on 28 Jan 2001. The rookie running back ran for 102 yards and a touchdown during the Baltimore Ravens' 34–7 romp over the New York Giants.

YOUNGEST WINNING COACH

Sean McVay (b. 24 Jan 1986) lifted the Vince Lombardi Trophy aged 36 years 20 days after his LA Rams' 23–20 win over the Cincinnati Bengals at Super Bowl LVI on 13 Feb 2022. McVay was already the **youngest coach**, having overseen the Rams' 13–3 loss to the Patriots three years earlier, aged 33 years 10 days.

Most appearances by a head coach

Bill Belichick led the New England Patriots to nine Super Bowls between the 2001 and 2018 seasons. They triumphed in six, giving Belichick the **most wins by a head coach**. He also registered two championship wins as defensive coordinator for the New York Giants at Super Bowls XXI and XXV.

Longest...

· **Field goal**: 54 yards, by Steve Christie (CAN) for the 1993 Buffalo Bills at Super Bowl XXVIII.
· **Punt return**: 61 yards, by Jordan Norwood at Super Bowl L for the 2015 Denver Broncos.
· **Punt**: 65 yards, by Johnny Hekker for the 2018 LA Rams at Super Bowl LIII.
· **Run from scrimmage**: 75 yards, by Willie Parker at Super Bowl XL for the 2005 Pittsburgh Steelers.
· **Pass reception**: 85 yards, by wide receiver Muhsin Muhammad for the 2003 Carolina Panthers at Super Bowl XXXVIII.
· **Touchdown**: 108 yards, on a kickoff return by Jacoby Jones for the 2012 Baltimore Ravens at Super Bowl XLVII.

MOST WINS

Tom Brady earned his seventh Super Bowl ring on 7 Feb 2021 as the Tampa Bay Buccaneers overcame the Kansas City Chiefs 31–9. The quarterback's previous six titles had come with the New England Patriots. Win No.7 came at the age of 43 years 188 days, meaning Brady (b. 3 Aug 1977) added **oldest Super Bowl player** to his lengthy list of records. Check out the table below for more.

Brady at the Super Bowl	
Most...	Total
Appearances	10
Yards passing	3,039
Yards passing (single game)	505
Passes completed	277
Passes completed (single game)	43
Touchdown passes	21
MVP awards	5

MOST RUSHING TOUCHDOWNS

Emmitt Smith ran in five TDs during three Super Bowl wins for the 1992, 1993 and 1995 Dallas Cowboys. The running back scored three times in two championship games against the Buffalo Bills and was named MVP after Super Bowl XXVIII, having rushed for 132 yards and two scores. Smith added two further TDs in Super Bowl XXX, against the Pittsburgh Steelers (pictured).

All players USA, unless stated otherwise. Team years refer to that season's commencement.

World Series

1
ALBERT PUJOLS
Most total bases
in a game: 14

2
DON LARSEN
Fewest hits allowed
in a game: 0

3
FREDDIE LINDSTROM
Youngest player:
18 years 318 days

4
BABE RUTH
Most innings pitched
in a game: 14

5
MADISON BUMGARNER
Lowest earned run
average (ERA): 0.25

6
GEORGE SPRINGER
Most home runs in a
single series: 5 (tied)

7
MARIANO RIVERA
Most saves
by a pitcher: 11

8
MICKEY MANTLE
Most home runs: 18
Most runs: 42

9
YOGI BERRA
Most championships: 10
Most games: 75

10
JACK QUINN
Oldest player:
47 years 95 days

11
REGGIE JACKSON
Most MVP awards:
2 (tied)

12
WHITEY FORD
Most strikeouts
by a pitcher: 94

Since 1903, an annual seven-game playoff between the winners of the American and National Leagues has provided the climax of the Major League Baseball season. The New York Yankees are out in front with the **most World Series wins by a team** – 27. Here, we examine the individual records of some of the legends to have graced the "Fall Classic".

All players USA, unless stated otherwise.

1. ALBERT PUJOLS
In Game 3 of the 2011 World Series on 22 Oct, Pujols (b. DOM) hit three home runs and two singles – 14 total bases – for the St Louis Cardinals.

2. DON LARSEN
On 8 Oct 1956, pitcher Larsen of the New York Yankees retired all 27 Brooklyn Dodgers batters he faced. Larsen threw just 97 pitches at Yankee Stadium, recording the only perfect game in a World Series.

3. FREDDIE LINDSTROM
Rookie phenom Lindstrom (b. 21 Nov 1905) was 18 years 318 days old when he played third baseman for the New York Giants against the Washington Senators in Game 1 of the 1924 World Series on 4 Oct.

4. BABE RUTH
Better known as a batter, George Herman "Babe" Ruth Jr also pitched a record 14 innings for the Boston Red Sox in Game 2 of the 1916 World Series on 9 Oct.

5. MADISON BUMGARNER
Lefty pitcher Bumgarner recorded a miserly ERA of just 0.25 across three World Series (2010, 2012 and 2014) for the San Francisco Giants.

6. GEORGE SPRINGER
Springer hit five home runs for the Houston Astros during their 2017 World Series against the LA Dodgers. This matched the feat of Reggie Jackson (Yankees; 1977) and Chase Utley (Philadelphia Phillies; 2009).

7. MARIANO RIVERA
Between 1996 and 2009, Yankees pitcher Rivera (b. PAN) was credited with 11 saves across seven World Series. The 1999 series MVP finished his career with five championship rings and a series ERA of 0.99.

8. MICKEY MANTLE
Mantle hit 18 home runs in 12 World Series between 1951 and 1964 for the New York Yankees. The switch-hitting slugger also recorded the **most runs** (42) and the **most runs batted in** (40).

9. YOGI BERRA
Yankees catcher Lawrence "Yogi" Berra won the World Series 10 times as a player between 1947 and 1962 – and added three more championships as a coach. Berra played in the **most World Series** (14) and the **most games** (75), and also recorded the **most hits** (71).

10. JACK QUINN
Quinn (b. SVK, 1 Jul 1883) was aged 47 years 95 days when he pitched in Game 3 of the 1930 World Series for the Philadelphia Athletics on 4 Oct.

11. REGGIE JACKSON
"Mr October" won the World Series MVP twice, with the Oakland Athletics in 1973 and the Yankees in 1977. He equalled Sandy Koufax (LA Dodgers; 1963, 1965) and Bob Gibson (St Louis Cardinals; 1964, 1967).

12. WHITEY FORD
Edward "Whitey" Ford threw 94 strikeouts for the Yankees in World Series between 1950 and 1964. He pitched the **most innings** (146) and racked up the **most wins by a pitcher** (10).

US Sports

MOST WOMEN'S BASKETBALL OLYMPIC GOLD MEDALS

At the Tokyo Games in 2021, Diana Taurasi (left) and Sue Bird claimed their fifth consecutive Olympic golds with Team USA. The pair first played together at UConn in 2000 and rewrote the record books in the Women's National Basketball Association (WNBA), playing for the Seattle Storm (Bird) and Phoenix Mercury (Taurasi) – see right.

Taurasi and Bird: WNBA record-breakers

DIANA TAURASI		SUE BIRD	
Most points scored	9,174	Most games played	549
Most field goals	2,891	Most minutes played	17,261
Most field goals attempted	6,719	Most assists	3,048
Most three-point field goals	1,205	Most assists (WNBA Finals game)	16
Most free throws	2,187	Most turnovers	1,333
Most free throws attempted	2,513	Most All-Star selections	12

YOUNGEST MVP IN AN MLB ALL-STAR GAME

On 13 Jul 2021, Vladimir Guerrero Jr (CAN, b. 16 Mar 1999) was named All-Star MVP aged 22 years 119 days. The slugger led the American League to a 5–2 victory over the National League at Coors Field in Denver, Colorado, hitting two RBIs and a 468-ft (142.6-m) home run.

MLB

Fewest innings for a pitcher to reach 100 strikeouts in a season

It took Jacob deGrom just 61⅔ innings to record a century of strikeouts for the New York Mets during the 2021 Major League Baseball season. He reached the landmark against the San Diego Padres on 11 Jun.

Fewest games for a pitcher to reach 1,500 career strikeouts

On 21 Jun 2021, Yu Darvish (JPN) fanned hitter No. 1,500 in his 197th MLB game – the San Diego Padres' 6–2 win over the Los Angeles Dodgers. Darvish eclipsed Randy Johnson's previous record of 206 by nine games.

Most consecutive hits to begin a season

Catcher Yermín Mercedes (DOM) began the 2021 MLB season with a bang, ripping off eight straight hits for the Chicago White Sox on 2–3 Apr.

NHL

Most face-offs contested

As of 16 Mar 2022, Sidney Crosby (CAN) had taken 23,694 face-offs for the Pittsburgh Penguins since the 2005/06 season – when the National Hockey League officially began tracking face-off statistics. Crosby had won 12,339 face-offs and lost 11,355.

The **most face-offs won** is 13,586, by Patrice Bergeron (CAN) for the Boston Bruins.

Most individual points in one period (regular season)

On 17 Mar 2021, Mika Zibanejad (SWE) scored six points during the second period of the New York Rangers' 9–0 win over the Philadelphia Flyers. Zibanejad scored a hat-trick (even-handed, short-handed and during a power play) and made three assists. He matched the feat of Bryan Trottier (CAN) in the second period of the New York Islanders' 9–4 victory against the New York Rangers on 23 Dec 1978.

All players USA, unless stated otherwise.

MOST CONSECUTIVE STRIKEOUTS BY AN MLB PITCHER

The 2021 MLB season saw two pitchers equal Tom Seaver's record of 10 successive strikeouts, which he set for the New York Mets against the San Diego Padres on 22 Apr 1970. Aaron Nola of the Philadelphia Phillies fanned 10 Mets hitters in a row on 25 Jun, and the Milwaukee Brewers' Corbin Burnes (inset) followed suit against the Chicago Cubs on 11 Aug.

MOST TOUCHDOWN CATCHES IN AN NFL POSTSEASON GAME

Gabriel Davis caught eight passes for 201 yards and four TDs during the Buffalo Bills' AFC divisional playoff game against the Kansas City Chiefs on 23 Jan 2022 at Arrowhead Stadium in Kansas City, Missouri. Despite Davis's fourth TD putting his team up by three with just 13 sec on the clock, the game ended in heartbreak for the Bills, who lost 42–36 in overtime.

MOST NBA THREE-POINT FIELD GOALS

Stephen Curry sank his 2,974th three-pointer for the Golden State Warriors on 14 Dec 2021, passing Ray Allen's mark for the all-time lead – and in 511 fewer games. Curry, who by 17 Mar 2022 had reached 3,117 three-pointers, also holds the **single-season** record of 402, from 2015/16.

GREATEST WINNING MARGIN IN AN NBA GAME

On 2 Dec 2021, the Memphis Grizzlies destroyed the Oklahoma City Thunder 152–79 – a winning margin of 73 points. The previous record (68, by the Cleveland Cavaliers against the Miami Heat) had stood for 30 years. Oklahoma have now suffered both the largest home and road losses in NBA history.

NFL

Longest field goal

Justin Tucker provided the National Football League Moment of the Year with his last-gasp 66-yard field goal for the Baltimore Ravens on 26 Sep 2021. His effort bounced off the crossbar before spinning through the uprights, sealing a 19–17 win over the Detroit Lions at Ford Field in Detroit, Michigan.

Most 100-yard receiving games in a season

Cooper Kupp of the Los Angeles Rams completed 11 games with 100+ receiving yards in 2021, equalling Michael Irvin for the Dallas Cowboys in 1995 and the Detroit Lions' Calvin Johnson in 2012. Kupp went on to record the **most postseason receptions** – 33 in four games – and was voted MVP at Super Bowl LVI as the Rams claimed the Vince Lombardi Trophy.

Most quarterback sacks in a season

Outside linebacker TJ Watt was credited with 22.5 sacks for the Pittsburgh Steelers in 2021. Watt equalled the mark set by the New York Giants' Michael Strahan in 2001.

Most passing yards

Tom Brady threw for 84,520 passing yards between 2000 and 2021 for the New England Patriots and the Tampa Bay Buccaneers. The legendary QB surpassed Drew Brees' mark on 3 Oct 2021, during the Bucs' 19–17 win over the Patriots.

NBA

Youngest player to achieve a triple-double

Josh Giddey (AUS, b. 10 Oct 2002) put up 17 points, 14 assists and 13 rebounds for the Oklahoma City Thunder aged 19 years 84 days on 2 Jan 2022. The 203.2-cm (6-ft 8-in) guard was playing against the Dallas Mavericks.

Most three-point field goals in a quarter (team)

Three teams sank 11 three-pointers in a single quarter in 2021: the Houston Rockets (1 Feb), the Charlotte Hornets (13 Mar) and the Atlanta Hawks (6 Apr). They equalled the feat of the Milwaukee Bucks on 28 Mar 2006 and the Cleveland Cavaliers on 31 Jan 2010.

WNBA

Most rebounds

Sylvia Fowles claimed 3,712 rebounds playing for the Minnesota Lynx and the Chicago Sky between 2008 and 2021. Fowles also had the **highest field goal percentage** – 59.7%, or 2,347 of 3,930 attempts.

Highest free throw percentage

Elena Delle Donne had converted 956 of 1,018 free throw attempts by the end of the 2021 season. Her success percentage of 93.9% was 3% higher than the **NBA** record of 90.7%, by Stephen Curry (see above).

MOST CONSECUTIVE NHL GAMES PLAYED

On 25 Jan 2022, defenseman Keith Yandle set a new NHL ironman record when he played his 965th consecutive regular-season game, for the Philadelphia Flyers against the New York Islanders. Yandle's streak – 981, as of 13 Mar – had lasted 13 years and featured more than 20,000 minutes on ice.

> In 2019, Lamar Jackson became NFL MVP aged 23 – the second-youngest ever, after Jim Brown.

MOST 100-YARD RUSHING GAMES FOR AN NFL QUARTERBACK

On 7 Nov 2021, Lamar Jackson equalled Michael Vick's record of 10 games with 100 yards' rushing. Between 18 Nov 2018 – his first QB start – and 11 Oct 2021, Jackson led the Baltimore Ravens to the **most consecutive 100-yard rushing games (team)** – 43, equalling the Pittsburgh Steelers in 1974–77.

Cricket

MOST WICKETS AT A SINGLE MEN'S T20 WORLD CUP
Wanindu Hasaranga de Silva (LKA) took 16 wickets in eight matches at the 2021 International Cricket Council Men's T20 World Cup in the UAE and Oman. The all-rounder struck at an average of 9.75 runs per wicket. See the table below for more T20 World Cup record holders.

MOST WINS OF THE ICC WOMEN'S WORLD CUP
Australia's women secured their seventh one-day World Cup title on 3 Apr 2022, defeating England by 71 runs in the final in Christchurch, New Zealand. Opener Alyssa Healy smashed the **most runs by a player in an ICC World Cup final** – 170.

ICC Men's T20 World Cup

Most...	Total	Name	Team
Matches	35	Tillakaratne Dilshan	Sri Lanka
Runs	1,016	Mahela Jayawardene	Sri Lanka
Wickets	41	Shakib Al Hasan	Pakistan
Dismissals (wicket-keeper)	32	MS Dhoni	India
Catches (fielder)	23	AB de Villiers	South Africa
Sixes	63	Chris Gayle	West Indies

Most sixes in an international over
On 9 Sep 2021, Jaskaran Malhotra (USA, b. IND) hit six sixes off an over during a One-Day International (ODI) match between the USA and Papua New Guinea at Oman's Al Amerat Cricket Ground. He became only the fourth player in history to do so in international cricket, along with Herschelle Gibbs (ZAF), Yuvraj Singh (IND) and the West Indies' Kieron Pollard (TTO).

Malhotra's innings of 173 contained a total of 16 sixes – just one shy of the record for **most sixes in an ODI**, by England's Eoin Morgan (b. IRL) in a Cricket World Cup match against Afghanistan on 18 Jun 2019.

Most consecutive international wickets
Jason Holder (BRB) took four wickets in successive deliveries during the West Indies' T20 match against England on 30 Jan 2022 in Bridgetown, Barbados. Holder equalled the feat of Lasith Malinga (LKA, twice), Rashid Khan (AFG), Anuradha Doddaballapur (DEU, b. IND) and Curtis Campher (IRL, b. ZAF).

Patel took 10 wickets for 119 runs in 47.5 overs. New Zealand, however, lost the match by 372 runs.

MOST WICKETS IN A TEST INNINGS
On 3–4 Dec 2021, Ajaz Patel (NZ, b. IND) took all 10 of India's first-innings wickets at Mumbai's Wankhede Stadium. The left-arm spinner became only the third player to perform such a feat, after England's Jim Laker against Australia on 30–31 Jul 1956, and Anil Kumble (IND) versus Pakistan on 7 Feb 1999.

Most international runs (female)
Mithali Raj (IND) had scored a combined total of 10,868 runs in international cricket as of 3 Apr 2022. This comprised 699 Test runs, 2,364 in T20 Internationals and the **most ODI runs (female)** – 7,805, which was 1,813 runs more than any other female cricketer in the 50-over format. Raj had also amassed the **most ODI fifties (female)** – 66.

Most catches taken by a wicket-keeper on Test debut
Gloveman Alex Carey (AUS) took eight catches in the First Ashes Test against England at Brisbane Cricket Ground in Australia on 8 and 10–11 Dec 2021. He pouched three in the first innings and five in the second.

Most wickets taken in a T20 International
On 26 Aug 2021, Frederique Overdijk (NLD) bagged seven wickets for three runs against France in an ICC Women's T20 World Cup Qualifier in Cartagena, Murcia, Spain. She clean-bowled six batters.

On 24 Oct 2021, Nigeria's Peter Aho recorded the **best bowling figures in a T20 International (male)**. He took six wickets for five runs in 3.4 overs against Sierra Leone, in a match staged at the University of Lagos Cricket Oval in Nigeria.

SHANE WARNE (1969–2022)
Cricket lost one of its greatest-ever players in 2022, when Australian leg-spinner Shane Warne died on 4 Mar aged 52. He took 708 Test wickets, behind only Muttiah Muralitharan, including the **most Test wickets against one team** – 195, versus England. Warne's first English dismissal, that of Mike Gatting on 4 Jun 1993, became known as the "Ball of the Century".

YOUNGEST PLAYER TO SCORE AN INTERNATIONAL CENTURY
Amy Hunter (IRL, b. 11 Oct 2005) celebrated her 16th birthday in style in 2021, making 121 not out in an ODI for Ireland against Zimbabwe at Harare Sports Club. Hunter became the youngest centurion – male or female – in any form of international cricket.

Tennis

Most ATP Masters 1000 singles titles
On 7 Nov 2021, Novak Djokovic (SRB) secured his 37th ATP (Association of Tennis Professionals) Tour Masters 1000 title, ousting Daniil Medvedev 4–6, 6–3, 6–3 at the Paris Masters in France. Djokovic moved one clear of his rival Rafael Nadal, just six months after the Spaniard had registered a record-tying 36th Masters 1000 win at the Rome Masters in Italy.

Also in 2021, Djokovic extended his record for **most ATP Player of the Year awards**, claiming his seventh. First presented – to Arthur Ashe – in 1975, since 1990 the accolade has been given exclusively to the man finishing the calendar year as the No.1-ranked player on the ATP Tour.

Most years winning an ATP title
Rafael Nadal won at least one ATP Tour title for 19 consecutive years between 2004 and 2022. He claimed the top prize at the Melbourne Summer Set 1 in Australia on 9 Jan 2022 to move one title year ahead of both Roger Federer (18 in 2001–15, 2017–19) and Andre Agassi (18 in 1987–96, 1998–2005).

Most ATP Tournament of the Year awards
California's Indian Wells Masters was named the ATP's Tournament of the Year seven years in a row between 2014 and 2021. One of nine Masters 1000 events on the tennis calendar, Indian Wells surpassed the six awards won by Florida's Miami Open in 2002–06 and 2008.

Most Olympic tennis women's singles appearances
Samantha Stosur (AUS) participated in her fifth Olympic singles tournament at the Tokyo Games in 2021. She equalled the mark set by Venus Williams between 2000 and 2016. Venus and sister Serena (both USA) share the record for **most Olympic tennis gold medals** – four – including three as a doubles pairing.

The **Olympic men's singles appearance** record was also extended to five in Tokyo, by Lu Yen-hsun (aka Rendy Lu) of Taiwan, China. The 37-year-old bowed out in the first round of the men's singles and immediately announced his retirement.

Latest finish to an ATP Tour singles match
A first-round match between Alexander Zverev (DEU) and Jenson Brooksby (USA) at the Mexican Open in Acapulco finished at 4:55 a.m. local time on 22 Feb 2022. Zverev prevailed 3–6, 7–6, 6–2 in the midnight marathon, which featured a 1-hr 51-min second set.

Most Grand Slam singles tournaments played
On 30 Jun 2021, Venus Williams made her 90th Grand Slam singles appearance – 24 years after her first, as a 16-year-old at the 1997 French Open. Williams recorded her 271st Grand Slam match win in Round 1 at Wimbledon, before falling in the next round.

Most Grand Slam wheelchair titles
Shingo Kunieda (JPN) won his 47th wheelchair tennis title at the Australian Open on 27 Jan 2022. Kunieda beat Alfie Hewett 7–5, 3–6, 6–2 in the singles final in Melbourne to make it 26 Grand Slam singles titles in all, with a further 21 in doubles.

Also at Melbourne, 47-year-old David Wagner (USA) extended his record for **most Grand Slam men's quad doubles titles** to 22. The **men's quad singles** record is 15, by Dylan Alcott (AUS, see right).

YOUNGEST WINNER OF AN ATP TOUR 500 EVENT
On 8 Aug 2021, Jannik Sinner (ITA, b. 16 Aug 2001) won the Citi Open in Washington, DC, USA, aged 19 years 357 days. Sinner defeated Mackenzie McDonald 7–5, 4–6, 7–5 in the final to become the first teenager to claim an Association of Tennis Professionals Tour 500 event.

FIRST GOLDEN SLAM (MALE)
On 12 Sep 2021, Dylan Alcott (AUS) won the US Open quad singles to complete a "Golden Slam" – winning all four Grand Slam singles or doubles titles and Olympic/Paralympic gold in the same year. His feat was matched by Diede de Groot (NLD, inset) at the same tournament, in the women's wheelchair singles. The **first Golden Slam** was achieved by Steffi Graf (DEU) in 1988.

MOST ACES IN A US OPEN MATCH (FEMALE)
Karolína Plíšková (CZE) served 24 aces during her second-round win against Amanda Anisimova on 3 Sep 2021 at the Arthur Ashe Stadium in New York City. Karolína's twin sister, Kristýna, holds the overall record for **most aces in a match (female)** – 31 – against Monica Puig at the Australian Open on 20 Jan 2016.

MOST GRAND SLAM SINGLES TITLES (MALE)
On 30 Jan 2022, Rafael Nadal (ESP) defeated Daniil Medvedev in the final of the Australian Open to seal his 21st Grand Slam singles title. He moved one clear of Roger Federer and Novak Djokovic, giving him sole ownership of the record for the first time. Nadal's 21 Slams include 13 French Open titles – the **most wins of a single Grand Slam (open era)**.

Track & Field

FASTEST...

100 m (T63, female)

Ambra Sabatini (ITA) won Paralympic gold in 14.11 sec on 4 Sep 2021 in Tokyo, Japan. The 19-year-old sprinter led home an Italian 1-2-3 in the women's T63 100 m. She only took up para athletics in 2020, having lost her left leg in a traffic accident the previous year.

200 m (T12, female)

Omara Durand (CUB) claimed three titles at the Tokyo Paralympics including the 200 m crown, which she won in a time of 23.02 sec on 4 Sep 2021. Durand has a career tally of eight Paralympic gold medals, competing in the T12 and T13 categories for visually impaired athletes. She also holds the **T12 400 m** record of 51.77 sec, while her 11.40-sec **T12 100 m** sprint at the 2016 Rio Paralympics is the fastest recorded by any female para athlete over that distance.

FASTEST INDOOR 60 M HURDLES (MALE)

On 24 Feb 2021, Grant Holloway (USA) clocked 7.29 sec for the 60 m hurdles at a World Athletics Indoor Tour meeting in Madrid, Spain. He broke Colin Jackson's 27-year-old record by 0.01 sec. At the time, Holloway had been unbeaten in the event for six years.

FASTEST 10 KM ROAD RUN (WOMEN-ONLY RACE)*

On 12 Sep 2021, Agnes Tirop (KEN) ran 10 km (6.2 mi) in 30 min 1 sec at the Road to Records event in Herzogenaurach, Germany. She took nearly 30 seconds off Asmae Leghzaoui's previous record, set in 2002. Tragically, Agnes was killed in Oct 2021; her funeral was attended by 1,000 mourners.

Wheelchair 800 m (T54, male)

Daniel Romanchuk (USA) completed two laps of the track in 1 min 29.54 sec at the Swiss Nationals in Arbon, Switzerland, on 24 May 2021.

2,000 m (female)

Burundi's Francine Niyonsaba ran 2,000 m in 5 min 21.56 sec on 14 Sep 2021 in Zagreb, Croatia. A former 800 m runner, Niyonsaba was forced to move up to longer distances on account of World Athletics' regulations banning female runners with naturally high levels of testosterone from competing between 400 m and one mile. She is the first athlete to have identified themselves as having DSD (differences in sex development) to break an official world record.

5 km road run (male)

On 31 Dec 2021, Berihu Aregawi (ETH) won the Cursa dels Nassos in Barcelona, Spain, in 12 min 49 sec. The **female** record fell in the same race, to Ejgayehu Taye (ETH) in 14 min 19 sec. World Athletics maintains separate road running records for mixed-gender and women-only races. The **fastest 5 km (women-only race)*** is 14 min 29 sec, by Senbere Teferi (ETH) on 12 Sep 2021 in Herzogenaurach, Germany.

The **fastest 10 km road run (female, mixed-gender race)*** is 29 min 14 sec, by Yalemzerf Yehualaw (ETH) on 27 Feb 2022 in Castellón, Spain.

10,000 m (female)

Letesenbet Gidey (ETH) won the Ethiopian Olympic trials in 29 min 1.03 sec on 8 Jun 2021 in Hengelo, Netherlands. She knocked five seconds off the women's 10,000 m record that had been set only two days earlier by Sifan Hassan at the same stadium.

Gidey also holds the **women's 5,000 m** record – 14 min 6.62 sec, set on 7 Oct 2020 – and clocked the **fastest women's half-marathon (mixed-gender race)** on 24 Oct 2021, running 21 km (13 mi) in just 1 hr 2 min 52 sec in Valencia, Spain.

FARTHEST SHOT PUT (MALE)

Ryan Crouser (USA) threw the shot 23.37 m (76 ft 8 in) on 18 Jun 2021 at the US Olympic Team Trials in Track & Field in Eugene, Oregon. He shattered the world record of 23.12 m (75 ft 10 in), which had stood for 31 years. Crouser, who stands 2.01 m (6 ft 7 in) tall, had a stellar 2021, setting the **indoor** record with his first throw of the season – 22.82 m (74 ft 10 in), on 24 Jan 2021. He also defended his Olympic shot put title in Tokyo.

FASTEST 400 M HURDLES

In an extraordinary final of the men's 400 m hurdles at the Tokyo Olympics on 3 Aug 2021, Karsten Warholm (NOR) finished in 45.94 sec to destroy his own **male** world record from July by three-quarters of a second. Bronze medallist Alison dos Santos ran 46.72 sec, which would have been a world record just five weeks earlier.

The next day, Sydney McLaughlin (USA) broke the **female** record on her way to gold in 51.46 sec. She edged out Dalilah Muhammad, her rival and former record holder, in a thrilling race.

*pending ratification by World Athletics

FASTEST 100 M (T62, FEMALE)

On 3 Jun 2021, Fleur Jong (NLD) clocked 12.64 sec at the World Para Athletics European Championships in Bydgoszcz, Poland. On 28 Aug, she claimed her first Paralympic gold medal with the **farthest long jump (T62, female)** – 6.16 m (20 ft 2 in). Jong lost both her legs below the knee, and eight of her fingertips, following a bacterial infection she contracted aged 16.

FARTHEST...

Indoor triple jump (male)

On 16 Jan 2021, Hugues Fabrice Zango (BFA) sailed out to 18.07 m (59 ft 3 in) at an event in Aubière, France. He beat the mark of 17.92 m (58 ft 9 in) set in 2011 by his coach, Teddy Tamgho. Zango is Burkina Faso's first-ever track and field world record holder.

Javelin (F46, male)

Dinesh Priyantha (LKA) became Sri Lanka's first-ever Paralympic gold medallist on 30 Aug 2021, thanks to a world-record throw of 67.79 m (222 ft 4 in).

The same day, former wrestler Sumit Antil (IND) set a new **F64** record three times in six throws. His fifth-round effort of 68.55 m (224 ft 10 in) secured Antil the F64 javelin title on his Paralympic debut.

MOST OLYMPIC ATHLETICS MEDALS (FEMALE)

Allyson Felix (USA) claimed her 10th and 11th Olympic medals at the delayed 2020 Tokyo Games, winning bronze in the 400 m and gold in the 4 x 400 m relay. Her career tally includes the **most Olympic athletics golds (female)** – seven. Tokyo was Felix's fifth Games; her first was Athens 2004, where she won silver in the 200 m at the age of just 18.

The **male** record is 12 (nine gold and three silver), by the "Flying Finn" Paavo Nurmi (inset) between 1920 and 1928.

HIGHEST...

Pole vault (male)*

On 7 Mar 2022, Armand Duplantis (SWE, b. USA) cleared 6.19 m (20 ft 3.7 in) at the Belgrade Indoor Meeting in Serbia. It was the third time that "Mondo" had set a new pole vault world record, and he estimated that he had taken as many as 50 attempts to clear this latest height in competition.

MOST...

Diamond League victories

Discus thrower Sandra Perković (HRV) recorded two meeting wins in the 2021 Diamond League to take her career total to 44, more than any other athlete. She shares the record for **most women's Diamond League titles** – six – with shot-putter Valerie Adams (NZ) and long/triple jumper Caterine Ibargüen (COL).

Olympic golds in the hammer throw (female)

Anita Włodarczyk (POL) confirmed her status as the greatest women's hammer thrower in history with her third consecutive Olympic title in Tokyo. Włodarczyk sealed victory with a throw of 78.48 m (257 ft 5 in) on 3 Aug 2021. Her world record for the **farthest hammer throw (female)** is 82.98 m (272 ft 2 in), set on 28 Aug 2016.

MOST OLYMPIC APPEARANCES IN ATHLETICS

Jesús Ángel García (ESP) competed in his eighth Olympic 50 km race walk on 6 Aug 2021, finishing 35th at the age of 51. He made his Games debut at Barcelona in 1992 and recorded his highest finish – fourth – at Beijing 2008. García will not take part at Paris 2024, as the 50 km race walk is no longer part of the Olympic programme.

See Stop Press (pp.246–47) for updates from the 2022 World Indoor Championships.

LONGEST TRIPLE JUMP (FEMALE)

On 1 Aug 2021, Yulimar Rojas (VEN) hopped, stepped and jumped 15.67 m (51 ft 4 in) to claim Olympic gold at the Tokyo Games. She was already assured of victory when she set off on her final jump of the competition, which broke Inessa Kravets' world record of 15.50 m (50 ft 10 in) from 1995. Rojas also holds the **indoor** record of 15.43 m (50 ft 7 in), which she set on 21 Feb 2020 in Madrid, Spain.

Para Sports

Fastest cycling 500 m time trial (C4, female)
At the Tokyo Paralympics, Kadeena Cox (UK) completed two laps of the Izu Velodrome in 34.812 sec to take gold in the women's time trial (C4–5) on 27 Aug 2021. The multidisciplinarian also teamed up with Jody Cundy and Jaco van Gass to set a new **mixed team sprint (C1–5)** record of 47.579 sec for Great Britain before turning to the athletics track. Cox finished fourth in the T38 400 m, won by Germany's Lindy Ave in exactly 1 min – the **fastest T38 400 m (female)**.

Fastest cycling 1 km time trial (C1, male)
Li Zhangyu (CHN) won gold in the men's time trial C1–3 with a time of 1 min 8.347 sec on 27 Aug 2021 in Tokyo. It was his third consecutive Paralympic title over the distance. Alexandre Léauté (FRA) took silver with the **C2** record of 1 min 9.211 sec, while Jaco van Gass (UK, b. ZAF) claimed bronze with the **C3** record of 1 min 5.569 sec. Competitors' times were adjusted according to their level of disability to determine their overall standings in the event.

Fastest 100 m (T12, male)
On 29 Aug 2021, Salum Ageze Kashafali (NOR, b. COD) sprinted to Paralympic glory in 10.43 sec in Tokyo. This was just 0.01 sec behind Petrucio Ferreira dos Santos's (BRA) **fastest 100 m (T46/47)** from the 2019 World Championships in Dubai, UAE – the fastest recorded by any para athlete over the distance.

FASTEST SHORT COURSE 1,500 M FREESTYLE (T21, FEMALE)
Dunia Camacho Marenco (MEX) swam 1,500 m in a 25-m pool in 23 min 55.27 sec in Nova Scotia, Canada, on 25 Jul 2018. In 2021, she was presented with four GWR certificates for swims in the T21 category, as recognized by the Down Syndrome International Swimming Organisation. Swimmers with Down syndrome face an uphill battle to qualify for the Paralympics, where they are placed in World Para Swimming's S14 class, against athletes with intellectual but no physical impairments.

MOST MEN'S SITTING VOLLEYBALL PARALYMPIC TITLES
Iran claimed its seventh men's sitting volleyball title at the Tokyo Paralympics, defeating the Russian Paralympic Committee by three sets to one in the final on 4 Sep 2021. Its team featured the **tallest Paralympian ever** – the 246-cm (8-ft 0.85-in) outside hitter Morteza Mehrzadselakjani (far left).

Fastest 200 m (T37, male)
Sprinter Nick Mayhugh (USA) clocked a time of 21.91 sec in the final of the 200 m in Tokyo on 4 Sep 2021. He had already recorded the **fastest T37 100 m** – 10.95 sec – eight days previously, and finished the Games with three gold medals and one silver. Mayhugh, who has cerebral palsy, is also a member of the US Para 7-a-Side National Soccer Team.

Farthest discus throw (F52, female)
Elizabeth Rodrigues Gomes (BRA) threw the discus 17.62 m to win Paralympic gold on 30 Aug 2021. Gomes, who has multiple sclerosis, was competing in her first Paralympics at the age of 56.

FASTEST WHEELCHAIR 100 M (T34, FEMALE)
On 29 Aug 2021, Hannah Cockroft (UK) secured her third consecutive Paralympic 100 m title in 16.39 sec in Tokyo. It sealed a record-breaking year for Cockroft, who in May had set new fastest times in the T34 class over **200 m** (29.27 sec), **400 m** (53.99 sec) and **800 m** (1 min 48.87 sec) – all in the Swiss town of Arbon.

FASTEST CYCLING 3 KM INDIVIDUAL PURSUIT (C5, FEMALE)
Dame Sarah Storey (UK) rode 3 km in 3 min 27.057 sec at the Tokyo Paralympics on 25 Aug 2021. She broke the women's C5 individual pursuit world record during qualifying at the Izu Velodrome and went on to catch compatriot Crystal Lane-Wright in just eight laps in the final to win gold. Competing at her eighth Paralympics, Storey won two golds to take her tally to 17, making her Britain's most successful Paralympian.

Storey won five of her 17 Paralympic golds in the swimming pool before switching to cycling in 2005.

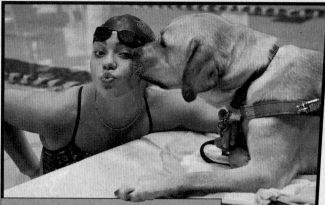

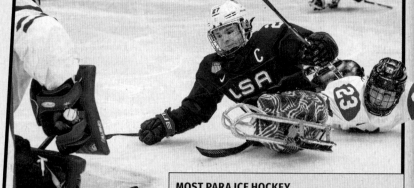

FASTEST 400 M FREESTYLE SWIM (S11, FEMALE)

Para swimmer Anastasia Pagonis (USA, with guide dog Radar above) lost her sight completely at the age of 14. She has built a following of millions on TikTok, sharing her everyday experiences of living with blindness. On 26 Aug 2021, the 17-year-old broke her own world record in the S11 400 m freestyle to win her first Paralympic gold medal in 4 min 54.49 sec.

Fastest 100 m freestyle swim (S10, male)

The most successful Paralympian in Tokyo was Maksym Krypak (UKR), who claimed seven medals, including five golds. He took the S10 100 m freestyle title in 50.64 sec on 28 Aug 2021 and also set new S10 bests for the **100 m backstroke** (57.19 sec) and the **100 m butterfly** (54.15 sec).

Another dominant swimmer in the S10 class was Aurélie Rivard (CAN). She clocked world records for the women's **100 m freestyle** (58.14 sec) and **400 m freestyle** (4 min 24.08 sec) on her way to double gold.

Fastest 50 m butterfly swim (S5, male)

Zheng Tao claimed the Paralympic 50 m butterfly title in 30.62 sec on 27 Aug 2021. It was one of four golds won in Tokyo by the Chinese para swimmer, who took up the sport aged 13 after an electric shock caused the loss of both of his arms. He also set the **fastest S5 50 m backstroke** in Tokyo, coming home in 31.42 sec.

HEAVIEST POWERLIFT (-41 KG, FEMALE)

On 28 Nov 2021, Lingling Guo (CHN, pictured at the Tokyo Paralympics) lifted 109.5 kg (241 lb 6 oz) at the World Para Powerlifting Championships in Tbilisi, Georgia. She is the only female para powerlifter to hold records in two current weight classes, having set the **-45 kg** record of 118 kg (260 lb 2 oz) in 2019.

MOST PARA ICE HOCKEY PARALYMPIC GOLD MEDALS

Defenseman Josh Pauls (USA) claimed his fourth consecutive Winter Paralympic gold at Beijing 2022, finding the net in the final as the USA defeated rivals Canada 5–0 on 13 Mar. Pauls was born without tibia bones and had both legs amputated at 10 months old. He won his first gold at Vancouver 2010 aged 17 and has played in 19 games at the Paralympics.

Heaviest powerlift (-88 kg, male)

On 4 Dec 2021, Abdelkareem Khattab (JOR) lifted 250 kg (551 lb 2 oz) at the World Para Powerlifting Championships in Tbilisi, Georgia. He destroyed his own world record, set in Dubai on 21 Jun, by 10 kg (22 lb) with his final lift of the competition. Other para powerlifting records to fall in Tbilisi were:
-55 kg, female: 133.5 kg (294 lb 5 oz), by Mariana Shevchuk (UKR) on 30 Nov. It was a third world record of the year for Shevchuk, who is short statured.
-79 kg, female: 144 kg (317 lb 7 oz), by Bose Omolayo (NGA) on 2 Dec.
-86 kg, female: 152.5 kg (336 lb 3 oz), by Folashade Oluwafemiayo (NGA) on 3 Dec. It was the fourth time she had broken the world record in 2021.
-107 kg, male: 251 kg (553 lb 5 oz), by Ali Akbar Gharibshahi (IRN) on 5 Dec.

Highest score in women's 10 m air pistol (SH1)

Para shooter Sareh Javanmardi (IRN) defended her Paralympic 10 m air pistol title in Tokyo, scoring 239.2 at the Asaka Shooting Range on 31 Aug 2021. Competitors in the SH1 classification can support the weight of their firearm themselves.

Another gold medallist was Dragan Ristić (SRB), who recorded a new best for the **mixed 50 m rifle prone (SH2)** – 252.7 – on 4 Sep 2021.

FARTHEST LONG JUMP (T64)

Markus Rehm (DEU) leapt out to 8.62 m (28 ft 3 in) on 1 Jun 2021 at the World Para Athletics European Championships in Bydgoszcz, Poland, smashing his own world record by 14 cm (5 in). This is the farthest long jump by any para athlete, and would have secured him gold at the previous six Olympic Games. Rehm, nicknamed the "Blade Jumper", went on to take his third Paralympic long jump title in Tokyo.

Golf

OLDEST MAJOR WINNER

Phil Mickelson (USA, b. 16 Jun 1970) became the oldest winner of a major tournament in 160 years when he lifted the 2021 PGA Championship trophy aged 50 years 341 days. Mickelson's victory at Kiawah Island in South Carolina, USA, came more than 30 years after his first win on the PGA Tour.

LOWEST SCORE IN A MAJOR ROUND

At the 2021 Evian Championship, Lee Jeong-eun (aka Jeongeun Lee6, KOR, pictured) and Leona Maguire (IRL) both shot rounds of 61 to equal Kim Hyo-joo's (KOR) major record from the 2014 Evian. Lee's second-round 61 helped her to the **lowest major score (first 36 holes)** of 127 (66, 61; 15 under par); she would go on to finish in second place.

Lowest total score on the PGA European Tour

On 25 Apr 2021, Garrick Higgo (ZAF) won his first European Tour event in record-breaking style, playing four rounds in just 255 strokes (65, 64, 63, 63; 25 strokes under par) at the Gran Canaria Lopesan Open in Spain. Thaworn Wiratchant also shot 255 at the 2005 Indonesia Open, but preferred lies were in operation – meaning that, on account of the weather conditions, players could improve the position of their ball by hand on certain parts of the course.

Youngest winner of a world-ranking tournament (male)

Ratchanon "TK" Chantananuwat (THA, b. 5 Mar 2007) was aged 15 years 36 days when he won the Trust Golf Asian Mixed Cup in Pattaya, Thailand, on 10 Apr 2022. He finished on 20 under par at Siam Country Club to become the youngest male winner of an Official World Golf Ranking-eligible tournament.

The **female** record is held by Atthaya Thitikul (THA, b. 20 Feb 2003), who was 14 years 139 days old when she triumphed at the Ladies European Thailand Championship on 6–9 Jul 2017 – also in Pattaya.

Lowest total score at The Open Championship (first 36 holes)

Louis Oosthuizen (ZAF) reached the halfway stage of the 2021 Open in just 129 strokes (64, 65; 11 under par) at Royal St George's in Kent, UK. He went on to finish tied for third, behind winner Collin Morikawa. Oosthuizen enjoyed a bittersweet 2021, earning $6,306,679 (£4.6 m) despite failing to claim a title – the **highest PGA Tour season's earnings without a victory**.

Greatest tournament prize money

Staged on 10–14 Mar at TPC Sawgrass in Ponte Vedra Beach, Florida, USA, the 2022 Players Championship had a total prize purse of $20 m (£15.3 m). The weather-affected tournament was won by Cameron Smith (AUS), who claimed the $3.6-m (£2.7-m) winner's purse with a 13-under-par score of 275.

The **women**'s record is $5.8 m (£4.2 m), offered by the 2021 Women's Open. It was held on 19–22 Aug at Carnoustie Golf Links in Angus, UK, and won by Anna Nordqvist, who took home $870,000 (£638,322).

Lowest score in a round at the Olympic Games (male)

On 1 Aug 2021, Rory Sabbatini (SVK, b. ZAF) shot a final-round 61 to earn himself an Olympic silver medal, sealed with a birdie at the 18th hole of the Kasumigaseki Country Club in Kawagoe, Saitama, Japan. Born in South Africa, Sabbatini qualified for Slovakian citizenship through his wife, Martina, who also caddied for him at the Games.

Fewest putts in a PGA Tour round

On 6 Aug 2021, Cameron Smith became only the 12th golfer in history to take 18 putts in 18 holes on the PGA Tour. He was competing in the second round of the WGC-FedEx St. Jude Invitational in Memphis, Tennessee, USA.

Oldest first-time winner on the PGA European Tour

Richard Bland (UK, b. 3 Feb 1973) was aged 48 years 101 days when he triumphed at the British Masters on 15 May 2021. Bland had played in 477 tournaments without success before finally tasting glory at The Belfry in Warwickshire, UK.

LOWEST SCORE TO PAR AT THE WOMEN'S PGA CHAMPIONSHIP

On 27 Jun 2021, Nelly Korda (USA) claimed the Women's PGA Championship – her first major – with a score of -19 in Johns Creek, Georgia, USA. Korda matched the winning scores of Cristie Kerr (USA) in 2010, Yani Tseng of Taiwan, China, in 2011 and Inbee Park (KOR) in 2015. First staged in 1955, the Women's PGA Championship was formerly known as the LPGA Championship.

Nelly's sister, Jessica, is also a pro golfer, while brother Sebastian has won a junior tennis Grand Slam.

LOWEST SCORE TO PAR ON THE PGA TOUR

On 9 Jan 2022, Cameron Smith (AUS) won the 2022 Tournament of Champions with a 72-hole score of -34 at the Kapalua Plantation Course in Maui, Hawaii, USA. Smith sank eight birdies in his final round to finish ahead of Jon Rahm and Matt Jones, who also finished inside the previous PGA Tour record of -31, set by Ernie Els at the same event in 2003.

MOST RYDER CUP POINTS

Sergio Garcia (ESP) earned 28.5 points for Europe in 10 appearances at the Ryder Cup between 1999 and 2021. His match record stood at 25 wins – the **most match wins** – seven halves and 13 defeats. Garcia claimed both records at the 2021 edition of the biennial event, despite Europe losing 19–9 to the USA.

MOST OLYMPIC TABLE TENNIS GOLD MEDALS
At the delayed 2020 Tokyo Games, table-tennis legend Ma Long (CHN) took his tally of Olympic titles to five. "The Dragon" won gold in the men's team and singles events for the second Games in a row, having also won the team event at London 2012.

MOST GOALS IN OLYMPIC MEN'S HANDBALL
Mikkel Hansen scored 165 times in four Olympic tournaments for Denmark between 2008 and 2021. The left-back broke the previous best of 127 goals at the Tokyo Games, racking up a **single-tournament** record of 61. Denmark lost out to France in the final (see below) to claim the silver medal.

MOST...

Olympic table tennis medals
Dimitrij Ovtcharov (DEU, b. UKR) won six medals at the Games between 2008 and 2021. Ovtcharov, the son of a Soviet table-tennis champion, claimed bronze in the singles and a team silver at the Tokyo Games in 2021.

The **female** record is five, by Wang Nan (CHN). She won four golds and a silver between 2000 and 2008.

Olympic handball gold medals (men)
France secured its third men's handball title at the Tokyo Games, defeating Denmark 25–23 on 7 Aug 2021. They also won back-to-back golds in 2008 and 2012.

The **women**'s record is also three, by Denmark between 1996 and 2004. Their 38–36 extra-time victory over South Korea in the final of Athens 2004 made them the first country to record three successive Olympic handball titles.

EHF Handball Champions League wins
On 13 Jun 2021, FC Barcelona (ESP) defeated Aalborg Håndbold 36–23 in the final of the 2021 EHF Champions League to secure their 10th title since 1991. It ended a six-year drought in the competition for the Spanish giants. Barcelona enjoyed a perfect Champions League season, winning all 20 matches they played.

MOST WINS OF RUGBY UNION'S CHAMPIONS CUP
Toulouse (FRA) claimed their fifth top-flight European title with a 22–17 victory over La Rochelle on 22 May 2021 at Twickenham in London, UK. Fly-half Romain Ntamack, who scored 17 points, followed in the footsteps of his father, Émile, a member of Toulouse's first Champions Cup-winning team in 1996 (when it was known as the Heineken Cup).

Heineken CHAMPIONS CUP

Fistball Women's World Championships
On 31 Jul 2021, Germany secured their fourth consecutive and seventh overall title with a straight-sets 3–0 (11–4, 11–3, 11–7) defeat of hosts Austria in Grieskirchen. Fistball is similar to volleyball, but the ball can only be struck with the fist or arms (rather than an open hand) and is permitted to bounce after each contact.

Women's World Floorball Championships
Sweden continued their domination of both floorball world championships (see below left) by recording their 10th victory in the women's competition in 2021. They overcame Finland 4–3 in overtime in the final on 5 Dec in Uppsala, Sweden.

Super League titles
St Helens (UK) claimed their ninth domestic rugby league title in 2021, defeating Catalan Dragons 12–10 in the Grand Final on 9 Oct. St Helens' first Super League title, in its inaugural year, was secured before the introduction of the Grand Final in 1998.

English Premiership tries
Chris Ashton touched down twice for Leicester Tigers against Exeter Chiefs on 27 Mar 2022 to equal Tom Varndell's (both UK) tally of 92 tries in top-flight English rugby union.

The **single-season** record is 20, by Exeter back row Sam Simmonds (UK) in 2020/21. He also scored a post-season try in the Premiership Final.

MOST MEN'S WORLD FLOORBALL CHAMPIONSHIPS
On 11 Dec 2021, Sweden defeated Finland 6–4 at the Hartwall Arena in Helsinki to claim their ninth men's floorball world title. Invented in Sweden in the 1960s, floorball is a form of indoor hockey that uses a plastic ball with holes.

MOST OLYMPIC WOMEN'S HOCKEY GOLDS
The Netherlands claimed their fourth Olympic women's hockey title at Tokyo 2020, beating Argentina 3–1 in the final on 6 Aug 2021. The team bounced back from their penalty shoot-out loss to Great Britain at Rio 2016 to win their third gold medal in four Games. Midfielder Eva de Goede and forward Lidewij Welten equalled the **individual** record of three, set by Rechelle Hawkes (AUS) in 1988, 1996 and 2000.

Cycling

MOST OLYMPIC TRACK CYCLING MEDALS

Jason and Laura Kenny (both UK) are the golden couple of Olympic track cycling. At the Tokyo Games, Jason increased the **male** record to nine – including the **most golds**, seven – with a silver in the team sprint and victory in the keirin. Laura equalled Anna Meares's (AUS) **female** record of six with a silver in the team pursuit and gold in the Madison, alongside Katie Archibald.

Farthest track distance in one hour (female)

On 30 Sep 2021, Joscelin Lowden (UK) rode 48.405 km (30.077 mi) in 60 min at the Tissot Velodrome in Grenchen, Switzerland. Lowden made her record attempt days after competing in three road races at the Union Cycliste Internationale (UCI) Road World Championships. She added almost 400 m (1,312 ft) to Vittoria Bussi's previous hour record and exceeded Jeannie Longo's "absolute record" of 48.159 km (29.924 mi), which the French rider set in 1996 using an aerodynamic position later banned by the UCI.

Fastest women's 500 m team sprint

Zhong Tianshi and Bao Shanju (both CHN) completed two laps of the Izu Velodrome in 31.804 sec at the Olympics on 2 Aug 2021. The rules for the women's team sprint changed following Tokyo, with teams of three riding three laps of the track. The **fastest women's 750 m team sprint** is 46.064 sec, by Germany (Pauline Grabosch, Lea Friedrich and Emma Hinze) on 20 Oct 2021.

MOST CONSECUTIVE WINS OF THE VUELTA A ESPAÑA

On 5 Sep 2021, Primož Roglič (SVN) celebrated his third victory in a row at the Spanish Grand Tour race, matching Tony Rominger (CHE) in 1992–94 and Roberto Heras (ESP) in 2003–05. Roglič capped a triumphant 2021 with gold in the Olympic road time trial on 28 Jul, finishing a minute ahead of the field.

FASTEST WOMEN'S 4 KM TEAM PURSUIT

On 3 Aug 2021, the German team of Franziska Brausse, Lisa Brennauer, Lisa Klein and Mieke Kröger won Olympic team pursuit gold in Japan in 4 min 4.242 sec. They broke the world record three times at the Izu Velodrome, overcoming defending champions Great Britain in the final.

FASTEST WOMEN'S 3 KM INDIVIDUAL PURSUIT (C4)

Competing at her first Paralympics at the age of 41, Emily Petricola (AUS) set a world record of 3 min 38.061 sec during qualifying for the C4 individual pursuit on 25 Aug 2021. She went on to win the gold medal by overlapping Shawn Morelli in the final. Petricola, a five-time world champion, was diagnosed with multiple sclerosis at the age of 27 and took up cycling training in 2015.

Fastest men's 4 km individual pursuit

Ashton Lambie (USA) cycled 4 km in 3 min 59.930 sec – an average of 60 km/h (37 mph), from a standing start – on 18 Aug 2021 in Aguascalientes, Mexico. The former gravel rider reclaimed the record from Filippo Ganna. In para track cycling, only the men's C4, C5 and B classes race over 4 km. All three world records were broken at the Tokyo Paralympics. Jozef Metelka (SVK) qualified for the **C4** final in 4 min 22.772 sec while Dorian Foulon (FRA) claimed the **C5** record in 4 min 18.274 sec. Tristan Bangma and pilot Patrick Bos (both NLD) qualified for the final of the **B** classification – for visually impaired athletes – in 3 min 59.470 sec.

Most elite women's road race medals at the UCI Road World Championships

Marianne Vos (NLD) has won nine world-championship medals in the women's one-day road race since 2006. She finished second at the 2021 edition in Belgium to take her total to three golds and six silvers.

Youngest Olympic mountain biking gold medallist

Tom Pidcock (UK, b. 30 Jul 1999) was aged 21 years 361 days when he won the men's cross-country on 26 Jul 2021 in Izu. He finished 20 sec clear of the field.

MOST STAGE WINS OF THE TOUR DE FRANCE

Mark Cavendish (UK) won four stages of the 2021 Tour de France to equal the overall record of 34, set by the great Eddy Merckx (BEL) between 1969 and 1975. It was a remarkable return to form for the veteran sprinter, who was only added to the Deceuninck–Quick-Step team as a late replacement and went on to claim the points classification.

Endurance

Fastest IRONMAN 70.3 triathlon (female)

Also known as "Half-IRONMANs", the 70.3 is staged over half the distance of a full race: a 1.2-mi (1.9-km) swim, a 56-mi (90-km) bike ride and a 13.1-mi (21.1-km) run. On 5 Aug 2018, Daniela Ryf (CHE) crossed the finish line at the IRONMAN 70.3 Gdynia in Poland in 3 hr 57 min 55 sec. Ryf is a five-time world champion at this distance.

The **fastest IRONMAN triathlon (female)** is 8 hr 22 min 41 sec, by Sara Svensk (SWE) at IRONMAN Cozumel in Mexico on 21 Nov 2021.

SMALLEST COUNTRY BY POPULATION TO WIN AN OLYMPIC GOLD MEDAL

On 27 Jul 2021, Flora Duffy won the women's triathlon in Tokyo to earn Olympic glory for Bermuda (population: 62,278). Duffy completed the 1.5-km (0.9-mi) swim, 40-km (24.8-mi) cycle and 10-km (6.2-mi) run in 1 hr 55 min 36 sec. For the **smallest country to win any Olympic medal**, turn to pp.244–45.

Also in 2021, Duffy equalled the **most wins of the World Triathlon Championship Series (female)** – three, first set by Emma Snowsill (AUS) in 2003 and 2005–06.

Most consecutive days running a marathon distance (female)

Between 31 Mar and 3 Jul 2020, Alyssa Clark (USA) ran 26.2 mi (42.1 km) for 95 successive days. At the start of the COVID-19 pandemic, Clark was locked down with her husband at a US Navy base in Naples, Italy. She began running a treadmill marathon every day and continued after lockdown – even squeezing in a run at 00.30 a.m. in Germany on her journey back to the USA.

Fastest time to complete the London Wheelchair Marathon

Marcel Hug (CHE) secured his third London Marathon title in record time on 3 Oct 2021, crossing the finish line in 1 hr 26 min 27 sec. It was the second year in a row that the race had been moved from its usual date in April, on account of COVID.

The **female** record also fell on the same day, to Hug's compatriot Manuela Schaar, in a time of 1 hr 39 min 52 sec. Schaar also holds the outright **fastest women's wheelchair marathon** time of 1 hr 35 min 42 sec, which she set on 17 Nov 2019 in Ōita, Japan.

Fastest 50 km

In Jan 2022, World Athletics ratified three inaugural 50 km world records. The **male** holder was Ketema Negasa (ETH), who won the Nedbank Runified 50k race in South Africa in 2 hr 42 min 7 sec on 23 May 2021. He recorded an average pace of 3:15 per km (5:13 per mi). Irvette van Zyl (ZAF) set the **female (women-only race)** record at the same event, in 3 hr 4 min 24 sec. The **female (mixed-gender race)** record was 2 hr 59 min 54 sec, clocked by Desiree Linden (USA) on 13 Apr 2021 at the Brooks 50K & Marathon in Eugene, Oregon, USA.

GREATEST DISTANCE RUN IN 24 HOURS*

On 28–29 Aug 2021, Aleksandr Sorokin (LTU) ran 309.399 km (192.251 mi) at the UltraPark Weekend 24 Hour race in Park Wolności, Pabianice, Poland. He shattered Yiannis Kouros's legendary mark of 303.506 km (188.589 mi), which had stood since 1997. Sorokin ran the equivalent of seven marathons in a day, averaging 4:39 per km (7:29 per mi).

FASTEST IRONMAN® TRIATHLON

Kristian Blummenfelt (NOR) triumphed at IRONMAN Cozumel in 7 hr 21 min 12 sec on 21 Nov 2021. The Olympic triathlon champion destroyed the world-best IRONMAN time on his debut over the distance. His splits were: 39:41 (swim); 4:02:35 (cycle) and 2:35:24 (run).

Blummenfelt also holds the record for the **IRONMAN 70.3** – 3 hr 29 min 5 sec – which he set in Bahrain in 2018.

Most laps completed in a backyard ultramarathon

Backyard ultras challenge competitors to complete a 4.167-mi (6.7-km) loop of track or road every hour, until only one runner remains. The distance is calculated to total 100 mi each 24 hr. On 16–19 Oct 2021, Harvey Lewis (USA) completed 85 laps to win Big's Backyard Ultra in Bell Buckle, Tennessee, USA. The event began at 7 a.m. on Saturday and finished at 9 p.m. on Tuesday; Lewis ran a total of 354.16 mi (569.96 km). He beat the previous record of 81 laps, set by John Stocker at the 2021 Suffolk Backyard Ultra on 5–8 Jun.

The **female** record is 68 laps, set by Courtney Dauwalter (USA) when she won 2020's virtual edition of Big's Backyard Ultra.

* pending ratification by the IAU

FASTEST TIME TO BAG ALL WAINWRIGHTS

On 11–17 Jun 2021, Sabrina Verjee (UK) conquered the 214 peaks of the Lake District National Park in Cumbria, UK, in 5 days 23 hr 49 min. The peaks, or fells, are listed in Alfred Wainwright's *A Pictorial Guide to the Lakeland Fells.* Verjee, a 40-year-old veterinary surgeon, slept for only 8 hr during her 325-mi (523-km) trek.

MOST WINS OF THE ULTRA-TRAIL DU MONT BLANC (MALE)

François D'Haene (FRA) claimed his fourth win of the single-stage Alpine ultramarathon on 28 Aug 2021, moving one clear of Kílian Jornet and Xavier Thévenard. D'Haene completed the 171.5-km (106.5-mi) course through the French, Swiss and Italian mountains in 20 hr 45 min 59 sec. The race takes place every year and attracts more than 2,000 entrants.

Need for Speed

FASTEST...

Formula One Grand Prix
Ferrari's Michael Schumacher (DEU) won the 2003 Italian Grand Prix at Monza with an average speed of 247.585 km/h (153.842 mph) for the entire 53-lap race. He took the chequered flag after just 1 hr 14 min 19 sec.

Over the course of his career, seven-time world champion Schumacher also recorded the **most Formula One fastest laps** – 77 – between 30 Aug 1992 and 22 Jul 2012.

World Rally Championship race
Kris Meeke (UK) completed the 2016 Rally Finland in Jyväskylä at an average speed of 126.62 km/h (78.67 mph) in his Citroën DS3 WRC. Dubbed the "Grand Prix on Gravel", Rally Finland is famous for its high speeds and fast times.

Lap at the Isle of Man TT Races
On 8 Jun 2018, Peter Hickman (UK) rode a circuit of the TT Senior race at an average speed of 217.989 km/h (135.452 mph) on his BMW S1000RR. The completed lap time was 16 min 42.778 sec.

Speed at a MotoGP event
Johann Zarco (FRA) hit 362.4 km/h (225.1 mph) during free practice for the Grand Prix of Qatar in Lusail on 27 Mar 2021. This was matched by Brad Binder (ZAF) in Scarperia e San Piero at the Grand Prix of Italy on 29 May, also during free practice.

MOST WORLD RALLY CHAMPIONSHIP RACE WINS (FEMALE)
Michèle Mouton (FRA) won four WRC rallies between 10 Oct 1981 and 14 Aug 1982. She claimed her first victory at the 1981 Rallye Sanremo in an Audi Quattro and added three more wins in 1982, when she finished second in the overall standings. Mouton is also the only woman to win the Pikes Peak International Hill Climb, in 1985.

MOST MOTOGP RACE WINS
Valentino Rossi (ITA) retired from MotoGP in 2021 after a stellar career in which he took the chequered flag 89 times (including 13 in MotoGP's predecessor, the 500cc championship). The flamboyant nine-time world champion (seven in MotoGP) rode for Honda, Yamaha and Ducati, and recorded the **most MotoGP starts** – 372 – while competing at 29 different circuits.

Most National Hot Rod Association wins
On 15 Aug 2021, John Force (USA) earned career victory No.154 in the Funny Car class at the Menards NHRA Nationals in Topeka, Kansas, USA – at the age of 72. Force – father of Brittany (see right) – went winless in his first nine seasons before becoming the first driver to record 100 wins in any class. See p.79 for more.

The **most NHRA wins (female)** is 45, by Angelle Sampey (USA) in the Pro Stock Motorcycle class. Her latest triumph came on 17 Oct 2021 at the NHRA Thunder Valley Nationals in Bristol, Tennessee, USA. She outpaced Karen Stoffer in an all-female final.

Most NASCAR race wins
Kyle Busch (USA) extended his record for victories across the three tiers of US stock-car racing to 222 in 2021. He had won 59 races in the top-tier NASCAR Cup Series along with the **most Xfinity Series wins** (102) and the **most Truck Series wins** (61). Busch surpassed Richard Petty's record of 200 victories – all achieved in the Cup Series between 1960 and 1984 – at the TruNorth Global 250 Truck Series race on 23 Mar 2019 in Ridgeway, Virginia, USA.

Most Superbike World Championship race wins
Jonathan Rea (UK) triumphed in 13 races during the 2021 Superbike season to take his career tally to 112 – almost twice as many as his nearest rival, Carl Fogarty (59). Rea became the first Superbike rider to record a century of victories on 22 May 2021, at MotorLand Aragón in Spain.

FASTEST FORMULA ONE LAP
Lewis Hamilton (UK) completed a circuit of the Autodromo Nazionale Monza at an average speed of 264.362 km/h (164.267 mph) for Mercedes during qualification for the 2020 Italian Grand Prix, driving 5.7 km (3.5 mi) in 1 min 18.887 sec. Hamilton has torn up the F1 record books, becoming the first driver to reach a century of race wins and pole positions.

Lewis Hamilton

Most...	Total
Race wins	103
Pole positions	103
Wins on different circuits	31
Poles on different circuits	32
Consecutive starts	265 (2007–20)

Figures correct as of the start of the 2022 F1 season

MOST WINS OF THE INDIANAPOLIS 500
Hélio Castroneves (BRA) equalled A J Foyt, Al Unser Sr and Rick Mears (all USA) with his fourth Indy 500 victory, recorded on 30 May 2021. His time of 2 hr 37 min 19.3846 sec was the **fastest Indy 500** for a full 200-lap race; his average speed around the Indianapolis Motor Speedway was 190.690 mph (306.885 km/h).

FASTEST COMPLETION OF THE MOUNT WASHINGTON HILLCLIMB AUTO RACE

On 15 Aug 2021, Travis Pastrana (USA) raced his 862-hp (642-kW) Subaru WRX STI to the summit of Mount Washington in 5 min 28.670 sec. First staged in 1904, the "Climb to the Clouds" is one of the USA's oldest motorsport races, and follows a 7.6-mi-long (12.2-km) stretch of road with a vertical gain of 4,650 ft (1,417 m).

LAND SPEED RECORD (FORMULA ONE, FIA-APPROVED)

On 20 Jul 2006, Alan van der Merwe (ZAF) drove a modified BAR Honda at 397.483 km/h (246.984 mph) over a flying kilometre at Bonneville Salt Flats in Utah, USA. It was part of Honda's "Bonneville 400" project, to see if an F1 car could reach 400 km/h (248 mph); test driver van der Merwe would later become F1's medical-car driver.

Most Formula One Grand Prix starts

Kimi Räikkönen (FIN) retired from F1 in 2021 after 349 Grand Prix starts and more than 18,000 laps in the sport. He made his F1 debut at the 2001 Australian Grand Prix and raced for Sauber, McLaren, Ferrari (twice), Lotus and Alfa Romeo. Räikkönen won the 2007 F1 Championship with Ferrari and recorded 21 race wins, 18 poles and 103 podium finishes.

Most Formula E Grand Prix starts

As of 12 Feb 2022, Lucas di Grassi (BRA) and Sam Bird (UK) had contested every race of the electric car championship since its inception – a total of 87. Di Grassi's entries all came for Audi Sport ABT Schaeffler, with whom he claimed the title in 2016/17. He has triumphed in 12 races, one behind Sébastien Buemi's (CHE) record for **most Formula E race wins**. Bird has raced for Envision Virgin Racing and Jaguar TCS Racing, notching up 11 victories.

MOST FORMULA DRIFT EVENT WINS

First staged in 2004, Formula Drift is a series of judged motorsport competitions in which entrants are rated on line, angle and style. Fredric Aasbø (NOR, left) is the king of the drifters, having racked up wins in 16 events between 21 Jun 2014 and 28 Aug 2021. In 2021, he claimed his second Formula Drift championship.

Youngest World Rally Championship race winner

On 18 Jul 2021, Kalle Rovanperä (FIN, b. 1 Oct 2000) won the Rally Estonia aged 20 years 290 days. He was behind the wheel of a Toyota Yaris WRC, alongside co-driver Jonne Halttunen, and finished a minute clear of the field.

FASTEST SPEED IN AN NHRA TOP FUEL RACE (1,000-FT)

On 1 Nov 2019, Brittany Force (USA) reached 338.17 mph (544.23 km/h) at the NHRA Nationals in Las Vegas, Nevada, USA. She covered 1,000 ft (304 m) in 3.659 sec. Speeds are measured using a 66-ft (20-m) speed trap that ends at the finish line, while "elapsed time" clocks the length of the entire run.

National Hot Rod Association records (1,000 ft and 1/4 mi)

Class	Elapsed Time	Speed	Driver	Location	Date
Top Fuel	3.623 sec		Brittany Force	Mohnton, Pennsylvania	14 Sep 2019
		338.17 mph	Brittany Force	Las Vegas, Nevada	1 Nov 2019
Funny Car	3.793 sec		Robert Hight	Brainerd, Minnesota	18 Aug 2017
		339.87 mph	Robert Hight	Sonoma, California	29 Jul 2017
Pro Stock	6.450 sec		Erica Enders	Gainesville, Florida	13 Mar 2022
		215.55 mph	Erica Enders	Englishtown, New Jersey	30 May 2014
Pro Stock Motorcycle	6.665 sec		Karen Stoffer	Gainesville, Florida	13 Mar 2022
		205.04 mph	Matthew Smith	Sonoma, California	24 Jul 2021
Pro Mod	5.621 sec		Jose Gonzalez (DOM)	Gainesville, Florida	14 Mar 2021
		261.22 mph	Erica Enders	Norwalk, Ohio	22 Jun 2019

All drivers and locations USA, unless otherwise stated

Combat Sports

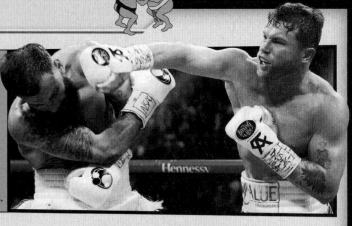

MOST UFC FIGHTS (FEMALE)

On 25 Sep 2021, Jéssica Andrade (BRA) became the first woman to step into the UFC octagon for the 20th time. She beat Cynthia Calvillo via a first-round TKO in their flyweight bout at UFC 266. A former strawweight world champion, Andrade's record stood at 13 wins and seven losses.

MOST OLYMPIC GOLD MEDALS IN...

Greco-Roman wrestling

Mijaín López (CUB) defeated Iakobi Kajaia 5–0 on 2 Aug 2021 to claim his fourth super-heavyweight Olympic title in a row. This is also the **most consecutive Olympic individual golds (male)**, matching sailor Paul Bert Elvstrøm (DNK), discus thrower Al Oerter (USA), Carl Lewis (USA) in the long jump, and swimmer Michael Phelps (USA) in the 200 m individual medley.

Judo

On 31 Jul 2021, Teddy Riner won his third Olympic title, as part of France's mixed judo team. He matched the feat of Tadahiro Nomura (JPN) at extra-lightweight in 1996, 2000 and 2004. Riner also claimed individual bronze at heavyweight in Tokyo to take his career medal tally to five – the **most Olympic judo medals**, equalling Ryoko Tani (JPN) in the women's extra-lightweight class between 1992 and 2008.

Taekwondo (women's heavyweight)

Milica Mandić (SRB) won her second Olympic gold at +67 kg in Tokyo, matching the feat of Chen Zhong (CHN) at Sydney 2000 and Athens 2004.

MOST OLYMPIC GOLD MEDALS IN AN INDIVIDUAL FENCING DISCIPLINE (MALE)

On 24 Jul 2021, Áron Szilágyi (HUN, right) claimed his third successive Olympic sabre title, defeating Luigi Samele 15–7 in the final in Tokyo. Two other male fencers, Ramón Fonst and Nedo Nadi, also have three individual golds to their name, but competing across different disciplines.

FIRST UNDISPUTED SUPER-MIDDLEWEIGHT BOXING WORLD CHAMPION

On 6 Nov 2021, Saúl "Canelo" Álvarez (MEX, far right) beat Caleb Plant to claim all four super-middleweight belts. Rated the world's best pound-for-pound boxer by *The Ring*, Álvarez's record stood at 57 wins, two draws and one loss.

Most UFC finishes

Charles Oliveira (BRA) had achieved 18 Ultimate Fighting Championship victories within the distance as of 11 Dec 2021. He extended his record at UFC 269, defeating Dustin Poirier with a third-round submission to defend his lightweight championship title. It was the 15th time that Oliveira had made an opponent tap out – the **most UFC submissions**.

The **most UFC finishes (female)** is 10, by Amanda Nunes (BRA) between 3 Aug 2013 and 6 Mar 2021. But her record for **most consecutive UFC wins (female)** – 12 – came to an end at UFC 269 with her shock defeat to Julianna Peña.

Most significant strikes landed in a UFC match

Max Holloway (USA) connected with 445 significant strikes in five rounds of his featherweight bout against Calvin Kattar on 16 Jan 2021, at UFC Fight Island 7 in Abu Dhabi, UAE.

MOST MATCHES WON BY A SUMO WRESTLER

In Dec 2021, GWR presented five certificates to sumo legend Hakuho Sho (JPN, b. MNG), who had recently retired after a glittering career. He won a total of 1,187 bouts, of which 1,093 were in the *makuuchi*, sumo's highest tier of competition: the **most top-division match wins**. Across sumo's six annual tournaments (*honbasho*), Hakuho recorded the **most top-division championship wins** (45) – including the **most undefeated** (16), where he won with a perfect record. He retired as the **longest-reigning yokozuna**, having competed at sumo's highest rank for 84 *honbasho*.

Most wins of the men's *kata* at the World Karate Championships

There are two main disciplines of competition at the World Karate Championships: *kata*, in which practitioners perform a sequence of correct forms and postures; and *kumite*, a sparring bout. On 20 Nov 2021, Ryo Kiyuna (JPN) claimed his fourth consecutive *kata* world championship title in Abu Dhabi, UAE.
- **Women's *kata***: four, by Yuki Mimura in 1988, 1990, 1992 and 1996; and Atsuko Wakai (both JPN), consecutively between 1998 and 2004.
- **Men's *kumite***: five, by Rafael Aghayev (AZE) between 2006 and 2016.
- **Women's *kumite***: four, by Guusje van Mourik (NLD) between 1982 and 1988.

Most International Judo Federation (IJF) World Tour gold medals

On 12 Jan 2021, Clarisse Agbegnenou (FRA) won her 18th gold in the women's -63 kg category on the IJF World Tour. She matched the tally of Kosovo's Majlinda Kelmendi in the women's -52 kg.

The **most medals** overall is 39, by Urantsetseg Munkhbat (MNG) in the women's -48 kg and -52 kg categories.

Hakuho's father, Jigjidiin, won a silver medal for Mongolia in freestyle wrestling at the 1968 Olympics.

Extreme Sports

FASTEST SPEED SKYDIVING (FEMALE, FAI-APPROVED)
On 29 Oct 2021, Maxine Tate (USA) achieved an average vertical speed over three seconds of 459.09 km/h (285.26 mph) at the 2021 United States Parachute Association National Championships in Eloy, Arizona, USA. Tate, a skydiving world champion, broke her own record four times in eight jumps.

YOUNGEST X GAMES GOLD MEDALLIST
Gui Khury (BRA, b. 18 Dec 2008) won Skateboard Vert Best Trick aged 12 years 210 days on 16 Jul 2021. Khury became the first to land a 1080 in competition on a vert ramp, seeing off a field including 10-time gold medallist Tony Hawk.

Fastest speed skydiving (male, FAI-approved)
Kyle Lobpries (USA) hit 512.97 km/h (318.74 mph) in freefall at the 2021 USPA National Championships on 28 Oct 2021 in Eloy, Arizona, USA. Speed skydivers use a GPS tracking device to record their fastest average vertical speed in a three-second period during the scoring window of freefall, which starts at the exit altitude (13,000–14,000 ft above ground level; 3,962–4,267 m) and ends at around 5,600 ft (1,706 m).

Fastest timbersports hot saw
On 21 Aug 2021, Robert Ebner (DEU) took just 4.87 sec to cut three complete discs ("cookies") from a horizontal 46-cm-diameter (1-ft 6-in) trunk at the STIHL TIMBERSPORTS German Pro Championship in Gelsenkirchen. Hot saw competitors use custom-built, high-powered chainsaws to slice through the wood, but must not cut outside a marked 15-cm (6-in) section.

A week after Ebner's effort, Ole Magnus Syljuberget (NOR) completed the **fastest timbersports stock saw** in 8.51 sec at the Nordic Pro Championship in Stenkullen, Sweden. Competitors cut two cookies from a 10-cm (4-in) section of a horizontal tree trunk.

Fastest Antarctic Ice Marathon (female)
On 17 Dec 2021, Evija Reine (LVA) battled soft snow underfoot and temperatures dipping to -15°C (5°F) to complete the world's **most southerly marathon** in 4 hr 6 min 11 sec. She finished more than an hour ahead of the next-fastest woman in the field. Reine, a 30-year-old student doctor, broke Fiona Oakes's record of 4:20:02, which had stood since 2013.

MOST WINS OF THE RED BULL WOMEN'S CLIFF DIVING WORLD SERIES
Rhiannan Iffland (AUS) claimed her fifth consecutive world series title in 2021. She has dominated the competition since entering as a wildcard in 2016. Following the abandoned 2020 World Series, Iffland completed her second perfect season in a row in 2021, recording her 13th consecutive event win.

FASTEST 15 M SPEED CLIMB (FEMALE)
Aleksandra Mirosław (POL) scaled a 15-m (49-ft) wall in 6.84 sec at the Olympics on 6 Aug 2021. Sport climbing debuted at the Tokyo Games, and also featured bouldering and lead climbing elements. Mirosław, a two-time speed-climbing world champion, finished the overall competition in fourth place.

The **male** record was also broken in 2021, by Indonesia's Veddriq Leonardo in 5.20 sec in Salt Lake City, Utah, USA, on 28 May.

Most X Games gold medals (summer sports)
On 16 Jul 2021, Garrett Reynolds (USA) won his 14th gold at X Games, extending his record of **most BMX Street gold medals** to 12. He has also twice topped the podium in Real BMX. Reynolds joined an elite club on 14 gold medals: Dave Mirra (USA) and Jamie Bestwick (UK), also in BMX; and skateboarder Bob Burnquist (BRA).

Most X Games medals (winter sports)
At X Games Aspen 2022, Mark McMorris (CAN) and Jamie Anderson (USA) both increased their career medal haul to 21. McMorris won gold in Men's Snowboard Slopestyle for a record sixth time, while Anderson won silver in Women's Snowboard Slopestyle and Big Air. Another star performer at Aspen was Estonia's Kelly Sildaru, who claimed the outright record for **most X Games medals by a teenager**. She took gold in Ski SuperPipe on 21 Jan, her 10th X Games medal before the age of 20.

MOST MEDALS IN X GAMES SUMMER DISCIPLINES (FEMALE)
Letícia Bufoni (BRA) has won 12 skateboarding medals at the X Games: six golds, three silvers and three bronze. On 17 Jul 2021, she claimed the women's record for **most Skateboard Street golds** with her fifth victory in the event. Bufoni also has a gold medal from the RWN Multi Sport event at X Games Barcelona 2013.

Most wins of the Red Bull Men's Cliff Diving World Series
High-diver Gary Hunt (FRA, b. UK) claimed his ninth King Kahekili Trophy in 12 seasons in 2021. Amazingly, Hunt admits that he has a fear of heights – but only when there is no water beneath him!

Swimming

FASTEST SHORT COURSE 200 M FREESTYLE (FEMALE)

On 16 Dec 2021, Siobhán Haughey became the first swimmer from Hong Kong, China, to set a world record, winning the 200 m freestyle in 1 min 50.31 sec at the FINA World Swimming Championships (25 m) in Abu Dhabi, UAE. Haughey also claimed the 100 m freestyle title.

MOST MEDALS WON AT AN OLYMPIC GAMES (FEMALE)

Emma McKeon (AUS) claimed seven medals at the Tokyo Games in 2021, equalling the feat of Soviet gymnast Maria Gorokhovskaya at Helsinki 1952. McKeon won four golds – in the 50 m, 100 m and 4 x 100 m freestyle and 4 x 100 m medley – together with three bronze.

Fastest 4 x 100 m medley relay (male)*

On 1 Aug 2021, the USA – Ryan Murphy (backstroke), Michael Andrew (breaststroke), Caeleb Dressel (butterfly) and Zach Apple (freestyle) – won Olympic gold in 3 min 26.78 sec. Several relay world records were set in Tokyo, including:
- **4 x 100 m freestyle (female)**: 3 min 29.69 sec, by Australia (Bronte Campbell, Meg Harris, Emma McKeon and Cate Campbell) on 25 Jul.
- **4 x 200 m freestyle (female)**: 7 min 40.33 sec, by China (Yang Junxuan, Tang Muhan, Zhang Yufei and Li Bingjie) on 29 Jul.

Fastest 200 m breaststroke (female)

Tatjana Schoenmaker (ZAF) swam to Olympic glory on 30 Jul 2021, winning the 200 m breaststroke in 2 min 18.95 sec in Tokyo. She broke Rikke Møller Pedersen's record of 2 min 19.11 sec, which had stood since 2013.

FASTEST 4 x 100 M MIXED MEDLEY

The final of the first-ever Olympic mixed swimming event took place on 31 Jul 2021 in Tokyo, and was won by Great Britain in 3 min 37.58 sec. The team comprised (from left to right): Kathleen Dawson (backstroke), Adam Peaty (breaststroke), Anna Hopkin (freestyle) and James Guy (butterfly). It was the third GB team with which Peaty had set a world record in the event.

MOST PARALYMPIC SWIMMING MEDALS (MALE)

Daniel Dias (BRA) won 27 medals in the Paralympic pool from 2008 to 2021: 14 gold, seven silver and six bronze. Born with impairments to his upper and lower limbs, Dias didn't learn to swim until he was 16. He won three bronze at his final Paralympics in Tokyo before retiring from the sport.

Fastest 50 m breaststroke (female)

On 22 May 2021, 16-year-old Benedetta Pilato (ITA) touched home in 29.30 sec at the European Aquatics Championships in Budapest, Hungary. She was competing in the same pool where Lilly King had set the previous record in 2017.

Fastest short course 100 m butterfly (female)

Kelsi Dahlia (USA) won the first race of the 2021 International Swimming League (ISL) final in 54.59 sec on 3 Dec 2021. Dahlia was competing for the Cali Condors in Eindhoven, Netherlands. Other short course records to fall in 2021 included:
- **100 m backstroke (male)**: 48.33 sec, by Coleman Stewart (USA) at the ISL on 29 Aug in Naples, Italy.
- **50 m backstroke (female)**: 25.27 sec, by Maggie Mac Neil (CAN, b. CHN) at the FINA World Swimming Championships (25 m) in Abu Dhabi, UAE, on 20 Dec 2021.
- **1,500 m freestyle (male)**: 14 min 6.88 sec, by Florian Wellbrock (DEU) in Abu Dhabi on 21 Dec 2021.

Most gold medals won at different FINA World Swimming Championships (25 m)

Ranomi Kromowidjojo (NLD) won titles at six editions of the short course world championships between 2008 and 2021, matching the feat of the USA's Ryan Lochte between 2004 and 2014. Kromowidjojo claimed two golds in Abu Dhabi in Dec 2021 before announcing her retirement the following month. She won a staggering 45 FINA world championship medals.

Fastest 400 m surface finswimming (male)

On 21 Mar 2021, Oleksii Zakharov (UKR) clocked 2 min 55.57 sec at the CMAS (Confédération Mondiale des Activités Subaquatiques) Finswimming World Cup in Lignano Sabbiadoro, Italy. Surface finswimmers compete wearing a mask, snorkel and monofin.
The **female** record is 3 min 12.10 sec, by Sun Yi Ting (CHN) on 16 Jul 2018 in Belgrade, Serbia.

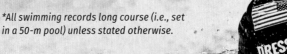

FASTEST 100 M BUTTERFLY (MALE)

On 31 Jul 2021, Caeleb Dressel (USA) won gold in the 100 m fly in 49.45 sec at the Tokyo Games in Japan, shaving 0.05 sec off his own 2019 world record. Dressel claimed five golds in Tokyo, cementing his position as one of the fastest swimmers in history. As of 1 Feb 2022, he held the **most current swimming world records** – nine.

All swimming records long course (i.e., set in a 50-m pool) unless stated otherwise.

Water Sports

First Olympic surfing gold medallists

On 27 Jul 2021, Ítalo Ferreira (BRA) and Carissa Moore (USA) were crowned men's and women's shortboard champions at the Tokyo Games. The competition took place at Tsurigasaki Beach in Chiba, Japan. Ferreira defeated home favourite Kanoa Igarashi in the men's final before Moore overcame Bianca Buitendag.

Most World Surf League event wins

Days before his 50th birthday, surfing legend Kelly Slater (USA) claimed the Billabong Pro Pipeline in Hawaii, USA, on 5 Feb 2022 – his 56th title in the World Surf League (formerly the Association of Surfing Professionals). Slater defeated Seth Moniz in the final to seal his eighth Billabong title, 30 years after his first. The 11-time world champion described it as "the best win of my life".

Fastest 1,000 m canoe sprint (C2, men)

Serguey Torres and Fernando Jorge (both CUB) won Olympic gold in the men's C2 in 3 min 24.995 sec on 3 Aug 2021 at Sea Forest Waterway in Tokyo. It was Cuba's first-ever Olympic gold in canoe sprint.

Most ICF Canoe Slalom World Championships individual gold medals

On 26 Sep 2021, Jessica Fox (AUS, b. FRA) took her tally of solo world titles to eight with gold in the extreme women's slalom at the 2021 International Canoe Federation Canoe Slalom World Championships in Bratislava, Slovakia. Fox had previously won the K1 class three times and the C1 class four times – along with three team world titles.

Highest-scoring Olympic dive

On 7 Aug 2021, Yang Jian (CHN) was awarded 112.75 points for his forward four-and-a-half somersaults dive during the final round of the men's 10 m platform at the Tokyo Games. Yang surpassed Matthew Mitcham's 112.10-point dive at Beijing 2008 but had to settle for silver behind Cao Yuan.

Deepest constant weight freedive with bi-fins (female)

On 2 Jul 2021, Jennifer Wendland (DEU) swam down to a depth of 93 m (305 ft 1 in) at the AIDA Limassol Depth Games in Cyprus. She beat Alenka Artnik's previous record by 1 m (3 ft 3 in).

Fastest men's kite surfing speed (nautical mile)

Sylvain Hoceini (FRA) reached 39.11 knots (72.43 km/h; 45 mph) over 1 nautical mi (1.8 km; 1.1 mi) on 15 Jul 2020 at La Palme in France. Hoceini's achievement was verified by the World Sailing Speed Record Council.

MOST DIVING MEDALS AT AN OLYMPIC GAMES (COUNTRY)

China earned 12 medals at the Tokyo Games, winning seven of eight events and adding five silvers. This equalled the USA's haul from the 1932 Games, where they swept all four events. Synchronized events were added to the Olympics in 2000, doubling the medals on offer.

MOST POINTS WATERSKIING (MALE)

On 14 Oct 2021, Joel Poland (UK) scored 2,660.12 points at the International Waterski & Wakeboard Federation World Championships at Sunset Lakes in Okahumpka, Florida, USA. Poland slalomed two buoys on a 10.25-m line at 58 km/h (36 mph), scored 11,620 points in tricks and jumped 69 m (226 ft 4 in).

MOST CANOEING GOLD MEDALS AT AN OLYMPIC GAMES

New Zealand's Lisa Carrington won three events at the Tokyo Games, matching Vladimir Parfenovich (USSR) in 1980, Ian Ferguson (NZ) in 1984 and Danuta Kozák (HUN) in 2016. Carrington – nicknamed the "GOAT in a boat" – triumphed in the K1 200 m and 500 m and K2 500 m on 3–5 Aug 2021.

Carrington was awarded the 2021 Lonsdale Cup by the New Zealand Olympic Committee in honour of her wins.

FASTEST 2,000 M MEN'S LIGHTWEIGHT DOUBLE SCULLS

Fintan McCarthy and Paul O'Donovan (both IRL) won their Olympic rowing semi-final in 6 min 5.33 sec on 28 Jul 2021. The pair went on to take gold the next day. A total of six world-best rowing times fell at Tokyo's Sea Forest Waterway on 28 Jul, helped by a strong tailwind.

MOST OLYMPIC WATER POLO GOALS (FEMALE)

Maggie Steffens (USA) scored 56 times in 19 Olympic water polo matches between 2012 and 2021. In Tokyo, Steffens overtook Tania Di Mario's record of 47 goals and became one of only two women, along with teammate Melissa Seidemann, to claim three gold medals in the event. She also holds the **single Games** record of 21 goals, set during London 2012.

Tokyo 2020 rowing record-breakers

Class	Time	Nationality	Crew
Men's quadruple sculls	5:32.03	Netherlands	Tone Wieten, Koen Metsemakers, Abe Wiersma and Dirk Uittenbogaard
Women's quadruple sculls	6:05.13	China	Cui Xiaotong, Lyu Yang, Zhang Ling and Chen Yunxia
Women's coxless pairs	6:47.41	New Zealand	Grace Prendergast and Kerri Gowler
Women's coxed eights	5:52.99	Romania	Viviana Iuliana Bejinariu, Maria Tivodariu, Amalia Bereş, Ioana Vrînceanu, Magdalena Rusu, Mădălina Bereş, Denisa Tîlvescu, Georgiana Dedu and cox Daniela Druncea
Women's lightweight double sculls	6:41.36	Italy	Valentina Rodini and Federica Cesarini

Round-Up

MOST...

Olympic appearances by a female athlete

Sport shooter Nino Salukvadze (GEO) competed at her ninth consecutive Olympics in Tokyo; she finished 31st in the 10 m air pistol and 25th in the 25 m pistol, and carried the Georgian flag at the opening ceremony. Salukvadze won a gold, silver and bronze over her 33-year Olympic career. The outright **Olympic appearance** record is 10, by equestrian Ian Millar (CAN) between 1972 and 2012.

Tokyo welcomed another age-defying athlete in 46-year-old gymnast Oksana Chusovitina (UZB), who participated in qualifying for the women's vault. It was her eighth Games in a row since 1992 – the **most Olympic appearances by a gymnast**.

Points scored in 60 m 36-arrow outdoor compound archery (female)

Ella Gibson (UK) shot 358 out of 360 on 12 Sep 2021 at the Battle of Britain 1440 event in Burnham-on-Sea, Somerset, UK. All World Archery 36-arrow records must be set as part of a full 1440 round, which comprises 144 arrows shot over four distances: 30 m, 50 m, 70 m and 90 m for men; and 30 m, 50 m, 60 m and 70 m for women.

Stage wins at the Dakar Rally

Stéphane Peterhansel (FRA) triumphed in 82 stages of the iconic off-road race between 1988 and 2022. He won stage 10 of the 2022 Dakar Rally in Saudi Arabia – his 49th victory in a car. Peterhansel also claimed 33 stage wins in the motorcycle class.

Medals won at the ISU World Synchronized Skating Championships by a team

Between 2000 and 2022, Marigold IceUnity (FIN) earned 14 world-championship medals: five golds, seven silvers and two bronze.

Open singles titles at the World Indoor Bowls Championships (female)

Katherine Rednall (UK) claimed a record fourth women's singles title on 20 Jan 2022, defeating Alison Merrien in two sets at Potters Leisure Resort in Hopton-on-Sea, Great Yarmouth, UK.

Horseshoe Pitching World Championships

Pitcher Alan Francis secured his 25th men's title in 2021, winning all 15 of his matches in Winnemucca, Nevada, USA. At the same event, Joan Elmore equalled the **female** record of 10, first set by Vicki Chapelle Winston (all USA) from 1956 to 1981.

SMALLEST COUNTRY BY POPULATION TO WIN AN OLYMPIC MEDAL

San Marino (population: 34,009) won three medals at the Tokyo Games in 2021. Alessandra Perilli (b. ITA) got the ball rolling with a bronze in the women's trap shooting on 29 Jul 2021, and then added a silver in the mixed trap team event with Gian Marco Berti two days later (above). Myles Amine (b. USA, inset) added a bronze in the 86 kg men's freestyle wrestling on 5 Aug.

UFC fights

On 19 Feb 2022, Jim Miller (USA) stepped into the octagon for the 39th time, taking on Nikolas Motta in a lightweight clash at UFC Vegas 48. Miller knocked out his opponent in the second round to record his 23rd victory in the championship – equalling Donald "Cowboy" Cerrone's (USA) record for **most UFC wins**. Cerrone had taken part in 37 UFC bouts.

UFC fights won by KO/TKO

Derrick Lewis (USA) knocked out 13 UFC opponents between 19 Apr 2014 and 18 Dec 2021. Heavyweight Lewis gained sole possession of the UFC KO record with his first-round stoppage of Chris Daukaus at UFC Fight Night 199 in Las Vegas, Nevada, USA.

MOST ARCHERY WORLD CUP WINS

Sara López (COL) sealed her sixth Archery World Cup title in the women's compound on 29 Sep 2021, beating Toja Ellison 147–145 in the final in Yankton, South Dakota, USA. López moved one clear of Brady Ellison's total of five men's recurve titles. The Archery World Cup began in 2006 and comprises four qualifying events and a final.

MOST TRIALS WORLD CHAMPIONSHIPS

Toni Bou (ESP) continued his domination of the sport of motorcycle trials in 2021, taking his total championships to 30. He has won 15 titles outdoors at the Fédération Internationale de Motocyclisme (FIM) Trial World Championships and 15 titles indoors at the FIM X-Trials – consecutively, since 2007.

HIGHEST SCORE IN UCI ARTISTIC CYCLING (MEN'S SINGLES)

Artistic cyclists present a five-minute programme set to music on fixed-gear bicycles. Lukas Kohl (DEU) scored 214.20 in Oberbüren, Switzerland, on 18 Sep 2021.

The **open pair** record also fell in 2021, to Max Hanselmann and Serafin Schefold (both DEU) with 173.50 in Öhringen, Germany, on 29 Aug.

MOST OLYMPIC EQUESTRIAN MEDALS

Isabell Werth (DEU) earned 12 medals across six Games between 1992 and 2021. Riding Bella Rose 2, she took gold in the team dressage and an individual silver on 27–28 Jul 2021 at Baji Koen Equestrian Park in Tokyo, Japan. Werth is one of only three athletes to win gold at six different Olympics, together with canoeist Birgit Fischer and fencer Aladár Gerevich.

FASTEST-RUN INDOOR 1,500 M (MALE)

On 17 Feb 2022, Jakob Ingebrigtsen (NOR) ran 1,500 m in 3 min 30.60 sec at a World Athletics Indoor Tour meeting in Liévin, France. The 21-year-old, the youngest of three middle-distance-running brothers, won gold in the 1,500 m at the Tokyo Olympics on 7 Aug 2021.

Heaviest weightlifting +87 kg total (female)

Li Wenwen (CHN) lifted a total of 335 kg (738 lb 8 oz) on 25 Apr 2021 at the Asian Weightlifting Championships in Tashkent, Uzbekistan. This comprised the **heaviest snatch** – 148 kg (326 lb 4 oz) – and the **heaviest clean & jerk** – 187 kg (412 lb 4 oz). Li went on to take the women's super-heavyweight gold at the Tokyo Olympics at the age of just 21.

Heaviest weightlifting 81 kg clean & jerk (male)

Teenage sensation Karlos Nasar (BGR) lifted 208 kg (458 lb 8 oz) on 12 Dec 2021 at the International Weightlifting Federation (IWF) World Championships in Tashkent. Nasar became 81-kg world champion aged 17, breaking the IWF Youth, Junior and Senior world records with his clean & jerk.

Highest score in a frame of professional snooker

Jimmy Robertson (UK) racked up a score of 178 in one frame at the 2021 Scottish Open in Llandudno, Wales, UK, on 7 Dec. During his second-round match with Lee Walker, Robertson made a clearance of 133, having accrued 44 points in fouls and potted a single red.

First person with Down's syndrome to complete a sprint triathlon (female)

On 7 Aug 2021, Jade Kingdom (UK) took part in the sprint distance race at the London Triathlon, swimming 750 m (0.4 mi), cycling 20 km (12.4 mi) and running 5 km (3.1 mi). She finished the event in 2 hr 39 min 55 sec, raising more than £15,000 ($19,600) for the North Devon Hospice.

Fastest-run 100 miles (female)

On 18 Feb 2022, Camille Herron (USA) finished the USATF 100 Mile Road Championships in Henderson, Nevada, USA, in 12 hr 41 min 11 sec. Competing in her first race in the Masters category (age 40–44), Herron sustained an average pace of a mile every 7.37 min to break her own world record. She won the race outright, finishing half an hour ahead of her nearest male competitor. Herron also broke the ultra-distance record for **farthest run in 12 hours (female)**, covering 152.83 km (94.96 mi).

Fastest wheelchair marathon (T53/54, male)

On 21 Nov 2021, Marcel Hug (CHE) took just 1 hr 17 min 47 sec to reach the finish line at the Oita International Marathon in Japan. He broke the 22-year-old men's wheelchair marathon record of 1 hr 20 min 14 sec – also set in Oita, by Hug's compatriot Heinz Frei – by more than two minutes.

MOST WINS OF BADMINTON'S SUDIRMAN CUP

On 3 Oct 2021, China secured its 12th international mixed-team championship with a 3–1 victory over Japan in Vantaa, Finland. First contested in 1989, the Sudirman Cup is a biennial badminton competition with ties consisting of up to five matches: men's and women's singles, doubles, and mixed doubles.

Shiffrin is the only skier, male or female, with World Cup wins in all six individual Alpine disciplines.

MOST FIS ALPINE SKI WORLD CUP RACE WINS IN ONE DISCIPLINE

On 11 Jan 2022, Mikaela Shiffrin (USA) won her 47th Fédération Internationale de Ski World Cup slalom race in Schladming, Austria – the most victories in a single discipline of Alpine skiing. Shiffrin moved one clear of Ingemar Stenmark, who won 46 giant slalom races in 1975–89. It was Shiffrin's 73rd World Cup triumph in total, consolidating third place on the all-time list.

Stop Press

The following entries were approved and added to our database after the official closing date for this year's submissions.

Highest-altitude fashion show on land
On 23 Sep 2021, an eco-friendly fashion show took place at 5,500 m (18,044 ft) at Gokyo 6th Lake View Point in Nepal. It was organized by Pankaj K Gupta (IND), Ramila Nemkul and Riken Maharjan (both NPL).

Largest washing-machine pyramid
To celebrate National Recycling Week, Currys and Ainscough Training Services (both UK) built a pyramid of 1,496 washing machines in Bury, Lancashire, UK, on 24 Sep 2021. The final structure was 13.6 m (44 ft 7 in) tall.

Most varieties of cheese on a pizza
On 25 Sep 2021, chef Julien Serri, cheesemaker François Robin and YouTuber Morgan Niquet (all FRA) prepared a pizza featuring 834 different types of cheese in Lyon, France. The dairy-drenched delight was prepared for the Sirha food-service trade fair.

Longest line of postcards
Viewspire (USA) arranged 23,446 postcards in a row in Commerce Township, Michigan, USA, on 9 Oct 2021. The event was part of Viewfest 2021, a psychologist-curated community event.

Fastest time to change four wheels on a car
On 16 Oct 2021, a team of four apprentices from the Lucky Car garage chain (AUT) changed four wheels on a Ford Focus in 49.03 sec in Vienna, Austria.

Largest body pillow
On 23 Oct 2021, That Pillow Guy unveiled a giant pillow in the likeness of YouTube vlogger David Dobrik (both USA) measuring 18.3 x 5.03 x 1.55 m (60 ft x 16 ft 6 in x 5 ft 1 in) in Vernon Hills, Illinois, USA.

Largest vegan burger
Finnebrogue Artisan (UK) created a 162.5-kg (358-lb 4-oz) vegan burger, as verified on 18 Nov 2021 in Downpatrick, County Down, UK. The patty was a scaled-up version of their Naked Evolution Burger, topped with vegan bacon, crispy onions, vegan cheese, burger sauce, lettuce, tomatoes and pickles.

Longest time standing on one leg (blindfolded)
On 21 Nov 2021, 12-year-old Max Petoe (AUS) balanced on one leg while blindfolded for 35 min in Melbourne, Victoria, Australia.

Fastest short course 50 m breaststroke (male)
Hüseyin Emre Sakçı (TUR) swam two lengths of a 25-m pool in 24.95 sec on 27 Dec 2021. He was competing in Gaziantep, Turkey.

Most countries identified from their outline in one minute
Adam Saeed (BHR) named 85 nations from their outlines on 11 Jan 2022 in Manama, Bahrain. He reclaimed the record, having first broken it with 70 on 8 Jul 2021.

Most basketball figure-eight moves in one minute
Luka Trpin (SVN) passed a basketball through his legs in a figure-of-eight shape 74 times in 60 sec in Ljubljana, Slovenia, on 15 Jan 2022.

Fastest half-marathon dressed as a ninja
On 15 Jan 2022, Kit Marlar (UK) ran 13.1 mi (21 km) in 1 hr 44 min 21 sec garbed as a *ninjutsu* warrior. He was competing at the Battersea Park Half Marathon in London, UK.

Fastest time to cut five apples in the air by sword
Moyin Xingluo, aka Liang Yizhi (CHN), sliced through five airborne apples in 11.13 sec on 17 Jan 2022 in Tai'an, Shandong, China. He threw the fruit up himself and sheathed his bamboo sword between cuts. His feat was live-streamed on the video platform Douyin.

First female referee in the Africa Cup of Nations
Salima Mukansanga (RWA) officiated Zimbabwe's 2–1 win over Guinea at the Stade Ahmadou Ahidjo in Youandé, Cameroon, on 18 Jan 2022. Mukansanga, who had previously refereed at the Olympics and the FIFA Women's World Cup, led an all-female officiating team.

Most YA authors identified by book title in one minute
On 24 Jan 2022, V Varun Sriram (IND) named 42 young-adult writers by their works in 60 sec in Chennai, India. He was just eight years old.

Largest gummy candy
On 27 Jan 2022, Shiba (IRN) unveiled a dolphin-shaped candy weighing 1,212.5 kg (2,673 lb) in Tehran, Iran. That's about six times the average weight of a bottlenose dolphin (*Tursiops truncatus*). The gummy was 3.5 m (11 ft 5 in) long and 2 m (6 ft 6 in) wide.

Largest donation of sweaters in one hour
Lakshyaraj Singh Mewar (IND) celebrated his birthday on 28 Jan 2022 by distributing 2,800 sweaters in 60 min in Udaipur, Rajasthan, India.

Most spiderman knuckle push-ups in one minute
On 29 Jan 2022, "Push-Up King" Luis Vargas (USA) completed 89 Spidey-style push-ups in 60 sec in Marblehead, Massachusetts, USA.

Two days earlier, Luis set the same record while encumbered with a **20-lb pack**, executing 71 reps in the time frame.

Longest lightning flash
A flash of lightning spanned a horizontal distance of 768 km (477.2 mi) across the US states of Mississippi, Louisiana and Texas on 29 Apr 2020. The event was verified by the World Meteorological Organization on 1 Feb 2022.

The **longest-lasting lightning flash** was also ratified on the same day. It occurred over Uruguay and northern Argentina on 18 Jun 2020 and lasted for 17.102 sec.

Most consecutive donuts (spins) in an electric car on ice
Stunt driver Terry Grant (UK) pulled off 69 successive spins on a frozen sea in Piteå, Sweden, on 3 Feb 2022. Terry, who was driving a standard-production Porsche Taycan 4S Cross Turismo electric car with winter tyres, had to keep within a circle with a diameter twice the length of his car.

Fastest 20-m tightrope walk (full-body burn)
On 3 Feb 2022, Maurizio Zavatta (ITA) traversed a 20-m (65-ft) tightrope 10.5 m (34 ft) off the ground in 14.34 sec – while on fire! The feat of fiery funambulism took place at the iconic Monza racetrack circuit in Italy for *Lo Show dei Record*.

Not to be outdone, on the same day Niklas Brennsund (NOR) completed the **most paper walls walked through during a full-body burn in one minute** – 13.

Most awareness ribbons made in one hour (team)
On 4 Feb 2022, a group of 54 volunteers from the Emirates Oncology Society (UAE) produced 2,828 ribbons in Dubai. The record was organized to raise awareness for World Cancer Day.

Most drinking glasses stacked on a ball balanced on a stick held in the mouth
On 6 Feb 2022, Richard Ljungman (SWE) kept 14 stacked glasses aloft in Gothenburg, Sweden. Richard is a professional balance artist and founder of Cirkusskolan, a circus school based in Sweden.

Fastest 1 km ice swim (male)
Marcin Szarpak (POL) swam 1 km (0.6 mi) in 11 min 48.1 sec at the 4th International Ice Swimming Association World Championship held in Głogów, Poland, on 7 Feb 2022. The water temperature during his swim was 3°C (37.4°F).

Most water balloons burst under the armpit in one minute
On 10 Feb 2022, Mr Cherry, aka Cherry Yoshitake (JPN), exploded 16 water balloons in 60 sec on the set of *Lo Show dei Record* in Milan, Italy.

Largest continuous GPS drawing by bicycle in 12 hours (individual)
On 14 Feb 2022, the Pedalling Picasso, aka Anthony Hoyte (UK), drew a picture on GPS exercise app Strava by riding 112 km (69.59 mi) around the Italian city of Milan. The image depicted an artist with a paintbrush behind his ear.

Fastest double ascent springboard chop
GWR was saddened to learn of the passing of timbersports competitor and world record holder Martin Komárek (CZE) in Mar 2022. On 18 Feb, Martin completed a double ascent springboard chop in 1 min 57 sec in Milan, Italy. Competitors have to climb a pole by cutting notches in the wood and inserting springboards on which to stand, before finally hacking through the top of the pole.

Most *udon* eaten in three minutes
Jeremy Lanig (USA) polished off 1,565 g (3 lb 7 oz) of *udon* noodles in 180 sec on the set of *Sekai no Hate Made ItteQ!* in Takamatsu, Kagawa, Japan, on 20 Feb 2022. The noodle-mad English-language teacher successfully returned the record to Kagawa Prefecture, which is known for *udon*.

Most pine boards broken in one minute by a team of two (mixed)
Taekwondo first-degree black belts – and married couple – Lisa and Chris Pitman (both UK) smashed through 316 wooden planks by hand in Milan, Italy, on 24 Feb 2022.

Most rollovers by a dog in one minute
On 24 Feb 2022, Maya rolled over 52 times in 60 sec in Stukenbrock, Germany. She was performing with trainer Wolfgang Lauenburger (DEU).

Fastest one-mile swim across the Drake Passage (Pacific Ocean to Atlantic Ocean)
The Drake Passage is a wild stretch of water between South America and Antarctica, linking the Pacific and Atlantic oceans. The quickest 1-mi (1.6-km) swim in this channel is 15 min 3 sec, by Bárbara Hernández Huerta (CHL) on 27 Feb 2022. Huerta's extreme open-water swims have earned her the nickname Ice Mermaid.

Largest collection of *Sonic the Hedgehog* memorabilia
Barry Evans (USA) has amassed 3,050 items relating to Sega's spiky speedster, as verified on 1 Mar 2022 in Dayton, Texas, USA. He has been collecting for more than 30 years.

Largest display of oil lamps
On 1 Mar 2022, a total of 1,171,078 oil lamps were arranged on the banks of the river Shipra in Ujjain, Madhya Pradesh, India, for the annual Maha Shivaratri festival. It was overseen by the Department of Culture, Government of Madhya Pradesh.

Fastest swim crossing of False Bay (male)

It took Kyle Stephens (ZAF, b. 17 Mar 2005) 8 hr 8 min 15 sec to swim the 32.8 km (20.4 mi; 17.7 nautical mi) between Miller's Point and Rooi Els in South Africa on 1 Mar 2022. Aged 16 years 349 days, he is also the **youngest** to cross it.

On 20 Feb 2022, Simon Ince (ZAF, b. 30 Jul 1959) became the **oldest person to swim across False Bay**, aged 62 years 205 days. The records were ratified by the Cape Long Distance Swimming Association and the False Bay Swimming Association.

Most money raised by an online campaign in one week

The UK Disasters Emergency Committee raised £61,997,547 ($81.5 m) between 3 and 10 Mar 2022. Fifteen UK aid agencies united to ask the public to donate towards relief efforts supporting those displaced by the conflict in Ukraine.

Most people unboxing at the same time (multiple venues)

Samsung India Electronics Private Ltd staged their "Epic Unboxing" event across India on 5 Mar 2022. In all, 1,820 people opened the new Samsung Galaxy S22 Ultra smartphone simultaneously.

Most skips by a robot in one minute

PENTA-X (JPN) jumped over a skipping rope 170 times in 60 sec in Kanagawa, Japan, on 5 Mar 2022. The robot, made by the Ricoh Company, smashed the previous record of 106.

Heaviest elephant bar deadlift (female)

On 6 Mar 2022, Tamara Walcott (USA) completed an elephant bar deadlift of 641 lb (290.7 kg) at the Arnold Sports Festival in Columbus, Ohio, USA.

Fastest marathon run by a married couple (aggregate time)

Mao Ichiyama and Kengo Suzuki (both JPN) clocked a combined running time of 4 hr 26 min 30 sec at the Tokyo Marathon in Japan on 6 Mar 2022. They beat the previous record from 2017 by just 35 sec.

Most soccer-ball rolls from eye to eye in one minute

Freestyler Yuuki Yoshinaga (JPN) rolled a football between his eyes 251 times in 60 sec in Katsushika, Tokyo, Japan, on 19 Mar 2022.

Largest collection of soft-drink cans (same brand)

Christian Cavaletti (ITA) had 12,402 Pepsi cans as of 19 Mar 2022. He began collecting with his brother in 1989, and has now amassed items from 81 different countries.

Longest triple jump (female)

Yulimar Rojas (VEN) hopped, stepped and jumped 15.74 m (51 ft 7.6 in) at the World Athletics Indoor Championships on 20 Mar 2022. Rojas smashed her own **indoor** and **outdoor** world records (see p.231) in Belgrade, Serbia.

On the same day, Armand Duplantis (SWE, b. USA) extended his **highest pole vault (male)** record to 6.20 m (20 ft 4 in), while Grant Holloway (USA) equalled his **fastest indoor 60 m hurdles (male)** time of 7.29 sec.

Most nationalities in a yoga lesson

Yoga instructor Nisha Agrawal led a 40-min class for people from 114 different nations in Doha, Qatar, on 25 Mar 2022. The lesson was organized by the Indian Sports Centre under the aegis of Qatar's Embassy of India.

Highest score in ice dance figure skating

Gabriella Papadakis and Guillaume Cizeron (both FRA) claimed their fifth world championship title with a score of 229.82 in Montpellier, France, on 25–26 Mar 2022. Their total – which beat their own record from the Winter Olympics (see p.220) – comprised both the **highest-scoring rhythm dance** (92.73) and **free dance** (137.09).

Largest LEGO®-brick word

On 26 Mar 2022, a trio of Boston University students – Luo Wenqi, Wei Xiaoya and Zhang Yufan (all CHN) – spelt the word "Terriers" using 9,697 LEGO pieces in Massachusetts, USA. Rhett the Boston Terrier is the university's mascot.

Most wins of the Women's Bandy World Championship

Sweden's women secured their 10th world bandy title on 27 Mar 2022, defeating Norway 12–0 in the final held in Åby, Sweden. The only year to date that they have failed to triumph was 2014, when they were beaten 3–1 in the final by Russia.

Most powerful energy beam in a cyclotron

On 28 Mar 2022, the Superconducting Ring Cyclotron (SRC) at RIKEN (JPN) in Wakō, Saitama, Japan, produced an energy beam of 82,400 MeV (mega electron-volts).

Longest rap marathon (individual)

On 1–3 Apr 2022, Dalcon, aka Daniel Alcon (UK), rapped a continuous flow of lyrics for 39 hr 37 min 54 sec at his home in Valencia, Spain. Alcon was permitted 30 sec between tunes, and a 5-min rest break for every hour that he performed.

Fastest Women's University Boat Race

Cambridge (UK) won the Women's Boat Race in 18 min 22 sec on 3 Apr 2022. It was the Light Blues' fifth consecutive victory in the event, which sees rival crews from Oxford and Cambridge race a 4-mi 374-yd (6.7-km) course along the Thames in London, UK.

Most WWE matches (female)

Natalya (b. Natalya Neidhart, CAN/USA) had appeared in 1,137 World Wrestling Entertainment bouts as of 3 Apr 2022. A third-generation professional wrestler, she is the daughter of Hart Foundation member and Hall of Famer Jim Neidhart.

◗ Tallest stack of M&M's®

On 7 Apr 2022, Ibrahim Sadeq (IRQ) built a tower of seven button-shaped chocolates in under two minutes in Nasiriyha, Iraq. Ibrahim is the co-holder of the record for **most eggs balanced on the back of the hand** – 18. (See pp.82–83 for more.)

Largest quilling paper mosaic image

On 8 Apr 2022, Quilling Card (VNM) unveiled a 26.73-m² (287.72-sq-ft) reproduction of the Vincent van Gogh painting *The Starry Night* using the ancient art of paper quilling in Ho Chi Minh City, Vietnam.

On the same day, they oversaw 300 people making quilled birthday cards – the **most people quilling simultaneously**.

Fastest standing skateboard speed downhill (team)

On 9 Apr 2022, four members of the Virgin Media Speed Demons team – Peter Dashwood-Connolly, Jonathan Braun, Aaron Skippings (all UK) and Jennifer Alina Schauerte (DEU, b. USA) – reached 84.95 km/h (52.78 mph) on skateboards. As per the rules, they formed a chain by linking hands along the 100-m (328-ft) downhill course in Dalby Forest, North Yorkshire, UK.

Fastest 100 m FISO obstacle-course race

On 10 Apr 2022, Mark Julius Rodelas (PHL) completed a 100-m course with 12 ninja obstacles in 27.12 sec at the Philippine OCR 100M Open in Pasig. The event was held by the Fédération Internationale de Sports d'Obstacles (FISO).

The **female** record of 39.42 sec was also set at the event on the same day, by Kaizen Dela Serna (PHL).

Oldest gorilla in captivity

Fatou the western lowland gorilla (*Gorilla gorilla gorilla*) celebrated her 65th birthday on 13 Apr 2022. Estimated to have been born in the wild *c.* 1957, she arrived at Zoo Berlin in Germany in May 1959 and has resided there for 63 years. The typical life expectancy of captive gorillas is between 40 and 50 years.

Fastest time to stand 10 pencils on end

On a visit to GWR headquarters in London, UK, on 13 Apr 2022, 10-year-old Lewis Woodhead (UK) tested the steadiness of his hand by standing 10 pencils on their end in just 16.35 sec. Each pencil measured a minimum of 15 cm (5.9 in) in length, and had to remain upright for at least 5 sec.

Heaviest chandelier

A chandelier in the Masjid Misr mosque in Egypt's New Administrative Capital weighs 24,300 kg (53,572 lb) – roughly the same as four elephants. Constructed by Asfour Crystal International (EGY), its weight was verified on 14 Apr 2022. At 22.7 m (74 ft 5 in) in its greatest dimension – taller than the height of the White House in Washington, DC – it is also the world's **largest chandelier**.

Fastest time to solve a rotating puzzle tetrahedron while in freefall

Chinmay Prabhu (IND) unscrambled a QiYi Pyraminx in 24.22 sec during his first ever skydive. He made the leap over Sri Racha in Chonburi, Thailand, on 14 Apr 2022.

Most views for a cat on YouTube

A ragdoll cat named Puff from New York City, USA, had accrued 7,532,180,184 views on his YouTube channel "That Little Puff" as of 21 Apr 2022. Owned by Lynch Zhang (USA), "Chef Puff" first rose to fame on TikTok thanks to his culinary-inspired videos, in which he appears to prepare and cook a variety of dishes.

Largest uncut emerald

On 22 Apr 2022, the weight of the Chipembele emerald was confirmed to be 7,525 carats (1.5 kg; 3 lb 4 oz). It was owned by Eshed–Gemstar and Avraham Eshed (both ISR). The name "Chipembele" translates as "Rhino" in the dialect of the Bemba people of Zambia, where the gigantic gem was mined.

Largest gathering of people dressed as astronauts

A crew of 716 cosmic cosplayers landed in Derry, UK, on 23 Apr 2022. The mission was organized to launch "Our Place in Space", a scale model of the Solar System designed by artist Oliver Jeffers with Professor Stephen Smartt and Nerve Centre, a media arts centre in Northern Ireland.

Most wins of the World Snooker Championship (modern era)

On 2 May 2022, Ronnie O'Sullivan secured his seventh world snooker title at the Crucible Theatre in Sheffield, South Yorkshire, UK, matching the feat of Stephen Hendry (both UK). O'Sullivan beat Judd Trump 18–13 in the final of the 2022 tournament, where "The Rocket" also matched Steve Davis's (UK) **most World Snooker Championship appearances** – 30.

Most licensed manga characters in a mobile game

Puzzle RPG *Jumputi Heroes* (LINE Corporation, 2018) features 1,010 characters from the Japanese manga anthology *Weekly Shōnen Jump*, as verified on 2 May 2022.

Most expensive sports memorabilia sold at auction

On 4 May 2022, the No.10 shirt worn by soccer legend Diego Maradona during Argentina's 2–1 defeat of England at the 1986 FIFA World Cup was purchased by a mystery buyer for £7,142,500 ($8.9 m) at Sotheby's in London, UK.

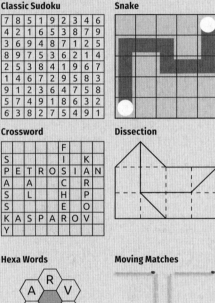

PUZZLE ANSWERS
Below are the solutions to the World Puzzle Federation challenges set on pp.176–77.

Classic Sudoku

Snake

Crossword

Dissection

Hexa Words

Moving Matches

Word Search

Diagonal Sudoku

Spot the Difference

CONSULTANTS

To help investigate and verify records across a broad spectrum of disciplines, GWR collaborates with many institutions, federated bodies and specialist groups. A few who assisted with this particular edition are highlighted below. For a full list, visit **www.guinnessworldrecords.com/records/partners.**

8000ers.com
Eberhard Jurgalski has developed the system of "Elevation Equality", a method of classifying mountain ranges and peaks. His website has become the main source of altitude statistics for the Himalayas and Karakoram ranges.

AbleGamers
Founded in 2004 by Mark Barlet, this US-based charity creates opportunities that enable play in order to combat social isolation, foster inclusive communities and improve the quality of life for people with disabilities. AbleGamers has empowered thousands of people to connect with the gaming world, and created multiple adaptive hardware solutions by working with engineering teams and research partners. #SoEveryoneCanGame

CANNA UK National Giant Vegetables Championship
Each year, Martyn Davis welcomes expert growers to the Malvern Autumn Show held in Worcestershire, UK. He ensures that all the vegetables comply with the strict criteria and are measured appropriately.

Channel Swimming Association
The CSA supports swimmers with the logistics of crossing the Strait of Dover and has been the governing body of Channel swimming since 1927. The CSA only ratifies swims that are conducted under its rules and that are accompanied by its observers.

Classic *Tetris* World Championship
Founded in 2010 by Vince Clemente and Adam Cornelius, the Classic *Tetris* World Championship is the premier international *Tetris* competition. Hundreds of players of all ages compete annually to be named the best *Tetris* player in the world. The CTWC is played using the 1989 version of *Tetris* on the original Nintendo Entertainment System.

Council on Tall Buildings and Urban Habitat
Based in Chicago, Illinois, USA, the CTBUH is the world's leading resource for professionals focused on the design, construction and operation of tall buildings and future cities.

ESPN X Games
Since 1995, ESPN's X Games has been the leading action-sports competition, spotlighting the world's best action-sports athletes in BMX, skateboard and Moto X in the summer as well as skiing, snowboarding and snowmobiling at its winter events.

Gerontology Research Group
Established in 1990, the GRG's mission is to slow and ultimately reverse ageing via the application and sharing of scientific knowledge. It also keeps the largest database of supercentenarians (i.e., people aged 110+), which is managed by GWR's senior gerontology consultant Robert Young.

Great Pumpkin Commonwealth
The GPC cultivates the growing of giant pumpkins – among other prodigious produce – by establishing universal standards and regulations that ensure quality of fruit and fairness of competition.

International Ice Swimming Association
Founded by Ram Barkai, the IISA was established in 2009 with a vision to formalize swimming in icy water – below a threshold of 5°C (41°F). It has put in place a set of rules to allow for maximum safety measures, and to regulate swim integrity in terms of distance, time and conditions.

International Slackline Association
The ISA aims to support and develop slackline communities of all sizes, as well as providing governance for slacklining as a competitive sport.

International Surfing Association
The ISA – founded in 1964 – is recognized by the International Olympic Committee as the world governing authority for surfing. The ISA crowned its first Men's and Women's World Champions in 1964; the first Big Wave World Champion in 1965; World Junior Champion in 1980; World Kneeboard Champions in 1982; Paddleboard Champions in 2012; and World Para Surfing Champions in 2015. ISA membership includes the surfing National Federations of 109 countries on five continents. The ISA is currently presided over by Fernando Aguerre.

The IRONMAN Group
The IRONMAN Group is the largest operator of mass-participation sports in the world. It provides more than a million participants annually the benefits of sport through its vast offerings across triathlon, cycling, running and trail/dirt events.

Metacritic
Since 2001, Metacritic has distilled opinions from the world's most respected and reliable entertainment critics into an easy-to-understand rating (i.e., the Metascore) to rank movies, music, videogames and television.

The Numbers
TheNumbers.com is the web's biggest database of cinema box-office information, with figures on 50,000 movies and 200,000 people in the film industry. It was founded in 1997 by Bruce Nash and is visited by more than 8 million people every year.

Ocean Rowing Society International
The ORSI was established in 1983 by Kenneth F Crutchlow and Peter Bird, later joined by Tom Lynch and Tatiana Rezvaya-Crutchlow. The organization documents all attempts to row the oceans and major bodies of water, and classifies, verifies and adjudicates ocean-rowing achievements.

Parrot Analytics
Parrot Analytics is the leading global content demand analytics company for the modern multi-platform TV business. It tracks more than 1.5 billion daily expressions of demand in over 100 languages.

Polar Expeditions Classification Scheme
PECS is a grading and labelling system for extended, unmotorized polar journeys that is overseen by a committee of polar-expedition specialists, managed by Eric Philips. Polar regions, modes of travel, routes and forms of aid are defined under the scheme, giving expeditioners guidance on how to classify, promote and immortalize their journeys.

Times Tables Rock Stars
Established in 2010 by maths teacher Bruno Reddy, *Times Tables Rock Stars* is a carefully sequenced programme – created by teachers for teachers, families and tutors – that successfully boosts the times-tables recall speed of more than 1 million children every year. It has been licensed to other educational institutions since 2013 and has been adopted by more than 16,000 schools (primary and secondary) worldwide.

VGChartz
Established in 2005 by Brett Walton, VGChartz is a business intelligence and research firm. It publishes over 7,000 unique weekly estimates relating to videogaming hardware and software sales/shipments, and hosts an ever-expanding games database.

World Cube Association
The WCA governs competitions for mechanical puzzles that are operated by twisting groups of pieces, such as the Rubik's Cube. Its mission is to have more competitions in more countries, all participating under fair and equal conditions.

World Jigsaw Puzzle Federation
The WJPF is an international organization dedicated to jigsaw puzzles, bringing together puzzlers from the world over for the World Jigsaw Puzzle Championship (WJPC). Its goals are to organize and supervise the WJPC, achieve the acknowledgement of jigsaw-puzzle competitions as a sport, establish a standard on rules and regulations for competitions, foster friendship among jigsaw-puzzle enthusiasts, and stimulate innovations in the field of jigsaw puzzles. The current chair is Alfonso Álvarez-Ossorio.

World Karate Federation
The WKF is the international governing body of karate. With 198 national federations and headquarters in Madrid, Spain, the WKF manages the sport of karate for its 100 million fans around the world and organizes events worldwide.

World Meteorological Organization
Dr Randall Cerveny is a President's Professor in Geographical Sciences who specializes in weather and climate. He has held the position of Rapporteur of Weather and Climate Extremes for the WMO since 2007.

World Open Water Swimming Association
Founded by Steven Munatones in 2005, WOWSA is the international governing body for the sport of open-water swimming. It provides membership and certification programmes as well as publications and online resources.

World Puzzle Federation
The WPF is an association of legal bodies with an interest in puzzles. The objects of the federation are to supervise the World Puzzle Championship, World Sudoku Championship and other WPF events; provide means for an international exchange of puzzle ideas; stimulate innovations in the field of puzzles; and foster friendship among puzzle enthusiasts worldwide.

World Sailing Speed Record Council
The WSSRC was recognized by the International Yacht Racing Union (now World Sailing) in 1972. The council of experts draws members from Australia, France, Great Britain and the USA.

World Ultracycling Association
WUCA is a non-profit organization dedicated to supporting ultracycling across the world. It holds the largest repository of cycling records for all bike types, and certifies successful rides for its members.

We also work with hundreds of individuals who know their subjects inside out. New experts to GWR this year specialize in cryptocurrency, rock climbing, political mobilizations, extinct megafauna and movie special effects, to name just a few. For a full list, visit **www.guinnessworldrecords.com/records/partners**.

Tom Beckerlegge is an award-winning writer whose books have been translated around the world. He is also GWR's lead sports consultant, updating hundreds of new records every year across athletic disciplines and liaising with numerous sporting federations to keep abreast of the latest stories. This year introduced him to backyard ultramarathons, Formula Drift and the trailblazing career of rally driver Michèle Mouton.

Yvette Cendes is a postdoctoral fellow in astronomy at Harvard & Smithsonian's Center for Astrophysics in Massachusetts, USA, specializing in radio astronomy and signals that vary over time, ranging from exoplanets to supernovae to black holes that shred stars. Yvette has written for publications such as *Astronomy* magazine and *Scientific American*, and is active on Reddit as u/Andromeda321, where her "astronomer here!" comments are read by millions around the world.

Erica Chenoweth is a professor at the Harvard Kennedy School and the Radcliffe Institute for Advanced Study at Harvard University. Chenoweth has authored/edited nine books and dozens of articles on mass movements, non-violent resistance and political activism. Chenoweth maintains the NAVCO Data Project and co-directs the Crowd Counting Consortium, analyzing the reach of US mobilizations. Their research has been featured in *The New York Times*, *The Washington Post* and *The Economist*.

Mike Chrimes retired as Director of Engineering Policy and Information at the Institution of Civil Engineers in 2014, after 37 years. A professional librarian and information scientist, he has contributed to many books and papers on engineering history and information services, such as *The Consulting Engineers* (2020), with Hugh Ferguson, and *Early Main Line Railways 2* (2019). He has an American Society of Civil Engineers History and Heritage Award, and was honoured with an MBE for services to engineering.

Ian Failes is the founder of *befores & afters*, a visual-effects and animation online magazine, print publication and podcast destination. He has also contributed to *fxguide*, *Cartoon Brew*, *VFX Voice*, *3D Artist*, *3D World*, *Syfy*, *Digital Arts*, *MovieMaker*, *Develop* and *Polygon*, and co-hosts the *VFX Notes* visual podcast. Ian is a regular speaker at conferences such as FMX, SIGGRAPH, Trojan Horse Was a Unicorn and SPARKFX. His first book – *Masters of FX* – was published in 2015.

Hugh Ferguson is a professional civil engineer who has worked as a contractor, consulting engineer, journalist and editor. After graduating with a civil-engineering degree, he worked in the industry before joining *New Civil Engineer* magazine, which he would go on to manage from 1976 to 1990. He is author (or co-author) of several books, including: *The Civil Engineers* (2011), *Engineers* (2012), *The Contractors* (2013), *Constructionarium* (2016) and *The Consulting Engineers* (2020).

David Fischer has been GWR's senior US sports consultant since 2006. He has written for *The New York Times* and *Sports Illustrated for Kids*, and has worked at *Sports Illustrated*, *The National Sports Daily* and NBC Sports. David has authored *Tom Brady: A Celebration of Greatness on the Gridiron* (2021), *The New York Yankees of the 1950s: Mantle, Stengel, Berra, and a Decade of Dominance* (2019) and *The Super Bowl: The First Fifty Years of America's Greatest Game* (2015).

John Fitzpatrick is a former Curator of Birds at Chicago's Field Museum of Natural History and was Executive Director of the Cornell Lab of Ornithology between 1995 and 2021. He has authored more than 150 scientific papers and co-authored four books – including the world's leading college-level textbook on ornithology. In 2002, he and colleagues launched the digital *eBird* platform, now one of the largest citizen-science projects.

Bryan G Fry holds a dual degree in Molecular Biology and Scientific Philosophy. Born in the USA, he was drawn to Australia by its numerous toxic creatures, and completed a PhD on the toxic peptides of the inland taipan (the **most venomous terrestrial snake**; see p.41). He is now associate professor at the University of Queensland, where he is group leader of the Venomics Laboratory. Bryan has led expeditions to over 40 countries and has also been inducted into The Explorers Club.

Robin Hutton has spent her adult life working in major event productions and the motion-picture business as a writer and producer. She is the author of the *NY Times* best-seller, *Sgt. Reckless: America's War Horse* (2014), and *War Animals: The Unsung Heroes of World War II* (2018), as well as the President of the non-profit Angels Without Wings. In 2019, Robin instituted the Animals in War & Peace Medal of Bravery and, in 2022, a new Distinguished Service Medal was added (see p.50).

Emily Lakdawalla is a science communicator, author and educator who specializes in planetary science and space exploration. She has contributed to Planetary Society publications since 2002, and is an associate editor for *Sky & Telescope*. Her first book, *The Design and Engineering of Curiosity*, is due to be followed up by the companion volume, *Curiosity and Its Science Mission: A Mars Rover Goes to Work*, in 2022. She also has an asteroid named after her: 274860 Emilylakdawalla.

Michael Levy is a freelance journalist as well as the editor-at-large for *Climbing* magazine. His work has also appeared in *The New York Times*, *Outside* and *Rock and Ice*, among other publications. Michael has climbed all over the world, from the big walls of Yosemite in California, USA, to the limestone cliffs of south-east Asia; from the lofty peaks in the Alaska Range to those in the Peruvian Cordillera Blanca.

Jonathan McDowell writes on the technical history of space exploration and maintains a comprehensive catalogue of space objects at his popular website **planet4589.org**. He is also an astrophysicist whose research publications include studies of cosmology, black holes, galaxies, quasars and asteroids, and he helps develop algorithms for X-ray astronomy as part of NASA's Chandra telescope team.

Merav Ozair is a global leading expert on blockchain and cryptocurrency, with an in-depth knowledge of global financial markets, and a background in data science and quant strategy. Currently, she applies her expertise to researching and experimenting with decentralized finance, non-fungible tokens (NFTs) and decentralized autonomous organizations, across different industries and business-use cases. She holds a PhD from NYU's Stern School of Business and is a co-founder of ChainVision.

Martin Pratt is an internationally respected expert in boundary-making, border management and territorial dispute resolution, and is the director of Bordermap Consulting. He is also an honorary professor at Durham University, UK, where he worked for over 20 years as director of research at the International Boundaries Research Unit. He is a geographer and cartographer by training, specializing in technical aspects of land and maritime boundary delimitation.

Robert Riener has been the professor for Sensory-Motor Systems at the Institute of Robotics at ETH Zurich, Switzerland, and professor of medicine at Balgrist University Hospital since 2003. Robert has published more than 400 peer-reviewed articles, 20 book chapters and filed 25 patents. He is also the initiator of the Cybathlon sports event for athletes that use, and engineers that develop, cutting-edge assistive technology.

Karl P N Shuker has a PhD in Zoology and Comparative Physiology from the University of Birmingham, UK, and is a Scientific Fellow of the Zoological Society of London, a Fellow of the Royal Entomological Society and a Member of The Society of Authors. He has penned 25 books as well as hundreds of articles covering many aspects of natural history. Karl's work has an emphasis on anomalous animals, including new, rediscovered and unrecognized species.

Maria Vassilopoulos is a publishing professional and book-trade historian, currently writing a PhD on the history of the British bookselling and publishing industry. She has previously worked for *The Bookseller*, the British Library and Waterstones, and has authored pieces on the history of the Publishers Association and The Book Society. Maria also holds the position of archivist for the Society of Young Publishers.

Matthew White is GWR's music, cricket and tennis consultant. Additionally, between 2009 and 2022, he pored over more than 50,000 published records as fact-checker and proofreader for the world's **best-selling annual**. After training as a journalist, Matthew landed his dream job as a member of the team that produced the final four editions of the *Guinness Book of British Hit Singles & Albums*. His latest project is a guide to musicians from his home county of Suffolk, UK.

Cassidy Zachary is a fashion historian specializing in the social and cultural significance of dress throughout history, right up to today. She is the creator and co-host (along with April Calahan) of the award-nominated iHeartRadio podcast *Dressed: The History of Fashion*, which *Vogue* has described as "the gold standard in fashion podcasting". Cassidy is also the co-author of the 2015 book *Fashion and the Art of Pochoir*.

Steven Zhang is a palaeontologist and Honorary Research Associate at the University of Bristol, UK. He is an expert in the evolution and fossil history of proboscideans – the group that contains elephants and their extinct cousins such as mammoths, mastodonts, stegodonts and deinotheres. Eager to tell the stories of these outlandish prehistoric beasts, he has conducted palaeontological outreach activities in museums and consulted for several TV documentaries.

Thanks also to...

Evan Ackerman (*IEEE Spectrum*); DC Agle, Ron Baalke, Glenn Orton (NASA/JPL); Rachael Anderson (Ekso Bionics); Scott Banks (Boardwalk Organ Restoration Committee); Mark Aston; Emmanuel Barraud (EPFL); Karl Battams (US Naval Research Laboratory); Edward Bell (Tiniest Babies Registry); Brian Bianco (Inspiration4); Annabelle Bozec (Herrenknecht AG); David Bruson; David Bruzon, Anna Burgess (Harvard University Library); Alice Carter (British Library); Martyn Chapman; Richard Chen (cryptoart.io); Brenna Connor, David Walter, Lee Graham (NPD Group); Philip Currie (University of Alberta); Tammie deVoogt Blaney (International Association of Structural Movers); Amy Dickin, Hattie Thorpe-Gunner (PDSA); Pádraig Egan; Taylah Egbers, Louise Baker, Sarah Cuthbert-Kerr (National Trust for Scotland); Kiah Erlich, Melinda Widlake, Michael Edmonds, Sarah Blask (Blue Origin); Federico Ferroni, Alex Reynolds (International Surfing Association); Barbara Finlay, Linda Beltz Glaser (Cornell University); Rosemary Firman, Abby Jones (Hereford Cathedral); Andrew Gallup (SUNY); Karla Grahn (Fly Denver); Victoria Grimsell; Bryony-Hope Green (British Esports Association); Thaneswar Guragai; Robert Gwynne, Simon Bayliss (National Railway Museum); Steven Haddock (Monterey Bay Aquarium Research Institute); JD Harrington, Sean Potter (NASA/HQ); Terry Harrison (New York University); Nick Hartwell (Nixus Sport and Entertainment); Suzanne Herrick, Joanna Danks (Minnesota Historical Society); Heidi Huebner (PUP Program, LAWA); Paul Hunn; Daniel Huot, Shaneequa Vereen, Courtney Beasley, Kathryn Hambleton (NASA/Johnson Space Center); Alan Jamieson (Minderoo-UWA Deep-Sea Research Centre); Sarah Jeffery (Martin-Baker); Rachel Jones; Steve Jones (Antarctic Logistics & Expeditions); Eliza Kavanagh (Publishers Association); Danny Klein (Food News Media); Louise Lee (Blue Cross); Tammy Lee Long, Madison Tuttle (NASA/Kennedy Space Center); Leah Linder, Benjamin Popkin (TikTok); Pedro Lopes (University of Chicago); Emma Lowe (*The Bookseller*); Jérôme Mallefet (Université catholique de Louvain); Pàdraig Mallon, Jacqueline McClelland (Irish Long Distance Swimming Association); Ray Mansell; Borislav Marinov (Exoskeleton Report); Rick Mayston; Mark McBride-Wright (Equal Engineers); Mary Melnyk; Thomas Mills, Tim Shephard (Dwarf Sports Association); Joël Minet (Muséum national d'Histoire naturelle); Monsters of Schlock (Burnaby Q Orbax and Sweet Pepper Klopek); François Moreau (Bouygues Construction); Peter Morris, David Allen, Henry Rzepa, Anna Simmons (Royal Society of Chemistry); Anushia Nair (data.ai); Greg Newby (Project Gutenberg); Kara O'Keeffe (Wisconsin Historical Society); Justin O'Schmidt (Southwest Biological Institute); Corina Oertli, Roland Sigrist (Cybathlon); Mariam Olayiwola; Matthew Oliver; Uffe Paulsen (Royal Danish Library); Gary Rendsburg (Rutgers University); Barry Rice (*Carnivorous Plant Newsletter*); Matthew Rogerson, Emma Beer (Institution of Civil Engineers); Ethan Ruparelia, Dan Schrieber (*QI/No Such Thing as a Fish*); William Ryan (Library of Congress); Eric Sakowski (Highest Bridges); Nancy Segal (Twin Studies Center); Tulsi Shah (Cambody Groarke); Lily Shallom (APOPO); Will Shortz, Matúš Demiger (American Crossword Puzzle Tournament); Nevan Simone, Amit Gupta, Jamie Stephens, Maria Esteva, Weijia Xu, Moriba Jah (University of Texas/ASTRIAGraph); Tina Smart; Christopher Smout (Institution of Mechanical Engineers); Samuel Stadler (Parrot Analytics); Jaclyn Swope (Nielsen IQ); Martyn Tovey; Gijs van der Velden, Merlin Moritz, Kasper Siderius (MX3D); Paul Walker-Emig; Heather Weintraub (Christie's); Annabel Williams (Guide Dogs); Nick Williamson, James Bartlett, Daryl Chapman, Helen Atwere, Denise Matthews, Rob Grant (RNIB); Mark Woods (Bible Society); Anatoly Zak (Russian Space Web); Lojdová Zdislava (Extreme Light Infrastructure Beamlines).

SVP Global Publishing
Nadine Causey

Editor-in-Chief
Craig Glenday

Managing Editor
Adam Millward

Editor
Ben Hollingum

Layout Editors
Tom Beckerlegge,
Rob Dimery

**Proofreading
& Fact-checking**
Matthew White

**Director of Publishing
& Book Production**
Jane Boatfield

Head of Studio
Fran Morales

Picture Researchers
Abby Taylor, Alice Jessop

Design
Paul Wylie-Deacon,
Rob Wilson, Jo Mansfield
at 55design.co.uk

Cover Design
Rod Hunt

Talent Researcher
Charlie Anderson

**Production & Distribution
Director**
Patricia Magill

Production Coordinator
Thomas McCurdy

Production Consultants
Roger Hawkins, Kevin
Sarney, Maximilian
Schonlau, Jens Pähler

**Head of
Commissioned Content**
Michael Whitty

Original Photography
Brien Adams, Dan Austin,
Alberto Bernasconi,
Felix Brandstetter, Dojo
Films, Jon Enoch, Rubén
Gil, Chuck Green, Laura
Grisamore, Paul Michael
Hughes, Diyan Kanardzhiev,
Edwin Koo, Kat Ku, Rob
Partis, Rod Penn, Kevin
Scott Ramos, Alex Regish,
Tim Stubbings

Indexer
Marie Lorimer

Global Sales Director
Joel Smith

**Head of Global Publishing
Licensing**
Helene Navarre

UK Key Account Manager
Mavis Sarfo

**Supply Chain &
Distribution Manager**
Isabel Sinagola

Global Marketing Director
Nicholas Brookes

**Head of Communications
(UK & International)**
Amber-Georgina Maskell

**PR Manager
(UK & International)**
Madalyn Bielfeld

**PR Executive
(UK & International)**
Alina Polianskaya

**Content Manager
(UK & International)**
Eleonora Pilastro

**Head of Communications
(Americas)**
Elizabeth Vaughan

**Senior PR Manager
(USA & Canada)**
Amanda Marcus

**Senior PR Manager
(LATAM)**
Alice Pagán

PR Executive (Americas)
Kylie Galloway

**Content Manager
(USA & Canada)**
Ali Rodriguez

**Content Manager
(LATAM)**
Luisa Sanchez

Reprographics
Resmiye Kahraman
at Born Group

Printing & Binding
MOHN Media Mohndruck
GmbH, Gütersloh,
Germany

British Library Cataloguing-in-publication data: a catalogue
record for this book is available from the British Library

UK: 978-1-913484-21-7
US: 978-1-913484-20-0
US PB: 978-1-913484-29-3
Middle East: 978-1-913484-22-4
Australia: 978-1-913484-23-1

Records are made to be broken – indeed, it is one of the key
criteria for a record category – so if you find a record that you
think you can beat, tell us about it by making a record claim.
Always contact us before making a record attempt.

Sustainability
At Guinness World Records, we continue to run our business
in the most sustainable, environmentally conscious way we
can. As part of that commitment, the pages of this book are
printed on a fully recycled paper, made of 100% reclaimed
paper and post-consumer de-inked pulp.

No chlorine bleaching is used in the
paper production process. It has
been awarded the Blue Angel and
EU Ecolabel recognition.

This paper is produced at the Steinbeis
Papier mill in Germany, which is one of
the most energy-efficient and low-emission
paper mills in Europe. The mill is focused on ecological
balance throughout the production process – from the
regional procurement of reclaimed paper as a raw material,
to production with an almost entirely closed energy and
water cycle.

GWR is committed to ethical and
responsible sourcing of paper, as well
as ink. We also work to ensure that all
our supply-chain partners meet the
highest international standards for
sustainable production and energy
management. For more information,
please contact us.

Thanks to innovative use of combined heat and power
technology, up to 52% less CO_2 was emitted in printing this
product when compared with conventional energy use.

Guinness World Records Limited has a very thorough
accreditation system for records verification. However, while
every effort is made to ensure accuracy, Guinness World
Records Limited cannot be held responsible for any errors
contained in this work. Feedback from our readers on any
point of accuracy is always welcomed.

Guinness World Records Limited uses metric and imperial
measurements. Exceptions are made for some scientific
data where metric measurements are universally accepted,
and some sports data. Where a specific date is given, the
exchange rate is calculated according to the currency values
at the time. Where only a year date is given, the exchange
rate is calculated from 31 Dec of that year.

Appropriate advice should always be taken when attempting
to break or set records. Participants undertake records
entirely at their own risk. Guinness World Records Limited
has complete discretion over whether or not to include any
particular record attempts in any of its publications. Being
a Guinness World Records record holder does not guarantee
you a place in any Guinness World Records publication.

PRINTED IN GERMANY

Global President
Alistair Richards

Governance
Alison Ozanne

Global Finance: Elizabeth Bishop,
Jess Blake, Lisa Gibbs, Lucy Hyland,
Kimberley Jones, Okan Keser, Jacob
Moss, Sutha Ramachandran, Ysanne
Rogers, Lorenzo Di Sciullo, Andrew
Wood
**Business Partnering & Product
Marketing:** Maryana Lovell, Blair
Rankin, Scott Shore, Louise Toms

Legal
Raymond Marshall
London: Matthew Knight, Mehreen
Moghul
Beijing: Mathew Alderson,
Greyson Huang, Jiayi Teng

IT & Operations
Rob Howe
Digital Technology & IT: Diogo Coito
Gomes, John Cvitanovic, Mike Emmott,
Adeyinka Folorunso, Sunil Gill,
Veronica Irons, Benjamin McLean,
Roelien Viljoen, Alex Waldu
Central Records Services: Adam Brown
Record Content Support: Lewis
Blakeman, Clea Lime, Mark McKinley,
Emma Salt, Mariana Sinotti Alves de
Lima, Dave Wilson, Melissa Wooton
Records Curation Team: Oliver de
Boer, Megan Bruce, Esther Mann, Will
Munford, Will Sinden, Luke Wakeham

Global People & Culture
Stephanie Lunn
London: Jackie Angus, Isabelle
Fanshawe, Matthew Niyazi,
Monika Tilani
Beijing: Crystal Xu, Nina Zhou
Tokyo: Emiko Yamamoto
New York: Rachel Gluck, Jennifer Olson
Dubai: Monisha Bimal

Brand & Digital
Katie Forde

Brand Strategy & Communications:
Juliet Dawson, Lucy Hunter, Doug Male
TV & Digital: Karen Gilchrist
Social Media: Josephine Boye, Lisha
Howen, Dominic Punt, Dan Thorne
Website Content: Sanj Atwal,
Connie Suggitt
Commissioned Content:
Michael Whitty
Video Production & Design:
Momoko Cunneen, Jesse Hargrave,
Aisheshek Magauina, Fran Morales,
Matthew Musson, Joseph O'Neil,
Alisa Zaytseva
Event Production: Alan Pixsley
Content Licensing: Kathryn Hubbard,
Catherine Pearce
Creative: Paul O'Neill

Global Consultancies
Marco Frigatti

Americas Consultancy
Carlos Martinez
Commercial Account Services:
Mackenzie Berry, Brittany Carpenter,
Carolina Guanabara, Ralph Hannah,
Nicole Pando, Kim Partrick, Michelle
Santucci, Joanna Weiss
Commercial Marketing: Alexia Argeros,
Ana Rahlves
Records Management: Raquel Assis,
Maddison Kulish, Callie Smith,
Carlos Tapia Rojas

Beijing Consultancy
Charles Wharton
Content Marketing: Chloe Liu
Editorial: Angela Wu
Commercial Account Services:
Catherine Gao, Xiaona Liu, Tina Ran,
Amelia Wang, Elaine Wang, Paige Wu
Commercial Marketing: Theresa Gao,
Lorraine Lin
Event Production: Fay Jiang
PR: Echo Zhan, Yvonne Zhang
Records Management: Ted Li, Vanessa
Tao, Alicia Zhao, Sibyl Zou

Dubai Consultancy
Talal Omar
Commercial Account Services:
Sara Abu-Saad, Naser Batat,
Mohammad Kiswani, Kamel Yassin
Commercial Marketing: Shaddy Gaad
Brand & Content Marketing:
Mohamad Kaddoura
Event Production: Daniel Hickson
PR: Hassan Alibrahim
Records Management: Reem Al
Ghussain, Sarah Alkholb, Hani
Gharamah, Karen Hamzeh

London Consultancy
Sam Prosser
Commercial Account Services:
Nicholas Adams, Monika Drobina, Fay
Edwards, Sirali Gandhi, Shanaye Howe,
Nikhil Shukla, Nataliia Solovei
Commercial Marketing: Amina Addow,
William Baxter-Hughes
Event Production: Fiona Gruchy-Craven
Records Management: Andrew Fanning,
Paul Hillman, Christopher Lynch,
Apekshita Kadam, Francesca Raggi
Global Demand Generation:
Angelique Begarin, Melissa Brown

Tokyo Consultancy
Kaoru Ishikawa
Brand & Content Marketing:
Masakazu Senda
Commercial Account Services:
Minami Ito, Wei Liang, Takuro
Maruyama, Yumiko Nakagawa, Nana
Nguyen, Masamichi Yazaki
Commercial Marketing: Hiroyuki
Tanaka, Eri Yuhira
Event Production: Yuki Uebo
PR: Kazami Kamioka
Records Management: Fumika
Fujibuchi, Aki Ichikawa, Mai McMillan,
Momoko Omori, Naomi-Emily Sakai,
Lala Teranishi, Kayo Ueda

Picture credits

1 Getty; **2** NASA/KSC, Rod Hunt; **3** Nintendo/Games Press; **4 (UK)** GWR; **5 (UK)** Jack Deery, BBC, GWR; **6 (UK)** GWR, Ethan Ruparelia/*QI*; **7 (UK)** Urdd Gobaith Cymru/Dafydd Owen, Shutterstock, Fun Kids Radio; **6 (US)** Shutterstock, Kevin Youngblood; **7 (US)** Getty; **4 (Aus/NZ)** Politix; **5 (Aus/NZ)** Shutterstock; **7 (Aus/NZ)** Alamy; **6 (MENA)** MDLBEAST Soundstorm; **8** Jon Enoch/GWR, Shutterstock; **9** Jon Enoch/GWR, Diyan Kantardzhiev/GWR, Games Press/Mojang, Games Press/Milestone, Shutterstock, Moby Games/EA, Games Press/Epic Games, YouTube; **10** GWR, Alex Regish/GWR, Alamy, Shutterstock; **11** Shutterstock; **12** Shutterstock, GWR; **13** GWR; **14** NASA; **15** Science Photo Library, NASA; **16** NASA, National Reconnaissance Office, Shutterstock; **17** NASA, NASA/KSC, NASA/Bill Ingalls, ATK, Shutterstock, NASA/Joel Kowsky, Amy Thompson; **18** Shutterstock, Getty, Virgin Galactic; **19** NASA, U.S. Army White Sands Missile Range/Applied Physics Laboratory, Shutterstock, Blue Origin; **20** Inspiration4/Twitter, NASA, Shutterstock; **21** SCH, NASA, Shutterstock, ESA, James Blair/NASA, Rod Hunt; **22** Tulsa World, Northrop Grumman, Getty; **23** CelesTrak, Brad Sease, NASA, Anatoly Zak/RussianSpaceWeb.com, Getty, Esperance Museum; **24** NASA, NASA/JPL-Caltech/University of Arizona, NASA/JPL-Caltech, Science Photo Library, CNSA, Shutterstock; **25** CNSA/EPA, NASA/JPL-Caltech, NASA/Johns Hopkins APL, NASA/JPL/Cornell University, Shutterstock; **26** ESO/M. Kornmesser, NASA/JPL-Caltech/ASI/USGS, NASA/JPL-Caltech/SSI; **27** NASA/MOLA Science Team/O. de Goursac, Adrian Lark, NASA/ESA/A. Simon, NASA/JPL-Caltech/MSSS, NASA/JHUAPL/SwRI, NASA/JPL-Caltech/Keck, NASA/ScienceCasts, Maxar/ASU/P. Rubin/NASA/JPL-Caltech; **28** Alamy, ESO/M. Kornmesser; **29** NASA/ESA/Zolt Levay, Science Photo Library, NASA/JPL-Caltech/STScI, ESO, Shutterstock, R. Sahai and J. Trauger (JPL)/NASA/ESA; **30** Thomas Shea/USA TODAY NETWORK; **31** ESA/ATG medialab, NASA/STScI; **32** SpaceX, Science Photo Library, NASA; **33** NASA, ESA, B. Welch (JHU) and D. Coe (STScI), ESA & NASA/*Solar Orbiter*/EUI team, NASA/Aubrey Gemignani; **34** Blue Origin, Getty, Shutterstock; **35** NASA, Shutterstock, Getty; **37** APOPO, Alamy, Brian Mckay, Shutterstock; **38** Shutterstock, Roman and Alexandra Uchytel, Prehistoric Fauna; **39** Roman and Alexandra Uchytel, Prehistoric Fauna, Roman Yevseyev, Science Photo Library, National Museum of Ireland; **40** Shutterstock, Brian Mckay, A. Palci/Flinders University; **41** Shutterstock, Alamy; **42** Alamy, Shutterstock, Tormod Amundsen/Biotope; **43** Shutterstock, Alamy, Angie Cederlund; **44** naturepl.com, Shutterstock, Science Photo Library; **45** Alamy, naturepl.com, Shutterstock; **46** Shutterstock, Alamy, Rajani Kurup/Anil John Johnson/Sabulal Baby, 2020 Walter de Gruyter GmbH, Berlin/Boston, Dr Steven Haddock; **47** NOAA, Alamy, Dr J. Mallefet - FNRS - UCLouvain, Science Photo Library, Discover Puerto Rico; **48** Kat Ku/GWR, Shadai Perez/GWR, Shutterstock; **49** Alberto Bernasconi/GWR, Shutterstock; **50** Nancy Latham Parkin, US War Dogs Association, Getty, National Archives, Dominika Frej for Gallop, Shutterstock; **51** Alamy, APOPO, Denver International Airport, Toronto Zoo, GWR; **52** Alamy, Shutterstock; **53** Alamy, Shutterstock; **54** Alamy, Qianshi Lin, Shutterstock; **55** Shutterstock, David Lees, Alamy, Zhao Chuang/PNSO; **56** GWR, Getty, Back to Healing/Damla Karaarslan; **57** GWR; **58** Brien Adams/GWR, GWR; **59** Shutterstock, Kevin Scott Ramos/GWR; **60** Martin Volken/moment.ch, Getty, Alzheimer's Research UK, Shutterstock; **61** Alamy, Shutterstock; **62** John Wright/GWR, Alberto Bernasconi/GWR, GWR, Paul Michael Hughes/GWR, Shutterstock; **63** Alberto Bernasconi/GWR, Kevin Scott Ramos/GWR, Shutterstock, Walter Succu/GWR; **64** Ranald Mackechnie/GWR, Paul Michael Hughes/GWR, Kevin Scott Ramos/GWR, Shutterstock; **65** Kevin Scott Ramos/GWR; **66** Shutterstock; **67** Dan Austin/GWR, Laura Grisamore/GWR, Shutterstock; **68** Penguin, Shutterstock; **69** Shutterstock; **70** Alamy, Shutterstock; **72** Kevin Scott Ramos/GWR, GWR, Mohammed Daw/GWR; **73** National University Hospital, Singapore, Kwek Family, Paul Michael Hughes/GWR, Peter Allen/DMG Media Licensing, Rob Partis; **74** Ryan Schude/GWR; **75** Alamy; **76** Go Visuals; **77** One Inch Dreams, onetotwo/Quirin Herterich, Shutterstock, SWNS, Rod Penn/GWR; **78** Piccard Family, Shutterstock, Photocall Ireland, Solar Impulse Foundation; **79** Getty, Alamy, GWR; **80** Paul Michael Hughes/GWR, Davide Canella/GWR, Shutterstock; **81** Rod Penn/GWR, Shutterstock, GWR; **82** Edwin Koo/GWR, Shutterstock, Alberto Bernasconi/GWR; **83** Shutterstock, GWR; **84** GWR, Diyan Kantardzhiev/GWR, Shutterstock; **85** Paul Michael Hughes/GWR, GWR, Shutterstock; **86** Shutterstock; **87** SWNS; **88** Diyan Kantardzhiev/GWR, GWR, Shutterstock; **89** Getty, Universal Pictures/Alamy, Alamy; **90** Alberto Bernasconi/GWR, Shutterstock, Paul Michael Hughes/GWR; **91** Captn Brandy/GWR, Shutterstock; **92** Shutterstock; **93** Richard Bradbury/GWR, Chukwuebuka Freestyle Entertainment, GWR, Shutterstock; **94** J. Chin/National Geographic/Shutterstock, John Bachar; **95** Pavel Blazek, Paolo Sartori, Javipec/ASP/Red Bull Content Pool, Chris Alstrin, Cheyne Lempe, Bobby Sorich, Alastair Lee/Posing Productions, Alamy; **96** Enrique Alvarez, Shutterstock; **97** Alamy, Shutterstock; **98–99** Miss Isle, International Surfing Association, Shutterstock, Getty, Marathon des Sables; **100** GWR, Alberto Bernasconi/GWR, Photos with Finesse, Ruben Gil/GWR; **101** Alberto Bernasconi/GWR, Ruben Gil/GWR; **102** Alamy, Shutterstock; **103** Shutterstock; **104** GWR; **105** Justin Clemons/Guardian/eyevine; **106** Rajiv Mundayat, Justin N Lane/Courtesy of US Chess, Shutterstock; **108** Casey Brooke Lawson, J-F Rioux, Marvel/Disney/Shutterstock; **109** Robert Partis/GWR; **110** ESA/NASA/SOHO; **111** Tim Stubbings/GWR; **112** Jon Enoch/GWR, Ranald Mackechnie/GWR, Drew Gardner/GWR, Shutterstock; **113** Shutterstock, Rod Hunt; **114** Shutterstock; **115** Shutterstock; **116** Cedar Point, Getty, Shutterstock, Alamy, Allison Missal Akright/Fridley Theatres; **117** Kevin Scott Ramos/GWR, David Torrence/GWR, Shutterstock; **118** Alamy, Getty, Shutterstock; **119** Shutterstock, Alamy; **120** Alamy, Jason deCaires Taylor, Shutterstock; **121** Alamy, Shutterstock; **122** Shutterstock, Alamy; **123** Shutterstock, Alamy; **124** Shutterstock, Alamy, Shakespeare Trust, Sportsfile pictures; **125** Getty, Alamy, Chris Parry/Ffestiniog Railway, Shutterstock; **126** Shutterstock; **127** Shutterstock; **128** Alamy, Shutterstock; **129** Shutterstock, Alamy, Getty; **130** Tommy Simonsen, Shutterstock, Janne Peräaho, Satu Härkönen, Alamy, VisitSamsø; **131** Asaf Kliger, Shutterstock, Getty, Alamy, Andreas Christoffer Nilson/Secretsoftheice.com, Bakken; **132** Shutterstock, Alamy; **133** Shutterstock, Martin De Jong, Alamy, Pinkpop, Diego Delso/delso.photo; **134** Shutterstock, CERN, Alamy; **135** Stefan Seelig, Alamy, Jakub Szczęsny/Forgemind ArchiMedia, Shutterstock; **136** Shutterstock, Alamy, Lotte; **137** Alamy, Shutterstock, Getty; **138** Shutterstock, Getty, Alamy; **139** Shutterstock; **140** Alamy, Getty, Shutterstock; **141** Alamy, Shutterstock; **142** Shutterstock, Alamy, Getty; **143** Shutterstock, Alamy, Oxalis Adventure; **144** Alamy, Getty, Shutterstock; **145** Shutterstock, Dick Thomas Johnson, Getty, Alamy; **146** Shutterstock, Alamy, Ian Moore/Evandale Village Fair, Getty; **147** Getty, Te Papa, Shutterstock, Alamy, Ellen Rykers, David Wall; **148** Getty; **149** Wlad SIMITCH/M6; **150** Chuck Green/GWR; **151** Shutterstock, Alamy; **152** Shutterstock, Sameer Regmi/Discover Parbat, Getty, Merlin Moritz/MX3D; **153** Alamy, Shutterstock; **154** Shutterstock, Alamy, Max Bögl Group, Marshall Gerometta; **155** Alamy, Stefan Fussan/Marshall Strabala and Jun Xia, Shutterstock; **156** EPFL, ReWalk Robotics, Alamy, Shutterstock; **157** ETH/Alessandro Della Bella, The University of Chicago, Ben Rollins/GWR, Sarcos Technology and Robotics Corporation, Innophys Co. Ltd; **158** Alamy, Shutterstock; **159** Getty, Alamy; **160** Shutterstock; **161** Shutterstock; **162** Geometrica, Inc., National Trust for Scotland, Alamy; **163** Rolls-Royce, Samo Vidic/Red Bull Content Pool, faroephoto.com; **164** Alamy, UNOCHA/David Gough, Getty, Kwaku Alston for Disney Studios, Shutterstock; **165** Shutterstock; **166** Netflix; **167** Netflix, Cameron Allen; **168** Stan Winston Studio, PIXOMONDO, LAIKA, Disney/Alamy, Makuta, Shutterstock, Getty; **169** Warner Bros./Shutterstock, Framestore, Marvel/Disney/Alamy, DreamWorks/Paramount/Alamy, Lucasfilm/Shutterstock, Lucasfilm/Disney, Shutterstock; **170** Disney/Alamy, Hudson Soft/Moby Games, Square/Games Press, Disney, Alamy, Pixar/Disney/Alamy; **171** Disney/Alamy, Pixar/Disney/Alamy, Marvel/Disney/Alamy, Lucasfilm/Disney/Alamy, Shutterstock; **172** NBCUniversal Media/Getty, CBS Entertainment, FX, ABC/Art Streiber, Alamy, National Geographic/Fox, MBS, Shutterstock; **173** Curtis Bonds Baker/Netflix, HBO Entertainment/Alamy, Sony Entertainment Television India (SET)/Studio Next, Marvel Studios/Disney Plus, Paramount+, Shutterstock, Apple TV+; **174** Alamy, Ryan Schude/GWR, Shutterstock; **175** Alamy, Shutterstock, Stephen J. Greenberg/NLM, NLM, Rod Hunt; **176** Shutterstock, World Puzzle Federation; **178** Shutterstock, Alamy; **179** Cameron Allen; **180** Getty, GWR, Alamy, Shutterstock; **181** Shutterstock, Getty; **182** Alamy, Getty, Warner Bros.Pictures/Alamy, FX Network TV/Alamy, Netflix, Shutterstock, Vice Studios/Alamy, Netflix/Alamy; **183** Shutterstock, Nickelodeon, Getty; **184** Blizzard/Games Press, Warner Bros./Games Press, Rockstar Games; **185** Capcom/Games Press, Koelnmesse GmbH/Oliver Wachenfeld, Shutterstock; **186** Activision, Ryan Schude/GWR, EA; **187** EA/Games Press, TiMi Studio Group, Shutterstock; **188** Shutterstock, Square Enix/Games Press, Square Enix/Moby Games, Nintendo/Games Press, Alamy; **189** Roblox/Games Press, Adopt Me, Rockstar/Games Press, Shutterstock; **190** The Pokémon Company/Games Press, Nintendo, Paul Michael Hughes/GWR, Epic Games; **191** Nintendo/Games Press, Heritage Auctions, Telltale Games/Games Press, Shutterstock; **192–93** Paul Michael Hughes/GWR, Kevin Scott Ramos/GWR, Ranald Mackechnie/GWR, Richard Bradbury/GWR, Alamy; **194** Getty, James Ellerker/GWR, Marvel/Disney/Alamy, Supergiant Games/Games Press; **195** Getty, Heritage Auctions, Marvel/Disney/Alamy; **196** Getty, Alamy, Shutterstock; **197** Shutterstock, Alamy; **198** Getty; **199** Alamy, Getty, Kevin Scott Ramos/GWR; **200** Getty, David Levene, Alamy, Aivars Liepiņš, Shutterstock; **201** Alamy, Shutterstock; **202** Shutterstock; **203** Shutterstock, Alamy, Dapper Labs, ASOBIMO/Games Press, Getty; **204** Kerameikos Archaeological Museum, Shutterstock, Getty, Bizmoune Cave, Essaouira Ministry of Youth, Culture and Communication, Julien's Auctions/Vincent Sandoval, Mouawad, Canadian Museum of History; **205** Daniel Buck Auctions, Shutterstock, University of Oregon Museum of Natural and Cultural History, David Jackson, dbking, Metropolitan Museum of Art, Rod Hunt; **206** Shutterstock, Christie's Images, Jos Buttler/Twitter, Heritage Auctions, Ashley Littlejohn Photography; **207** Shutterstock, Goldin Auctions, Sotheby's/SquareMoose, Getty, Sotheby's, Hake's Auctions, Rod Hunt; **208** Shutterstock, Maximum Games/Games Press; **209** Kevin Scott Ramos/GWR, Drew Gardner/GWR, Brian Braun/GWR, Al Diaz/GWR; **210** Shutterstock, Getty; **211** Zachary Fu & Dustin Ong, Alamy, Getty, Max Morse for TechCrunch, Shutterstock; **212–13** Getty, Dmitriy Kuznietsov, Shutterstock; **214** Alamy, Kevin Galvan; **215** Alamy, Alberto Bernasconi/GWR, Getty; **216** Getty, Shutterstock; **217** Getty, Shutterstock; **218** Shutterstock, Getty; **219** Shutterstock, Getty, Guide Dog Foundation; **220** Shutterstock, Getty; **221** Shutterstock, Getty; **222** Shutterstock; **223** Alamy, Shutterstock, Getty; **224** Shutterstock, Alamy, Getty; **225** Getty, Shutterstock, Alamy; **226** Getty, Shutterstock; **227** Getty, Shutterstock; **228** Alamy, Getty, Shutterstock, iZimPhoto/Jekesai Njikizana; **229** Shutterstock, Getty; **230** Getty, Shutterstock, Alamy; **231** Imago Images, Shutterstock, Alamy; **232** Shutterstock; **233** Guide Dog Foundation, Shutterstock, Alamy, Getty; **234** Shutterstock, Getty; **235** Shutterstock; **236** Rod Hunt, Shutterstock, Getty, Alamy; **237** Shutterstock, Rod Hunt, Mexican Triathlon Federation, Marek Janiak/UltraPark Weekend, Stephen Wilson, Getty; **238** LAT Images, Getty, Shutterstock, Alamy; **239** Getty, Shutterstock; **240** Shutterstock, Getty, GWR; **241** United States Parachutist Association/David Cherry, ESPN, Shutterstock, Getty; **242** Getty, Shutterstock; **243** Shutterstock, Alamy, Getty; **244** Getty, Pep Segalés/FIM, Imago Images; **245** Shutterstock, Alamy; **256** Rod Hunt

Every effort has been made to trace copyright holders and gain permission for use of the images in this publication. We welcome notifications from copyright holders who may have been omitted.

Official adjudicators: Alfredo Arista, Camila Borenstain, Joanne Brent, Jack Brockbank, Ahmed Bucheeri, Spencer Cammarano, Sarah Casson, Swapnil Dangarikar, Brittany Dunn, Kanzy El Defrawy, Michael Empric, Pete Fairbairn, Victor Fenes, Fumika Fujibuchi, Michael Furnari, John Garland, Andrew Glass, Iris Hou, Louis Jelinek, Lena Kuhlmann, Maggie Luo, Rishi Nath, Hannah Ortman, Kellie Parise, Pravin Patel, Justin Patterson, Glenn Pollard, Natalia Ramirez, Susana Reyes, Philip Robertson, Paulina Sapinska, Tomomi Sekioka, Lucia Sinigagliesi, Brian Sobel, Richard Stenning, Claire Stephens, Sheila Mella Suárez, Şeyda Subaşı Gemici, Lorenzo Veltri, Xiong Wen, Peter Yang

Acknowledgements: 55 Design Ltd (Hayley Wylie-Deacon, Tobias Wylie-Deacon, Rueben Wylie-Deacon, Linda Wylie, Vidette Burniston, Lewis Burniston, Paul Geldeart, Sue Geldeart), After Party Studios (Richard Mansell), Amanda Joiner, Banijay Italy, Carlotta Rossi Spencer, Cepak Ltd, Charlie Burland in memoriam, Chris Theriault, Codex Solutions Ltd, Coventry Communications (Jon Coventry), Della Galton, Devonte Roper, Dojo Films, Duncan Hart, Electric Robin, Exhibit Hosts, Facebook (Dan Biddle), FJT Logistics Ltd (Ray Harper), Gabriela Ventura, Georgia & Peter I'anson, Gracie & Jack Lewis, Imagination Station Toledo, Integrated Colour Editions Europe Ltd (Roger Hawkins, Susie Hawkins), Jim Pattison Jr, John Corcoran, Julie Moskalyk, Kathryn Huneault, Kidoodle (Brenda Bisner), Mintaka (Tim Stuart, Torquil Macneal), Mohn Media (Astrid Renders, Kevin Sarney, Maximilian Schonlau, Jeanette Sio), Montreal Science Center, Orchard Media & Events, Prestige Design (Jackie Ginger), Production Suite (Beverley Williams), Ripley Entertainment, Rob Partis, Science North, Snapchat (Rebecca Ozarow, Lucy Luke), Stark RFID, Steinbeis Papier GmbH, SLB Enterprises (Susan Bender, Sally Treibel), Tacita Barrera, TikTok (Normanno Pisani, Sanjit Sarkar), US Space & Rocket Center, William Anthony, YouGov

Special thanks: We dedicate this year's book to Production Consultant Roger Hawkins (above), who is retiring after 35 years. Uncle Rog has been a central member of the team since the 1989 edition, ensuring the smooth running of the production process and overseeing the printing of more than 70 million books! His unrivalled technical knowledge and unflappable enthusiasm for GWR will be sorely missed. Cheers, Roger!

Abbreviations

ABW	Aruba
AFG	Afghanistan
AGO	Angola
AIA	Anguilla
ALB	Albania
AND	Andorra
ANT	Netherlands Antilles
ARG	Argentina
ARM	Armenia
ASM	American Samoa
ATG	Antigua and Barbuda
AUS	Australia
AUT	Austria
AZE	Azerbaijan
BDI	Burundi
BEL	Belgium
BEN	Benin
BFA	Burkina Faso
BGD	Bangladesh
BGR	Bulgaria
BHR	Bahrain
BHS	The Bahamas
BIH	Bosnia and Herzegovina
BLR	Belarus
BLZ	Belize
BMU	Bermuda
BOL	Bolivia
BRA	Brazil
BRB	Barbados
BRN	Brunei Darussalam
BTN	Bhutan
BWA	Botswana
CAF	Central African Republic
CAN	Canada
CHE	Switzerland
CHL	Chile
CHN	China
CIV	Côte d'Ivoire
CMR	Cameroon
COD	Congo, DR of the
COG	Congo
COK	Cook Islands
COL	Colombia
COM	Comoros
CPV	Cape Verde
CRI	Costa Rica
CUB	Cuba
CYM	Cayman Islands
CYP	Cyprus
CZE	Czech Republic
DEU	Germany
DJI	Djibouti
DMA	Dominica
DNK	Denmark
DOM	Dominican Republic
DZA	Algeria
ECU	Ecuador
EGY	Egypt
ERI	Eritrea
ESP	Spain
EST	Estonia
ETH	Ethiopia
FIN	Finland
FJI	Fiji
FRA	France
FSM	Micronesia, Federated States of
GAB	Gabon
GEO	Georgia
GHA	Ghana
GIB	Gibraltar
GIN	Guinea
GMB	Gambia
GNB	Guinea-Bissau
GNQ	Equatorial Guinea
GRC	Greece
GRD	Grenada
GRL	Greenland
GTM	Guatemala
GUM	Guam
GUY	Guyana
HND	Honduras
HRV	Croatia (Hrvatska)
HTI	Haiti
HUN	Hungary
IDN	Indonesia
IND	India
IRL	Ireland
IRN	Iran
IRQ	Iraq
ISL	Iceland
ISR	Israel
ITA	Italy
JAM	Jamaica
JOR	Jordan
JPN	Japan
KAZ	Kazakhstan
KEN	Kenya
KGZ	Kyrgyzstan
KHM	Cambodia
KIR	Kiribati
KNA	Saint Kitts and Nevis
KOR	Korea, Republic of
KWT	Kuwait
LAO	Laos
LBN	Lebanon
LBR	Liberia
LBY	Libya
LCA	Saint Lucia
LIE	Liechtenstein
LKA	Sri Lanka
LSO	Lesotho
LTU	Lithuania
LUX	Luxembourg
LVA	Latvia
MAR	Morocco
MCO	Monaco
MDA	Moldova
MDG	Madagascar
MDV	Maldives
MEX	Mexico
MHL	Marshall Islands
MKD	North Macedonia
MLI	Mali
MLT	Malta
MMR	Myanmar
MNE	Montenegro
MNG	Mongolia
MNP	Northern Mariana Islands
MOZ	Mozambique
MRT	Mauritania
MSR	Montserrat
MUS	Mauritius
MWI	Malawi
MYS	Malaysia
NAM	Namibia
NER	Niger
NGA	Nigeria
NIC	Nicaragua
NIU	Niue
NLD	Netherlands
NOR	Norway
NPL	Nepal
NRU	Nauru
NZ	New Zealand
OMN	Oman
PAK	Pakistan
PAN	Panama
PER	Peru
PHL	Philippines
PLW	Palau
PNG	Papua New Guinea
POL	Poland
PRI	Puerto Rico
PRK	Korea, DPRO
PRT	Portugal
PRY	Paraguay
QAT	Qatar
ROM	Romania
RUS	Russian Federation
RWA	Rwanda
SAU	Saudi Arabia
SDN	Sudan
SEN	Senegal
SGP	Singapore
SHN	Saint Helena
SLB	Solomon Islands
SLE	Sierra Leone
SLV	El Salvador
SMR	San Marino
SOM	Somalia
SRB	Serbia
SSD	South Sudan
STP	São Tomé and Príncipe
SUR	Suriname
SVK	Slovakia
SVN	Slovenia
SWE	Sweden
SWZ	Eswatini
SYC	Seychelles
SYR	Syrian Arab Republic
TCA	Turks and Caicos Islands
TCD	Chad
TGO	Togo
THA	Thailand
TJK	Tajikistan
TKM	Turkmenistan
TMP	East Timor
TON	Tonga
TTO	Trinidad and Tobago
TUN	Tunisia
TUR	Turkey
TUV	Tuvalu
TZA	Tanzania
UAE	United Arab Emirates
UGA	Uganda
UK	United Kingdom
UKR	Ukraine
UMI	US Minor Islands
URY	Uruguay
USA	United States of America
UZB	Uzbekistan
VAT	Vatican City
VCT	Saint Vincent and the Grenadines
VEN	Venezuela
VGB	Virgin Islands (British)
VIR	Virgin Islands (US)
VNM	Vietnam
VUT	Vanuatu
WSM	Samoa
YEM	Yemen
ZAF	South Africa
ZMB	Zambia
ZWE	Zimbabwe

Where's Wadlow?

This year's book cover design continues the "Discover Your World" theme that we've explored with our past two editions. Award-winning artist Rod Hunt has once again created a stellar illustration for us – and this time, his action-packed artwork launches GWR into space...

Rod has devised a sparkling constellation of record-breaking individuals, animals and objects for *GWR 2023*. Nearly every detail on this cosmic cover is associated with a record – there are about 200 GWR title holders in all. They once again include the **tallest man ever**, 272-cm (8-ft 11.1-in) Robert Wadlow (USA) –

although this time he's wearing a spacesuit! Below, we present 20 record holders that appear somewhere on the front and back of the book (see the inside covers for a version without any text). For a bit of fun, how quickly can you find them all? And for a bonus point, can you spot the Tesla Roadster that became the **first mass-produced car in space** in 2018?

GUINNESS WORLD RECORDS 2023

2021

2022

This year's cover can be joined with those for 2021 and 2022 to reveal Rod Hunt's artwork in all its glory!

Tallest woman
Rumeysa Gelgi (TUR): 215.16 cm (7 ft 0.7 in). *See p.56*

Largest horn spread on a goat
Albino (CHE): 1.44 m (4 ft 8.6 in). *See p.36*

Most consecutive cars jumped over on a pogo stick
Tyler "TPhil" Phillips (USA): six cars. *See p.12*

First music video filmed in space
Commander Chris Hadfield (CAN): 12 May 2013. *See p.21*

Fastest wheelchair 100 m (T34, female)
Hannah Cockroft (UK): 16.39 sec. *See p.232*

Most tattooed man
Lucky Diamond Rich (NZ): over 200% skin coverage. *See p.112*

Fastest time to solve a 3x3x3 rotating puzzle cube with one hand
Max Park (USA): 6.82 sec. *See p.74*

Largest group of life-size statues
Terracotta Army (CHN): *c.* 8,000 figures. *See p.144*

Most flesh tunnels (face)
James Goss (UK): 15 flesh tunnels. *See p.62*

Largest mouth gape (female)
Samantha Ramsdell (USA): 6.52 cm (2.56 in). *See p.58*

Most guide dogs trained
The Guide Dogs for the Blind Association (UK): 36,670 dogs. *See p.51*

Heaviest jack o'lantern
Grown by Travis Gienger (USA): 2,350 lb (1,065.9 kg). *See p.87*

Farthest distance travelled in a single Martian day
Perseverance rover: 319.79 m (1,049 ft 2 in). *See p.25*

Appear on the cover of *Guinness World Records 2024*! We're thrilled to announce that next year Rod Hunt will be diving to the depths of the oceans to complete his quadrilogy of *Guinness World Records* covers. To celebrate, we're giving YOU the chance to feature on the final cover, where you'll see yourself submerged in a sea of superlative submariners. To find out how you can win this special prize, visit **guinnessworldrecords.com/2023**

First collision between two satellites
Iridium 33 struck by *Kosmos-2251* (both RUS): 10 Feb 2009. *See p.22*

Largest ukulele
Lawrence Stump (USA): 3.99 m (13 ft 1 in). *See p.193*

First commercial passenger rocket plane
Virgin Galactic SpaceShipTwo *Unity*: 11 Jul 2021. *See p.18*

First functional LEGO® prosthetic arm
David Aguilar (AND): 2017. *See p.148*

Tallest domestic cat
Fenrir Antares Powers (USA): 47.83 cm (1 ft 6.8 in) *See p.48*

Farthest distance jumping a canal
Jaco de Groot (NLD): 22.21 m (72 ft 10 in). *See p.133*

Largest telescope mirror in space
James Webb Space Telescope: 6.5 m (21 ft 4 in). *See p.30*

ABOUT THE ILLUSTRATOR

Not surprisingly, Rod Hunt was passionate about comics as a child. They inspired him to start drawing, and by the time he was a teenager he had begun to consider a career as an illustrator. Over the years, Rod has honed his artistic technique. Firstly, he mulls over the project and doodles simple pencil sketches; then he creates a more complete drawing. Next, he scans this into his computer and builds it up, layer by layer, using digital-illustration software. Find out more about Rod at www.rodhunt.com